DISCARDED

D1456848

Agricultural Economics

Principles and Policy

Agricultural Economics

Principles and Policy

Christopher Ritson

Department of Agricultural Economics and Management
University of Reading

HD
1411
·R48
1977b

Crosby Lockwood Staples London

121490

Granada Publishing Limited
First published in Great Britain 1977 by
Crosby Lockwood Staples
Frogmore St Albans Hertfordshire AL2 2NF and
3 Upper James Street London W1R 4BP

Copyright © 1977 by Christopher Ritson

All rights reserved. No part of this publication may be
reproduced, stored in a retrieval system, or transmitted,
in any form or by any means, electronic, mechanical,
photocopying, recording, or otherwise, without the prior
permission of the publishers.

ISBN 0 258 96938 5

Printed in Great Britain at The Spottiswoode Ballantyne Press
By William Clowes & Sons Limited, London, Colchester and Beccles

Preface

This book is intended for use by university students as a general textbook in agricultural economics. I hope that it will be of value to students of agricultural economics, to economics students who are taking a course in agricultural economics or who are interested in seeing economic theory explained in the context of agricultural activities, and to students of agriculture whose degrees include an economics component. The book is about economic theory and its application to agriculture. I have not attempted to provide a comprehensive account of organisational or institutional aspects of agriculture.

At the onset of writing a textbook, crucial decisions have to be taken concerning the level and approach to be adopted, as well as the subject matter to be covered. From my own experience, and in the light of remarks made by other teachers of agricultural economics, it seemed to me that what was required most was a general text in agricultural economics pitched at what one might call an intermediate level. The book is therefore aimed mainly at students who have already taken a basic introductory course in economics.

The past ten years have seen rapid developments in the use of economic theory in agricultural economics. A level of sophistication in the use of economic theory, long regarded as appropriate in farm production economics, has gradually spread to other areas, most particularly to the economic analysis of agricultural policies. I have attempted wherever possible to include these developments, but no demands on mathematical understanding are made of the reader beyond familiarity with elementary algebra and geometry (except in the appendix to Chapter 2 and in an occasional footnote).

Two themes underlie the approach I have taken. The first is the close relationship between understanding economic theory and successfully applying it. As a discipline, 'agricultural economics' can be interpreted either as the application of economic theory to agriculture, or as the development of a theoretical approach to the economic problems of agriculture – which does not really matter; in either case we are trying to equip ourselves to be able to understand more about the real world. For this reason the theoretical argument is illustrated throughout with applications to individual economic problems in agriculture. Most of the examples used relate to Western Europe and North America. However, the particular choice of examples is not important. The intention is to illustrate an approach to the solution of economic problems, and the book should therefore be applicable to any part of the world where the market mechanism has a significant influence on the distribution of resources and products and where the starting point for a government's agricultural policy is seen predominantly in terms of intervention in order to modify a market solution. (Arguably, much of what is said is also relevant to those countries where the market mechanism is seen mainly as a means of supplementing the role of central planning in controlling the distribution of resources and products.)

The second theme is the importance of distinguishing clearly between the use of economic theory to help us to understand the agricultural aspects of an economic system and its use in attempting to assess the merits of alternative economic situations. It is this distinction which separates the material covered in Parts I and II of the book. In Part II I have attempted to make accessible to students of agricultural economics those aspects of welfare economics which seem to me to have important implications for the economist's study of agricultural policy. There is implicit in much contemporary writing on agricultural policy a familiarity with the central notions of formal welfare economics, but this is often not appreciated by the student when he reads policy articles. Most students will probably find much of the material in Part II more difficult than the contents of Part I, but I believe a reasonable grasp of the theoretical ideas outlined in Chapters 5 and 6 to be an increasingly important part of the equipment required by any agricultural economist who is concerned with the economic analysis of agricultural policies.

Historically 'agricultural economics' has included a third subject area in addition to those covered respectively in Parts I and II of this book. This is the study of techniques for assisting the private decision-maker in agricultural production and marketing to meet his objectives – in other words, *private* (as opposed to *public*) agricultural policy, but usually called *farm management* (or *farm planning*) in the case of on-farm decisions, and *marketing management* in the case of decisions relating to agricultural produce once it has left the 'farm gate'. This subject area is quite well covered in other texts.

A textbook is not something which should be read quickly; if it is to be useful it requires *work*. The student should expect to encounter difficulties, to have to reread sections, and on occasions to have to devote perhaps thirty minutes to one diagram. If this is not the case, then the textbook will not be serving its intended purpose. At the end of each chapter there is a list of publications referenced consecutively through the chapter by numbers in parenthesis. The references are intended to help the student to pursue in greater depth those issues which particularly interest him or which relate to some assignment he has been set. Wherever possible I have included references which themselves refer to a number of other publications on the same topic. In order to minimise printing costs, the 'footnotes' are also listed at the end of each chapter and referred to by superscript numbers. Many of these notes contain qualifications or elaborations which are important, but which would have proved distracting if included in the text.

Many of my colleagues at Reading have helped me by commenting on early drafts, and I would like in particular to thank Jim Burns, Tim Josling, Stefan Tangermann (University of Göttingen), Ronald Tuck, and Martin Upton, all of whom did more than their fair share. Of course I alone remain responsible for the errors and defects that remain. I would also like to thank Mary Gray for so carefully typing what I had written (and sometimes being careful not to type what I had written), Ginnie Hume, who produced the illustrations, and my wife, Sandra, whose welfare was severely impaired by the externalities of the project (see Chapter 6).

University of Reading
August, 1976

Contents

Introduction

It is sometimes said that economics possesses as many definitions as there are economists. Certainly, attempts at defining the subject precisely usually seem unsatisfactory. As one writer has put it:

We all talk about the same things, but we have not yet agreed what it is we are talking about (1).

The same writer (Lord Robbins) is responsible for the most frequently quoted definition:

Economics is the science which studies human behaviour as a relationship between ends and scarce means which have alternative uses (1).

There is perhaps more agreement concerning the use of the term *economic system*. This usually refers to the system developed by a society in order to satisfy some of the wants of its members, whereby what are called *productive resources* (or *factors of production*) are converted into forms suitable for consumption (then called variously *products, commodities*, or *goods and services*). In economics we study such systems.

A common theme in most definitions of economics is *scarcity* and *choice*. Society must choose between competing uses when resources are wanted for different productive activities, and must choose between competing ends when products are desired by different individuals. The science of economics is therefore concerned with the way society organises the allocation of scarce resources in order to satisfy alternative wants.

An agricultural activity is one in which mankind attempts to control groups of plants or animals in order to fulfil certain human wants, mainly by producing food. This process of control normally takes a form which we know as farming, but farming is often only the start of a long sequence of productive operations. The agricultural economist retains an interest in the process which leads ultimately to the satisfaction of a human want as long as a major part of what is produced is derived from agricultural activity. In the case of most food products, this means following the process through to the point of final consumption. On the other hand, the agricultural economist would normally not retain an interest in many non-food products beyond the point at which these products are purchased as raw materials by manufacturing industry.

The diagram opposite describes, in a simplified form, those components of an economic system which are normally regarded as being within the *agricultural economist's* sphere of interest. In Part I of this book we attempt to show how the principles of economics can help us to understand the operation of this part of an economic system. In the first chapter we investigate how man's desire for the consumption of food leads to a *demand* for agricultural products. Chapter 2 is concerned with the theory of farm production and with how decisions taken within the farm firm lead to a *supply* of agricultural products. Chapter 3 explores the interaction of supply and demand in agricultural *markets*, and in the final chapter of Part I we discuss the use of *resources* in agricultural production.

In Part II we turn to the question of Government involvement in the operation of an economic system. Chapter 5 provides an introduction to the branch of economics – called welfare economics – which provides the basic theory for much of what agricultural economics has to offer as a discipline to the study of government agricultural policies. The remaining chapters cover three broad aspects of the interaction between government policy and agriculture, namely, the assessment of public agricultural projects, agricultural trade policy, and methods of supporting farm incomes.

Reference

(1) Robbins, L. *An Essay on the Nature and Significance of Economic Science*, 2nd edn. London, Macmillan, 1935.

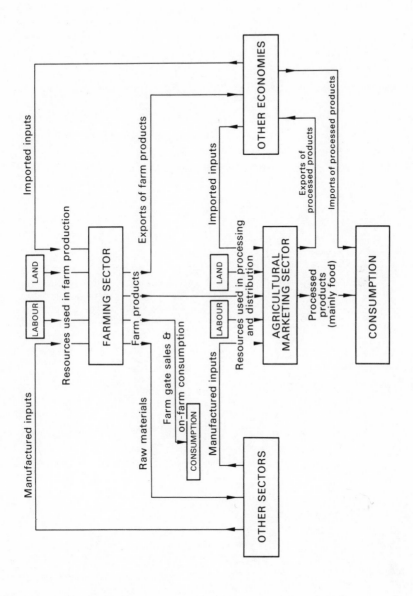

PART I

Principles

CHAPTER 1

The Demand for Agricultural Products

1 The theory of household behaviour

1.1 Utility

We have identified the ultimate function of economic activity as being the satisfaction of human wants through consumption. Let us suppose, for the moment, that the amount of satisfaction (or *utility*) derived from the consumption of a product is quantitatively measurable. We will use the word *util* (a name invented by Boulding (1)) to describe 1 unit of utility. How will an individual's utility vary in relation to his consumption of different products?

Consider first the case where the quantities of all goods consumed by an individual except one, bread, are held constant. Even if the individual eats no bread, as long as he consumes some food we would expect him to experience some positive level of utility. Figure 1.1 describes an imaginary relationship between this individual's level of utility and variations in the number of loaves he consumes each week. The number of utils per week derived from bread consumption are measured on the vertical axes. In Fig. 1.1a the heights of the bars indicate the *total utility* derived from the consumption of successively increasing numbers of loaves per week. In a similar way, Fig. 1.1b shows *marginal utility*, which is defined here as the increase in total utility resulting from the consumption of each additional loaf. Marginal utility declines from 5 utils for the first loaf to 1 util for the fifth, the total utility derived from the consumption of five loaves per week being 15 utils. The sixth loaf does not add to total utility and our consumer finds the practice of eating more than six loaves per week distasteful – additional loaves would render negative marginal utility and reduce total utility from bread consumption below its maximum of 15 utils.

Where the consumption of a product can be varied by very small amounts, we can illustrate the relationship between consumption and utility by means of smooth curves. In Fig. 1.2a the curve TU_1 shows the same total utility from the

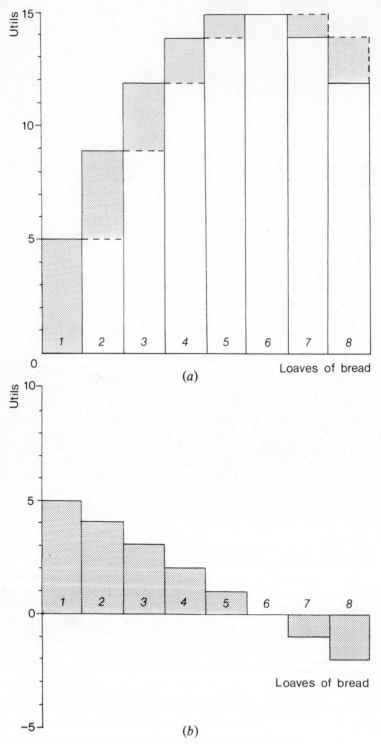

Figure 1.1   (a) Total utility, (b) Marginal utility

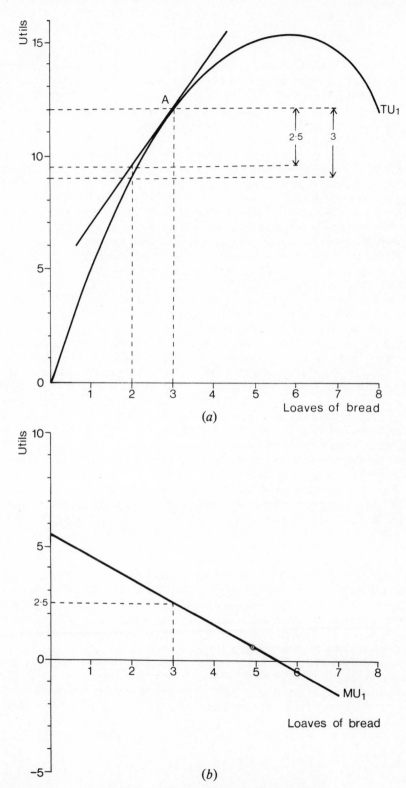

Figure 1.2   (a) Total utility, (b) Marginal utility

consumption of whole loaves of bread as Fig. 1.1a – 5 utils from one loaf, 9 utils from two loaves, and so on – but includes additional information relating to fractions of loaves. We discover, for example, that when we allow our consumer to eat five and a half loaves during the week, rather than forcing him to complete the sixth loaf once he has decided to embark upon it, the total utility from bread consumption is slightly higher than 15 utils.

When it is possible to vary the consumption of a product continuously, the concept of marginal utility is redefined as being the rate of change of total utility as quantity consumed increases. Diagrammatically this is represented by the slope of the total utility curve.[1] If for example we take the consumption of three loaves per week, and draw a tangent to TU_1 at point A, it is clear that when consumption is precisely three loaves per week, utility is increasing at a rate of $2\frac{1}{2}$ utils per loaf, and marginal utility is therefore shown in Fig. 1.2b as 2·5 for three loaves. (If on the other hand we define marginal utility as the increase in total utility resulting from the consumption of each successive loaf, then it takes the value 3, as in Fig. 1.1b.) A small increase in consumption above three loaves – say to three and a quarter – means that utility is increasing at a slightly lower rate; marginal utility has decreased.

The utility derived from bread consumption will of course depend on which and how much of other products are also consumed. If all other food products were excluded from the consumer we would expect the amount of utility derived from a particular level of bread consumption, and the number of loaves required to render marginal utility zero, to be much higher than if other food products were being consumed. The utility derived from bread would remain largely unaffected by the amount consumed of most non-food products – the utilities would be independent. For some products, which are known as *complements*, an increase in the quantity consumed of one product might increase the utility derived from the consumption of another product. This is probably the case for example with bread and butter.

Figure 1.3 illustrates the relationship between utility and the consumption of two products taken together, bread and meat. (The quantities consumed of all other products are held constant.) The axis OX measures kilogrammes of meat, the axis OY loaves of bread, and the axis OU utils of utility. Any point in the XY plane (such as for example point A) represents a combination of the weekly consumption of bread and meat, and the amount of utility derived from consuming that combined quantity of bread and meat is measured by a point vertically above the plane. (In the case of A, this is point B.) The curve TU_1 is taken from Fig. 1.2a and describes the total utility from bread consumption when no meat is consumed. Curve TU_2 shows the total utility from the consumption of bread and meat taken together when the consumption of meat is always 1 kg per week and only the number of loaves varies. Point B lies on TU_2 and the vertical distance AB gives us the total utility when 1 kg meat and four loaves are consumed. Similarly, point D represents the total utility when 1 kg meat and two loaves are consumed. Repeating this procedure for every possible combination of meat and bread traces out a *utility surface* above the XY plane.

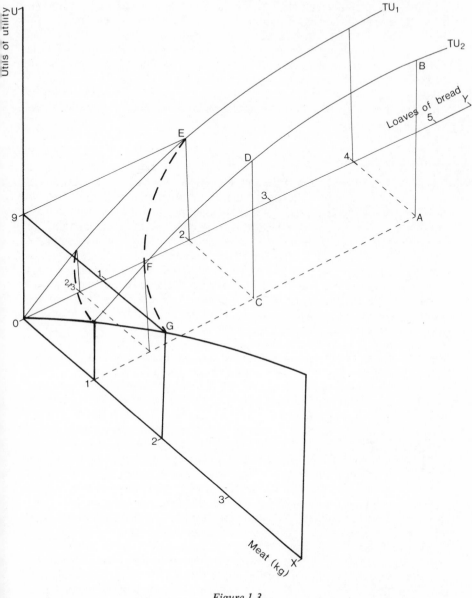

Figure 1.3

Three-dimensional diagrams like Fig. 1.3 are difficult to construct and limited in the amount of information they can convey. To overcome this problem, economists have developed a technique which is similar to that employed by map-makers when they show height above sea level by contour lines. In our case the two products, bread and meat, are measured on the horizontal and vertical axes, and the third dimension – utility – is represented by contour lines joining different combinations of the two products which yield the same level of utility. One such line is shown in Fig. 1.3, that for 9 utils (EFG), and is labelled I_0 in Fig. 1.4. Combinations of no bread and 2 kg meat, 1 kg meat and two-thirds of a loaf, and no meat and two loaves all yield a total utility of 9 utils. In this way we could build a contour map of the three-dimensional Fig. 1.3.

1.2 Indifference curves

The contour map method of representing utility possesses the added advantage that it allows us now to abandon the assumption that was made at the beginning of the previous section – that the amount of satisfaction derived from consumption is quantitatively measurable. In other words, there is in fact no need to specify that each contour line is associated with a particular number of utility units (or utils), only that each contour represents a series of combinations of the two products which are preferred to all combinations lying on lower contours. We call this *ordinal* as opposed to *cardinal* measurement. If, for example, we take the combination of three loaves and 3 kg meat (point A in Fig. 1.4) we would expect the consumer to prefer A to any combination of meat and bread which lies both below and to the left of A, as all such points represent less of both meat and bread. Similarly, combinations above and to the right of A will be preferred to A (unless they represent quantities of bread or meat which are so high that our consumer has become satiated). It follows that there will be a series of points lying in the remaining two quadrants which are equally preferred to A. Two such points in Fig. 1.4 are C and B – one might say that the consumer is indifferent between combinations A, B, and C, and the line joining all these combinations (I_2) is therefore usually known as an *indifference curve*.

Most economists have welcomed this opportunity to avoid the assumption of cardinal utility. From our own experience we are constantly aware of the necessity to take decisions on the basis of a preference for more of one good rather than another, and sometimes the choice is extremely difficult. We would perhaps be less comfortable if our theory of demand required us to assume that one activity created – say – twice as much satisfaction as another. If, of course, it turned out that the indifference curve technique was markedly inferior to the idea of measurable utility as a basis for understanding the observed behaviour of consumers in the market, then being 'comfortable' about its assumptions would be little consolation. But as it happens, to assume merely that a consumer has an ordered pattern of preferences is perfectly adequate. It is only in occasional applications of demand theory that it is more convenient to be able to assume that utility is quantitatively measurable.[2]

The indifference curves in Fig. 1.4 are shown as being shaped convex to the origin. This means that we are implying something about the character of the

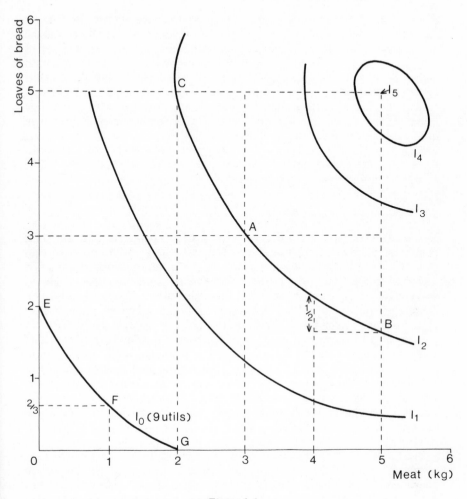

Figure 1.4

consumer's preferences for bread and meat in addition to the assumption that he will normally prefer more of both products. If we take the slope of any indifference curve, this shows the rate at which the product measured on the vertical axis can be substituted for the other product to leave the consumer indifferent about the change.

The slope of an indifference curve is sometimes called the *marginal rate of substitution* between the products and the marginal rate of substitution will have a negative value when indifference curves are downward sloping – an increase in the quantity consumed of one of the products is associated with a decrease in the quantity consumed of the other. The fact that the indifference curves become steeper as the quantity of the product measured on the horizontal axis decreases means that, if we successively reduce the quantity consumed of one product by equal amounts, it requires increasing quantities of the other product to leave the consumer indifferent regarding the change. For example, taking the level of utility represented by I_2, we are suggesting that a reasonable preference pattern for our consumer would be one in which he would accept about half a loaf as compensation for a reduction in weekly meat consumption from 5 kg to 4 kg, but that it would take two loaves if it were a case of reducing meat consumption from 3 kg to 2 kg. When meat consumption falls below 2 kg a week, I_2 begins to bend back on itself implying that there simply is no quantity of bread which will allow the consumer to achieve a level of utility I_2 if he cannot eat at least 2 kg of meat per week.

1.3   The consumer in equilibrium

The indifference curve map describes an individual's pattern of preferences for the consumption of different products. The next question to be answered concerns the actual choice of consumption that will result. Most consumption decisions are in fact not taken by individual consumers but relate to households. In this respect, however, consumer theory makes no distinction between single-person and other households. When a household consists of more than one person it is assumed that an ordered preference pattern for the household as a whole emerges. Clearly this assumption involves a number of complex matters, including the question of commodities which are consumed jointly by the household and the extent to which the head of the household (if any) exercises authority over household consumption. These intrafamily problems are usually regarded as being the concern of disciplines other than economics. In this chapter we shall find it convenient to regard the consumer as the decision-taker, but the analysis applies equally well to the case where consumption decisions relate to 'the household'.

The fundamental assumption upon which demand theory is based is that the consumer acts in such a way as to maximise his satisfaction. If there is no constraint placed upon the quantities of goods that can be consumed, then this assumption will lead the consumer to move to his most preferred position. In the case of meat and bread consumption, this is the level of utility I_5 in Fig. 1.4, which is attained only with five loaves and 5 kg meat per week. This combination is preferred to all others, including those combinations containing more of both bread and meat.

There is, however, a constraint upon the consumption possibilities open to the consumer – money is required to purchase commodities (and his income is finite). Consider first the case where there are only two products, say food and cloth. In Fig. 1.5 the consumer's preferences for different quantities of these two products are shown by the set of indifference curves I_0, I_1, etc. The range of possible combinations of food and cloth open to the consumer during a particular time period can be shown by a *budget line*. If for example the price of food is £1 per unit and the price of cloth £2 per unit, with £2 our consumer

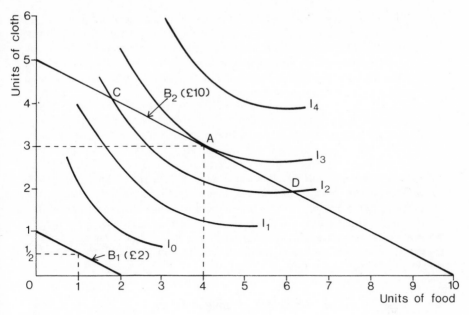

Figure 1.5

could purchase either 2 units of food, 1 unit of cloth, or any combination of food and cloth on the line B_1. (One such combination is 1 unit of food and $\frac{1}{2}$ unit of cloth.) With a weekly income of £10 the consumer could purchase either 10 units of food, 5 units of cloth, or any combination of food and cloth lying on (or within) the budget line B_2. Since each of the indifference curves I_1, I_2, etc. represent a series of combinations of food and cloth which are preferred to all combinations lying on lower indifference curves, it follows that the consumer will maximise his satisfaction by choosing the combination which lies on the highest attainable indifference curve. In the case of a weekly income of £10, this is 4 units of food and 3 units of cloth (point A). All other attainable combinations, such as those represented by points C and D, lie on lower indifference curves.

All points on the budget line B_2 lie on some indifference curve but it is only at point A that the budget line has the same slope as the associated indifference curve. The slope of the indifference curve – the marginal rate of substitution between the products – gives us the rate at which one product can be substituted for the other to leave the consumer indifferent. The slope of the budget line is given by the quantity of cloth that can be bought if all income is devoted to cloth (5 units), divided by the quantity of food that can be purchased if all income is spent on food (10 units):

$$\frac{\text{(Weekly income)/Price of cloth}}{\text{(Weekly income)/Price of food}} \left(\frac{10/2}{-10/1} \right) = -\frac{\text{Price of food}}{\text{Price of cloth}} \left(-\frac{1}{2} \right)$$

The negative signs are there because the budget line is downward sloping – an increase in the quantity purchased of food means a decrease in the quantity purchased of cloth. We may say more formally therefore that the consumer will be in equilibrium when the marginal rate of substitution between food and cloth is equal to the inverse ratio of their prices. Since there is likely to be one combination of food and cloth where this is the case, for every level of income, and each level of income is represented by a different budget line, we must add the requirement that all income is spent.

This argument can be extended in a non-graphical form to include as many products as necessary, e.g. for three products A, B, and C, satisfaction is maximised when the marginal rates of substitution between A and B, B and C, and C and A are all equal to the inverse ratio of their prices. In other words, where more than two products are involved, the condition must apply simultaneously for any *pair* of products. When cardinal utility is assumed, the utility maximising position for a consumer is usually presented in a slightly different form, known as the *equimarginal principle*. The two versions of the argument concerning the consumer in equilibrium are entirely consistent. See, for example, Cole (4).

1.4 Price–consumption and income–consumption lines

Our argument so far has taken us to a position where we can say that the quantity of a product purchased by the consumer will be related to four factors. These are:

(a) His pattern of tastes and preferences.
(b) His income.
(c) The price of the product.
(d) The price of another product.

In Fig. 1.5, (a) is represented by the consumer's set of indifference curves and (b), (c) and (d) by the budget line B_2.

We can conveniently illustrate the manner in which the consumer will alter his purchases of a product in response to price and income changes if we use a slightly different form of the indifference curve diagram. In Fig. 1.6 quantity of product A per week is measured on the horizontal axis and the consumer's weekly income on the vertical axis. The indifference curves I_0, I_1, etc. show the individual's preferences for different combinations of product A and remaining money income, which is available for spending on all other products. We treat remaining money income in Fig. 1.6 in the same way as we did units of cloth in Fig. 1.5. The budget line B_1 is that for a weekly income of £40 and a price for product A of £1 per unit. If the whole of income was spent on product A, 40 units per week could be purchased; conversely, if none of product A is consumed, £40 is available for the purchase of other products. The slope of the budget line B_1 is therefore £40/40 = (−)1 and, ignoring the negative sign, this also gives the price of product A. Thus when we measure quantity consumed on the horizontal axis, and remaining money income on the vertical axis, the absolute value of the slope of any budget line is also the price of the product. The consumer's preferred position is at point *E* where he purchases 20 units of product A leaving him £20 to spend on other commodities.

We can now draw a series of lines parallel to the budget line B_1, each one representing a different level of income, the price of product A remaining £1 per unit. In Fig. 1.6 budget lines for weekly incomes of £20 to £70 are shown and the line joining the points where these budget lines are tangential to indifference curves – the *income–consumption line* – indicates the way in which the consumption of product A changes as income increases. An

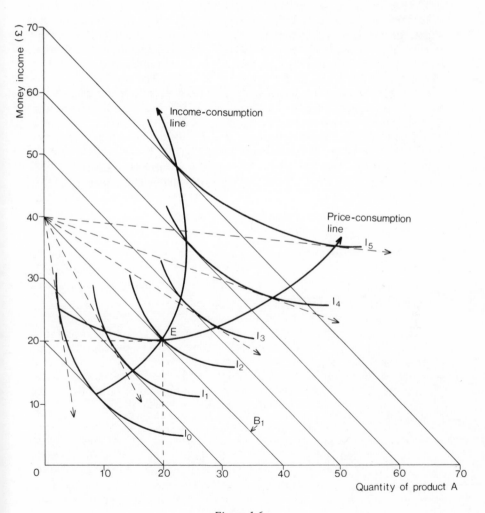

Figure 1.6

individual's income–consumption curve will of course vary depending on the characteristics of the product in question. Later in this chapter we investigate the likely relationships between income and consumption of food products, and the reader may care at this stage to glance at Fig. 1.14, which contains hypothetical income–consumption curves for selected food products. The income–consumption line in Fig. 1.6 shows consumption of product A increasing until income reaches £60 per week but declining at income levels above £60. A product for which consumption declines as income increases is known as an *inferior good*; when consumption increases with income the product is sometimes referred to as a *normal good*.

The possibility that an individual might reduce his consumption of a product in response to an increase in his income occurs because increasing affluence allows the consumer to switch purchases within a broad commodity group, for example meat in place of bread. Bread might therefore be a normal good when consumer income is low but become an inferior good at higher levels of income.

In a similar way to the derivation of an income–consumption line, we can derive a *price–consumption line* by constructing a series of budget lines representing different price levels for product A, income remaining constant at £40. These budget lines are shown in Fig. 1.6 by the broken lines radiating from the £40 point on the vertical axis. Budget lines to the left of B_1 are steeper than B_1 and thus represent prices for product A of more than £1 per unit. Budget lines to the right of B_1 indicate prices which are becoming successively lower than £1 per unit.

1.5 Income and substitution effects

It is sometimes useful to distinguish two components of the change in quantity consumed which follows a price change. These are:

(a) An element which can be attributed to the change in the price of the product relative to the prices of other products.

(b) An element which is related to the fact that, if the consumer's money income remains the same, a change in the price of one of the products he normally purchases will alter his real income – that is, the capacity which his money income gives him to purchase commodities, and thus the level of utility he can attain with any given money income. The change in his real income will lead him to alter the quantities purchased of some or all of the commodities available to him, probably including the one which has changed in price.

Component (a) is known as the *substitution effect* and (b) the *income effect*; these are illustrated in Fig. 1.7. Initially the price of product A, for a weekly income of £OC, is given by the budget line CE. If the price of product A falls to £OC/OD per unit, giving the new budget line CD, the quantity purchased per week increases from Q_1 to Q_4.[3] In order to distinguish the income and substitution effects of this price fall we draw the line FG, parallel to CD, which

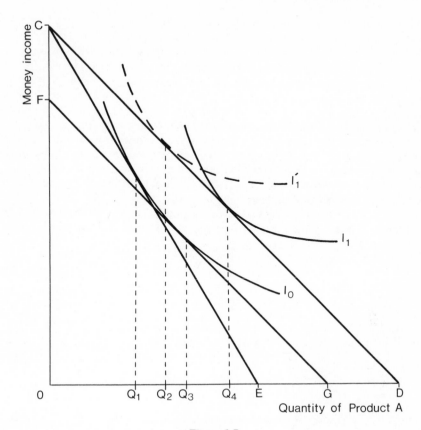

Figure 1.7

maintains the new price for product A but reduces the consumer's money income until, by purchasing Q_3, he is just able to achieve the same level of utility (I_0) as he did before the price change. The increase in consumption from Q_1 to Q_3 can therefore be attributed solely to the change in the price of product A relative to the prices of other products, and the further increase in consumption to Q_4 is the result of the income effect of the price change. Product A is a normal good, so the income effect is positive. If it had been an inferior good, as would be the case if we replaced indifference curve I_1 by the broken line I'_1, the income effect would be negative – that is, the substitution effect increases consumption from Q_1 to Q_3 but the income effect reduces it to Q_2.

The distinction between the income and substitution effects provides an explanation of a phenomenon known as the '*Giffen paradox*'. The Victorian economist Sir Robert Giffen is reputed to have observed that an increase in the price of wheat led to an increase in the consumption of bread among nineteenth-century English peasants (5). It is conceivable that this could have occurred if the negative income effect (bread being an inferior good) was to exceed the increase in consumption attributable to the substitution effect.

In Fig. 1.8, the initial price is represented, for OC money income, by the budget line CD, and Q_2 is purchased. An increase in the price of bread to OC/OE gives the new budget line CE and consumption increases to Q_3. The impact of the substitution effect of the rise in the price of bread is to reduce consumption to Q_1, but the income effect raises consumption from Q_1 to Q_3.

Giffen goods are probably very rare creatures indeed. It would require a family to be sufficiently poor for one basic foodstuff to constitute a substantial proportion of family expenditure (so that an increase in the price of the foodstuff would have a significant income effect) but nevertheless to have reached a sufficiently high level of income to be regularly supplementing the family diet with less basic food products (as the negative income effect requires the existence of better quality foods which the inferior good replaces when income

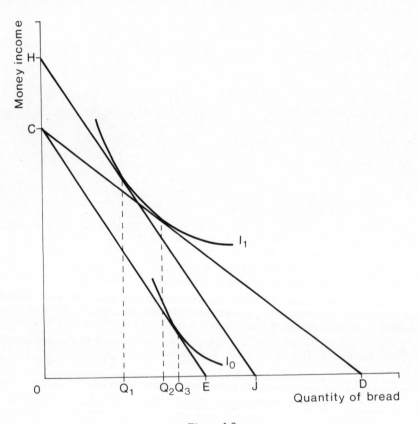

Figure 1.8

falls). However, as we shall see in section 5 below, there is substantial evidence to support the view that many basic foodstuffs have become inferior goods for the majority of the population in the advanced countries of Europe and North America.

2 Market demand

The *quantity demanded* of a product is the amount that will be purchased per time period under a given set of circumstances. Thus Fig. 1.6 showed that, given the set of preferences described by the indifference curves I_0, I_1, etc., an income of £40 per week, and a price of product A of £1 per unit, the quantity of product A 'demanded' each week by our consumer would be 20 units. The word 'demand' on its own is usually taken to mean the array of different quantities that would be purchased per time period under alternative sets of circumstances so that, taken as a whole, Fig. 1.6 in a sense describes our consumer's demand for product A.

In the remainder of this chapter we are concerned with *market demand*, which is the aggregated demand of a large number of individual consumers. We are here regarding the study of the market demand for agricultural products as following logically from the theory of household behaviour by aggregating the behavioural characteristics of a group of consumers. An alternative approach would have been to regard the study of market demand as the starting point of the economist's investigation, with the theory of household behaviour providing a view of the behaviour of households which is consistent with the observed characteristics of market demand.

The function of a market is to bring together buyers and sellers who wish to exchange goods for money. A market can be said to be performing this function efficiently if it is not possible to buy a good and immediately sell it in the same market at a higher price, otherwise buyers would be paying more for a good than they need, and sellers receiving less. One major distinguishing feature of a market may therefore be a single price for the good in question. Where a third party is necessarily involved in the transfer of goods from sellers to buyers the (uniform) selling price will diverge from the (uniform) buying price. For example, we find that different prices are quoted for purchase and sale on commodity or stock exchanges.

Historically, large numbers of markets for agricultural produce developed selling mainly local produce, and until quite recently 'market demand' would normally have meant the aggregated demand of the population surrounding a market town. It would rarely have been sensible to talk about the market demand of country, or even region; the high transport costs of most agricultural products meant that prices had to diverge substantially before interaction between the markets was likely to take place and poor communications meant that price differences, over and above those accounted for by transport costs, could perpetuate.

With the improvement in communications it has become more and more possible for a market to contain buyers and sellers located over greater areas and it is now sometimes more useful to replace the idea of a single market price by a price band relating to the costs of transporting the good. Thus commodity exchanges have developed in commercial centres of the world, such as London and Chicago, and it is possible to conceive of a 'world market' and a 'world demand' for – say – wheat.

However, the existence of manmade barriers to trade leads to the separation of the world market for a product into individual country markets. In some cases a country market can be completely isolated from world events and the term market demand now most commonly refers to the aggregate demand of a country's population. On occasions market demand may refer to the demand from a group of individuals distinguished by some characteristic, such as location, social class, age, sex or race.

To the four variables that were isolated in section 1 as having a major influence upon the amount of a product purchased by our consumer (which were his pattern of tastes and preferences, the price of the product, the prices of other products, and the consumer's income) we must add two more in order to complete a list of the main factors influencing market demand. These are the size of the population being considered and the distribution of income among that population. The factors affecting market demand for a particular product can be expressed symbolically by a *demand function*:

$$Q_d = f(P_p, P_1 \cdots P_n, Y, N, T, G)$$

where Q_d is the quantity demanded per time period
P_p is the price of the product
$P_1 \ldots P_n$ represents the prices of (n) other products
Y is the average income per head of the population
N is the number of individuals in the population
T represents the tastes and preferences of the population
G describes the distribution of income within the population

The quantity demanded of a product is said to depend on these factors and we therefore refer in this case to Q_d as the *dependent variable* and the other factors as *independent variables*.

A convenient way to investigate demand relationships for agricultural products is to consider the influence of each of these independent variables in turn. In order to do this we will normally have to be prepared to assume that the other five independent variables remain constant. It would also be useful if we had some simple measure of the significance of each variable in relation to potential changes in the quantity demanded of the product. For this purpose economists conventionally use a measure of the responsiveness of demand to changes in the independent variables which is known as *elasticity*. This can be defined as:

$$\frac{\text{Proportionate change in quantity demanded of a product}}{\text{Proportionate change in independent variable}}$$

or

$$\frac{\text{Percentage change in quantity demanded of a product}}{\text{Percentage change in independent variable}}$$

These amount to the same thing since 'percentage change' is simply 'proportionate change' multiplied by 100.

We use *proportionate change*, rather than just change, so as to have a measure of responsiveness which is independent of the units chosen for measuring price and quantity.

Coefficients of elasticity are usually calculated only for the price of the product itself (*own-price elasticity*, but sometimes referred to as *price elasticity* or even just *elasticity* of demand), the prices of other specified products (*cross-price elasticity* of demand) and income (*income elasticity* of demand).

3 The price of the product

3.1 Price elasticity of demand

We find that in almost every case the quantity demanded of a product falls when price increases – demand is inversely related to price. This is a result that we would expect from section 1 where it was only in the very rare case of the 'Giffen good' that the theory of household behaviour predicted that an individual consumer would increase his consumption of a product following an increase in its price.

The relationship between the quantity demanded of a product and the price of the product can be presented either in tabular form – known as a *demand schedule* – or on a graph, whereupon it is called a *demand curve*. A hypothetical demand curve[4] for apples is given in Fig. 1.9. Table 1.1 contains the corresponding demand schedule. This shows the quantity of apples per week which will be demanded at various prices (with given income, prices of other products, etc.) For example, when the price is 30p per kg, the demand for apples is 2000 kg per week. The coefficient of price elasticity of demand will give us the responsiveness of demand to some change from the price of 30p per kg. Suppose the price increases to 40p per kg; demand will fall to 1000 kg per week.

The proportionate change in demand is:

$$\frac{\text{Change in quantity demanded}}{\text{Original quantity demanded}} = \frac{-1000}{2000}$$

$$= \frac{-1}{2}$$

The proportionate change in price is:

$$\frac{\text{Change in price}}{\text{Original price}} = \frac{10}{30}$$

$$= \frac{1}{3}$$

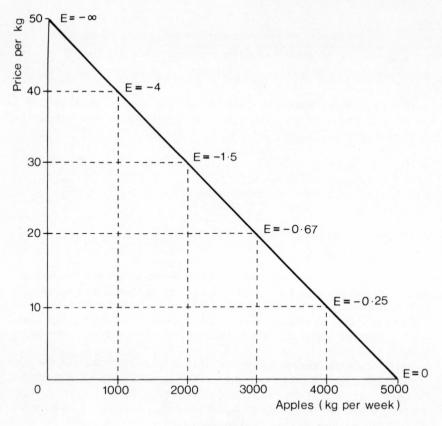

Figure 1.9

The coefficient of price elasticity of demand (*E*) is therefore:

$$\frac{\text{Proportionate change in quantity demanded}}{\text{Proportionate change in price}} = \frac{-1/2}{1/3}$$

$$= \frac{-3}{2} \text{ (or } -1\cdot5)$$

In Table 1.1, elasticity coefficients are calculated for a series of points on the demand curve. Except at those points where either price or quantity equals zero the calculation is shown for both an upward and a downward movement along the curve. All the coefficients are negative because an increase in price is always associated with a decrease in quantity (and vice versa) and the coefficients range from 0 at the intersection with the quantity axis, to $-\infty$ at the intersection with the price axis.

Table 1.1

Price (pence per kg)	Quantity (kg)	Elasticity (E)		
0	5000	$\dfrac{-1000/5000}{10/0}$		$= 0$
10	4000	$\dfrac{-1000/4000}{10/10}$	or $\dfrac{1000/4000}{-10/10}$	$= -0 \cdot 25$
20	3000	$\dfrac{-1000/3000}{-10/20}$	or $\dfrac{1000/3000}{10/20}$	$= -0 \cdot 67$
30	2000	$\dfrac{-1000/2000}{10/30}$	or $\dfrac{1000/2000}{-10/30}$	$= -1 \cdot 5$
40	1000	$\dfrac{-1000/1000}{10/40}$	or $\dfrac{1000/1000}{-10/40}$	$= -4 \cdot 0$
50	0		$\dfrac{1000/0}{-10/50}$	$= -\infty$

Demand is said to be *elastic* when the absolute value of the coefficient of price elasticity is greater than −1 and *inelastic* when the coefficient is between 0 and −1. A coefficient of −1 signifies *unitary* elasticity of demand. When demand is elastic, a given percentage change in price is associated with a larger percentage change in quantity, and when demand is inelastic, a given percentage change in price is associated with a smaller percentage change in the quantity demanded. With unitary elasticity, a given percentage change in price is associated with the same percentage change in the quantity demanded.

The calculations of elasticity at any point on the demand curve in Fig. 1.9 can be made using either a price rise or a price fall (except of course at the axes, where a calculation in one direction only is possible): the same value is obtained. The reason for this becomes apparent if we rewrite somewhat the elasticity formula. Consider the same point on the demand curve as before and call the original price and quantity (30p and 2000 kg) P and Q, and the change in price and quantity (10p and 1000 kg) ΔP and ΔQ. Then:

$$E = \frac{\Delta Q/Q}{\Delta P/P}$$

$$= P/Q \times \Delta Q/\Delta P$$

Since $\Delta P/\Delta Q$ is the slope of the demand curve, this can be rewritten:

$$\frac{P}{Q} \times \frac{1}{\text{Slope of demand curve}}$$

As the slope of a straight line demand curve is constant (and, as it happens, equal to -1 in the case of Fig. 1.9) the elasticity varies along the length of the curve as P/Q varies, $\Delta P/\Delta Q$ remaining constant.

If the relationship between price and quantity is curvilinear, then it is preferable to use this reformulation in order to calculate elasticity at a point on the curve. Taking the curve DD in Fig. 1.10, the elasticity at point Z will be

$$\frac{P_1}{Q_1} \times \frac{1}{\text{slope of curve at point } Z} = \frac{P_1}{Q_1} \times \frac{1}{(-a/b)} = -\left(\frac{P_1}{Q_1} \times \frac{b}{a}\right)$$

The formula (percentage change in quantity)/(percentage change in price) will only give the same value for very small changes in price and quantity and will become increasingly inaccurate as a measure of elasticity at a point on a curvilinear demand curve when the price and quantity changes become greater. (Because of this, some economists prefer to include 'for a very small change' in

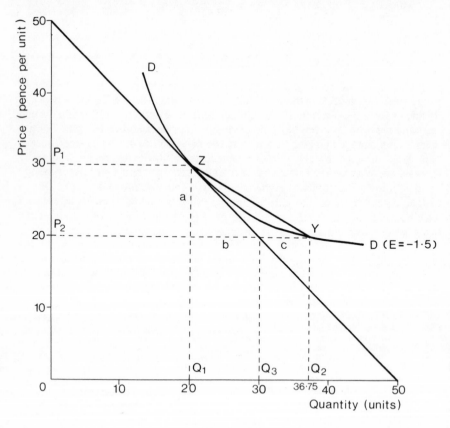

Figure 1.10

the definition of elasticity.) For example, taking the decrease in price from P_1 to P_2 (a movement from Z to Y on the demand curve),

$$\frac{\text{Percentage change in quantity}}{\text{Percentage change in price}} = \frac{(b + c/Q_1)}{-a/P_1}$$

$$= -\left(\frac{P_1}{Q_1} \times \frac{b+c}{a}\right)$$

This latter method of measuring elasticity at a point on a demand curve is known as *arc elasticity* and the value of the coefficient will vary depending on the direction and extent of the price change (except, as already seen, in the case of the straight line demand curve).

It will sometimes be the case that information is available concerning demand at only two alternative prices and quantities – say at points Z and Y in Fig. 1.10. There are an infinite number of demand curves that could be consistent with this information, including DD and the straight line passing through Z and Y. A method of estimating elasticity, known as the 'Allen formula' (7) is sometimes used in these circumstances. This is to take

$$\frac{\text{(Change in quantity)/(average quantity demanded)}}{\text{(Change in price)/(average price)}}$$

or

$$\left(\frac{(Q_1 - Q_2)/\frac{1}{2}(Q_1 + Q_2)}{(P_1 - P_2)/\frac{1}{2}(P_1 + P_2)}\right)$$

In our example, this would give an elasticity coefficient of:

$$\frac{-(b + c)/\frac{1}{2}(Q_1 + Q_2)}{a/\frac{1}{2}(P_1 + P_2)} = -\left(\frac{P_1 + P_2}{Q_1 + Q_2} \times \frac{b+c}{a}\right)$$

This gives, in effect, the elasticity at a point halfway between Z and Y on the straight line joining these two points.

We have so far gone no further than to say that demand will normally be inversely related to price, and that price elasticity coefficients will therefore be negative. Is there anything else that can be said about the likely shape of a demand curve? One plausible suggestion, which is supported by a certain amount of empirical evidence, is that price elasticity coefficients might remain roughly constant along the length of a demand curve. This would mean that, for a small percentage change in price, the percentage change in quantity demanded would be the same at high or low prices. This demand relationship can be contrasted with the implications of the straight line demand curve shown in Fig. 1.9 which requires the same absolute change in the quantity demanded to result when price changes by some given amount, whether the initial price is relatively high or low.

For a demand curve to have constant elasticity, its slope must change continually along the length of the curve to compensate for changes in the value of P/Q in the formula:

$$E = P/Q \times \frac{1}{\text{slope of demand curve}}$$

For example, in Fig. 1.10, P_1 is 30p per unit, Q_1 is 20 units, and the slope of DD at point Z is -1. Elasticity at point Z is therefore:

$$\frac{30}{20} \times \frac{1}{-1} = -1 \cdot 5$$

P_2 is 20p per unit and Q_2 is $36\frac{3}{4}$ units. For the demand curve DD to have a constant elasticity of $-1 \cdot 5$:

$$\frac{20}{36 \cdot 75} \times \frac{1}{\text{slope of curve at } Y}$$

must equal $-1 \cdot 5$, i.e. the slope of DD at point Y must be:

$$\frac{20}{36 \cdot 75} \times -\frac{2}{3} = -0 \cdot 363 \text{ (approx.)}.$$

In Fig. 1.11 the curve D_1D_1 has constant elasticity of $-0 \cdot 5$, and because this coefficient relates to every point on the curve, D_1D_1 can be called an *inelastic demand curve*. Similarly, the curve D_2D_2 has constant elasticity equal to -2 and is therefore an *elastic demand curve*. Curve D_3D_3 is of constant unitary elasticity which means that a given small percentage change in price will always be associated with the same percentage change in quantity demanded. Thus with a *unitary demand curve*, revenue (price × quantity) is always the same. In terms of Fig. 1.11, area OP_1AQ_1 ($= £4000$) = area OP_2BQ_2 = area OP_3GQ_3, and so on. In the case of the inelastic demand curve, revenue increases continuously as price increases (i.e. area OP_3HQ_4 (£5656) > area OP_1AQ_1) and with the elastic demand curve, revenue decreases continuously as price increases (area OP_3FQ_5 (£2000) < area OP_1AQ_1).

When elasticity is thought to be constant and equal to a particular value, the impact on quantity demanded of a relatively large price change can only be calculated accurately by reference to the appropriate equation of the demand curve. (For example, the equation of a unitary demand curve will be $P \times Q = R$, where R (revenue) is a constant in this case, since P and Q must always vary so as to leave revenue unchanged.)[6] The use of the formula:

$$\frac{\text{Percentage change in quantity}}{\text{Percentage change in price}}$$

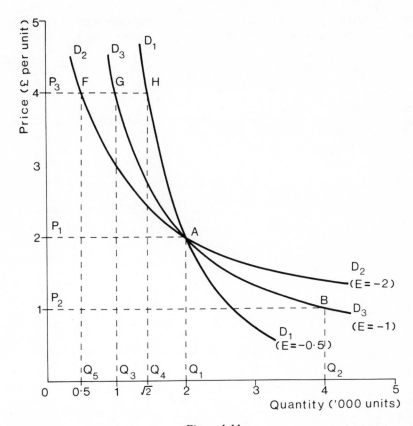

Figure 1.11

will give an increasingly incorrect estimate of demand response as the percentage change in price increases. Returning to Fig. 1.10, with *DD* representing a demand curve of uniform elasticity equal to $-1\cdot5$, the percentage change formula underestimates by about 20 per cent (Q_3 rather than Q_2) the increase in quantity demanded that follows the fall in price from P_1 to P_2.

3.2 Price elasticities for food products

Table 1.2 gives estimates made by the UK Ministry of Agriculture, Fisheries and Food of price elasticities of demand for the main food products and food product groups in Britain. The figures should not, of course, be regarded as precise price elasticity coefficients; they are, rather, broad indications of the order of magnitude likely to have been involved in each case.

The most obvious characteristic of Table 1.2 is that the majority of the coefficients are between 0 and -1. In other words, for most food products, a

Table 1.2   Estimates of price elasticities of demand for major food products and product groups in Britain (1968–73)

Product	Price elasticity
Beef and veal	−1·57
Mutton and lamb	−0·91
Pork	−1·06
All carcase meat	−0·62
Bacon and ham (uncooked)	−0·49
Broiler chicken	−0·88
Sausages	−0·48
All meat and meat products	−0·21
Butter	−0·40
All fats	−0·04
Milk	−0·09
Fish*	−0·71
Eggs	−0·09
Sugar and preserves*	−0·21
Cheese*	−0·25
Potatoes (excluding potato products)	−0·12
Cauliflowers	−1·43
Tomatoes	−0·28
Frozen peas	−0·70
All vegetables* (excluding potatoes)	−0·34
Oranges	−1·07
Apples	−0·57
Bananas	−1·41
All fresh fruit*	−0·57
Bread	−0·32
Other cereals*	−0·71
Tea	−0·34
Coffee	−1·10
All beverages*	−0·64

Source: MAFF (8).   * 1966–73.

proportionate change in price is associated with a less than proportionate change in the quantity demanded. Table 1.2 is consistent with one other normal characteristic – that the demand for a product will tend to be more elastic the better or more numerous are the substitutes for it. Thus products such as milk, eggs, cheese, butter, bread, sugar, potatoes and tomatoes – all of which lack good substitutes – are very price inelastic. This feature of demand means that the more we attempt to break food consumption down into individual product categories, the more price elastic the demand for each product is likely to become. It is for this reason that the demand for all carcase meat is less elastic than that for beef and veal, pork, or mutton and lamb, taken separately. (The weighted average elasticity of beef and veal, mutton and lamb, and pork is −1·30 compared to a coefficient of −0·62 for all carcase meat.) Similarly, the demand (by weight) for all meat and meat products is much less elastic than that for any individual meat product.

Demand is more elastic for some fruits and vegetables for which closer substitutes are available, but again 'all fruit' and 'all vegetables' are much less price elastic than the weighted average elasticity of individual fruits and vegetables.

It is also sometimes argued that the price elasticity of a product will be greater the greater the proportion of consumers' income devoted to it. This is because the income effect for a normal good will strengthen the substitution effect, and the income effect of a price change will have a greater impact upon real income the more significant the product is in the overall purchasing pattern of the consumer. There is some evidence in Table 1.2 to support this view but it is not possible to distinguish statistically the influence on the degree of elasticity, on the one hand, of the existence, or otherwise, of close substitutes, and on the other hand, of the proportion of consumers' income spent on the product.

Earlier we stated that for virtually every food product we would expect the quantity demanded to be inversely related to price. There are three possible exceptions to this generalisation. The first of these was mentioned in section 1 of this chapter − the case of a 'Giffen good'. If in a particular market there are enough individuals for whom the income effect exceeds the substitution effect for some basic foodstuff, then the effect of an increase in price would be to increase the quantity demanded in the market.

The second possibility is that a rise in price might be taken by consumers as evidence that further price rises are likely to follow. Over a small part of the demand curve, and for a short period of time only, quantity demanded and price might therefore be positively related.

A third case is where the price of the product is taken as an indicator of quality. The conventional textbook examples of this refer to luxury goods − where the consumer is only satisfied that the product is a luxury if it 'really is expensive'. Thus, over a particular price range, it is possible that the quantity demanded of − say − champagne or caviar might be positively related to changes in price.

Evidence has been provided by research carried out at Nottingham University (9) which suggests that price might be taken as an indicator of quality in the case of some everyday products. This study investigated the hypothesis that

The typical consumer enters the market with a price bracket in mind, and this is what gives rise to the phenomenon of the market demand curve.

The authors claim that

Our results clearly indicate that the typical short-run demand curve for competitive branded products has a substantial backward sloping portion.

Among the six goods investigated were two food products and for one of these

> There was strong evidence of a breaking point at three shillings, indicating that ... housewives have a (possibly rational) distrust of brands priced below three shillings, which is in fact the price of the cheapest category produced by leading manufacturers.

Unfortunately (because of a request by the organisation which financed and assisted in the investigation) the identity of the food product was not given, but we might surmise that a meat product – say sausages – could display the same kind of demand characteristics. The UK National Food Survey shows that the average price for pork sausages in the United Kingdom at the time of this investigation (mid-1960s) was about three shillings and fourpence (16½p) so that housewives might well have been suspicious of pork sausages priced at less than three shillings per pound. (British pork sausages are traditionally of a better quality than beef sausages and have a higher meat content.) If then the implications of this study are correct – and one must be a little sceptical about

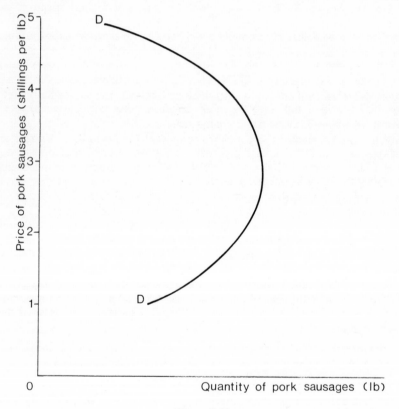

Figure 1.12

results which are based on housewives being questioned as regards their purchasing behaviour rather than based on observed behaviour in the market – the demand curve for pork sausages in the United Kingdom at the time of the survey would have looked something like that shown in Fig. 1.12. Quantity demanded increases in the 'normal way' as the price declines towards three shillings per pound but decreases if the price falls below three shillings.

The important message of these examples of a 'backward sloping' demand curve is to indicate just how unlikely it probably is that the quantity demanded of a food product could be positively related to its price. The examples also emphasise the importance in demand theory of the assumption that all other factors affecting demand, apart from the variable under consideration, should remain constant. When a change in price is taken by a consumer as evidence that further price changes will follow, strictly speaking, all other things do not remain constant. There has been a change in the expected future price of the product, and although we did not include this in our list (section 2) of the major factors affecting demand, changes in future price expectations can have a significant impact upon the quantity purchased of a product in some circumstances. In the case of the example of price as an indicator of quality, if the cheap sausages were in fact inferior, then we would not be dealing with precisely the same product, which is a necessary assumption for the identification of a single demand curve.

Any demand curve is defined for some given set of constant values for all variables affecting the demand for a product, apart from product price. A change in the value of one of these other variables, such as for example a rise in average income or a fall in the price of a substitute product, is likely to mean a different quantity purchased at any given price, or to put it in graphical terms, a shift in the demand curve to a new position. It is to these other factors that we now turn.

4 The prices of other products

The responsiveness of the quantity demanded of one product (A) to a change in the price of another product (B) is known as *cross price elasticity of demand* and is defined as:

$$\frac{\text{Proportionate change in quantity demanded of product A}}{\text{Proportionate change in price of product B}}$$

The cross price elasticity of demand might be positive or negative – that is, an increase in the price of product B might cause the quantity demanded of product A either to increase or decrease, depending mainly on whether the products are *complements* or *substitutes*. Complements are goods which are customarily consumed together, for example gin and tonic, bread and jam, and bacon and eggs. An increase in the price of jam might therefore cause a decrease in the quantity of bread purchased (as well as a decrease in the quantity of jam itself).

Most food products are, to a greater or lesser extent, substitutes for one another and demonstrate positive cross price elasticities of demand. Table 1.3 gives calculations of cross price elasticities for carcase meats in Britain. Reading down the first column of coefficients, an increase of 1 per cent in the average price of beef and veal, other things remaining equal, would be expected to result in a decrease of 1·56 per cent in the average quantity of beef and veal bought, together with an increase of 0·62 per cent in average purchases of mutton and lamb, and increases of 0·25 per cent and 0·29 per cent respectively in purchases of pork and broiler chicken.

One rather surprising feature of Table 1.3 is the suggestion that pork and chicken might demonstrate the characteristics of complements. Although it would not be impossible to devise a rational explanation for this, the figures should certainly be treated with caution for some of the values in the table do not attain formal statistical significance and it is probably wise to discount the smaller values.

Two products might, of course, act either as complements or substitutes depending on the manner of their use. Bread and butter are complements when the butter is spread on the bread, but may act as substitutes when butter is used for making cakes. Whether these products demonstrate positive or negative cross price elasticities, and are therefore regarded as complements or substitutes, will depend on the net effect.

In associating positive cross price elasticities with substitutes, and negative cross price elasticities with complements we have, in effect, ignored the income effect of a price change. In market terms, the income effect – where a rise in the price of one good, by reducing the real income of consumers, causes them to reduce their purchases of other goods – will strengthen the cross price relationship for complements but offset it for substitutes.

Table 1.3   Own price, and cross price elasticities of demand: Great Britain (1966–73)

| | Elasticity with respect to the price of: | | | |
	Beef and veal	Mutton and lamb	Pork	Broiler chicken
Beef and veal	−1·56	0·32	0·26	0·07
Mutton and lamb	0·62	−1·19	0·16	0·32
Pork	0·85	0·26	−1·29	−0·08
Broiler chicken	0·29	0·71	−0·11	−1·21

Source: MAFF (8).

NB   The own-price elasticities differ somewhat from those given in Table 1.2, both because the two tables relate to different time periods and because they were derived using different estimation techniques.

If the product under consideration is an inferior good then the income effect will strengthen the cross price effect for a substitute. For example, suppose that there is an increase in the price of meat. If bread is an inferior good then consumers will tend to increase their consumption of bread, both because they are substituting bread for another product (meat), the price of which has risen, and because their real incomes have been reduced by the increase in the price of meat, the effect of which is to lead to a reduction in the consumption of normal goods, but an increase in the consumption of inferior goods.

For products which represent only a small proportion of the consumer's total budget the income effect is likely to be slight in relation to the cross price effect, but for products which do represent a significant item in consumer expenditure, the income effect might well have a perceptual impact upon estimates of cross price elasticities. For example, referring to Table 1.3, it is not inconceivable that, if pork and chicken are regarded by consumers as only mild substitutes, the income effect might be sufficient to produce negative values of cross price elasticities between pork and chicken. For an empirical study which took account of this effect, see Ferris *et al.* (10).

The concept of cross price elasticity of demand provides a convenient basis for defining a commodity. If for example all consumers regard Guernsey and Jersey tomatoes as perfect substitutes for one another, then, as far as market demand is concerned, they are a *homogenous product* and would possess infinite coefficients of cross price elasticity. (The cheaper tomato would always be purchased in preference to the more expensive.) We might then expect to find quite high cross price elasticity coefficients between Channel Islands and – say – Canary Island tomatoes, and moderate coefficients between tomatoes and vegetables. For other food products we would expect positive, but very low coefficients, except for those foods which constitute a significant proportion of total household budgets, where the income effect might possibly cause negative cross price coefficients. Finally, if we could find a product which is normally consumed jointly with tomatoes, then we would expect to find negative cross price elasticity coefficients.

5 Consumer income

The relationship between the market demand for a product and the average income of consumers can be represented by an *income–demand curve* which is analogous to the income–consumption curve of an individual consumer. A form of income–demand curve, demonstrating the various possible relationships, is shown in Fig. 1.13. If total income is fairly evenly distributed among individuals, only the barest necessities will be demanded at very low average levels of income. In Fig. 1.13 therefore, average income increases to level A before the product begins to be demanded. The quantity purchased increases with income between A and C, first at an increasing and then at a decreasing rate. Between C and D extra income does not alter the amount purchased, and

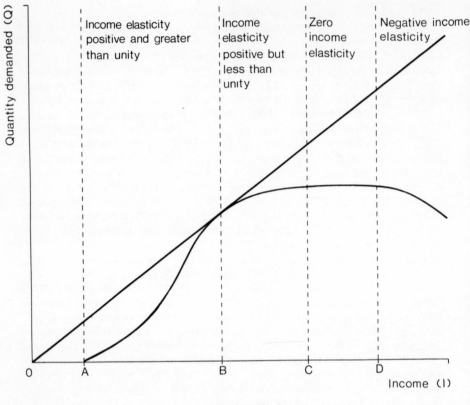

Figure 1.13

when income increases beyond D demand declines as other more expensive goods are substituted for this product, which has become an inferior good.

Income elasticity of demand (E_i) is the conventional measure of the responsiveness of demand for a product to a change in the average income of the population, and is defined as:

$$E_i = \frac{\text{Percentage change in quantity demanded}}{\text{Percentage change in income}}$$

The various possible relationships between demand and income are classified according to the numerical measure of income elasticity in Table 1.4.

Thus in Fig. 1.13 income elasticity is not defined between 0 and A (since percentage change in quantity demanded involves dividing zero by zero); is positive betweeen A and C; zero between C and D; and negative when income is higher than D. For income levels between A and C it is not immediately obvious, from inspection of the income demand curve, when E_i is greater and when it is less than unity. This is because the coefficient of income elasticity

Table 1.4

E_i	Nature of relationship between demand and income
Greater than unity	Demand for the product increases more than in proportion to the increase in income
Unity	Demand for the product increases in the same proportion as the increase in income
Between zero and unity	Demand for the product increases less than in proportion to the increase in income
Zero	Demand for the product does not change as income increases
Negative	Demand for the product decreases as income increases

varies with both the slope of, and position on, the income–demand curve. If we rewrite the formula for income elasticity as:

$$E_i = \frac{\Delta Q/Q}{\Delta I/I}$$

Then E_i will be greater than unity ($E_1 > 1$) if:

$$\Delta Q/Q > \Delta I/I \text{ or } \Delta Q/\Delta I > Q/I$$

Since for very small changes in income $\Delta Q/\Delta I$ becomes the slope of the income–demand curve, if the slope at a point on the curve exceeds the ratio Q/I (which is the slope of a line drawn from the origin to that point on the curve), the income elasticity coefficient will be greater than unity. Thus in the case of Fig. 1.13, the coefficient of income elasticity is above one between A and B and less than one between B and C.

Table 1.5 lists estimates of income elasticities of demand for various agricultural products in a selected group of countries. The coefficients are those that were used by the Food and Agricultural Organisation of the United Nations (FAO) when attempting to predict growth in demand for agricultural products between 1970 and 1980, and as with the price elasticity coefficients discussed earlier, the figures should be regarded as giving only a broad indication of the order of magnitude likely to have been involved in each case. Nevertheless they provide an extremely valuable picture of the way demand for food products changes in response to growth in real income per head.

The most notable characteristic of Table 1.5 is that the majority of the coefficients are positive but less than unity, indicating that an increase in income is associated with a less than proportionate increase in the demand for the product in question. This feature of food consumption was noted in the nineteenth century by the German statistician Ernst Engel and has since become widely known as 'Engel's law' (income–demand curves are correspondingly sometimes referred to as 'Engel curves').[7] There are also a

Table 1.5   Income elasticities of demand

Product	USA	Sweden	France	Australia	UK	Italy	Spain	Brazil	Kenya	India	Indonesia
Wheat	−0.3	−0.3	−0.4	−0.1	−0.2	−0.2	−0.3	0.4	0.8	0.5	1.0
Coarse grain	−0.1	−0.3	−0.1	0	−0.1	−0.4	−0.1	−0.3	0.4	−0.2	0.4
Sugar	0.1	0	0.3	−0.1	0	0.4	0.6	0.1	1.0	1.0	1.4
Vegetables	0.1	0.5	0.3	0.2	0.3	0.3	0.5	0.5	0.5	0.7	0.6
Fruit	0.2	0.6	0.5	0.7	0.5	0.6	0.7	0.5	0.5	0.8	0.8
Meat	0.2	0.2	0.4	0.1	0.2	0.7	0.7	0.5	1.0	1.2	1.3
Eggs	−0.1	0.1	0.2	0	0	0.5	0.6	0.6	1.0	1.0	1.2
Fish	0.3	0.3	0.6	0.3	0.3	0.4	0.7	0.5	0.8	1.5	1.0
Milk	−0.5	−0.2	0.1	0	−0.1	0.3	0.5	0.6	0.8	0.8	2.0
Butter	−0.5	−0.2	0.2	−0.1	0	0.4	0.5	1.1	0.9	0.6	n.a.
Coffee	0	0.3	0.5	0.8	0.8	1.0	1.0	0.1	1.0	0.4	0.2
Farm value	0.04	0.1	0.2	0.1	0.1	0.3	0.4	0.3	0.6	0.6	0.7
GNP per head (1971, $)	5160	4240	3360	2870	2430	1860	1100	460	160	110	80

Source: FAO (11), IBRD (12).

number of negative coefficients, indicating products which have, on balance, become inferior goods in the country concerned. This is only a common occurrence with cereals, but milk, butter, sugar and eggs all appear to be inferior goods in at least one country. (Many food products will, of course, be inferior goods for some members of the population but, for a negative income elasticity coefficient to emerge from analysis of national data, a sufficient proportion of the population must reduce their purchases of the product when their incomes rise so as to more than offset the action of those consumers for whom the product remains a normal good.) In general the highest coefficients are shown for meat, fish, fruit and vegetables; it is these products that consumers tend to substitute for staple foodstuffs, such as bread, potatoes and rice, when incomes rise.

The figure given for income elasticity of demand of *farm value* is an estimate of the relationship between increase in average income per head and the demand for all agricultural products valued at 1965 prices. It is thus a kind of income elasticity of demand for all agricultural products taken together.[8] All the 'farm value' coefficients are consistent with 'Engel's law', implying that an increase in income will bring forth a less than proportionate demand for all food products (valued at constant prices), or, to put it another way, that the proportion of income spent on food products declines as income rises.

If it were possible to estimate income elasticity coefficients from data relating to the same population over an extensive range of average incomes per head, a much more uniform picture would be attained than that presented by Table 1.5. Intercountry differences in tradition, culture, climate and Government policy will all affect demand patterns for food products, and the GNP per head figures, when converted to US dollars, are themselves very imperfect indications of levels of income per head. Nevertheless, with the aid of these elasticity coefficients and the associated FAO data on per caput consumption of food products in different countries, together with figures for food consumption among different income groups in the same country and information concerning historical trends in consumption, it is possible to build up a picture which allows us to construct plausible income–demand curves for the main agricultural products. Four examples of these are shown in Fig. 1.14.

Figure 1.14a is the kind of income–demand curve that one might expect for any basic foodstuff, such as bread, potatoes, rice or cassava. Consumption rises rapidly at very low levels of income but quickly reaches a maximum and then consistently declines. The income–demand curve for butter (Fig. 1.14c) is perhaps the most speculative of the four. There is substantial evidence of declining butter consumption in some high income countries but one cannot be sure of the extent to which this can be attributed to income growth as opposed to a shift in taste patterns (following publicity over the supposed health hazards of animal fats).

A distinction is sometimes made between 'income elasticity of quantity demanded' and 'income elasticity of expenditure'. Strictly speaking, if a product is precisely defined, these measures should be identical since if all other things remain equal, including the price and specifications of the product, a

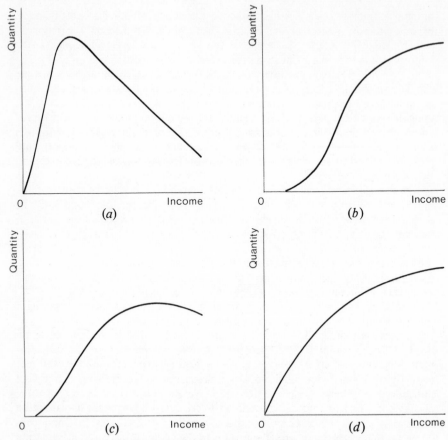

Figure 1.14   (a) Cereal product, (b) Meat, (c) Butter (d) Fruit or vegetable

certain percentage increase in the quantity purchased must result in the same percentage increase in expenditure on the product. However, when an income elasticity coefficient is calculated for a broader commodity group, the measures will tend to diverge as there is a tendency for consumers to switch to higher quality (and higher priced) varieties within the broad food groups when their incomes rise; in other words, the income elasticity of quantity demanded tends to be higher for higher priced varieties and thus the income elasticity of expenditure for the product group will exceed the income elasticity of quantity demanded.

This distinction can be illustrated by the use of a simple example. Suppose there are two varieties of green beans sold, fresh and frozen. Fresh beans sell at 10p per kg and frozen beans at 20p per kg. In Table 1.6 the quantities of both categories of beans sold in time period T_1 are shown in the second column and the quantities sold in time period T_2 in the fourth column; it is assumed that

Table 1.6

Product	Time period T_1 Quantity	Expenditure	Time period T_2 Quantity	Expenditure	Income elasticity of: Quantity	Expenditure
Frozen beans	100	2000	110	2200	1·0	1·0
Fresh beans	100	1000	105	1050	0·5	0·5
Total beans	200	3000	215	3250	0·75	0·833

average income has increased by 10 per cent between the two time periods but that prices remain unchanged. The expenditure on beans in the two time periods is shown in columns 3 and 5. The 10 per cent increase in income has led to a 10 per cent increase in quantity demanded and expenditure for frozen beans but to only a 5 per cent increase in the case of fresh beans, so the income elasticities of quantity demanded and expenditure are 1·0 and 0·5 respectively. The income elasticity of quantity demanded of all beans is 0·75 (the weighted average of the individual elasticities). However, the income elasticity of expenditure for all beans (which equals $(250/3000)/(10/100) = 0.833$, exceeds the equivalent income elasticity of quantity demanded because of the increased proportion of frozen beans purchased in time period two.

The UK Ministry of Agriculture estimates income elasticities of both quantity (in terms of weight) and expenditure using data from its survey of household food expenditure. It is reassuring to note that the Ministry's calculations are generally in accord with those made for the United Kingdom by the FAO. Some of the estimates made for 1971 are shown in Table 1.7. It

Table 1.7   Income elasticities of quantity demanded and expenditure for major food products (UK, 1971)

Product	Income elasticity of quantity demanded	Income elasticity of expenditure
Milk	0·17	0·18
Cheese	0·24	0·28
Carcase meat	0·21	0·27
Fish	0·04	0·17
Eggs	0·09	0·12
Butter	0·18	0·19
Sugar	−0·09	−0·05
Potatoes	−0·17	−0·09
Green vegetables	0·34	0·50
Bread	−0·20	−0·16
Beverages	0	0·10
ALL FOODS	n.a.	0·20

Source: MAFF (14).

will be seen that the coefficients for expenditure are consistently, though not substantially, higher than those for quantity. The coefficients are closest for those products for which there is little scope for switching to higher priced varieties, such as liquid milk, butter, sugar, bread and eggs. (A switch by consumers to higher priced large eggs would, of course, be reflected by an increase in quantity demanded (by weight).) The difference between coefficients of income elasticity of quantity and expenditure therefore represents a useful indication of the extent to which consumers are purchasing better qualities and more processed products as their incomes rise.

6 The distribution of income

In textbooks of economics income distribution is normally specified as one of the factors which influences demand but its relationship with the quantity purchased of a commodity is not investigated in the same way as it is with prices or average income. The most important reason for this is that the distribution of income is one of those factors which most people believe it is reasonable to assume remains constant over fairly long periods of time. In the developed countries, average levels of income increased a few per cent per annum for more than one hundred years, with the distribution of income probably not changing very much. It is only in the more recent past that governments have become extensively involved in distribution, and the possibility that a government might now contemplate a tax programme which is a radical departure from previous practice means that, in some circumstances, aggregate demand for a food product could be altered more rapidly in the short term by changing income distribution than by growth in average income per head.

A second reason for the neglect of income distribution as a factor affecting demand is the lack of a single acceptable method of measuring it. In this chapter the conventional *Lorenz curve/Gini coefficient* method is used, and although this technique is not entirely satisfactory it does at least allow us to investigate the impact of different income distributions on the demand for a food product.

A Lorenz curve relates the cumulative percentage of aggregate income to the cumulative percentage of the population receiving that income. If every member of the population received the same income, the Lorenz curve would coincide with the diagonal line *OC* shown in Fig. 1.15a – that is, 25 per cent of the population receive 25 per cent of aggregate income, 50 per cent of the population receive 50 per cent of aggregate income, and so on. In Fig. 1.15, the population are ranked according to income level along the horizontal axes, with those with the lowest incomes to the left and those with the highest to the right. The shape of any Lorenz curve must be such that it rises continually at an increasing rate since, if the 10 per cent of the population with the lowest incomes have – say – 5 per cent of aggregate income, the 10 per cent with the next lowest incomes cannot have less than 5 per cent of aggregate income. The

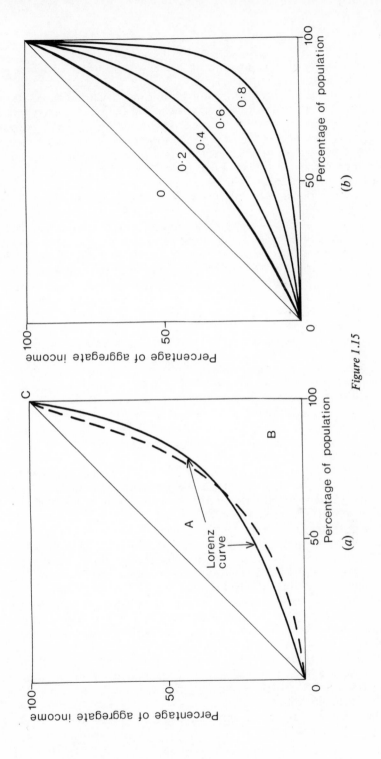

Figure 1.15

more unequal the distribution of income, the further below the diagonal will lie the Lorenz curve.

While the Lorenz curve has the useful property of illustrating the degree of inequality it does not provide a precise value that can be used for comparative purposes. A measure which does have this property is the *inequality coefficient* (or '*Gini coefficient*'), which is defined as the ratio of the area between the diagonal and a Lorenz curve to the total area under the diagonal; in Fig. 1.15a this is area $A/(\text{area } A + B)$ for the Lorenz curve shown. An inequality coefficient computed in this way will always assume a positive value, and its limits will be zero, denoting a completely equal income distribution and 1 implying complete inequality.

Since there are other Lorenz curves, such as that shown by the broken line in Fig. 1.15a, which will generate the same value as $A/(A + B)$ when the ratio of the area between the curve and diagonal to the total area is calculated, an inequality coefficient will not be uniquely associated with a particular Lorenz curve. However, if, as in Fig. 1.15b, we progressively alter the shape of the Lorenz curve in a uniform manner, ensuring that none of the curves cross, we obtain a range of income distributions which can be represented by a series of inequality coefficients.

We are now in a position to relate a series of alternative distributions of income to the demand for a food product. Before doing so, it is perhaps worth pausing to enquire why there should be a demand response to changing income distribution. This will be the case if those who are made worse off by the redistribution reduce their purchases of the product by a different amount from the increase in consumption by those who are made better off. (In the case of an inferior good it will be if those who are made worse off increase their purchases by a different amount from the reduction in purchases by those who are made better off.)

Suppose for example that redistribution is possible anywhere within the range £20 to £100 per week and that the population all demonstrate the same purchasing patterns at different income levels. In these circumstances, only a linear income–consumption relationship, such as AB in Fig. 1.16, means no change in aggregate consumption following a change in income distribution. If the income–consumption curve is a straight line over the relevant income range, then £1 added to any individual whose income lies anywhere within that income range will lead to an increase in consumption which is the same as the reduction in consumption which results when £1 is taken from any of the individuals whose income also lies within the range. Most available evidence suggests, however, that for most food products, the individual's income consumption curve, over an income range which excludes very low and very high incomes, is most likely to take the form of a curve, the slope of which is declining, such as that illustrated by the broken line in Fig. 1.16. If this hypothesis is correct, then we would expect the quantity demanded of a product to be inversely related to the inequality coefficient – that is, demand falls as income inequality is increased.

Note that there is no straightforward relationship between coefficients of

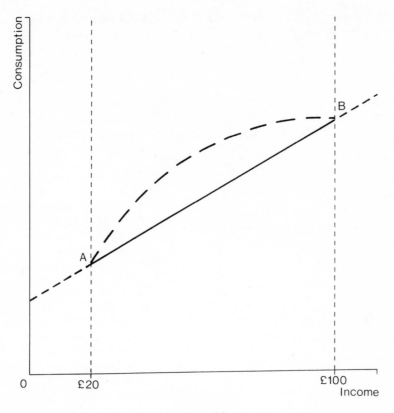

Figure 1.16

income elasticity and the response of demand to changing income distribution. A straight line income–consumption curve over the relevant range, such as *AB* in Fig. 1.16, will be associated with a constant income elasticity coefficient (of unity) if, and only if, it passes through the origin when extended back. If, when extended, it cuts the consumption axes, the income elasticity coefficient increases along the length of the line. Similarly, if it cuts the income axes, the income elasticity coefficient decreases consistently. In general, however, an income–consumption curve with declining slope, such as the broken line in Fig. 1.16, will be associated with a declining coefficient of income elasticity.

We can further illustrate the relationship between income distribution and demand by using information concerning the quantities of food products purchased at different levels of income in the United Kingdom. The annual report of the National Food Survey (15) provides figures for weekly consumption of food products divided into five income groups,[9] classified according to the gross weekly income of the head of the household, ranging (in 1972) from 'over £80 per week' to 'less than £17 per week'. In Fig. 1.17, consumption (ounces per person per week) has been plotted against income (£ per week earned by head of household) for four products – carcase meat, frozen vegetables, butter and potatoes.

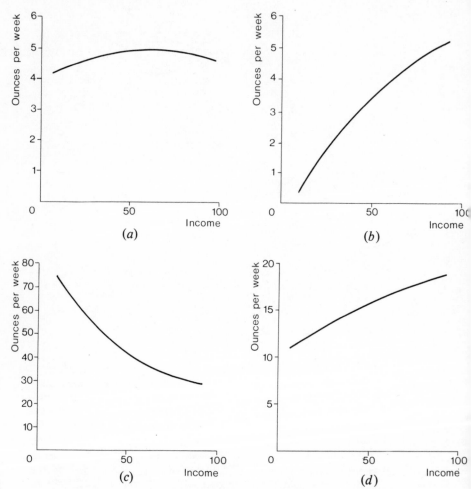

Figure 1.17   (a) *Butter,* (b) *Frozen vegetables,* (c) *Potatoes,* (d) *Meat*

If we assume that these relationships represent income–consumption curves for the 'average' British consumer, the same information can be used to estimate *income distribution–demand curves*, as in Fig. 1.18. Inequality coefficients ranging from 0 to 1, which have been generated from a series of Lorenz curves constructed in the same way as those illustrated in Fig. 1.15b, are measured along the horizontal axis, and consumption (ounces per person

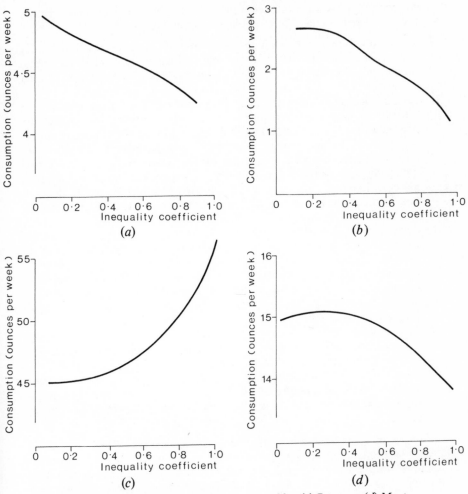

Figure 1.18   (a) Butter, (b) Frozen vegetables, (c) Potatoes, (d) Meat

per week) measured on the vertical axis. The average consumption per week for each of the four products has been estimated by noting the proportion of the population falling into each of the five income groups under the alternative income distributions indicated by different Gini-coefficients. This allows an estimate to be made of average consumption per head for each product under a range of income distributions. The curves therefore attempt to show the way average consumption per head of each of the four products might be expected to change following a change in the distribution of income in the United Kingdom which altered the associated Gini coefficient.

It must be emphasised that these estimates are intended only as illustrations of the concept of an income distribution–demand curve. A number of issues would require further investigation if this kind of approach were to be expected to produce reliable results. For example, we should note that:

(a) The assumption is made (which may be quite reasonable) that individuals who change groups as a result of redistribution display the same purchasing characteristics as those individuals who were in that income group in 1972.

(b) The 'gross income of the head of the household' is far from ideal as the measure of income for our purposes. Earners other than the head of the household might not add to household income in a uniform manner across the different income groups, and the progressive nature of income tax means that the proportion of gross income which must be deducted to obtain the sum available for consumption expenditure increases as 'gross income' increases. Similarly it is likely that the average composition of households, in terms of age and sex, varies among the different income groups.

(c) Perhaps most important of all we do not have sufficient information concerning food purchases at the extremes of the income range. In particular, some of the high inequality coefficients imply a significant proportion of the population at lower levels of income than any reported by the National Food Survey. The income distribution–demand curves shown in Fig. 1.18 are therefore probably less reliable for the higher inequality coefficients.

(d) As mentioned earlier, the same Gini coefficient can be achieved in different ways and this might influence the way quantity demanded is estimated to change as the income distribution is altered.

(e) Finally, we have assumed that redistribution can take place without affecting the total quantity of income available for consumer spending – i.e. average income remains constant, and we have also assumed constant prices.

In spite of these reservations, the National Food Survey does provide very useful information concerning the probable approximate relationship between food consumption and income levels in the United Kingdom, and in particular, a comparison of Figs. 1.17 and 1.18 illustrates very well the kind of income–consumption curve which is likely to lead to a significant demand response when the distribution of income is changed. The income–consumption curve for carcase meat has a slope which declines only slightly, and correspondingly the aggregate demand for meat changes proportionately by only a small amount as the distribution of income is altered. The slope of the income con-sumption curve for frozen vegetables declines by a somewhat greater amount, and the response of the demand for vegetables to changing income distribution is correspondingly somewhat greater. In the case of butter, consumption, although not changing very much over the observed income range, first increases as income increases, but subsequently declines. (In other words butter in the United Kingdom appears to be a normal good at low levels of income and an inferior good at higher levels.) The shape of the income–consumption curve tells us that butter consumption is responsive to changing income distribution. For potatoes we have a 'backward sloping' distribution–demand curve. Note that this is because the decline in the consumption of potatoes levels off at higher incomes – not just because potatoes are an inferior good.

Finally, we should perhaps consider what magnitude of income distribution changes are likely to be feasible in practice. It has been calculated (16) that the imposition of taxes and the distribution of state benefits in the United Kingdom reduces the inequality coefficient for income distribution from 0·385 to 0·282. The distribution–demand curves shown in Fig. 1.18 therefore indicate that the application of a government programme of redistribution of this order of magnitude would imply an increase in the demand for meat of 2 per cent, for butter of 3 per cent and for frozen vegetables of 17 per cent. The consumption of potatoes might be expected to fall by about 4 per cent. These changes in demand can be compared with the number of years likely to be required for the same changes in demand if we assumed an increase in average real income per head of – say – 3 per cent per annum. On the basis of the coefficients of income elasticity of demand calculated by the UK Ministry of Agriculture, this would be something like two years for meat, three and a half years for butter, five years for frozen vegetables, and thirteen years for potatoes.

7 Population and tastes

We have now considered four factors which influence the demand for a product – the price of the product, the prices of other products, the average income per head of the population, and the distribution of income among the population. The remaining two factors specified on page 18 were the size of the population and the tastes and preferences of the population.

Investigating the relationship between population size and the demand for food products is not a particularly useful exercise. This is because, *if there is no change in the other factors*, an increase in the size of the population must result in a pro rata increase in the demand for all products. It was this fact that allowed us in the previous two sections to represent market demand by 'consumption per head' without postulating a particular population size. Total demand would be expected to vary with population size but *under the assumption of 'other things remaining equal'*, consumption per person remains the same with different sizes of population. Now of course it is extremely likely that there will be changes in some of the factors affecting demand associated with changes in population size. For example a change in the size of the population may imply a change in average income and/or a different distribution of income. A growing population will almost certainly be associated with a shift in the taste factor because of alterations in the composition of the population. There might be a greater proportion of young people, of women, of people who live in urban rather than rural areas, or just people who like potatoes. These demand changes which result from changes in the age, sex or locational composition of a population are in fact one of the few aspects of taste shifts which can be incorporated in any meaningful way into the economist's analysis of demand. This is because they are potentially measurable in the sense that they are derived from a change in the number of people who are known to demonstrate a particular type of taste pattern. A growing population may thus be associated with a shift in the population's 'taste' for baby foods, with individual babies assumed to have a constant pattern of tastes and preferences. (If the babies themselves decide to go off strained apples, then that is another matter.)

Changes in the taste factor of a population which are derived from shifts in individual taste patterns lie largely outside the scope of the economist's predictive ability. There is no satisfactory method of measuring this kind of change in taste except by its impact upon demand itself. It is the 'residual' change in demand which is left unexplained when the statistician is satisfied that he has eliminated the demand changes which can be explained on account of the measurable factors. For example, the consumption of imported table wine in the United Kingdom rose from 18·7 million gallons in 1960 to 35·4 million gallons in 1970, and had nearly doubled again at 63·6 million gallons in 1973. It is quite clear that only a small part of this increase can be attributed to income, price, and population changes. In the main, there had been a rapid and massive increase in the demand for wine simply because of a shift in the taste factor. Sometimes it might be very difficult to distinguish statistically, within an overall change in the quantity purchased of a product, the element which should correctly be attributed to a shift in tastes. A case in point is the decline in butter consumption mentioned earlier (Fig. 1.14). We simply do not know the extent to which this is caused by a change in tastes. There must be some suspicion that the negative income elasticities shown in Table 1.5 for butter occur because the statistical techniques used by the FAO were not sensitive enough to avoid attributing the decline in consumption of butter to growth in average income per head.

There is, however, one further aspect of personal taste patterns which is open to demand analysis. This is seasonal shifts in demand. Professor J. A. C. Brown, who developed a technique for eliminating seasonal shifts in demand when calculating elasticity coefficients (17), illustrates the effect on demand of seasonal shifts in the taste factor by comparing the monthly quantities purchased of tomatoes and eggs (shown in Fig. 1.19). He interprets the price–quantity relationships shown as follows:

> Supplies of tomatoes gradually increase from a low level in January until June, but demand increases more quickly so that an increasing level of price (per lb) can be supported. After June, demand begins to recede as other fresh fruit and vegetables and self-supplied tomatoes become available, and the market price drops back sharply while purchases rise to a peak in July; after September, supplies fall off more rapidly than demand and the price again increases. This seasonal pattern in demand must be removed in order to form estimates of the true elasticity of demand in relation to price.

With eggs, on the other hand, though there is of course a marked seasonal variation in supply,[10] the relation between prices and purchases is much more simple; as supplies increase the price falls, and vice versa; the graph of monthly prices plotted against monthly purchases looks plausibly like a demand curve (18).

The UK National Food Survey reports significant seasonal shifts in demand for most food products. The UK climate can perhaps be held largely responsible for this, but culture and tradition also play a part. Some 'traditional' seasonal patterns of food consumption may in fact originate in supply variations – the (sensible) tradition develops of demanding certain foods when they are available. Modern production and marketing techniques reduce supply variations, but the seasonal pattern of demand lives on.

8 Conclusion

The demand function summarises the relationship between a number of independent variables, which determine how much of a product consumers will buy from a market, and the dependent variable – the amount which is bought. An understanding of the way the demand for food products is likely to respond to changes in the independent variables is one of the most important pieces of equipment possessed by agricultural economists. In order to facilitate such an understanding it is convenient to consider the effect on demand of changes in each of the independent variables in isolation, assuming fixed values for all other independent variables. It must be remembered, however, that when applying demand theory we will frequently be called upon to estimate the demand response occasioned by simultaneous changes in a number of the independent variables. A particular problem in this case, which can cause both conceptual and empirical complications, is that the relationship between one independent variable and quantity demanded may vary with the values of the other independent variables. For example, we tend to find that for many food products demand becomes more price inelastic as the average level of consumer income rises.

Simultaneous changes in a number of independent variables will sometimes be mutually reinforcing and in other cases they will counteract one another. An example of the latter kind is where there is a general inflation of all prices. An annual rise in beef prices of – say – 10 per cent might be accompanied by similar price rises for other food products as well as a 10 per cent rise in average consumer incomes. The net effect is most likely to be little change in the quantity demanded of beef. In contrast, if money incomes and other prices remain constant the implications of Table 1.2 are that, in Great Britain anyway, a rise in beef prices of 10 per cent might be expected to lead to a 15 or 16 per cent fall in the demand for beef.

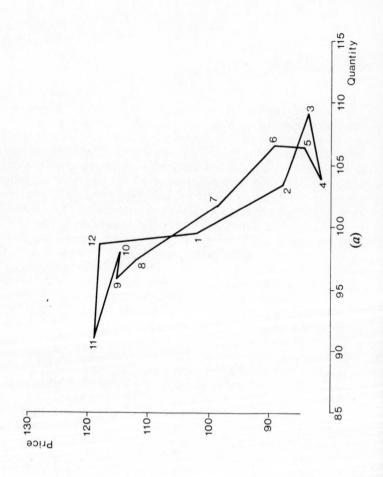

(a)

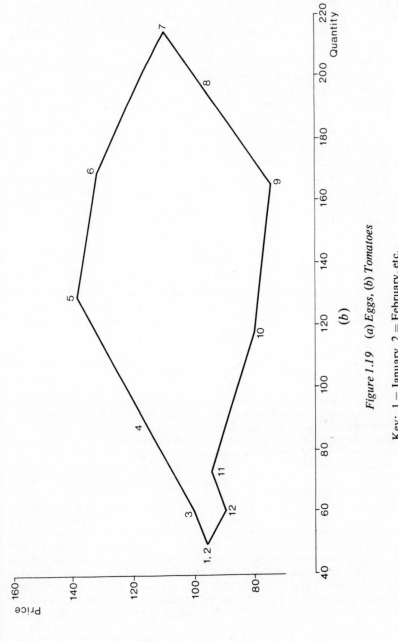

Figure 1.19   (a) Eggs, (b) Tomatoes

Key: 1 = January, 2 = February, etc.
      Annual average retail price = 100
      Annual average quantity purchased = 100

In other words, when considering the response of demand to price changes in the presence of general price inflation, it is more important than ever to remember that an estimate of the response of demand to a change in one of the independent variables assumes that *all other independent variables affecting demand remain constant.*

In most writings on demand theory, there is an implicit assumption that the general rate of price inflation (or deflation) is small enough to be ignored when compared to relative price movements. It may be that, in the presence of a significant degree of general price inflation, it would be preferable to redefine the concepts of a demand curve and an income–demand curve to relate quantity demand to changes in real prices or in real income, by dividing money price and money income by some estimate of the average change in all prices. As yet however, such an approach has not gained widespread support and the more common practice is to take account of general price inflation by recognising that it involves the simultaneous movement in a number of (so-called) independent variables, all of which influence the quantity demanded of the product.

Notes

[1] For the reader who is familiar with differential calculus this idea will not present any problems. Marginal utility is simply the first derivative of total utility with respect to quantity consumed. In fact, total utility in Fig. 1.2a is defined by the equation:

$$U = 5 \cdot 5L - 0 \cdot 5L^2$$

Marginal utility is therefore:

$$\frac{dU}{dL} = 5 \cdot 5 - L$$

[2] An example of where this is the case will be found in Chapter 5, section 2.3. Much of the debate over which approach to use is based upon the desire of economists to have a theory which is consistent with observed consumer behaviour using the minimum number of assumptions. Another approach, originated by Samuelson (2) (called *revealed preference*) removes the concept of utility from consumer theory. The various approaches are compared by Majumdar (3), who comes out in favour of indifference curves on the grounds that this is the most useful relative to the number of assumptions made.

[3] Strictly this should read OQ_1 and OQ_4. It is, however, convenient to refer to quantities or prices as just Q_1, Q_2, etc. or P_1, P_2, etc., except in those cases where ambiguity might result. Ambiguity can arise because 'Q_1' can be interpreted to mean either a specific number of units of product A or a point on the quantity axis which indicates a number of units of product A measured by the distance OQ_1. In the latter case 'Q_1Q_2' then indicates the difference between OQ_2 and OQ_1 units, but in the former case 'Q_1Q_2' would mean Q_1 units multiplied by Q_2 units. In this text, unless otherwise stated, Q_1Q_2, P_1P_2, etc. always indicate the distance between points marked on the axes (i.e. $OQ_2 - OQ_1$, $OP_2 - OP_1$, etc.) and Q_1, P_1, etc. is shorthand for OQ_1, OP_1, etc.

[4] The *Shorter Oxford Dictionary* defines 'curve' as 'line of which no part is straight'

and 'straight' as 'without curves'. In spite of this, *straight line curves* are allowed in economics! In Fig. 1.9, quantity demanded (the dependent variable) is measured on the horizontal axis. In fact it is conventional to measure a dependent variable on the vertical axis, but whoever drew the first demand curve (Marshall (5) is usually blamed) got it wrong, and the mistake has been perpetuated by economists ever since.

[5] Though because they are assumed always to be negative, the minus signs are sometimes quietly forgotten. Some economists (for example, Lipsey (6)) in fact prefer to define price elasticity of demand as

$$- \left(\frac{\text{Percentage change in quantity}}{\text{Percentage change in price}} \right)$$

so that they can legitimately use positive coefficients.

[6] The equation of a demand curve of constant elasticity is:

$$Q = CP^E$$

where Q is quantity demanded, P is price, C is a constant, and E is the constant elasticity coefficient. In much theoretical and empirical work it is found convenient to use the double logarithmic form of this equation, i.e.:

$$\log Q = \log C + E \log P$$

Thus a demand curve of constant elasticity, when expressed in this logarithmic form, is a straight line with a slope equal to the elasticity coefficient.

[7] Engel's formulation (in 1857) was:

> The poorer a family is, the greater the proportion of total expenditures which it must use to procure food (13).

Similarly, he asserted that the wealthier a people, the smaller the proportion of food to total expenditure. Subsequently, the 'law' has been used to describe a number of related features of relationships between income and food consumption. 'Engel's law' cannot therefore be given a precise definition which would find universal acceptance.

[8] The calculation of an income elasticity of demand coefficient for 'all food' requires some basis for bringing different products together in a common measure, and there really is no such measure which can be regarded as entirely satisfactory. For example, the use of weight does not make much sense when one is aggregating such things as bread, meat, butter and coffee. Market prices during some base period are more satisfactory, but prices will vary in different countries and between different time periods. A high elasticity coefficient for – say – eggs will therefore have a greater weight in the calculation of the 'all food' elasticity in a country where eggs are relatively high priced. Another possibility would be to break food products down into their chemical components, and FAO do in fact estimate, for each country, income elasticities of demand for 'calories', 'protein' and 'fats'.

It is perhaps worth noting that, however calculated, the income elasticity for all food, unlike the case of price elasticity, will not be less elastic than that implied by the individual product elasticities. The income elasticity of demand for all carcase meat will be the same as the weighted average of the individual income elasticities of beef, pork, and so on.

[9] The lowest income group is further divided into three subgroups, 'with earners', 'without earners', and 'old age pensioners'. In this example, we use only the 'with

earners' category.

10 Brown's data related to a period before controlled environment production techniques reduced most of the seasonal variation in egg supplies.

11 This is not to suggest that the implications of a general inflation of food prices are unimportant. As we shall see in Part II, Governments are often more concerned about a general rise in food prices than they are about relative movements between food product prices – particularly when the rate of change of food prices exceeds the rate of change of other prices. It is not necessarily the case that the quantities purchased of all products will remain unchanged if money incomes and all prices change by the same proportionate amount. Consumers may not fully appreciate that a change in money income is balanced by equivalent changes in product prices, and they may act as if there had been a change in real income or real prices. This effect is called *money illusion*, but it is not thought to be a significant influence in the case of the demand for food products.

References

(1) Boulding, K. E. *Economic Analysis*, 3rd edn. London, Hamish Hamilton, 1955.
(2) Samuelson, P. A. 'Consumption theory in terms of revealed preference.' *Economica*, Vol. XV, Nov. 1948.
(3) Majumdar, T. *The Measurement of Utility*. London, Macmillan, 1966.
(4) Cole, C. L. *Microeconomics: A Contemporary Approach*, pp. 68–69. New York, Harcourt Brace Jovanovich, 1973.
(5) Marshall, A. *Principles of Economics*, 8th edn., p. 132. London, Macmillan, 1920.
(6) Lipsey, R. G. *An Introduction to Positive Economics*, 4th edn. London, Weidenfeld & Nicolson, 1975.
(7) Allen, R. G. D. 'The concept of arc elasticity of demand.' *Review of Economic Studies*, 1934.
(8) Ministry of Agriculture, Fisheries and Food. '*Household food consumption and expenditure:* 1973'. Annual Report of the National Food Survey Committee. London, HMSO, 1975.
(9) Gabor, A. & Granger, C. W. J. 'Price as an indicator of quality: report of an enquiry.' *Economica*, Feb. 1966.
(10) Ferris, J., *et al.* 'The impact on US agricultural trade of the accession of the United Kingdom, Ireland, Denmark and Norway to the European Economic Community.' Research Report No. 11, Appendix F. Institute of International Agriculture, Michigan State University, 1971.
(11) *Agricultural Commodity Projections 1970–80*, Vol. II. Rome, FAO, 1971.
(12) *World Bank Atlas*. Washington, IBRD, 1973.
(13) Burk, M. C. 'Ramifications of the relationship between income and food.' *Journal of Farm Economics*, Vol. XLIV, No. 1, Feb. 1962.
(14) Ministry of Agriculture, Fisheries and Food. *Household Food Consumption and Expenditure 1970 and 1971*. HMSO, 1973.
(15) Ministry of Agriculture, Fisheries and Food. *Household Food Consumption and Expenditure 1972*. HMSO, 1974.
(16) Josling, T. E. & Hamway, D. 'Distribution of costs and benefits of farm support policy.' In *Burdens and Benefits of Farm Support Policies*. Trade Policy Research Centre, 1972.
(17) Ministry of Agriculture, Fisheries and Food. *Household Food Consumption and Expenditure 1969*, Appendix B. HMSO, 1971.
(18) Brown, J. A. C. 'Seasonality and elasticity of the demand for food in Great Britain since derationing.' *Journal of Agricultural Economics*, Vol. XIII, No. 3, June 1959.

CHAPTER 2

The Supply of Agricultural Products

1 Introduction

1.1

It is sometimes helpful to think of the household and the farm firm as representing the twin centres of decision-making upon which the principles of agricultural economics are built. In the first chapter we saw how decisions taken by households concerning consumption lead to a market demand for agricultural products. In this chapter we are concerned with *agricultural production and market supply*. Production is the name given to the process of conversion of certain *inputs* (also called *resources* or *factors of production*) into a consumable form, and the farm firm is a unit within the economy which takes decisions concerning the use of resources to produce agricultural products. The output of the farm firm can be in a form suitable for consumption by households or may require further conversion, in which case it represents an input for another firm which 'processes' it into a consumable form. Thus production decisions taken within the farm firm lead to a supply of agricultural products coming onto the market.

Although it is useful to draw an analogy between consumption, as the process where products are converted into utilities, and production, where resources are converted into products, there is one important respect in which the analogy is incomplete. This is that, whereas the amount of satisfaction derived from the consumption of a product cannot be measured directly – indeed it was pointed out in the previous chapter that many economists are reluctant even to suggest that utility is something which might in principle be measurable – the output of productive activity can be observed and described in physical terms. If a producer chooses one group of inputs rather than another on the grounds that more output will result, the economist does not have to rely solely on this piece of information as evidence of the production relationships involved; output can be recorded and it may be possible to show that the producer was incorrect.

1.2

Factors of production are conventionally grouped into three categories, *land*, *labour* and *capital*. Land is the name given by economists to those productive factors which are natural resources or 'the free gifts of nature'. Labour represents the efforts, both physical and mental, of human beings in the production process. Capital inputs are those resources which are themselves the outcome of past productive effort. As far as the farm firm is concerned capital items, such as machinery, buildings, tools and stocks of seed or fertiliser, will often be the products of other (non-farm) firms.

It should be emphasised that the distinction between these groups of factors, while helpful, and indeed essential, to an understanding of many aspects of the organisation of production, is not always straightforward to apply in practice. There are few natural resources used in the production process which have not by now been altered by past human endeavour. The most significant 'natural' resource used in agriculture is the soil and in most cases it will have been made more productive over time by cultivation. Similarly, the agricultural labour force has embodied in it past human effort in the form of general education and the specialist training required for the acquisition of farming skills.

A fourth factor of production is sometimes distinguished from land, labour and capital, namely *management* or *entrepreneurship* (though, as we shall see, these words do not describe quite the same function), to identify the process of taking decisions about the use of the other factors.

It has also been found useful to distinguish between fixed factors of production and variable factors of production. This distinction refers to the time period within which a decision to alter the quantity used of an input can become effective. There are two reasons why an input may be regarded as a fixed factor. First, it is sometimes physically impossible to pursue all the stages required for an input to become involved in the production process in less than a period of years. Second, where the productive life of an input lasts for several years, there may well also be a period of years before a new decision regarding its use is implemented.

Again the distinction between the two groups of inputs is far from clear cut, but with agricultural production the crop year (or for animal production, the life cycle) helps us to distinguish a *short run* for which certain factors of production can be regarded as fixed. For example, if at the beginning of a crop year, a farmer decides he wishes to increase output he can increase the quantities used of seed, fertiliser, fuel and certain categories of labour, and thus these can be regarded as variable factors of production. He will probably find it impossible to increase his land area significantly for the coming season (this might well involve moving to another farm); nor will he find it easy to increase large capital items. If a farmer decides to add to his farm buildings, he must draw up plans, obtain planning permission, find a contractor and then wait for building work to commence and eventually be completed. Even where it is feasible to obtain a large item of equipment in time for the coming season his decision on whether or not to do so will be affected by the fact that its productive life will continue into future crop years. Thus items such as land, buildings and machinery are usually regarded as fixed factors of production, and decision affecting the quantity of them used taken with respect to a time period known as *the long run*.[1]

1.3

The fact that agricultural output is to some degree measurable in physical terms means that results observed from experimental data can be used to throw light upon some aspects of the organisation of agricultural production. Figure 2.1 shows an estimate, based on experimental data (1), of the relationship between output of corn and the application of different quantities of nitrogen and phosphate, the use of all other inputs being held constant. The application of nitrogen (pounds per acre) is measured on the horizontal axis and the application of phosphate on the vertical axis. The third variable, output of corn (bushels per acre), is depicted by the same graphical technique as that used in Chapter 1 to show the levels of utility associated with the consumption of alternative combinations of two products. In this case the 'contour' lines join different combinations of the two fertilisers which yield the same output, and are known as *iso-product lines* or *iso-quants* (meaning equal product or equal quantity).

The iso-product curves shown in Fig. 2.1 present a pattern which is thought to be typical of many input/output relationships in agriculture.

The experiment investigates a complex production situation of two variable inputs used in conjunction with a fixed bundle of other inputs, such as machinery, labour and land. It will aid our discussion of agricultural production if temporarily we think of productive activity in the simplest possible form which still retains the essential characteristics of the kind of input/output relationship demonstrated in Fig. 2.1. In this chapter therefore, the argument is illustrated in sections 2.1 and 3.1 by a simple two input/one product example of production, the mathematical details of which are given in an appendix to the chapter. The example demonstrates similar input/output characteristics to those shown in Fig. 2.1 and we are able to use it to illustrate many aspects of agricultural production. A single elementary example cannot of course provide a complete picture of agricultural production. The chapter therefore also explores in a more general way the implications of alternative production situations where there are more than two inputs or more than one product.

The remainder of the chapter is divided into four parts. First we consider typical production relationships in agriculture, measuring resources and products in physical units. Next we introduce input and product prices. This enables us to express causal relationships between resources and products in terms of the money cost of production and the revenue from the sale of

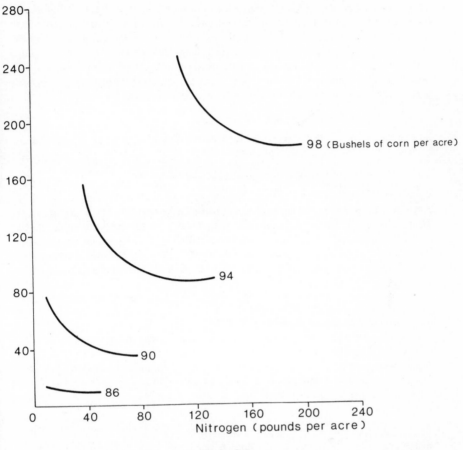

Figure 2.1

produce. In section 4 we turn to the question of what quantity of output will be produced by the individual farm firm, and what quantities of resources it will use to produce it. This requires the identification of the objectives upon which production decisions are based. In fact, it is implicit in much of the argument of sections 2 and 3 that there is some significance in the choice of a production plan which maximises the excess of revenue over cost per time period. In section 4 we discuss the implications for agricultural supply of an objective of profit maximisation, as well as considering the case for assuming alternative producer objectives and the extent to which such objectives might lead to different production decisions in any given situation. Finally we describe some common characteristics of the market supply of agricultural products.

It is probably true to say that more has been written on the theory of the farm firm than on any other major area of agricultural economics. The subject has received several thorough textbook treatments (e.g. 2–6). It is inevitable therefore that the argument in this chapter should be very condensed. Our intention is to cover that part of the economics of farm production which provides a theory of the behaviour of farm firms so that we can understand the way the firms comprising an agricultural industry are likely to alter the quantity they supply of a farm product, and the quantity of resources they use, in the face of some change in their economic environment.

2 The theory of the farm firm: (i) Physical relationships between inputs and products in the production process

2.1 A simple two-input/one-product production example

2.1.1

Assume that a particular agricultural product (A) is produced using only two inputs, X and Y. Both the inputs and the product are perfectly divisible, that is (like fertiliser and grain) they can be divided into very small amounts. In symbolic form we can represent the relationship between the maximum obtainable quantities of the product and given quantities of the two inputs as follows:

$$a = f(x,y)$$

where a is the quantity of product A produced per time period, and x and y are quantities used respectively of input X and input Y per time period.

This is called the *production function* of product A; the amount produced of A is some function (or is dependent upon) the quantities used of X and Y (which are the independent variables). For example, a very simple functional relationship between one product and two inputs could be:

$$a = \tfrac{1}{2}x^{1/2}y^{1/2}$$

which says that the output of product A per time period is equal to one-half of the square root of the amount of input X used multiplied by the square root of the amount of input Y used. Thus if $x = 4$ units and $y = 9$ units, output would be $\tfrac{1}{4} \times 2 \times 3 = 3$ units of A, and if $x = 16$ units and $y = 4$ units, output would be $\tfrac{1}{2} \times 4 \times 2 = 4$ units of A, and so on.

The particular functional relationship between product A and inputs X and Y which forms the basis for the numerical example of production used in this chapter is defined by the equation:

$$a = x^{2/5}y^{2/5}$$

Figure 2.2a is derived from this production function and it will be seen that the relationship regularises the iso-product curve pattern of Fig. 2.1.

Both the equations $a = \tfrac{1}{2}x^{1/2}y^{1/2}$ and $a = x^{2/5}y^{2/5}$ are examples of a particular form of production function known as the *Cobb–Douglas*[2] (7). This has been used extensively by agricultural economists when attempting to estimate relationships between inputs and outputs in agricultural production. Its popularity is partly because it is thought to be sufficiently flexible to encompass many typical production situations, but also partly due to certain characteristics which simplify the mathematical manipulations required when it is used.

We can divide the main input/output characteristics of our simple two-input one-product example into three kinds. These are:

(a) the relationship between one input and output, with the other input held constant, usually called the *factor/product* relationship;

(b) the relationship between one input and the other input, with output held constant – the *factor/factor* relationship; and

(c) *returns to scale*, usually defined as the relationship between output and all inputs applied in some fixed proportion.

In the text, these input/output relationships are examined in diagrammatical form. For the student who wishes to follow the parallel steps in elementary mathematical notation, these are given in the appendix to the chapter.

2.1.2

The graph of relationship between total output and one input, with all other inputs held constant, is known as a *total product* (*TP*) curve.

If we construct horizontal lines at levels $y = 4$ and $y = 8$ in Fig. 2.2a, the points of intersection with the iso-product curves give the quantities of input X required to achieve the level of output of A defined by each iso-product curve. Using this information, in Fig. 2.2b we construct two alternative total product curves for input X, those for input Y held constant at 4 units and for input Y held constant at 8 units. For example, the input combination $x = 4$ and $y = 8$ lies on the iso-product curve for 4 units of A, and in Fig. 2.2b the total product curve for X ($y = 8$) shows that the output of A will be 4 units when 4 units of input X are applied.

Figure 2.2c shows *marginal product* (*MP*) curves for input X, again with input Y held constant at 4 units and 8 units respectively. We will remember from Chapter 1 (section 1.1) that there were two alternative approaches to the concept of *marginal utility*, depending upon whether or not the product can be consumed in very small amounts. Similar considerations apply with production. In our example, it is possible to divide the inputs into very small amounts, so marginal product is defined as the rate of increase of output as the use of one input is changed, the use of all other inputs being held constant, expressed per unit of the variable input – in other words, the slope of the *TP* curve. Thus with Y held constant at level eight, when 4 units of X are applied, output is increasing at the rate of 0·4 units of A for every unit of X applied.

If it were only possible to apply input X in discrete units, the concept of marginal product would still retain its validity as long as the units were relatively small. In this case the appropriate definition of *MP* becomes 'the extra output which results from each additional unit of input X applied'. Thus *MP* when $x = 4$ would be the difference between *TP* when $x = 4$ and *TP* when

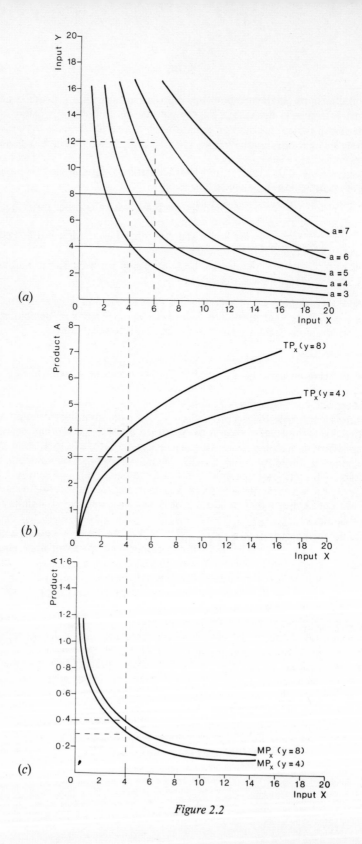

Figure 2.2

$x = 3$. This is slightly higher than 'the rate of increase of total product' when $x = 4$. This difference is illustrated diagrammatically for marginal utility in Fig. 1.2 and demonstrated numerically in the appendix to this chapter.

The marginal product curves shown in Fig. 2.2c are consistent with a general proposition about agricultural production known as the *law of diminishing marginal returns*. This states that if the use of one input is increased by successively equal amounts, the rates of use of all other inputs held constant, the marginal product per unit of the variable input will eventually decline. The 'law' is central to agricultural production theory in the sense that most of the conclusions we will come to concerning agricultural supply and resource use are valid only if diminishing marginal returns apply. It is, however, virtually impossible to conceive of a production situation for which the proposition would not hold. In our example, the rate of increase of output as input X increases, decreases throughout (the total product curve gradually gets flatter and flatter). Thus marginal product declines throughout – diminishing marginal returns are always present.

2.1.3

Total and marginal product curves describe the relationship between one input and output with the other input held constant. An *iso-product curve* describes the relationship between one input and the other input with the level of output held constant. The slope of an iso-product curve – known as the *marginal rate of substitution* (*MRS*) between the inputs – describes the rate at which one input must be substituted for the other input if the level of output is to remain unchanged. Because an increase in the use of one input is associated with a decrease in the use of the other input, the iso-product curves in our example are downward sloping – marginal rates of substitution are negative. The iso-product curve for $a = 4$ is reproduced in Fig. 2.3a. The 'convex to the origin' property means that the marginal rate of substitution between the inputs decreases absolutely as the amount of the input measured on the horizontal axis is increased; in other words, if the quantity of input X used is reduced by successively equal increments, increasing increments of Y must be substituted for X if output is to remain unchanged. Thus when 8 units of X are being applied, the marginal rate of substitution between the inputs is 1 unit of Y for 2 units of X and the slope of the iso-product curve is $-\frac{1}{2}$. When the quantity of input X used is reduced to 4 units, the rate at which one input must replace the other, if output is to remain unchanged at 4 units, is 2 units of Y for 1 unit of X – the *MRS* between the inputs has increased (absolutely) to -2.

2.1.4

If all inputs are increased by the same proportionate amount we say that the *scale* of production has increased. The resulting impact on output may conveniently be described as *returns to scale*. It is usual to distinguish three different scale situations; *increasing returns to scale*, where a proportionate increase in the use of all inputs results in a more than proportionate increase in output; *decreasing returns to scale*, where a proportionate increase in the use

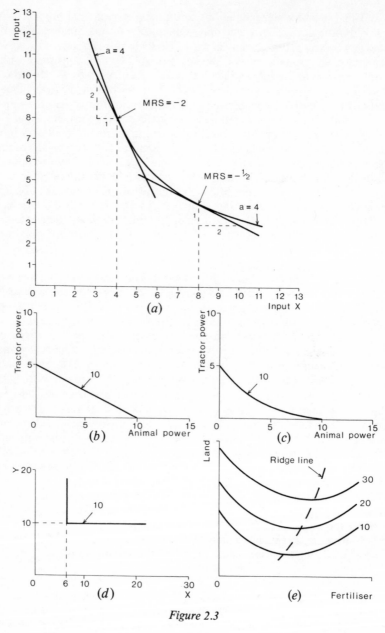

Figure 2.3

of all inputs results in a less than proportionate increase in output; and *constant returns to scale*, where a proportionate increase in the use of all inputs results in the same proportionate increase in output.

Our numerical production example demonstrates decreasing returns to scale. If we take any combination of X and Y in Fig. 2.2a and then increase the use of both the inputs by the same proportion we will find that the new level of output of product A has increased by an amount which is less in proportion than the increase in the inputs. For example, the combination of 4 units of X and 8 units of Y lies on the iso-product curve for 4 units of A. If we increase the use of both inputs by 50 per cent to 6 units of X and 12 units of Y, the new level of output of product A is approximately 5·5 units – an increase of about 38 per cent.

2.2 Some further aspects of input/output relationships in agriculture

2.2.1

Figure 2.3 also shows some alternative possible iso-product relationships. The iso-product curves in our numerical example do not intersect either of the axes, indicating that the product cannot be produced using only one of the inputs. When we take account of the presence of fixed factors of production, it is quite possible that a particular level of output could be produced using only one of the variable inputs. Figure 2.3b gives an example of this for animal power and tractor power. The iso-product curve shown depicts a *constant marginal rate of substitution* between the inputs – it is always possible to substitute 2 units of animal power for 1 unit of tractor power in order to achieve 10 units of output, and at the extremes 10 units of output can be produced using either 10 units of animal power and no tractor power or 5 units of tractor power and no animal power. In practice it is likely that there will be some farm activities for which animal power can be more easily substituted for tractor power. A more probable shape for the iso-product curve is therefore that shown in Fig. 2.3c which indicates a decreasing marginal rate of substitution between the inputs as animal power is increased from zero units to 10 units.

Occasionally, productive activity requires the use of two inputs in fixed proportions with no substitution between the inputs possible. This case is illustrated in Fig. 2.3d. In order to produce 10 units of output, 6 units of X and 10 units of Y are required. It is not possible to reduce the quantity of Y required for the production of 10 units of output by an increase in the amount used of X above 6 units; nor is it possible to reduce the quantity of X required below 6 units by using more than 10 units of Y. This situation is usually described as *fixed technical coefficients of production* and a typical example in agriculture could be one man in charge of one tractor.

The iso-product curves shown in Fig. 2.3e describe a production situation where excessive use of one of the inputs is counterproductive – that is, beyond a certain point it is no longer possible to maintain a given level of output by substituting this input for the other, and we may even find that more of both inputs must be used if output is not to fall. The iso-product curves therefore begin to bend back upon themselves. The line joining the points on the iso-product curves where further substitution becomes irrational – characterised by a zero marginal rate of substitution when the input in question is measured on the horizontal axis – is known as a *ridge line*. Experience suggests that many production situations will take this form. Figure 2.3e gives an example relating to land and fertiliser. It is possible to achieve all the levels of output shown with no fertiliser as long as sufficient land is available and the iso-product curves therefore intersect the land axis. On the other hand, clearly no output is possible with no land, but over a certain range it is possible to substitute more fertiliser for less land. Beyond a certain point, however, further application of fertiliser causes the land to become toxic reducing yield, so that if we are determined to use more and more fertiliser, more and more land is also required if output is not to fall.

2.2.2
Turning now to the nature of returns to scale where there are more than two inputs, most economists take the view that, if it really were possible to increase the use of all inputs in the same proportion, then constant returns to scale would ensue. After all, if the output of grain on a 200 hectare farm is 800 tonnes, why should it not be 1600 tonnes on a 400 hectare farm if all other inputs are doubled, or 400 tonnes on a 100 hectare farm if all other inputs are halved? In practice, it is rarely possible to change the use of all inputs in precisely the same proportion. Some inputs cannot be divided into small amounts – they are known as '*lumpy*' or '*indivisible*' resources. The smallest available unit of a particular input required for grain production may be adequate for the 200 hectare farm and more than adequate for the 100 hectare farm. It is not possible to have half a man driving half a tractor (though the hiring of machinery and the use of casual labour can overcome some problems of indivisibilities on small farms).

When we consider larger and larger farms, resource indivisibilities present less of a restriction on the possibilities for increasing the use of all inputs in the same proportion but the problem remains that the time period within which it is possible to alter the use of inputs varies with different inputs. Even when we consider a long period of time, it has been argued that there is one input – the factor of production which aims to provide adequate supervision for the large farm – which it may prove extremely difficult to increase in the same proportion as other inputs. (This is a point which we pursue in more detail in Chapter 4.)

These considerations have led to a rather looser use of the term 'returns to scale' to refer to the relationship between output and changes in the use of a group of inputs with one or more other inputs held constant. Just which inputs will be included in the 'returns to scale' will depend on both the size of the farm – and thus whether or not a particular resource has to be regarded as indivisible or not – and the time period under consideration, which affects which factors can be varied. This interpretation of scale is rather imprecise but it does have the advantage that it allows returns to scale to refer to something which can happen rather than something which very probably cannot.

When we consider a proportionate increase in a group of factors with one or more other factors held constant, the logical conclusion is that decreasing 'returns to scale' must ultimately apply, since similar forces operate as in the case of diminishing marginal returns to a single factor of production. This, anyway, is the finding of the experiment into fertiliser use shown in Fig. 2.1. A proportionate increase in the use of *both* phosphate and nitrogen, with all other inputs held constant, results in a less than proportionate increase in corn yield.

It also seems likely that in many cases decreasing returns to a group of variable factors will be preceded by increasing returns. Higher levels of output can cause specialisation in the use of both labour and capital such that at low levels of output a proportional change in the use of all variable factors could result in a more than proportionate increase in output. Suppose we have an area of land in which we wish to dig drainage ditches. Our two variable inputs are men and hand tools. We hire one worker and he begins to dig with a spade. If a second worker is added with a pick the rate of progress may be more than doubled because the workers can specialise, one loosening the earth, the other shovelling it out. More specialisation may be possible with the third worker so that output increases by more than one-half. When more workers plus implements are added, output will probably continue to increase but now in proportion to the increase in inputs, since all the possibilities for specialisation of function are used up. At some stage, however, extra workers will begin to get in each other's way and eventually there may be so many workers and so much equipment on the land that any additional inputs will cause output to decline.

Figure 2.4a shows an iso-product pattern for two variable inputs for which a proportionate change in the use of both inputs demonstrates first increasing and then decreasing returns to scale. This can be seen if we increase the use of both inputs along the *scale line ORST*. At point R, 30 units of product B are produced using 10 units of X and 20 units of Y. If the use of both inputs is increased by 50 per cent, to 15 of X and 30 of Y, the new level of output is 90 units of B, an increase of 200 per cent. If we now increase the use of both inputs again, this time to 20 of X and 40 of Y, the new level of output (110 units of B) represents an increase of 22·2 per cent compared with the increase in inputs of $33\frac{1}{3}$ per cent.

2.2.3

The production situation illustrated in Fig. 2.4a results in the kind of total and marginal product curves frequently found in elementary economics textbooks. If we hold input Y constant at − say − level 20 we can, as before, derive the total product curve for input X $(y = 20)$. This is shown in Fig. 2.4b, and the second column in Table 2.1 gives some specific quantities of total product for the alternative level of application of input X shown in the first column. Total product increases as input X is increased, first at an increasing and then at a decreasing rate, reaches a maximum of just over 90 units when $26\frac{2}{3}$ units of X are applied and then subsequently declines.

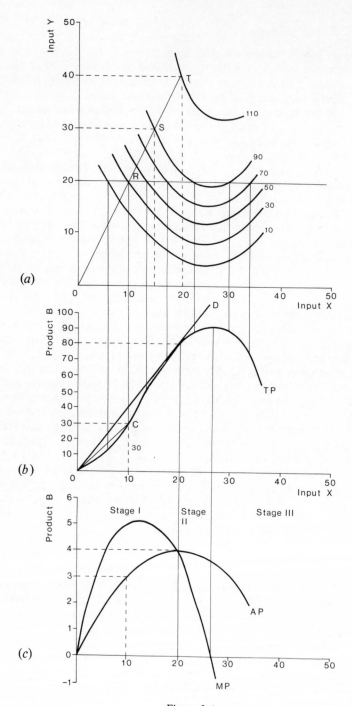

Figure 2.4

Table 2.1

(1) Units of input X	(2) Total product	(3) Marginal product	(4) Average product
0	0	—	—
5·00	8·75	3·75	1·75
10·00	30·00	5·00	3·00
13·33		5·33 (max.)	
15·00	56·25	5·25	3·75
20·00	80·00	4·00	4·00 (max.)
25·00	93·75	0·25	3·75
26·67	94·83 (max.)	0·00	
30·00	90·00	−3·00	3·00

The corresponding marginal product relationship is shown in Fig. 2.4c and column three of Table 2.1. Marginal product first increases (total product increasing at an increasing rate) and reaches a maximum when $x = 13\frac{1}{3}$. It then declines to equal zero when total product is at a maximum, and becomes negative as total product declines.

Figure 2.4c also shows the *average product* of input X which is defined as (total product)/(quantity of input X); it is the total output per unit of variable input. Thus when $x = 10$, total product is 30 and average product is therefore $30/10 = 3$. Average product reaches a maximum of 4 when $x = 20$.

A convenient way of diagrammatically relating marginal and average product to total product is to remember first that, for a perfectly divisible input, marginal product is the *slope of the total product* curve (i.e. the rate of change of total product as x changes). Marginal product therefore rises when the slope of the *TP* curve increases, and reaches a maximum when the slope of the *TP* curve stops increasing and begins to decrease (known as a 'point of inflection'). When *TP* reaches a maximum, the slope of the *TP* curve is zero and thus *MP* is zero, and when the slope of *TP* curve is negative so is *MP*.

Similarly, average product can be represented on the *TP* diagram by the *slope* of a line *drawn from the origin to the relevant point on the curve*. Thus when $x = 10$, $AP = 30/10$, which is also the slope of the line *OC* in Fig. 2.4b. Average product is at a maximum when the line drawn from origin to the *TP* curve is a tangent to that curve – in Fig. 2.4b this tangent is line *OD*. At this point the line drawn from the origin to the curve has the same slope as the *TP* curve itself, and thus $AP = MP$ (when 20 units of input X are applied). When x is less than 20, the slope at any point on the *TP* curve is greater than, and when x exceeds 20 it is less than, the slope of a line drawn from the origin to the curve. For this reason the *MP* curve in Fig. 2.4c passes through the maximum point of the *AP* curve, cutting it from above.

The kind of production relationship between one input and output shown in Fig. 2.4c is sometimes divided into three stages. In the first stage marginal product exceeds average product. In the second stage average product exceeds marginal product, but marginal product is positive. In the third stage marginal product is negative. The reason for distinguishing these three stages is that, as we shall see in the next section, considerations of *economic efficiency in production* leads to the conclusion that input X should be applied at some point in stage II. In contrast the traditional idea of *technical efficiency in production* (which is defined solely in terms of physical input/output relationships) might apply to either the onset or the end of the second stage. When the crop scientist talks about 'fertilising for maximum yield' he means *maximising the total product* of the input fertiliser, for a given quantity of land and other inputs. On the other hand the concept of maximum efficiency in feed conversion is more likely to mean *maximum average product* of the input feed, all other inputs held constant.

Some recent literature views technical efficiency as being related to whether a producer is operating on or below the relevant production function. This would mean that, in terms of Fig. 2.4b, for a given level of application of input X, as long as he obtains the level of output indicated by the *TP* curve, the producer would be regarded as 'technically' efficient.

2.2.4

To complete our discussion of physical relationships in the production process we need to consider the implications of the possibility of producing more than one product. The important aspect of production where there are two or more products concerns the allocation of fixed factors. If all factors are variable, and there is therefore no limit to the quantity of inputs which can be used in the production of any product, the decision to increase the output of one product does not imply any reduction in the quantity produced of another product. When there is some limit to the total quantity of an input available for use by a farm firm – which is the case in the short run with fixed factors – it may nevertheless be possible to vary the way the fixed factor is allocated between different products. In this case an increase in the amount of the fixed factor allocated to the production of one product is likely to imply less produced of some other product.

Consider therefore a production situation where there are two products, A and B, one fixed factor of production Z, and a number of variable factors. In total, 10 units of factor Z are available for use in the production of either A or B. The second row in Table 2.2 shows the quantity of product A that results from the application of the alternative quantities of input Z (from 1 to 10) shown in the first row, for some given constant level of application of other

Table 2.2

(1) Input Z	1	2	3	4	5	6	7	8	9	10
(2) Product A	14	26	36	44	50	54	56	56	54	50
(3) Product B	19	36	51	64	75	84	91	96	99	100

inputs in the production of A. This relationship between input Z and product A
is plotted in Fig. 2.5b giving a total product curve of Z in the production of A.
Similarly, the third row of Table 2.2 gives the total output of product B which
results from alternative applications of input Z. Again, all other factors used in
B production are held constant. The associated total product curve of input Z
in the production of product B is plotted in Fig. 2.5c.

In Fig. 2.5a we plot the various possible alternative combinations of the two
products which can be produced. For example, if 10 units of Z are allocated to

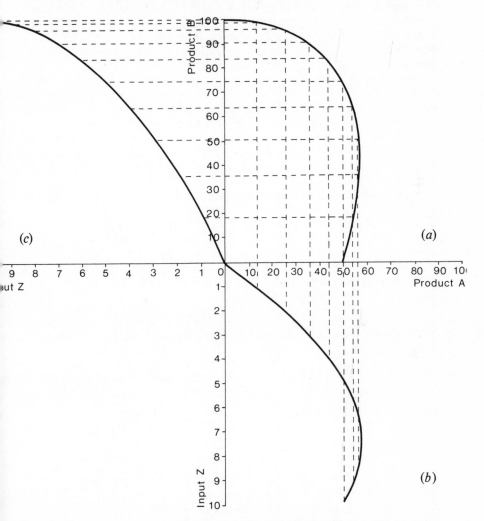

*Figure 2.5   (a) Production possibility curve, (b) Total product curve of Z in A, (c)
Total product curve of Z in B*

B production, none is available for A production and we get an output combination of 100 units B and zero A. If 8 units of Z are allocated to B production, two units are available for A production and we get an output combination of 96 units of B and 26 of A. The line joining the alternative possible combination of two products is called a *production possibility curve*. In Fig. 2.5a it is shaped concave to the origin because of diminishing marginal returns to Z in the production of both A and B. This means that as we switch units of input Z from one product to the other, the increments of output gained of one product get progressively smaller and the increments of output lost of the other product get progressively larger. When a production possibility curve slopes down from left to right the products are said to be competitive – that is an increase in the output of one product can only be brought about by a reduction in the output of the other product. Two products are said to be complementary if an increase in the output of one product is associated with an increase in the output of the other product, with the same total quantity of inputs used in the production of both. In our example, the two products are complementary over a short range because of negative marginal returns in A production. When we move from an allocation of all Z to A, to one where 1 or 2 units of Z are allocated to B, the output of both products is increased, but when the allocation of Z to A production falls below 8, the products become competitive.

Apart from negative marginal returns, there is another reason why two agricultural products might be complementary – where the production of one of the products provides an input for the other product. In this case, the two total product curves would not be independent. An example of this kind of complementarity is field beans grown as a break crop in a cereal rotation. The crop leaves residual nitrogen in the soil which increases the yield of wheat grown subsequently on the same land (though the benefit would usually be expressed as a fertiliser saving) (8).

3 The theory of the farm firm: (ii) Financial relationships in the production process

3.1 Costs, revenue and profit in the simple two-input/one-product production example

3.1.1

We now add to our simple two-input/one-product production example information concerning the prices per unit paid for the inputs X and Y (P_x and P_y) and the price received for the product A (P_a). These prices are as follows:

$$P_x = £4 \text{ per unit}; P_y = £8 \text{ per unit}; \text{and } P_a = £20 \text{ per unit}$$

We assume that these prices remain constant.

The total monetary value of the inputs used per time period is called the *total cost* (*TC*) of production. Thus

$$TC = P_x x + P_y y = 4x + 8y$$

where x and y are the quantities of X and Y used per time period.

The total monetary value of the product produced per time period is called the *total revenue* (TR) of production. Thus

$$TR = P_a a = 20a$$

where a is the amount of A produced per time period.

We define *profit* (π) as the difference between total revenue and total cost. Thus

$$\pi = TR - TC = 20a - 4x - 8y$$

In section 2.1 we examined physical input/output relationships by first holding one input constant. Next we looked at the relationship between the two inputs for a given level of output. Finally, we considered the impact upon output if both inputs were varied. Our examination of the financial relationships follows a similar course.

3.1.2

The relationship between total revenue and alternative applications of one input, all other inputs held constant, is called a *total value product* (TVP) curve. Correspondingly, the rate of change of total revenue as one input changes, all other inputs held constant, we call *marginal value product* (MVP).

We can convert total product and marginal product curves into monetary values by multiplying by the price of the product, and in Fig. 2.6 we thereby obtain a TVP and MVP curve for input X, input Y held constant at 8 units. For example, if we take a level of application of input X of 4 units, we can see from Fig. 2.2 that the total product is 4 units and the marginal product 0·4 units. Since product A sells at £20 per unit, total value product must be £80, and marginal value product £8 when $x = 4$.

The relationship between the total amount of money paid for an input and the quantity of the input we call *total factor cost* (TFC).

The total factor cost of input X is shown in Fig. 2.6a by the line TFC_x, which is obtained by multiplying each alternative level of application of input X by the price of X. Thus when $x = 10$ the cost of input X is $10 \times £4 = £40$. The maximum profit level of application of input X will be when the value of total product exceeds the total cost of input X by the greatest amount. Diagrammatically this is found in Fig. 2.6a by drawing a tangent to the TVP curve with the same slope as the line TFC_x. This point on the TVP curve occurs when x is approximately equal to 12·7 units.

In terms of the marginal relationships, the maximum profit level of application of input X occurs when the marginal value product of X is equal to the marginal factor cost (MFC) of X. Since MFC is the rate of change of TFC as input X changes, and TFC is increasing at a constant rate of £4 for every unit of input X used, MFC equals the price of input X. If MVP exceeds the price of X, an increase in the quantity of X used will contribute more to total revenue than to total cost. For example, when $x = 4$, the value of output is

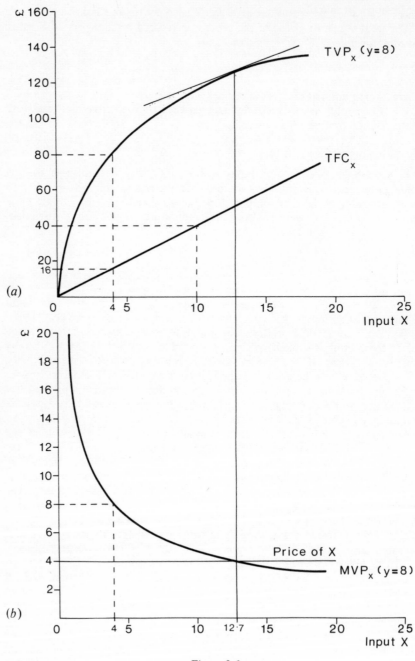

Figure 2.6

increasing at a rate of £8 for every unit of X applied. Since each unit of X costs only £4 – that is the cost of X increases at a rate of £4 for every unit of X applied – profit can be increased by adding more units of X. Only when *MVP* has fallen to the same level as the price of X (which occurs when x is approximately equal to 12·7 units) will further applications of input X add more to total cost than to total revenue.

It is worth noting that the maximum profit level of application of input X in Fig. 2.6b could have been derived directly from Fig. 2.5a simply by remembering that *MVP* is the slope of *TVP* and that the price of X (the marginal factor cost) is the slope of *TFC*. In Fig. 2.6a we identified the maximum profit level of application of X by equating the slope of *TVP* with the slope of *TFC*.

3.1.3

Let us now turn to the financial aspects of the second relationship discussed in section 2.1, that between two inputs for a constant level of output. In Fig. 2.7 we reproduce the iso-product curve for 4 units of A, and add to the diagram information concerning the cost of purchasing alternative combinations of the two inputs.

If we take a sum of money of – say – £20, with it we could purchase either 5 units of input X or $2\frac{1}{2}$ units of input Y, or any combination of the two inputs located on the line joining the points marking 5 units on the X axis and $2\frac{1}{2}$ units on the Y axis. This line is known as an *iso-cost line*; for any given set of input prices, an iso-cost line joins different combinations of the two inputs which can be purchased with a given sum of money. In Fig. 2.7, iso-cost lines are drawn for £20, £40, £60, and so on. The points of intersection of the iso-product curve with the iso-cost lines gives us a set of alternative total costs of producing 4 units of A, the cost depending on which combination of X and Y is used. For example, we can see from Fig. 2.7 that one combination which lies on the iso-product curve for $a = 4$ is 16 units of X and two units of Y, and this combination costs £80. Another such combination is 4 units of X and 8 units of Y, and this also costs £80. However, if we choose the combination of the inputs on the iso-product curve which lies on the lowest possible iso-cost curve we will have located the *least cost* combination of inputs for producing 4 units of A. This is 8 units of X and 4 units of Y (which costs £64).

The least cost combination is characterised by the fact that it is the only point on the iso-product curve where this curve has the same slope as have the iso-cost lines. The slope of the iso-product curve – the marginal rate of substitution between the inputs – gives us the rate at which one input must be substituted for the other input if output is to remain unchanged. The slope of the iso-cost lines is the amount of input Y that can be purchased for a given sum of money divided by the amount of input X which can be purchased for the same sum of money, and this gives us the rate at which it is possible to substitute one input for the other input if the total cost of purchasing both inputs is

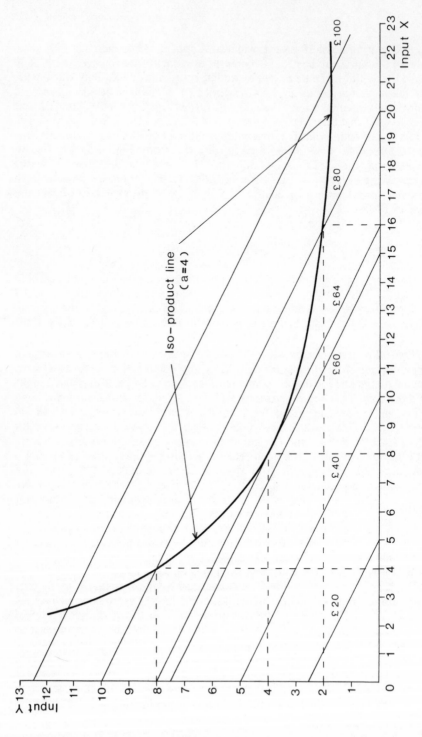

Figure 2.7

to remain unchanged. Formally, the slope of an iso-cost curve for a sum of money of £N is:

$$\frac{£N/P_y}{-£N/P_x} = -\frac{P_x}{P_y}$$

The least cost combination of inputs to produce a given level of output therefore occurs when the absolute value of marginal rate of substitution between the inputs is equal to the inverse ratio of input prices. In our example, the inverse price ratio is $\frac{1}{2}$, and we will remember from Fig. 2.4 that the MRS between X and Y was $-\frac{1}{2}$ when $x = 4$ and $y = 8$.

3.1.4

It remains to consider the relationship between costs and revenue when output is allowed to respond to variations in the use of both inputs. In Fig. 2.8 the least cost combination of inputs for the levels of output $a = 1$ to $a = 7$ have been located by finding the lowest iso-cost curve touched by each of the iso-product curves. These minimum total costs are listed in the second row of Table 2.3 and give us the (*minimum*) *total cost* curve shown in Fig. 2.9a. The word 'minimum' attached to total cost here is important because we are examining the relationship between revenue and cost under the assumption that the least cost method of producing each level of output is chosen. However, the relationship is usually just referred to as a *total cost* (*TC*) curve – the word minimum is implicit.

Table 2.3

Output (units of A)	1	2	3	4	5	6	7
Total cost (£)	11·3	26·9	44·7	64	84·6	106·2	128·9
Total revenue (£)	20·0	40·0	60·0	80	100·0	120·0	140·0
Profit (*TR–TC*) (£)	8·7	13·1	15·3	16	15·4	13·8	11·1
Marginal cost (£)	14·1	16·8	18·6	20	21·1	22·1	23·0
Marginal revenue (£)	20·0	20·0	20·0	20	20·0	20·0	20·0

Source: Production function $a = x^{2/5}y^{2/5}$, $P_a = £20$ per unit, $P_x = £4$ per unit; $P_y = £8$ per unit.

The *total revenue* (*TR*) curve in Fig. 2.9a shows the amount of money brought in from the sale of alternative quantities of the product. Maximum profit is when total revenue exceeds total cost by the maximum amount. This occurs with an output level of 4 units of product A, which gives a total revenue of £80 and (if the least cost method of producing 4 units of A – 8 units of X and 4 units of Y – is chosen) total cost is £64. Maximum profit is therefore £16.

Figure 2.9b shows the relationship between cost and revenue in marginal terms. *Marginal cost* (*MC*) is the rate of increase of total (minimum) cost as output increases. *Marginal revenue* (*MR*) is the rate of increase of total

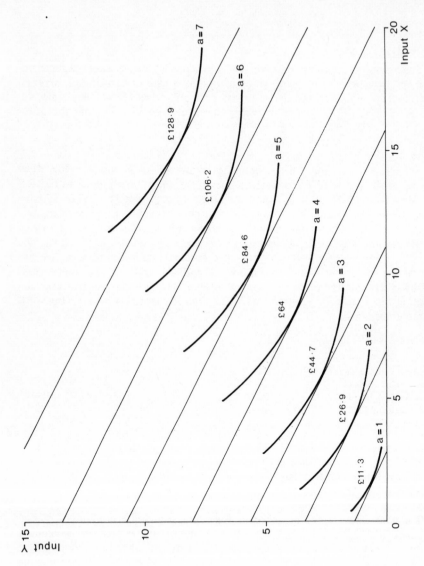

Figure 2.8

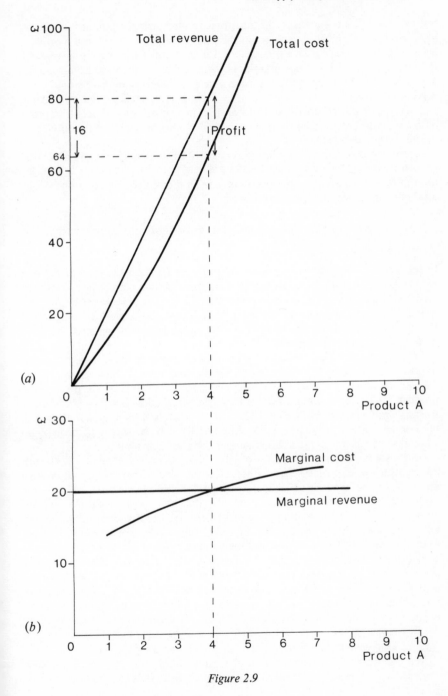

Figure 2.9

revenue as output increases. If the price of the product remains constant, marginal revenue must always equal the price of the product – with a product price of £20 per unit, total revenue increases at a rate of £20 per unit produced. If marginal cost is less than marginal revenue, a small increase in output will add more to total revenue than to total cost and will thus increase profit. Conversely, if marginal cost exceeds marginal revenue, a small increase in output will add more to total cost than to total revenue and will reduce profit. In terms of the marginal relationship, therefore, profit is maximised when marginal cost equals marginal revenue

Again, we can derive this result directly from Fig. 2.9a if we remember that total revenue exceeds total cost by the greatest amount when the slope of the total cost curve (which is the same as marginal cost) equals the slope of the total revenue curve (marginal revenue).

3.2 Some further aspects of costs and revenue in agricultural production

3.2.1

In section 2.2 we noted that the more complex production situation of a group of variable factors used in conjunction with fixed factors could lead to different input output patterns from that demonstrated by the simple two-input/one-product production example. We went on to investigate a production relationship which demonstrated, in turn, increasing, decreasing and negative marginal returns to a factor of production.

In Fig. 2.10 this same kind of production relationship is expressed in terms of costs and revenue. We can convert the physical relationships shown in Fig. 2.4 into value terms simply by multiplying each output level by the price of the product. *The total value product (TVP)*, *Marginal value product (MVP)* and *Average value product (AVP)* in Fig. 2.10 will therefore have similar shapes to the corresponding physical relationships, and the three *stages of production* will refer to the same areas of application of the variable input.

Now suppose that the price of the input is $£P_1$ per unit. With this information we can represent in Fig. 2.10a the cost of purchasing alternative amounts of the input by the line TFC_1. We established with respect to the numerical production example (Fig. 2.6) that the most profitable level of application of an input would be the one which equates marginal value product with the price of the input. In the case now under consideration, where marginal product first increases and then declines, there are two such points of equality – shown in Fig. 2.10 as q_1 and q_3. Clearly however, it is the point of intersection with the declining section of the MVP curve which gives us the maximum profit level of application of this input. The point of intersection with the rising part of the MVP curve gives a minimum profit (maximum loss) position; q_1 is the point where the application of units of the input begins, for the first time, to add more to total revenue, by the sale of the product, than it does to total cost, in the form of the price per unit paid for the input.

We can now see the relevance of distinguishing the three stages of production. Let us assume, for the moment, that our objective is to apply the input at

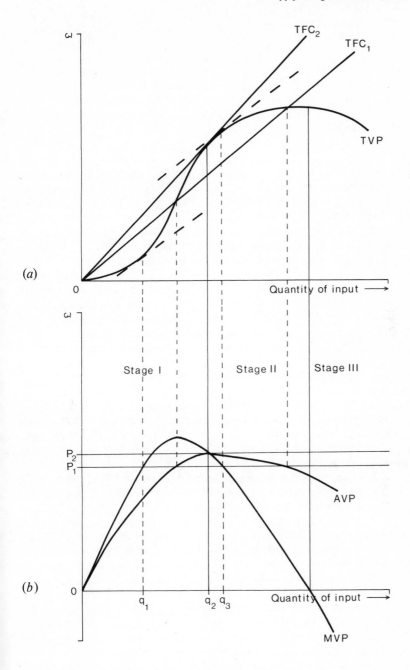

Figure 2.10

a level which maximises profit. If the price of the input is positive, clearly its optimum application cannot lie in stage III.[3] If on the other hand the price of the input exceeds P_2, there is no level of application for which the total revenue from the sale of the product exceeds the total cost of purchasing the input (the average value per unit of output is always less than the price per unit of input). Thus it is contended that, whatever the product and input prices, if it is profitable to use the input in the production process, it will be applied somewhere in stage II of production.

3.2.2

Turning now to the case where output is allowed to respond to changes in the use of all variable inputs, the more complex production situation means two major departures from the simple cost structure of the two-input production example. First, there are now costs associated with the fixed factors of production, called *fixed costs*. Second, a production relationship which demonstrates first increasing and then decreasing returns to scale for a group of variable inputs means that the marginal cost of production will initially decline.

This kind of cost structure is illustrated in Fig. 2.11. Fixed costs are shown in Fig. 2.11a by the horizontal line *FC* and the costs associated with the variable factors (*variable costs*) are added to fixed costs to give the *total cost curve*. Total cost increases first at a decreasing rate and then at an increasing rate. Marginal cost correspondingly declines to reach a minimum (at q_2).

Again we are assuming that the *least cost combination* of variable inputs is chosen for any level of output. We saw that, for two variable inputs, this requires that a combination of inputs be chosen such that (the absolute value of) the marginal rate of substitution between the inputs equals the inverse ratio of their prices. For three or more inputs the condition is that the marginal rate of substitution between *any pair* of inputs must equal the inverse ratio of their prices. Thus for three inputs, W, X and Y, *MRS* between W and X must equal P_x/P_w; *MRS* between X and Y must equal P_y/P_x; and *MRS* between Y and W must equal P_w/P_y.

Figure 2.11b also shows the *average cost* (AC) of producing the product. Average cost per unit of output is defined as total cost divided by quantity produced. We will remember from Fig. 2.4 that average product could be represented by the slope of a line drawn from the origin to a point on the total product curve. By a similar argument average cost is given by the slope of a line drawn from the origin to a point on the total cost curve. We can see from Fig. 2.11a that if we were to construct a series of such lines, each one drawn to a higher point on the total cost curve, the slope of each successive line would first be less than the previous one, but eventually each successive line will have a greater slope. Average cost reaches a minimum at q_4 units of output, where the slope of a line drawn from the origin to the *TC* curve is tangential to the curve; thus average cost must equal marginal cost at the minimum point on the average cost curve.

Average cost per unit of output is equal to the price of the product when total revenue is equal to total cost – at output levels q_3 and q_6. Output level q_3 is

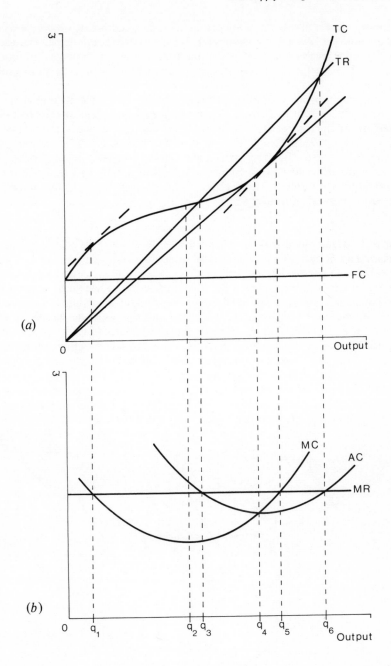

Figure 2.11

sometimes called a breakeven point – it is the level of output at which a small increase in output beyond q_3 causes total revenue to exceed total cost, whereas at lower output levels an overall loss is made. At output levels beyond q_6 total cost again exceeds total revenue. Between output levels q_3 and q_6 an overall profit is made.

The maximum profit level of output is q_5 units, given by the maximum vertical distance between the TR and TC curves in Fig. 2.11a and by the point of intersection of the rising part of the marginal cost curve with the marginal revenue curve in Fig. 2.11b. The point of intersection of the declining part of the marginal cost curve with the marginal revenue curve (at q_1 units of output) gives a minimum profit (or maximum loss) level of output. In Fig. 2.11a this level of output shows total cost exceeding total revenue by the greatest amount in the output range of zero to q_6.

3.2.3

Let us now extend our discussion of the cost structure of the typical farm firm to include output and input use decisions in the *long run*. The firm depicted in Fig. 2.11 is characterised by the fact that its cost structure is circumscribed by past decisions (which may or may not have turned out to have been appropriate ones) concerning its use of fixed factors of production. Figure 2.12 shows three alternative sets of average and marginal cost curves, under the assumption that for a given set of input prices, the quantity of fixed factors of production used in each case is such as to minimise the average cost of producing, respectively, q_1, q_2 and q_3 units of output per time period. A line which envelopes

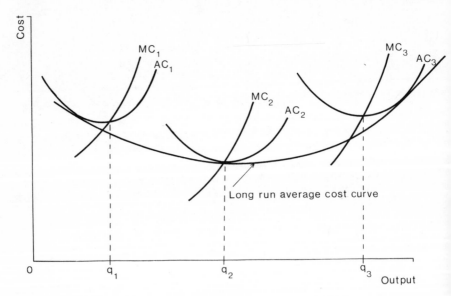

Figure 2.12

such a series of (short run) average cost curves is known as a *long run average cost curve.*

It is the nature of returns to scale which will determine, in the long run, whether or not the minimum average cost of producing a specific level of output will be the same as the minimum average cost of producing alternative levels of output. If, when the use of all inputs is increased by some proportionate amount, the level of output increases by a more than proportionate amount (increasing returns to scale) then long run average cost will fall as output is increased. Conversely, if decreasing returns to scale are applicable, long run average cost will rise as output increases.

3.2.4

We have so far restricted our investigation of the relationships between costs and revenue to the case where revenue is derived from the sale of one product only. In section 2.2 we mentioned that, inasmuch as the production process involves fixed factors, an increase in the amount produced of one product may in the short run imply a reduction in the amount produced of another product. A simple extension of Fig. 2.5a allows us to examine the financial implications of alternative allocations of a fixed factor of production.

Figure 2.13 reproduces the production possibility curve of Fig. 2.5a; it shows the various combinations of the products A and B which can be produced with alternative allocations of the fixed factor Z, assuming that the quantities of all other factors used in the production of A and B are held constant. Suppose now that product A and B both sell at £1 per unit. With this information we can construct in Fig. 2.13 a series of *iso-revenue lines*, showing different combinations of the two products which yield the same aggregate revenue. We can now identify the aggregate revenue associated with any point on the production possibility curve by reference to the iso-revenue line passing through the same point. The allocation of the fixed input which maximises the aggregate revenue from the sale of both products will be given by the point on the production possibility curve which lies on the highest attainable iso-revenue line. In our example this maximum revenue is £128 derived from an output of 44 units of product A and 84 units of product B. If we return to Fig. 2.5, we see that this point on the production possibility curve comes from allocation of 6 units of input Z to the production of product B and 4 units to product A.

More formally then, the revenue maximising allocation of a fixed factor occurs when the slope of the production possibility curve – known as the *marginal rate of transformation* (*MRT*) between the products – is equal to the slope of the iso-revenue lines, which is given by the inverse ratio of product prices; in other words, when $MRT = -(P_a/P_b)$.

Note that the production possibility curve in Fig. 2.13 is defined for specific quantities of variable factors used in the production of A and B. For the revenue maximising allocation of a fixed factor to be an overall position of profit maximisation these quantities of variable factors used must be such that marginal cost equals marginal revenue in the case of both products. Thus the two-product firm will maximise profits when marginal cost equals marginal

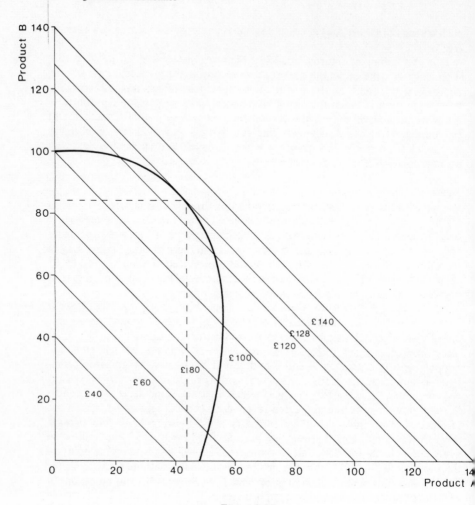

Figure 2.13

revenue for each product and when the marginal rate of transformation between the products, for any fixed factor, equals the inverse ratio of product
prices. In principle this conclusion is fairly straightforward, but the solution is
more complex than it first seems because the level of output for which marginal
cost equals marginal revenue will vary depending on the allocation of fixed factors to each product; conversely, the shape of the production possibility curve,
and thus the revenue maximising combination of products, varies depending on
the quantities of variable factors used in the production of each product.

4 Agricultural supply and the objectives of the farm firm

4.1 The supply function

The material covered in the previous two sections of this chapter, which we have referred to as the theory of the farm firm, provides us with the basis for now developing a theory of agricultural supply. The quantity supplied of an agricultural product is the amount of the product which will be offered for sale per time period under a given set of circumstances. The farm firm is a unit within the economy which generates a supply of agricultural products; it does so by employing a group of resources in agricultural production.

We can list the main factors affecting the market supply of an agricultural product in the same way as we did with market demand, and we can express market supply symbolically as a *supply function*, thus

$$Q_s = f(T, P_p, P_{1...n}, I_{1...m}, O, N, R)$$

where Q_s is the quantity of an agricultural product supplied to a market per time period

T represents the production function of the product, sometimes referred to as the technological conditions of production

P_p is the price of the product

$P_{1...n}$ are the prices of (n) other products

$I_{1...m}$ are the prices of (m) inputs

O represents the objectives of the farm firms

N is the number of firms supplying the market

R represents the size distribution of farms supplying the market, sometimes called the 'structure' of the agricultural industry

Our discussion so far has been concerned with the first four of these factors, with the view of production relationships in terms of costs and revenue bringing the influence of all four together. To extend this discussion to include a theory of supply by the individual farm firm, and thus, in a sense, 'to complete' the theory of the farm firm, we must examine one further aspect of agricultural production, the objectives of the farm firm. In other words, for a given technological and price environment, what considerations motivate the farm firm in coming to a decision on what to produce, how much to produce, and in what way to produce it. The remaining two factors – the number of firms and the size structure of the agricultural industry, will need to be included when we extend the theory of supply by the individual farm firm to a theory of market supply.

With a few exceptions, the theory of agricultural supply has been based on the assumption that the farm firm acts in such a way as to maximise profits. This assumption has certainly not lacked its critics and before we discuss the implications for agricultural supply of profit maximising behaviour we must consider whether or not the assumption is a realistic one.

First, we can dispose summarily with one kind of criticism. The word profit arouses strong emotions. Profits are regarded as an admirable aspect of an economic system by some, and as fundamentally antisocial by others. In this chapter, however, we are concerned with what happens, not with what ought to happen. This does not mean that we are going to avoid confronting the question of the extent to which a particular pattern of agricultural supply is in a 'society's interest'. We accept that agricultural economics has an important contribution to make in this area. The student of economics is quite rightly irritated and frustrated if every economics teacher refuses to tackle what the student often regards as the crucial and interesting questions. It is however extremely important that these two issues are not confused. There is a danger of assuming that what does happen is what ought to happen, or alternatively that what ought to happen does happen. For this reason, a discussion of the way agricultural economic principles might be applied to the question of what is and what is not in a 'society's interest' is postponed to the second part of this book.

Another criticism of the profit maximising assumption is that, put crudely, because farmers have never heard of marginal revenue or marginal cost curves, therefore they do not maximise profits. Such a criticism is derived from a failure to appreciate the function of formulating the profit maximising solution in terms of the marginal cost and marginal revenue of production. We can clarify this point if we distinguish three rather different approaches to the study of the farm firm.

(a) The first is the approach taken in this chapter which is to investigate production relationships in order to have a basis for developing a theory of agricultural supply. If we are going to be able to predict how the farm firm will react to some change in its economic environment we must have a hypothesis concerning the behaviour of the farm firm. One such behavioural hypothesis is that of profit maximisation, and the formulation of the profit maximising solution in terms of marginal cost and marginal revenue happens to be convenient from the point of view of identifying the supply response of a firm in the face of changes in prices or technology.

(b) Second, there is an approach to agricultural production which is designed to assist the individual farm firm in meeting its objectives. This branch of agricultural economics is known as *farm management* or *farm planning* and, as it happens, most farm planning techniques do take profit maxi-misation, in one form or another, as the primary goal. Similarly, the theory of the farm firm can provide the basis for a textbook discussion of farm planning techniques, though it is virtually unrecognisable by the time it has been moulded to meet the practical requirements of the decision-maker and his adviser. (And sometimes his computer as well. One way in which the presentation of agricultural production in farm planning books differs from the conventional theory of the farm firm, as described in this chapter, is that both farm advisers and computers prefer to work with linear (straight line) relationships. Upton (4) shows how the theory of the farm firm can be developed using linear relationships. A comprehensive coverage of farm planning techniques will be found in Barnard and Nix (9).)

(c) A third approach is to study the decision-making process itself; to investigate the way decisions are taken and to identify the objectives which appear to motivate them. Ultimately, such a study is not merely for its own sake, since a better understanding of the decision-making process can be of assistance in formulating a more accurate behavioural hypothesis for the theory of agricultural supply, and information concerning the way decisions are taken can help the farm planning exercise to be more effective.

Thus the criticism of the profit maximising assumption on account of the way it is presented in the theory of the farm firm is not legitimate because the marginal cost/marginal revenue formulation is intended neither as an aid to the farm planning exercise nor as a description of how decisions are taken (this is not to say, of course, that a successful profit maximising producer might not arrive at a decision concerning what level of output to aim for by a thought process which could be described approximately as a comparison of marginal costs and marginal revenue). This is a relatively straightforward point, but it is one that needs to be made; every economics teacher must sometime have been confronted with a student essay containing something like '. . . and then the producer looks at his marginal cost curve and compares it with his marginal revenue curve and . . .'.

A somewhat firmer criticism of the profit maximising assumption in the theory of agricultural supply is one that accepts that firms seek to maximise profits but argues that they are markedly unsuccessful in doing so. If this view is correct, it perhaps emphasises the potential scope for a more effective application of farm planning techniques, but it cannot fundamentally alter the theory of agricultural supply. Unless firms fail to maximise profits in some systematic way – say all fertilising for maximum yield, rather than applying this input to the point where its marginal value product equals the price per unit of fertiliser – it is difficult to see how we could improve on a theory which takes what firms try to do as the best available approximation to what they actually do do. To improve upon this approach would require knowledge of in which way, and to what extent, each individual firm failed to meet its objective.

The most substantial area of criticism of the profit maximising assumption emphasises that, for much of the world's agriculture, decisions concerning the use of factors of production are taken by one individual, the farmer. It is then pointed out that what the farmer will seek to maximise is the satisfaction derived by his household, the farm household possessing a utility function like any other. Now, on the face of it, higher profits increase the potential consumption of the farm family and therefore, other things being equal, the objective of maximising profits is quite consistent with that of maximising the utility of the farm household. There are however other factors apart from the consumption of purchasable goods which will enter this utility function. Two which seem most likely to conflict with profit maximising behaviour are the desire on the part of the farmer for, respectively, *leisure* and *certainty*. We will consider these in turn.

4.2 Leisure

In farming circles, the economist's assumption of profit maximising behaviour is often decried. Few farmers, it is said, are prepared to work themselves off their feet in order to maximise profits. What many want, to a greater or lesser extent, is some time for relaxation and they will forego a considerable degree of financial reward to obtain it. This particular criticism appears to arise in part because of a confusion between the concept of profit in the theory of the farm firm and the components of farm income. The total cost of production comprises payments to all resources used in production including those owned by the farm family. When we wish to value a resource which is owned by the farm firm we use a concept known as *opportunity cost*. The opportunity cost of a resource is the return it could earn in its best alternative use. The farmer may own his land, and the cost of land is the rent he could receive if he did not farm the land himself. The farmer and his family may contribute to the family labour force; they could as an alternative have been employed on other farms. Usually the farmer will act as his own manager, supervising the labour force and ensuring that overall policy decisions are converted into day-to-day decisions. All these are cost items, so that even if total revenue only just equals total cost, the farmer is paid for the use of the resources which he owns. Accounting conventions vary but all include some of these items as farm 'profit'. Some economists like to refer to those items of costs, appearing in accounts as 'profit', as *normal profit* and any surplus remaining after all resources are 'paid' as, *supernormal* or *pure profit*. However, in this book, profit is taken to mean the surplus (or deficit, as profit can be negative) after all resources have been paid.

Profit, as we have defined it, is received by the individual who initiates the production process, decides on the overall policy objectives of the firm and thereby takes decisions on what to produce, how much to produce and in what way to produce it. This role in the production process is known as *entrepreneurship*. The entrepreneur differs from other factors of production in that he cannot be hired, and therefore cannot be a cost of production. The entrepreneur is the individual who contracts to pay for certain inputs in the expectation that he will earn a surplus over the cost of production. In a world of perfect knowledge there would be no scope for the entrepreneurial function. If production functions and future prices were known with complete certainty, no special talent would be required in order to initiate the appropriate production plan and no reward would be expected for doing so. In the uncertain world, pure profit can be thought of as a reward for bearing the main risks in production.

Now, on the question of the goal of profit maximisation and leisure, the point is that the average farmer will probably only spend a small proportion of his time on entrepreneurial activity. It seems likely that the view that a farmer does not maximise profits because of a desire for leisure is, in terms of the theory of the farm firm, a remark about how long the farmer is prepared to work as a manager or farm worker. If a farmer decides to switch from – say – milk to beef production and in so doing accepts a reduction in farm income, this is not necessarily evidence of non-profit maximising behaviour. More probably, it will be a decision to accept a lower wage in return for a less strenuous job.

This does not, of course, mean that there will never be a conflict between profit maximising behaviour and leisure, though one suspects that in most cases the relationship between the level of profit and the time devoted to entrepreneurial activity will not be a particularly strong one. However, for those cases where profit is related to the time spent on entrepreneurial activity, Scitovsky (10) has shown, by constructing an entrepreneur's indifference map between money and leisure, how we can identify his optimum level of production.

4.3 Uncertainty

Undoubtedly, the most serious question mark against profit maximising behaviour has been raised in connection with recent work by agricultural economists into decision-making under risk and uncertainty.

The financial outcome of a particular production decision cannot be predicted with complete accuracy, first because the relevant production function will not be perfectly known, second because the quantities applied of some biological and climatic inputs lie outside the control of the decision-maker, and third because the prices paid for inputs and received for products vary through time. Thus, because of variations in the quantity of output which results from the use of a specific quantity of 'controllable' resources, and because of fluctuating prices, no production decision has a unique financial outcome. There will, rather, be a range of outcomes relating to all alternative production decisions and therefore a *range of profit outcomes* relating to each planned resource combination.

There are two ways in which the theory of agricultural supply might need to be modified to take account of the presence of production uncertainty. We need to ask, first, 'Does uncertainty make the representation of the farm firm in the form of a unique cost/revenue relationship misleading?', and second, 'Does uncertainty affect the realism of the profit maximising assumption?'.

In attempting to answer these questions it has been found helpful to distinguish a form of uncertainty called *risk*, which refers to a situation where, although the outcome of a particular event is uncertain, nevertheless the relative *probability* of each alternative outcome is known. The word *uncertainty* is then reserved for cases where the probabilities of each outcome occurring are not accurately known. In fact, the relative probabilities of alternative outcomes will never be known with complete certainty. However, much of the uncertainty in agricultural production is caused by random variables for which probabilities can be estimated to some extent. The most significant of these are climatic in origin. Experience of weather patterns means that sufficient information is often available to know how often a particular rainfall or temperature value has occurred in the past, but one cannot of course be certain that weather patterns observed in the past will continue to be experienced in the future. On the other hand it will rarely be the case that the probability of a particular outcome is completely unknown and, since decisions *have* to be taken, the decision-maker may be forced to use whatever information is available to attach *subjective probabilities* to alternative outcomes.

Thus the distinction between risk and uncertainty refers not to two completely different situations but to differences in the accuracy with which the relative probabilities of the alternative outcomes of a particular event are known.

Where it is thought reasonable to attach probabilities to alternative outcomes, one can calculate an *expected value* for output and prices. This is defined as the average value that the variable would take if the production situation was repeated a large number of times. To take a simple example, suppose that the output from a particular resource combination is 100 units unless a drought occurs, in which case it is 40 units. Droughts are known to occur on average once every four years. The probability of there being a drought can be expressed by a number – 0·25 – there is a 25 per cent chance in any year of a drought occurring. Similarly, the probability of there not being a drought in any year is 0·75. The expected value of output is therefore:

$$(0·25 \times 40) + (0·75 \times 100) = 85 \text{ units}$$

Thus when risk is taken into account, the objective of profit maximisation becomes in practice an objective of maximising *expected profit*. This is the same as saying the objective is to maximise actual profit when it is averaged over a long period. To answer the questions posed above therefore, by inserting expected values, the farm firm can still be viewed in terms of cost and revenue relationships when risk is present, and risk itself does not destroy the credibility of assuming profit maximising behaviour in the theory of agricultural supply, though there is the problem that maximum expected profit will not always result if expected (average) yields and expected (average) prices are manipulated as though they were actual yields and prices. (See Upton and Casey (11).)

A complication arises, however, because most decision-makers are thought to be *risk averse*. That is, given for example a choice between a certain £50, or the equal chance of receiving either £100 or nothing, they will always choose the £50, and there will be sums of money of less than £50 which will be chosen in preference to an equal chance of £100 or nothing. The implication is that a farmer may not aim for the production plan with the highest expected profit if this expected profit is associated with a wide range of alternative profit outcomes; he may instead opt for a lower expected profit if this involves a narrower range of profit outcomes.

The concept of risk aversity has led agricultural economists to develop a variety of mathematical models of agricultural production, which incorporate alternative outcomes for each potential production decision, and to attach probabilities to these outcomes. Risk aversion can be incorporated by the use of a statistical measure of the 'variance' of expected profit from the particular production plan – in other words a measure of the range of possible outcomes from which each expected profit is obtained. If the variance of a particular production plan exceeds some limit, that plan can be excluded from the optimising procedure.

Another approach is to assume that each decision maker subjectively converts each expected value into a *certainty equivalent*. A certainty equivalent is the risk-free sum of money which the decision-maker would just be prepared to exchange for the set of alternative possible returns from which the expected value is calculated. He may, for instance, be just prepared to accept the certainty of receiving £45 rather than the equal chance of £100 or nothing. If he is offered anything less than £45 he will take the chance of receiving £100. The sum of £45 is the certainty equivalent of an equal chance of receiving £100 or nothing. The objective of the decision maker then becomes the maximisation of expected profit expressed in terms of certainty equivalents.

Agricultural economists have also explored the possibility of developing mathematical models of production in the face of 'pure' uncertainty – where it is assumed that the possible outcomes from decisions are known but that the probabilities attached to these outcomes are not. One such approach is the application of *game theory*.[4] The various possible outcomes of a production decision in the form of yields and prices are called *states of nature* and the alternative production choices called *strategies*. All possible financial outcomes (called *pay-offs*) are then calculated using mathematical programming techniques. The production plan that should be chosen, or the one that is predicted will be chosen (depending on whether the procedure is directed towards farm planning or predicting producer behaviour), can then be derived by incorporating a *decision rule* into the procedure. Examples of decision rules are 'maximising the best that can reasonably be expected' (*maximax*) and 'maximising the worst that can reasonably be expected' (*maximin*). The latter of these has been applied to cases of small peasant farmers in low income countries where it is argued that production decisions will be directed towards survival. A decision rule which combines both considerations is one that assumes that farmers maximise profits provided the possibility of ruin is reduced to negligible proportions.

Note that this approach does not remove probability entirely from the decision-making framework. The identification of a set of *outcomes* involves the elimination of those outcomes which are regarded as very improbable. Thus we have 'maximising the worst that can *reasonably* be expected'.

Uncertainty is an everpresent feature of the real world which should not be ignored when developing a theoretical view of the farm firm which is intended to help us to understand the characteristics of agricultural supply. We have seen that some of the ways of viewing decision making under conditions of risk and uncertainty do not radically disturb the conclusions which are reached by applying the conventional theory of the farm firm, but that this theory becomes less realistic when the firm is assumed to face 'pure' uncertainty, and when the decision-maker is thought to be significantly risk-averse. The ability to simulate farm production in the face of 'pure' uncertainty, and in the presence of risk aversion, has fascinated many agricultural economists in recent years but it is not yet clear whether their work will have its main impact in the form of a restatement of the theory of agricultural supply and resource use, as an integrated part of the main body of farm planning techniques, or in throwing light on the decision-making process itself – the three alternative approaches to the study of the farm firm mentioned earlier. At times, game theory and related approaches have appeared to be doing no more than describing how a farmer will take production decisions in the face of uncertainty if he also happens to be an agricultural economist who is pretty good at maths, keeps a computer in his barn, and possesses an independent income.

When we come to ask how does the presence of risk and uncertainty affect the theory of agricultural supply we find that it is perhaps more fruitful to draw attention to some traditional views of the action that farmers may take to combat production and price uncertainty. These ideas have the advantage that they can, in general, be expressed as departures from the action that decision-makers would take if they acted solely on the basis of the profit maximising criteria in a risk-free world. This allows us to proceed to develop the theory of agricultural supply using the profit maximising assumption, but equipped with the ability to modify the implications of the theory if we feel that, in a particular case, considerations of risk and uncertainty are important.

Perhaps the best known traditional solution to reducing production uncertainty is diversification. The 'mixed farm' is thought to provide more security than the specialist one because the farmer believes that a 'bad year' for one crop will be offset by a 'good year' for another. It is necessary to remember, though, that the financial returns for some enterprises vary more than for others, and that the choice of a single reliable activity may yield less variable returns than a combination of activities, particularly because it can turn out to be a 'bad year' for all enterprises. Another possible course of action is for the farmer to plan for a lower level of output than the one which maximises expected profit. This reduces the extent of the loss experienced in bad years at the expense of a lower profit averaged over many years.

The choice of a flexible production system can also reduce risk. Some products may require a lot of specialist equipment whereas others can be produced using, in the main, general purpose buildings and equipment, so that it is easy to switch to an alternative product at short notice. It is even the case that alternative methods of producing the same product vary in the extent to which the inputs used can be switched to alternative farming activities. Finally, a farmer may *contract* to sell his produce in advance of production. As a result he may receive a lower return, when averaged over a period of years, but he reduces the uncertainty over the monetary value of his production in the coming year.

In the light of the various courses of action described above, we can summarise the ways in which the presence of risk and uncertainty may cause the individual farm firm to depart from a profit maximising production solution. The farm firm may choose:

(a) a greater number of products;
(b) a greater number of 'reliable' products;
(c) a lower level of output of all products, but particularly of 'risky' ones;
(d) a more flexible production system; and
(e) to contract the sale of produce in advance.

4.4 The firm's supply under an assumption of profit maximising behaviour

4.4.1
Earlier we suggested that the main factors affecting the firm's supply of an agricultural product could be divided into four groups, namely the state of technology, the price of the product, the prices of competing products, and the prices of inputs. The influence of all these factors is brought together in the view of the farm firm in terms of the cost and revenue of producing alternative levels of output; this facilitates the identification of the profit maximising (or 'optimum') level of output. An assumption of profit maximising behaviour means that we can postulate that, for a given state of technological knowledge, input prices and product prices, the quantity of a product supplied by a farm firm will be given by the level of output for which the marginal cost of producing the product equals the marginal revenue from the sale of the product.

Our interest is in the impact upon quantity supplied of some change in prices or in the physical conditions of production, and our starting point is to ask, 'In what direction will the profit maximising level of output change as a consequence of some change in the price of an input, the price of the product, the price of a competing product, or the production function?' In each case we assume that all factors affecting quantity supplied, apart from the one under consideration, remain constant. Although this assumption is a helpful one for the purpose of identifying the supply response of the farm firm to some change in its economic environment, it should be emphasised that the assumption may not remain valid when the supply response of a large number of firms is aggregated to give *market supply*. In section 4.5 we show, when deriving the market supply response to a change in product price, that it may be necessary to take account of subsequent changes in input prices. The market implications of a large number of firms simultaneously reacting to a change in the price of an input are discussed in Chapter 4.

Consider first a change in the price of a variable input. If there is no change in the production function or in the prices of other inputs, a fall in the price of one input must mean a fall in the total cost of producing any given level of output. Furthermore, since the quantity used of a variable input increases with the level of output, the fall in total cost will itself increase as output increases. This means that the marginal cost of producing any level of output also declines. For example, in Fig. 2.14 suppose that, prior to the input price change, the total cost of producing product A is shown by the curve TC_1 (in Fig. 2.14a) and the marginal cost by the curve MC_1 (Fig. 2.14b). The maximum profit level of output is q_1 units of product A. The fall in costs gives

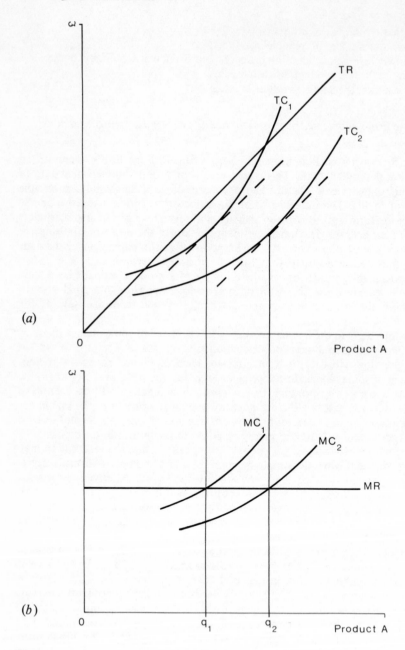

Figure 2.14

the lower total costs curve TC_2 and the lower marginal cost curve MC_2. Thus, under the assumption of profit maximising behaviour, the theory of the farm firm predicts that a fall in the price of one of the variable inputs used in the production of a product, other things remaining equal, will cause an increase in the firm's supply of the product. The converse also follows, i.e. an increase in the price of an input will cause a decrease in supply.

A technological (or productivity) improvement is defined as a change in the state of human knowledge which allows more of a product to be produced from a given combination of inputs, or alternatively, allows the same level of output to be produced using less of at least one input, with no increase in the use of other inputs. Diagrammatically, a productivity improvement can be expressed by a shift in a set of iso-product curves towards the origin so that, following the change, any given combination of inputs will lie upon a higher iso-product curve. Clearly if there is no change in input prices, any change in the physical conditions of production which allows the same level of output to be produced using less of at least one, and no more of any other input, means that the cost of producing any level of output will be less but in the case of a productivity improvement we have to be a little more careful about coming to the conclusions that, because costs are reduced, quantity supplied will increase. The reason for this is that it is not necessarily the case (though it is likely) that the fall in total cost associated with the productivity improvement will itself increase with output. If, for example, a productivity improvement were, over a range of output, to reduce total cost by the same amount whatever the level of output, then in terms of Fig. 2.14 TC_2 would be below but parallel to TC_1 and marginal costs would be unchanged.

Third, what happens if there is a change in the price of a competing product? In Fig. 2.15 we show a firm's production possibility curve between product A and product B. The initial prices of A and B give the set of iso-revenue lines R_1, R_2, etc., and the most profitable combination of A and B is a_1 of A and b_1 of B. If the price of product A now rises to give the new set of iso-revenue line R'_1, R'_2, etc. (shown by the broken lines) the new profit maximising allocation of the fixed resource implies a decrease in the quantity produced of product B. An increase in the price of a product which competes with a second product for the use of some fixed resource, other things remaining equal, will therefore cause a decrease in the firm's supply of the second product. Conversely, a fall in the price of the competing product will cause a rise in supply.

4.4.2
It remains to investigate the relationship between the firm's supply and the price of the product. Figure 2.16 describes a numerical example of a farm firm's marginal cost curve. We can construct four horizontal lines to represent the marginal revenue curves associated with four alternative product prices, £2, £3, £4 and £5 respectively. The profit maximising level of output (given by the intersection of the marginal cost curve with the marginal revenue curves) increases from ten units of product A when the price of A is £2 per unit, to 28 units when the price of A is £5 per unit.

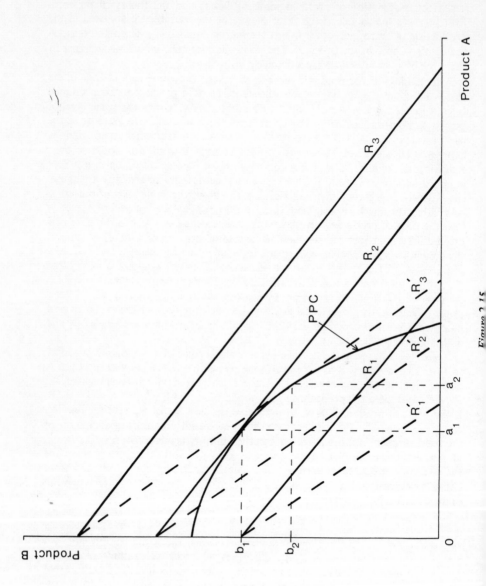

Figure 2.15

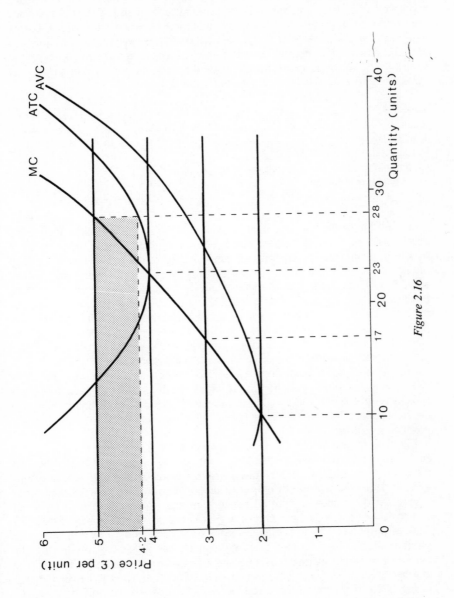

Figure 2.16

The relationship between the quantity supplied of a product and the price of the product is known as a *supply curve*. From Fig. 2.16 we can see that a firm's supply curve in the short run will be identical to its marginal cost curve since the profit maximising level of output for any price occurs when marginal cost is equal to that price.[5] Alternatively, the relationship between price and quantity supplied can be presented in tabular form whereupon it is known as a supply schedule. A simple supply schedule using the same numerical example as that upon which Fig. 2.16 is based is given in Table 2.4.

Table 2.4

Price of product A (£ per unit)	£2	£3	£4	£5
Quantity of product A supplied by the firm, per time period (units)	10	17	23	28

In addition to the marginal cost curve, Fig. 2.16 shows the *average variable cost (AVC)* per unit of output. The *AVC* curve gives a 'floor' price beneath which the profit maximising firm will cease production. The firm has always the option of producing nothing. If it chooses not to produce, it will sustain a loss equal to its fixed costs. If producing the product contributes more to costs than to revenue – i.e. if total variable cost should exceed total revenue at the optimum level of output – the firm will sustain a greater loss in production than if it produced nothing. Thus in terms of the numerical example shown in Fig. 2.16, when the product price falls to £2 per unit the average revenue per unit of output (which is the same as the price) equals the average variable cost per unit of output at the profit maximising (loss minimising) level of output. The firm would have sustained the same loss if it had decided not to produce at all, and if the price of the product should fall beneath £2 per unit, revenue from the sale of the product fails to cover variable costs and the firm will lose less by producing nothing.

Figure 2.16 also shows the *average total cost (ATC)* per unit of output. This enables us to see whether the firm is making an overall profit or loss. When the price of the product is £4 per unit, average revenue per unit of output equals average total cost per unit of output (total cost equals total revenue) and profit is zero. At the higher price of £5 per unit, average revenue per unit of output exceeds the average cost per unit of output at the profit maximising level of 28 units of output (i.e. total revenue exceeds total cost) and an overall operating profit is made. The amount of profit can be calculated by multiplying the difference between average revenue and average total cost (£5–£4·2) by the number of units produced (28), which equals £22·4, shown by the shaded area in Fig. 2.16. If the price of the product falls beneath £4 per unit, however, an overall loss is made (which can also be calculated by multiplying the difference between average revenue and average total cost – in this case a negative amount – by the quantity produced).

4.5 The industry supply curve

4.5.1

At the beginning of this section we said that knowledge of the number of firms supplying the market and size structure of the agricultural industry was required to extend the theory of supply by an individual farm firm to a theory of market supply. 'Size structure' refers to the quantity and distribution of land and other fixed factors throughout the agricultural sector and each individual firm's marginal cost curve will differ in relation to its own particular allocation of fixed factors. We can derive an industry supply curve for the product by a simple process of aggregating the individual firms' supply schedules. A numerical example of such an aggregation procedure is illustrated by Fig. 2.17. Suppose that the marginal cost curves of producing product A for three individual firms are as depicted in Fig. 2.17. These marginal cost curves enable us to derive each individual firm's supply schedule for product A as in Table 2.5. By adding together the quantity supplied at any given price by each of the three firms we obtain a supply curve for the industry – a relationship between the price of the product and the total quantity supplied to the market per time period.

Table 2.5

Price of product A (£ per unit)	Quantity supplied by firm 1	Quantity supplied by firm 2	Quantity supplied by firm 3	Aggregate (market) supply
1	—	—	—	—
2	10	—	—	10
3	17	15	—	32
4	23	20	7	50
5	28	24	11	63
6	32	27	14	73
7	35	29	16	80

The relationship between quantity supplied to a market and product price is, however, rather more complicated than is indicated by the aggregation of the marginal cost curves of the firms supplying the market. First, when a large number of farm firms simultaneously increase their levels of output, this may have repercussions for the economic environment within which the firms operate – in other words, other things may not remain equal. In particular, it is likely that the increased use of variable inputs which follows a rise in product price will lead to some increases in the prices of these inputs. If this is the case, the increase in quantity supplied to a market which follows a rise in product price will be less than is indicated prior to the price change, by the marginal cost curves of the individual firms supplying the market. Economists are not in agreement about whether this kind of effect should be included as part of the supply curve of an agricultural product, or should be accounted for by 'shifts'

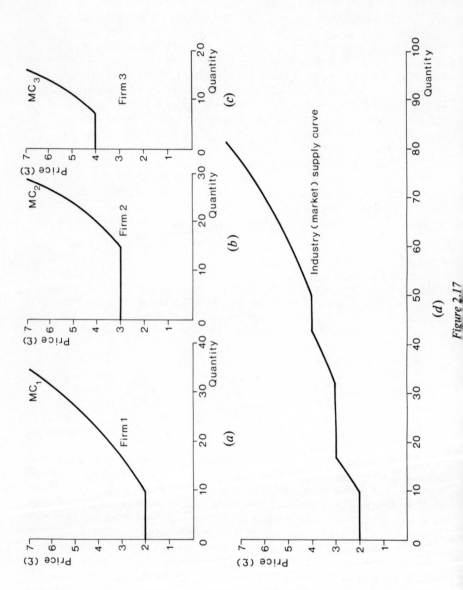

Figure 2.17

in supply curves, with each supply curve defined for a constant level of input prices. The latter approach is theoretically more acceptable, the former operationally more useful.

Second, a market supply curve like that shown in Fig. 2.17 is sometimes called the short-run supply curve of the product. This is to draw attention to the fact that it shows changes in the quantity supplied resulting solely from changes in the quantity of variable factors used by individual firms. In the long run we might expect a change in the price of the product to influence the quantity of fixed factors allocated to its production.

The relevant consideration here would appear to be the overall level of profit derived from the production of the product. Suppose for example that Fig. 2.16 describes a 'typical' farm firm producing product A. When the price of the product is £4 per unit, the overall profit level is zero. (Remember that we include in costs all payments for resources owned by the farmer, including his own labour and management.) In these circumstances we might expect the farm to maintain its stock of fixed resources, as there would be little incentive to increase the amount of investment in the production of this product, but neither would there be any reason to reduce output or to cease producing the product. If, however, the price increases to £5 per unit, we might expect the stock of fixed resources in the production of the product throughout the agricultural sector gradually to increase, both because of new firms setting up in production of this product and because of existing producers investing in more fixed equipment, land, and buildings. Conversely, if the price should decline to £3 per unit we might expect existing firms to begin to withdraw from the production of the product, or at least to reduce their commitment of fixed resources to it.

Clearly, therefore, the response of quantity supplied to a change in product price will be greater in the long run than in the short run because in the long run it is possible to alter the quantity of fixed factors employed in the production of the product. Some economists like to refer to the response of supply, which includes the impact of all changes in the use of fixed factors, as *the long-run supply curve* for the product. Others prefer to see the long-run supply response in terms of 'shifts' in the short-run supply curve.

The relationship between supply response in the short and longer run can perhaps be seen more clearly if we consider the sequence of events that might follow an increase in the price of product A from £4 per unit to £5 per unit, assuming the 'typical' farm firm to have the cost structure described by Fig. 2.16.

(*a*) Existing firms find that it is more profitable to increase output and do so until marginal cost has risen to equal the higher level of product price. The aggregate impact of all firms currently producing the product taking this action gives the short-run market supply response to the rise in price – the increase in quantity supplied from q_1 to q_2 along the short-run supply curve SRC_1 in Fig. 2.18.

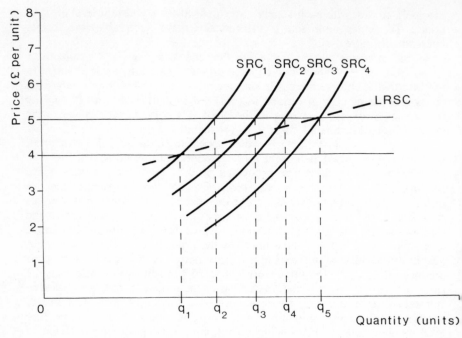

Figure 2.18

(b) In the longer term, if the price rise is sustained, there is a further supply response from existing firms who find that the revenue from the sale of product A is in excess of that necessary to cover all costs, and they are thereby induced to increase the quantity of fixed factors employed in its production. This causes the short-run supply curve for product A to shift to the right. The greater quantity of fixed factors now committed to the production of product A means that, *for any given price*, a greater quantity of the product will be supplied to the market *in the short run* than was the case prior to the initial rise in price from £4 per unit to £5 per unit.

(c) In the longer term, new firms may decide to enter the production of product A. As the time horizon is lengthened therefore, the short-run supply curve for product A will shift to the right both because new firms decide to produce this product and because existing firms invest in more fixed factors. This process is illustrated in Fig. 2.18. The rise in product price to £5 per unit promotes a movement of the short-run supply curve to SRC_2, SRC_3, and so on. If we wish, we can now construct a *long-run supply curve* (*LRSC*) to depict the response of quantity supplied (to the increase in price from £4 per unit to £5 per unit) after a period of time which is sufficient to allow changes in the quantity used of all fixed factors.

(d) The long-run supply response to a rise in product price will be finite – that is, the long-run supply curve will be upward sloping – if the average cost of producing the product rises as more is supplied, since this will remove the incentive for further increases in the quantity of fixed factors employed in the production of the product. There are two reasons why this is likely to be the case with agricultural production. First, as we saw in Fig. 2.12, if decreasing returns to scale apply, the firm's long-run average cost curve will slope upwards. There are grounds for believing that decreasing returns to scale do apply in agriculture, but a discussion of this issue is reserved for Chapter 4. Second, costs will rise as output is increased in the long run if the increased use of both fixed and variable factors leads to increases in the prices of these inputs.

4.5.2

The concept of *price elasticity of supply* is used in an analogous way to demand elasticity to measure the responsiveness of quantity supplied to changes in the price of the product. It is defined as:

$$\text{Elasticity of supply } (E_s) = \frac{\text{Proportionate change in quantity supplied of a product}}{\text{Proportionate change in price of a product}}$$

We have seen that a supply curve will normally slope upwards to the right, so supply elasticity coefficients are positive. Supply is said to be elastic if the coefficient of elasticity exceeds one and to be inelastic if the coefficient is less than one.

Some examples of supply elasticities are given in Fig. 2.19. Zero elasticity, or a *perfectly inelastic supply curve*, is where the quantity supplied does not change in response to price changes, and it is therefore shown by a vertical line. Infinite elasticity, or a *perfectly elastic supply curve*, is represented by a horizontal line; below a certain price, nothing is supplied, but a small increase in price above that level is sufficient to cause the quantity supplied to increase from zero to an infinite quantity. Any straight line supply curve which passes through the origin must have constant elasticity of unit ($E_s = 1$) since all such lines trace a locus of points such that a given proportionate change in price is always associated with the same proportionate change in quantity supplied. A straight line supply curve which cuts the quantity axis will have zero elasticity at its point of intersection with the axis and the coefficient of supply elasticity will approach unity as the quantity supplied becomes large. Similarly, any straight line supply curve which cuts the price axis will have infinite elasticity at its point of intersection with the axis but the coefficient of elasticity will approach unity as the quantity supplied becomes large.

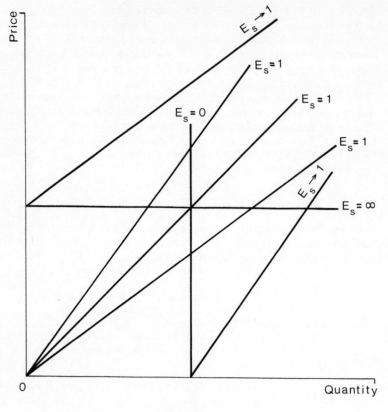

Figure 2.19

If we rewrite the supply elasticity formula as:

$$E_s = \frac{\Delta Q/Q}{\Delta P/P} = \frac{P}{Q} \times \frac{\Delta Q}{\Delta P} = \frac{P}{Q} \times \frac{1}{\text{Slope of supply curve}}$$

we can see that, for a supply curve to have a constant elasticity (other than $E_s = 0$, $E_s = 1$, or $E_s = \infty$) its slope must change along the length of the curve to compensate for changes in the value of P/Q. To illustrate this, Fig. 2.20 shows two supply curves of constant elasticity, equal to $\frac{1}{2}$ and 2 respectively. In the diagram, a comparison is made between the impact upon quantity supplied of a rise in price (from 30p per unit to 33p per unit, and 50p per unit to 53p per unit) when the elasticity of supply equals $\frac{1}{2}$ or 2, and the corresponding change

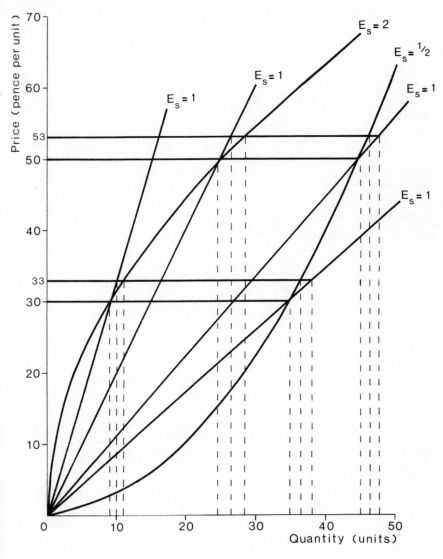

Figure 2.20

in quantity supplied which results when elasticity of supply equals unity. It can be seen that, for the supply curve for which $E_s = 2$, the increment in quantity supplied is double the increment if supply elasticity is unity, and that for the supply curve $E_s = \frac{1}{2}$, the increment in quantity supplied is one-half that which occurs in the case of unity elasticity.

5 Characteristics of agricultural supply

5.1

We may usefully divide the characteristics of agricultural supply into those which are concerned with the response of supply to changes in product price – in other words, the kind of supply curves that are likely to apply for individual agricultural products – and those which are concerned with other factors affecting agricultural supply. The latter will be associated with 'shifts' in the supply curves for individual agricultural products.

There are two features of agricultural supply involving shifts in supply curves which merit special mention. These are *unplanned variations in output* and *technological change*.

Agricultural production is subject to a number of climatic and biological factors which cannot be controlled by individual producers. These random elements cause fluctuations in supply which are not related to the quantities of 'controllable' inputs used. To illustrate this feature of agricultural supply, Fig. 2.21 shows the estimated yield of wheat (cwt per acre) in the United Kingdom between 1935 and 1974. The fluctuations in yield from year to year are mainly the result of variations in weather conditions. When we take into account the fact that the yields are averages for the whole of the United Kingdom (output fluctuations are greater for individual regions, and much greater for individual farms) the significance of the random element in agricultural supply is made clear.

United Kingdom cereal production is not as vulnerable to natural factors as is much of the world's agriculture. The British weather may be notorious but it is not subject to the violent excesses that can distinguish tropical climates, and the application of modern technology, particularly with respect to pest and disease control, water supply control, and mechanised harvesting, reduces the vulnerability of agricultural supply to natural elements. Much more variable yields than those shown in Fig. 2.21 can be experienced for tropical products in the less developed regions of the world.

The other feature of agricultural supply illustrated by Fig. 2.21 is the way technological change can cause a rapid increase in supply. Between 1950 and 1960, wheat yield, averaging a little under 20 cwt per acre during the 1930s and 1940s, was transformed into one that has averaged well over 30 cwt per acre since 1962. During the same period, total UK wheat production increased by about 50 per cent (there being some reduction in wheat acreage). These yield increases were due to many factors, including the introduction of better varieties, the control of soil fertility by the use of artificial fertilisers, the development of plant protecting herbicides, and mechanisation, which allowed farmers to gain a reasonably good crop when previously bad weather would have meant a poor one. All these come under the heading 'technological change' in our list of factors affecting agricultural supply; in little more than ten years, a radical change in the production function for wheat in the United Kingdom virtually doubled output per acre.

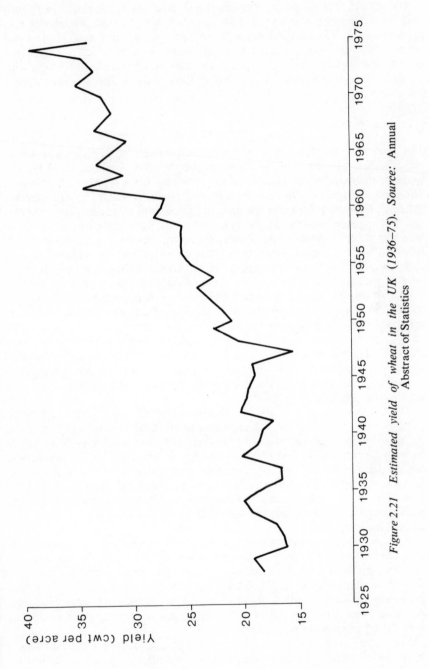

Figure 2.21   Estimated yield of wheat in the UK (1936–75). Source: Annual
Abstract of Statistics

The impact of this kind of technological change will be felt at different times both for different products and for the same product in different countries, and apparently can end as suddenly as it begins. The rise in cereal yields came about somewhat later in other European countries. A more recent example is the introduction of new high yielding varieties of wheat and rice, along with changed production methods, in South-East Asia – the so-called 'green revolution'.

5.2

The theory of the farm firm under an assumption of profit maximisation indicated that the shape of the short run supply curve would be related to the shape of the marginal cost curves of the individual firms supplying the market. There is one aspect of the cost structure of farm firms which has an important influence upon this short run response of agricultural supply to price changes. It is that in general, for most agricultural products, fixed costs are thought to be high relative to variable costs. Two conclusions regarding agricultural supply follow. The first is that, since in the short run output can respond only to changes in the use of variable inputs, we will expect the short run supply curve for an agricultural product to be less elastic than the supply curve for a product for which variable costs represent a high proportion of total costs. The second conclusion is that, since the theory of the farm firm predicts that individual firms will continue to supply the market in the short run as long as revenue covers variable costs, prices may have to fall to very low levels before individual firms cease production. This latter conclusion provides an explanation for the observed tendency for agricultural prices to fall more than other prices in periods of general economic depression, such as that experienced in most advanced countries during the 1930s.[6]

Two exceptions to the above generalisations are eggs and some horticultural products. More than 70 per cent of the cost of producing an egg is made up by feed, and egg prices do not therefore have to fall very much before some producers decide that they will lose less in the short run by abandoning egg production. In the case of some fruit and vegetable products, the casual labour required for harvesting constitutes a substantial proportion of total costs. This is why apples are sometimes 'left to rot on the trees'; at prevailing market prices, revenue from the sale of the crop does not cover the variable costs of harvesting it.

Both these supply characteristics are however affected by the ability of the multiproduct firm to increase the supply of individual products in the short run by switching fixed resources from one product to another within the firm (this was illustrated by Fig. 2.15). Thus the twin characteristics of short run inelasticity of supply, and supply continuing when prices fall to very low levels, are most likely to be prevalent when the prices of a number of competing agricultural products move together.

Another much discussed feature of agricultural production is its dependence upon the life cycles of plants and animals. This causes an inevitable time lag between the decision to commit resources to the production process and the resulting produce becoming available for sale to the market. For this reason the supply of an agricultural product is sometimes described as *perfectly inelastic* in the *very short run*. The 'very short run' can be thought of as a period of time which does not encompass a full crop year or animal life cycle. Some elasticity of supply in the very short run can be introduced by the accumulation or running down of stocks but only if it is the practice to hold 'carry-over' or 'year to year' stocks. Otherwise farmers (and others) holding stocks from the most recent harvest can influence the timing of supply throughout the very short run, but not the total quantity supplied during that period. Similarly, the main impact of the ability to alter the slaughter age for livestock is to influence the timing of sales during the very short run.

There is one curious supply feature associated with the timing of livestock slaughter. The optimum timing of slaughter can be viewed in terms of the relation between the marginal cost of extending the life of an animal and the marginal revenue from the associated life-weight gain. The effect of a rise in product price is to extend the optimum life of an animal whereas a fall in price reduces it. Thus the immediate impact of a rise in – say – cattle prices can be to reduce the quantity supplied to the market in the period immediately following the price change. Eventually, of course, the total quantity supplied during the very short run is increased somewhat by the extended life of the animals.

It has already been mentioned that we will expect the response of quantity supplied to a change in product price to be more elastic in the long run than in the short run; over a period of years, the short run supply curve for a product 'shifts' as some producers alter the quantity of fixed resources committed to the product and other producers enter or leave the industry. It has however been argued, particularly in the context of US agriculture, that a characteristic feature of agricultural supply will be that, for a given period of years, the response of supply will be more elastic for a price rise than for a price fall. There are two versions of this particular argument. The first suggests that farmers will be induced to make productivity improvements when prices rise, so that the long run response of supply to a rise in price will include three elements, namely:

(*a*) a movement along the short run supply curve;
(*b*) a shift in the short run supply curve due to the use of increased quantities of fixed factors;
(*c*) a further shift attributable to productivity improvement.[7]

Once adopted, however, new techniques are retained so that, following a subsequent price fall, quantity supplied will decline in relation only to the first two of these factors.

The second version of this argument is known as the *fixed asset theory* (19, 20). This draws attention to the fact that many agricultural inputs – land, buildings, machinery and even family labour – have low alternative use values outside the agricultural industry. A rise in price will bring these factors into agricultural production but their higher value in agriculture rather than outside the industry means that they will continue to contribute to agricultural supply at prices which are lower than those necessary to induce them into the sector.

The characteristics of agricultural supply discussed above have in common that they are consistent with an assumption of profit maximisation. The one aspect of non-maximising behaviour that has proved of great fascination to those interested in agricultural supply is the supposed conflict between maximising income and the attraction of leisure, for the reason that this conflict might conceivably be responsible for the occurrence of a 'backward sloping' or 'perverse' supply curve. It is contended that, if producers aim to achieve what they conceive of as a satisfactory income, a fall in product price may induce them to increase output (and work harder) in order to sustain that income. Again it should be noted that this argument seems to refer in the main to producers acting as part of their labour force, rather than as entrepreneurs, and that therefore from a 'purist's' point of view any 'perverse' impact upon quantity supplied of a change in price is the result of a change in the implicit price attached by the farmer to additional labour supplied by himself and his family. From the practical point of view of attempting to predict supply response, however, the existence or otherwise of perverse supply relationships is clearly an important question, but it must be said that, in spite of numerous attempts to discover backward sloping supply curves, there is no evidence to suggest that they are anything other than a very rare occurrence indeed. They rank, with the 'Giffen good' mentioned in the previous chapter, as something which attracts the theorist but are probably of little practical significance.

It is nevertheless important that agricultural economists should continue to search for perverse supply relationships, even if it is most unlikely that many will be found, simply because their existence is sometimes assumed unless the contrary is proven. If a government proposes a price cut in order to reduce the supply of a particular product, farmer organisations often reply that the result will be more output because of producers trying to sustain incomes.

The aspect of non-maximising behaviour, to which most attention was devoted in section 4 above, was the influence of risk and uncertainty. Although, as we saw, uncertainty may cause the amount supplied at any product price to differ from that predicted under a simple assumption of profit maximisation, there is no suggestion that uncertainty might cause a perverse supply relationship. What uncertainty, and the factors causing it, has done is to make the task of estimating agricultural supply relationships an exceedingly difficult one, more so than the corresponding demand exercise. First, unplanned variations in output can mask the response of planned supply to price changes, and this tends to introduce wide margins of error when estimates are made of supply elasticities. Second, fluctuating product prices mean that producers may regard the market price applying at the time production decisions have to be taken as only part of the evidence contributing to their expectations of the price likely to apply when their produce becomes available for supply to the market.

To take account of this second factor, Nerlove (21, 22) has developed a technique for estimating the response of supply to changes in price which incorporates the idea that producers base their output decisions upon expected future rather than existing market prices. The technique may be interpreted in a number of ways from a theoretical point of view, but the expected price is perhaps best understood as a weighted average of all past market prices. The more recent prices are given most weight, so that, in effect, the expected price is continually being modified towards the price received in the most recent time period. This technique, with some refinements, has been widely used in estimates of supply response in crop and livestock production.

One of the most comprehensive investigations of agricultural supply response using Nerlove's theory of 'adaptive expectations' was that attempted some years ago for the United Kingdom by G. T. Jones of Oxford University (23). Some of his estimates are given in Table 2.6. Supply in a particular period is approximated to by either crop acreage or livestock numbers. (The number of fowls is related to egg prices, and cow numbers to milk prices.) The short run elasticity of supply is defined as 'the effect of price in a particular year (or other time period) on supply in another particular year (or time period) the length of the gap between the two years being implicit in the kind of situation analysed'. In other words, as argued earlier in this chapter, the length of time which it is appropriate to regard as the short run will vary from product to product, but in most cases the short run supply elasticity can be thought of as representing the proportionate change in supply in year n as a result of a pro-

Table 2.6 Estimated short and long run elasticities of supply for agricultural products in the UK

Product	Short run supply elasticity	Long run supply elasticity	Rate of adjustment	Time period
Sows	0·90	4·5	0·20	1924–39
Fowls (over 6 months)	0·28	1·17	0·24	1927–39
Ewes	0·26	2·31	0·13	1907–58
Cows	0·06	0·46	0·12	1924–39 & 1946–58
Wheat	0·33	0·46	0·71	1924–39
Barley	0·63	1·75	0·36	1924–39
All grain	0·12	0·52	0·23	1924–39
Potatoes	0·11	0·33	0·33	1924–39
Tomatoes	0·17	1·05	0·16	1936–58
Soft fruit	0·18	0·58	0·31	1924–39 & 1946–58
Vegetables	0·28	0·78	0·36	1924–58

Source: G. T. Jones (19).

portionate change in price in year $n - 1$. The long run supply elasticity is the 'difference in supply caused by a difference between two prices which are both supposed to have been maintained over an indefinitely long period'. The long run elasticity therefore estimates supply response over a time period which is long enough to accommodate all changes in factor use and for which all uncertainty over whether the price change is to be a permanent one has been removed. The 'rate of adjustment' is the short run supply response expressed as a proportion of the long run response; other things being equal, we would expect a low rate of adjustment if a product is produced using a high proportion of fixed factors and/or where the product is subject to price instability (whereupon we would expect producers to require a price change to be sustained for a longer period before altering their production plans following the price change).

It should be emphasised that the estimates of supply elasticities quoted in Table 2.6 are included in this chapter, not because they are thought to provide a unique or precise tabulation of supply response for agricultural products. The intention rather is to show how a picture of the character of agricultural supply in a particular country, and during a specific time period, can be built up using the concepts of short and long run elasticity of supply. At the end of his article, Jones uses the elasticity coefficients obtained to describe the supply pattern that he sees emerging from his work:

There is a high supply elasticity for pigs – probably about 4·0 – and a moderate supply elasticity for eggs, mutton and beef – probably more than 1·0 in every case. The supply elasticity for milk is probably 0·50 and may even be augmented if more intensive feeding practices are used as prices rise. . . . There is some degree of complementarity in the supply of beef and milk, some substitution in the supply of eggs and pig meat and probably a mild degree of substitution between all the other pairs of products. . . .

The supply response of the main cereal crops to price was fairly clear indicating a price elasticity of rather less than unity for oats and wheat and more than unity for barley. The long run price elasticity for grain as a whole is probably 0·50.

The supply elasticity for open-air vegetables as a whole is moderately high, probably over 1·0. The evidence of competition within the vegetable group is remarkably small.

The supply elasticity of individual types of soft fruit and for soft fruit as a whole seems to be about 1·0 or somewhat less.

The effect of price on the scale of farm production as a whole does seem to be measurable and positive . . . [it] appears to be about 0·3 in the long run.

Notes

[1] It should be pointed out that there are alternative ways of distinguishing between the short run and the long run in economic analysis.

[2] The general form of the Cobb–Douglas production function is $a = kx^p y^q z^r \ldots$, where $k, p, q, r \ldots$ are constants.

[3] Very occasionally an input could possess a negative price. A poultry farmer might be prepared to pay an arable farmer for permission to deposit poultry manure on the arable farm. In this case, the use of an extra ton of manure could still be adding to profit when MVP is negative if the payment by the poultry farmer on account of this extra ton of manure more than outweighs the resulting reduction in crop output.

[4] Game theory was originated by von Neumann in 1928, but only became widely known following the publication in 1944 of a book von Neumann wrote in collaboration with Morgenstern (12). After years of sporadic attempts at applying it to various agricultural economic problems, disillusionment developed and in 1962, Dillon, in 'Applications of game theory in agricultural economics: review and requiem' (14), concluded that 'like Marshall, it has had its day' (arguably, he was wrong on both counts). More recently, McInerney (15, 16) has stimulated renewed interest in its application to farm production, particularly in the context of small peasant producers in low-income countries.

It should be emphasised that the application of game theory in agricultural economics is only a small part of what is a very extensive subject. Also, although game theory has found most of its applications to economic behaviour in situations where traditional theory was thought to be inadequate, it is not necessarily inconsistent with conventional economic analysis, which, mathematically speaking, it could be said to include as a special case.

[5] This assumes that there are no opportunities for switching fixed factors between products. If it is possible for the firm to reallocate its stock of fixed factors in the short run, the response of quantity supplied by the firm to a change in product price will be greater than is indicated by the marginal cost curve of the product, when this curve is defined for the quantity of fixed factors allocated to the product prior to the price change.

[6] For a discussion of this feature of agricultural supply, see (17, 18).

[7] Strictly speaking, the impact of productivity improvement is not part of long run supply elasticity if the supply curve is defined as the relationship between quantity supplied and product price, all other factors affecting supply, including the production function, remaining constant.

References

(1) Doll, J. P., Heady, E. O. & Pesek, J. T. 'Fertilizer production functions for corn and oats.' Research Bulletin No. 463. Agricultural and Home Economics Experimental Station, Iowa State College, 1958.

(2) Heady, E. O. *Economics of Agricultural Production and Resource Use*. New Jersey, Prentice-Hall, 1952.

(3) Doll, J. P., Rhodes, V. J. & West, J. G. *Economics of Agricultural Production, Markets, and Policy*. Homewood, Illinois, Irwin, 1968.

(4) Upton, M. *Farm Production Economics and Resource–use*. Oxford University Press, 1976.

(5) Rae, A. N. *Crop Management Economics*. London, Crosby Lockwood Staples, 1977.

(6) Dillon, J. L. *The Analysis of Response in Crop and Livestock Production*. Oxford, Pergamon, 1968.

(7) Cobb, C. W. & Douglas, P. H. 'A theory of production.' *American Economic Review*, 1928.

(8) Dench, J. A. L., *et al*. 'Break crops.' Agricultural Enterprise Studies in England and Wales. Economic Report No. 13. University of Reading, Department of Agricultural Economics and Management, 1972.

(9) Barnard, C. S. & Nix, J. S. *Farm Planning and Control*. Cambridge University Press, 1973.

(10) Scitovsky, T. 'A note on profit maximisation and its implications.' *Review of Economic Studies*, Vol. XI, 1943.

(11) Upton, M. & Casey, H. 'Risk and some pitfalls in the use of averages in farm planning.' *Journal of Agricultural Economics*, Vol. XXV, No. 2, May 1974.

(12) Neuman, J. von & Morgenstern, O. *Theory of Games and Economic Behaviour*. Princeton University Press, 1944. (This book is very difficult. For a more readable account of Game Theory see (13).

(13) Williams, J. D. *The Complete Strategyst*. New York, McGraw-Hill, 1954.

(14) Dillon, J. L. 'Applications of game theory in agricultural economics: review and requiem.' *Australian Journal of Agricultural Economics*, Vol. 6, No. 2, 1962.

(15) McInerney, J. P. 'Maximin programming – an approach to farm planning under uncertainty.' *Journal of Agricultural Economics*, Vol. XVIII, No. 2, May 1967.

(16) McInerney, J. P. 'Linear programming and game theory models – some extensions.' *Journal of Agricultural Economics*, Vol. XX, No. 2, May 1969.

(17) Galbraith, J. K. & Black, J. D. 'The maintenance of agricultural production during depression: the explanations reviewed.' *Journal of Political Economy*, Vol. 46, June 1938.

(18) Johnson, D. G. 'The nature of the supply function for agricultural products.' *American Economic Review*, Vol. XL, No. 4, Sept. 1950.

(19) Johnson, G. L. 'Supply functions – some facts and notions.' In *Agricultural Adjustment Problems in a Growing Economy* (eds. Heady *et al.*). Iowa State College Press, 1958.

(20) Edwards, C. 'Resource fixity and farm organisation.' *Journal of Farm Economics*, Vol. XLI, Nov. 1959.

(21) Nerlove, M. 'Estimates of the elasticities of supply of selected agricultural commodities.' *Journal of Farm Economics*, Vol. XXXVIII, No. 2, May 1956.

(22) Nerlove, M. 'Distributed lags and estimation of long-run supply and demand elasticities: theoretical considerations.' *Journal of Farm Economics*, Vol. XL, No. 2, May 1958.

(23) Jones, G. T. 'The response of the supply of agricultural products in the United Kingdom to price.' Part I: *The Farm Economist*, Vol. IX, No. 12, 1961. Part II: *The Farm Economist*, Vol. X, No. 1, 1962.

A Simple Two-Input One-Product Production Example

(This appendix has the limited purpose of helping those readers who are familiar with the simple mathematical notations used to understand more readily the argument of the main text. It is not concerned with deeper theoretical matters such as, for example, the identification of the conditions under which solutions will exist for any set of simultaneous equations which occurs, or the conditions required for maximum values to be unique. A treatment aimed at this degree of rigour would make demands upon mathematical understanding inconsistent with the aim of this book.)

Let the conditions of production for a commodity be given by the production function:

$$a = x^{2/5} y^{2/5} \qquad (1)$$

where x and y represent the quantities used respectively of input X and input Y per time period, and a represents the maximum quantity of output of product A obtainable from these quantities of inputs.

Let price of X (P_x) be £4 per unit
price of Y (P_y) be £8 per unit
price of A (P_a) be £20 per unit

Then:
$$\text{Total cost } (TC) = 4x + 8y$$
$$\text{Total revenue } (TR) = 20a$$
$$\text{Profit } (\pi) = TR - TC = 20a - 4x - 8y \qquad (2)$$

By substituting eqn (1) in eqn (2) we have:

$$\pi = 20x^{2/5} y^{2/5} - 4x - 8y \qquad (3)$$

Profit (π) will be at a maximum when $\partial\pi/\partial x = 0$ and $\partial\pi/\partial y = 0$ (assuming second-order conditions are fulfilled). By differentiating eqn (3):

$$\frac{\partial\pi}{\partial x} = 8x^{-3/5}y^{2/5} - 4$$

$$\frac{\partial\pi}{\partial y} = 8x^{2/5}y^{-3/5} - 8$$

On putting $\partial\pi/\partial x = 0$ and $\partial\pi/\partial y = 0$ (for maximum profit π), we have

$$8x^{-3/5}y^{2/5} = 4 \tag{4}$$

$$8x^{2/5}y^{-3/5} = 8 \tag{5}$$

Equations (4) and (5) may be solved simultaneously to obtain $x = 8$, $y = 4$. Substituting these values in eqn (1) gives $a = 4$.

NB   An 'economic' interpretation of this solution would be to say that we are ensuring that the marginal value product of X equals the price of X (eqn (4)) and that, simultaneously, the marginal value product of Y equals the price of Y (eqn (5)).

The calculations upon which sections 2.1 and 3.1 were based are as follows:

The factor/product relationship (2.1.2)

By holding input Y constant at 8 units we obtain the equation for the total product (*TP*) of X ($y = 8$):

$$TP = x^{2/5}8^{2/5}$$

When $x = 4$, $TP = 4^{2/5}8^{2/5} = 4$ units of A.

Marginal product (*MP*) of X ($y = 8$) is obtained by differentiating the expression for total product:

$$\frac{d(TP)}{dx} = \tfrac{2}{5}x^{-3/5}8^{2/5}$$

Marginal product (*MP*) of X when $x = 4$ is therefore:

$$MP = \tfrac{2}{5}4^{-3/5}8^{2/5}$$

$$= 0{\cdot}4 \text{ units of A (per unit of X)}$$

If, alternatively, marginal product is thought of approximately as the increment in total product for each additional unit of input X applied, then, when $x = 4$,

$$MP = TP(x = 4) - TP(x = 3)$$

$$= 4 - 3^{2/5}8^{2/5}$$

$$= 0{\cdot}435 \text{ units of A}$$

The factor/factor relationship (2.1.3)

By holding product A constant at level 4 we obtain the equation for the iso-product curve $a = 4$:

$$4 = x^{2/5} y^{2/5}$$

i.e.

$$y = \frac{32}{x}$$

The marginal rate of substitution (*MRS*) between the inputs when $a = 4$ may be found by differentiating this expression:

$$\frac{dy}{dx} = -\frac{32}{x^2} \qquad (6)$$

When $x = 4$

$$MRS = -32/4^2$$
$$= -2$$

When $x = 8$

$$MRS = -32/8^2$$
$$= -\tfrac{1}{2}$$

Returns to scale (2.1.4)

Let $x = 4$ and $y = 8$, then (from eqn (1)):

$$a = 4^{2/5} 8^{2/5}$$
$$= 4$$

Let $x = 6$ and $y = 12$ (an increase of 50 per cent in both inputs), then:

$$a = 6^{2/5} 12^{2/5}$$
$$= 5 \cdot 534$$

an increase of $38 \cdot 35$ per cent in output.

More generally, take a production function of the form:

$$a = k x^p y^q z^r$$

Let the initial values of a, x, y and z be a_1, x_1, y_1 and z_1 units respectively. Increase the application of all inputs by some factor, $n\,(>1)$. Then:

$$a = k (nx_1)^p (ny_1)^q (nz_1)^r$$
$$= n^{p+q+r} k x_1^p y_1^q z_1^r$$
$$= n^{p+q+r} a_1$$

Thus, if $p + q + r < 1$, then $n^{p+q+r} < n$, and decreasing returns to scale apply
  if $p + q + r > 1$, then $n^{p+q+r} > n$, and increasing returns to scale apply
  if $p + q + r = 1$, then $n^{p+q+r} = n$, and constant returns to scale apply

The optimum application of a single variable input (3.1.2)

Total value product (*TVP*) of X with Y held constant at 8 units is given by:

$$P_a \times TP(y = 8) = 20x^{2/5}\, 8^{2/5}$$

and, on differentiating with respect to x, marginal value product (*MVP*) is given by:

$$P_a \times MP(y = 8) = 8x^{-3/5}\, 8^{2/5}$$

Thus if, for example, we put $x = 4$, we have:

$$TVP = 20(4^{2/5}8^{2/5})$$
$$= £80$$

$$MVP = 8(4^{-3/5}8^{2/5})$$
$$= £8$$

On the other hand, the profit maximising level of application of input $X\,(y = 8)$ is given by:

$$MVP(y = 8) = P_x$$

i.e.

$$8x^{-3/5}y^{2/5} = 4$$
$$x^3 = 2^5\, 8^2$$
$$x = 12 \cdot 69$$

The optimum combination of inputs (3.1.3)

The least cost combination of X and Y to produce 4 units of A is given by:

$$MRS(a = 4) = - P_x/P_y$$

i.e. (using eqn (6))

$$-\frac{32}{x^2} = -\frac{4}{8}$$
$$x = 8$$

To find Y, substitute in eqn (1)

$$4 = 8^{2/5}\, y^{2/5}$$
$$y = 4$$

The optimum level of output (3.1.4)

MRS is found by partially differentiating y with respect to x.
From eqn (1)

$$y = \frac{a^{5/2}}{x}$$

$$\frac{\partial y}{\partial x} = -\frac{a^{5/2}}{x^2}$$

The least-cost combination of X and Y for any particular quantity a of product A is given by:

$$MRS = -\frac{P_x}{P_y}$$

i.e.

$$-\frac{a^{5/2}}{x^2} = -\frac{4}{8}$$

i.e.

$$x = 2^{1/2} a^{5/4} \tag{7}$$

Substituting eqn (7) in eqn (1), we have

$$y = 2^{-1/2} a^{5/4} \tag{8}$$

On substituting eqns (7) and (8) in profit eqn (3), we have:

$$\pi = 20a - 4(2^{1/2} a^{5/4}) - 8(2^{-1/2} a^{5/4})$$
$$= 20a - 8(2^{1/2} a^{5/4})$$

Profit (π) will be at a maximum when $d\pi/da = 0$ (assuming second-order conditions are fulfilled)

$$\frac{d\pi}{da} = 20 - 10(2^{1/2} a^{1/4})$$

Now put $d\pi/da = 0$, and we have

$$20 = 10(2^{1/2} a^{1/4}) \tag{9}$$

i.e.

$$a = 4$$

Now substitute in eqns (7) and (8) to find

$$x = 8, y = 4$$

NB   The 'economic' interpretation of the reasoning behind eqn (9) is that profit will be at a maximum when marginal cost is equal to marginal revenue.

CHAPTER 3

The Market Mechanism for Agricultural Products

1 Introduction

The concept of a market was introduced in Chapter 1 where it was described as the interaction of buyers and sellers exchanging goods for money. An explanation of the emergence of markets for agricultural goods is provided by one of the longest standing ideas in the history of economic thought – that of the *division of labour*. Individuals find that they can consume a greater quantity and a greater variety of goods if they specialise in one productive activity, exchanging part of their output for other products, rather than by attempting to provide for all their needs by their own productive efforts. Even in very primitive societies therefore, simple markets will develop with individuals exchanging their produce by barter. The appearance of a currency facilitates exchange and allows markets to specialise in single commodities. Modern telecommunication systems mean that it is now no longer necessary for buyers and sellers to meet in the same place, and the most appropriate definition of a modern market is perhaps the *totality of arrangements* whereby buyers and sellers exchange goods for money.

In this chapter, then, we explore the interaction of supply and demand in agricultural markets. This process of interaction can vary from that found in the simplest agricultural market, where producers congregate to sell their produce directly to those who wish to consume it, to the extremely complex economic activity constituted by the procedure of transportation, processing, storage, and distribution through which an agricultural product can pass in developed economies. Supply and demand relationships for commodities such as wheat, cocoa, coffee, tea and vegetable oils are often described in the context of a *world market*, but as suggested in Chapter 1, both transport costs and political barriers to the free movement of goods and factors mean that, for much agricultural produce, production and consumption in different parts of the world are separated by geographical barriers and country boundaries. The relationship between domestic and world markets is reserved for a later chapter. The majority of the argument of this chapter can apply to either domestic or world markets.

The subject matter of the chapter is divided into three parts. First, we consider market price as the mechanism which tends to equate quantity supplied to a market with quantity demanded from the market. Next we discuss how the characteristics of agricultural supply and demand outlined in the first two chapters themselves cause certain characteristic developments in the operation of agricultural markets. Finally, we investigate some aspects of the structure of the firms which process, distribute, and store agricultural commodities and we consider the way their activities can influence the operation of the market mechanism for agricultural products.

It should perhaps be emphasised that this chapter covers only a part of the subject matter to which agricultural economists can refer when they use the term *agricultural marketing*. Our approach to the 'marketing' of agricultural products is the same as our approach in the previous two chapters to the demand for agricultural products and to the supply of agricultural products – that is, to attempt to provide a theoretical framework to aid the understanding of the operation of agricultural markets and to illustrate the application of this theory using both 'real world' and hypothetical examples. The chapter does not attempt to describe the particular marketing channels through which individual farm products pass in different countries, neither is it concerned with the business management aspects of the firms which process and distribute the produce of farm firms, nor does it discuss ways in which farmers can 'improve' the marketing of their produce.

2 The equilibrium of the perfectly competitive market

In this section we consider the interaction of supply and demand in the context of the most basic model of a market used by economists – the *perfectly competitive market*. No one suggests that a perfectly competitive market exists in the real world though, as we shall see, many agricultural markets approximate more closely to the perfectly competitive model than do most markets for non-agricultural goods; but the concept of a perfectly competitive market requires our attention because many of the important characteristics of agricultural markets can best be understood by reference to the manner and extent to which a particular market departs from the perfectly competitive model. We can summarise the nature of a perfectly competitive market[1] by stating five conditions required for its attainment:

Condition 1   There are many buyers and sellers such that the action of no one individual buyer or seller can have a perceptible influence upon market price.

2   Producers and consumers have perfect knowledge of events on the market and act on this knowledge.

3 The product is homogeneous so that customers are indifferent between the produce of alternative suppliers.

4 Firms act independently of each other in such a way as to maximise their individual profits and each consumer acts similarly so as to maximise utility from consumption.

5 There are no barriers to the movement of goods or factors of production. Firms are therefore free to enter or leave the production of the product and are able to supply to the market whatever quantity they wish.

The term *pure competition* is sometimes used to describe a market for which all but the second of these conditions apply.

We will begin by considering the idea of equilibrium in a perfectly competitive market. In Fig. 3.1 and Table 3.1 we reproduce from Chapter 1

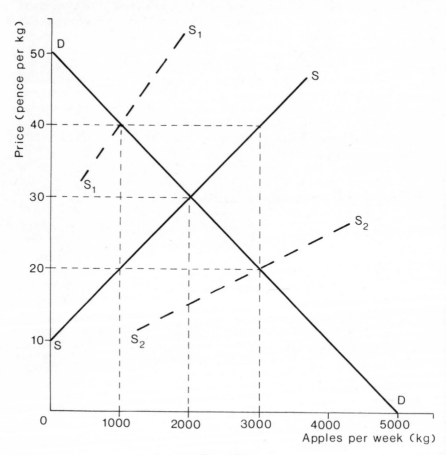

Figure 3.1

Table 3.1

Price (p per kg)	Quantity demanded (kg per week)	Quantity supplied (kg per week)
0	5000	0
10	4000	0
20	3000	1000
30	2000	2000
40	1000	3000
50	0	4000

(Fig. 1.9 and Table 1.1) the hypothetical numerical example of the relationship between the market demand for apples and the market price of apples, and we add to it corresponding information concerning the conditions of supply for apples, given by the supply curve *SS* in Fig. 3.1; it is postulated that, at a price of 10p per kg or less, no apples will be supplied per week, that 1000 apples per week will be supplied at a price of 20p per kg, 2000 at 30p per kg, 3000 at 40p per kg, and so on. Condition 1 above tells us that no buyer or seller contributes sufficiently to aggregate supply or demand for his action alone to have a perceptible influence upon the market.

Suppose price is initially established arbitrarily at 40p per kg; sellers wish to supply 3000 apples per week but buyers are only prepared to purchase 1000. If there were no change in price unsold apples would begin to accumulate. Each seller finds, however, that if he drops his price he is able to dispose of his supply to buyers who have, by virtue of condition 2, perfect knowledge of all selling prices in the market, and who will always buy from the cheapest source as the product is homogeneous (condition 3). Thus an incentive exists for sellers to lower their prices, and the price ruling in the market declines. Quantity demanded per week increases and quantity supplied decreases until a market price of 30p per kg is reached, when consumers are willing to purchase exactly the same quantity of apples per week as producers are willing to supply.

Alternatively, suppose price is established initially at 20p per kg. Buyers then find that they are unable to obtain as many apples as they wish to purchase at that price and individual buyers begin to offer slightly more. This forces up the market price towards 30p per kg, where quantity supplied equals quantity demanded.

The price of 30p per kg is called the *equilibrium price*. For the given conditions of demand and supply depicted in Fig. 3.1, it is the only price which, if attained, will then be maintained, as long as there is no change in the conditions of supply or demand. If price deviates from 30p per kg, *market forces* are set in motion to restore equilibrium. It is worth noting, therefore, that such frequently heard statements as 'demand exceeds supply' or 'supply was much greater than demand' are, if unqualified, quite meaningless. Demand can only exceed, equal or be less than supply *at a price*. For instance, in our example, supply exceeds demand at a price of 40p per kg. If, for some reason, price is prevented from falling beneath 40p per kg, then a quantity of 2000 apples per week would remain unsold. This is usually called a *market surplus*. Similarly, if the price is prevented from rising above 20p per kg, there is a *market shortage* of 2000 kg per week. But the perfectly competitive market cannot remain in surplus or shortage; in the perfect market, price moves so as to *equate* quantity demanded and quantity supplied.

The next question then, is what happens to equilibrium price in the perfectly competitive market if there is some change in the conditions of demand or supply. In Fig. 3.1 we see that a reduction in supply to S_1S_1 – that is, a change in one of the factors affecting the supply of apples such that less is supplied at any price – causes the equilibrium price to increase to 40p per kg, if there is no change in the demand curve. At the original price of 30p per kg, a potential shortage develops which forces up market price. Similarly, a shift in the supply curve to S_2S_2 causes the equilibrium market price to fall to 20p per kg.

The re-establishment of equilibrium following a shift in the demand curve is more complex because it is often necessary to take note of the distinction between supply response in the short and long term. This process is illustrated in Fig. 3.2. Initial market equilibrium is shown in Fig. 3.2b, with Q_1 units of product A sold per time period at price P_1. The associated equilibrium position of a 'typical' firm supplying the market is shown in Fig. 3.2a. At its profit maximising level of output (condition 4 contains an assumption of profit maximising behaviour) the firm produces q_1 units of product A per time period and all costs are just covered (the firm is making only 'normal' profits). There is no incentive either to reduce or increase the firm's use of fixed resources in the production of product A.

Suppose that there now occurs some change in one of the factors affecting the market demand for product A – perhaps a change in taste – which shifts the market demand curve to D_2D_2. A potential shortage develops in the market (of Q_1Q_3) and market price rises. The quantity demanded declines from Q_3 to Q_2 and the quantity supplied increases from Q_1 to Q_2, to establish a new equilibrium, with Q_2 sold at price P_2. For the individual firm, the higher price in the market has increased the profit maximising level of output. The firm depicted in Fig. 3.2a has responded by increasing output from q_1 units to q_2 units. The aggregate impact of all the firms supplying the market simultaneously increasing their output levels in the face of rising product price *constitutes* the increase in supply to the market along the (short run) supply curve S_1S_1 from Q_1 to Q_2.

The fifth condition for the existence of a perfectly competitive market specified that there should be no barrier to firms entering or leaving the industry. The rise in market price means that the typical firm supplying the market is making more than normal (or 'supernormal') profits. In the previous chapter it was argued that the consequence of this for a market supplied by profit maximising firms would be a shift of the short run supply curve to the right. Market price in the longer run therefore declines down the demand curve D_2D_2, and the shift in market supply curve will cease when price has fallen to the level where the typical firm again only makes normal profits in the production of product A.

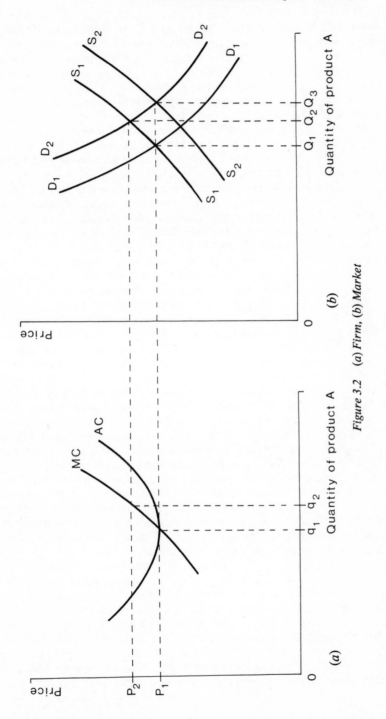

Figure 3.2   (a) Firm, (b) Market

In Fig. 3.2, the new long run equilibrium price is shown as P_1, the same as that pertaining prior to the increase in demand – in other words, supply is perfectly elastic in the long run. This occurs in the rather special case where the average cost of producing the product, after all long run adjustments are complete, remains constant as supply increases. This would require new firms having similar cost structures to existing firms and no change in input prices. However, it was suggested in the previous chapter that, for most agricultural products, long run supply elasticities are thought to be positive but less than infinite. In general, therefore, we would expect the new long run equilibrium price in the perfectly competitive market, following an increase in demand, to be somewhat higher than the previous equilibrium price.

The straightforward application of the equilibrating process in a perfectly competitive market can in itself often provide an adequate explanation of the behaviour of prices in agricultural markets, and can help us to predict the market consequences of some change in the conditions of supply and demand. At the time of writing, for instance, a dry summer has reduced potato yields in the United Kingdom and potato prices are very much higher, relative to other food prices, than they were in the previous year. To give another example, the rise in average incomes in Western Europe in the post-1945 period increased the demand for beef relative to the demand for most other agricultural products, and part of the growth in world beef production can perhaps be attributed to the effect of periods when beef producers earned more than normal profits; one would expect such periods to be followed by an expansion of beef output and a moderation in prices. Innumerable other examples could be cited where, with sufficient information concerning any significant changes in the factors underlying supply and demand, agricultural product price movements could be explained by assuming that the market in question had behaved in a manner consistent with perfect competition.[2]

The reason may very well be that many agricultural markets *do* conform quite closely to the perfectly competitive model. Inasmuch as the market involves farmers and final consumers, then there will usually be many buyers and sellers. In most cases, the produce sold on an agricultural market can be said to be more or less homogeneous and there are seldom any barriers to setting up business as a farmer if it seems attractive financially to do so. In general, licences are not required to produce farm products (there are of course exceptions) and existing farmers do not combine to prevent newcomers entering the industry. As we saw in the previous chapter, in many cases, profit maximisation is thought to be an acceptable behavioural assumption. There is never, of course, perfect knowledge, but nevertheless it can be argued that many farmers are surprisingly well informed about prices ruling in alternative localised markets. In the market which lacks perfect knowledge but for which the other conditions apply – the 'purely competitive market' – price differences for identical products will remain and time will be taken while adjustments take place. But as long as the other conditions apply, and knowledge is not 'too imperfect', then all these considerations suggest that the perfect competition model may very well provide a quite acceptable approximation to the real world behaviour of many agricultural markets. The major departure from such an approximation has occurred in the developed economies with the growth of large firms and institutions providing the marketing services which transform agricultural products from the time they leave the farmer to when purchased by the ultimate consumer. For this reason, we shall find it convenient to divide our investigation of agricultural markets into two sections. The latter part of the chapter discusses some aspects of the complex market structure which can characterise the provision of such market services as transport, distribution, processing and storage in advanced countries. But first we concentrate upon the characteristics of 'simple' agricultural markets. Much of what will be said under this heading applies also to more complex market situations.

As it happens, there are two issues which have tended to dominate the application of the principles of agricultural economics to the study of agricultural markets and both can be explained by simple analysis of farm product supply and final consumer demand. The two issues are the problems associated with, respectively, short term fluctuations in agricultural product prices and longer term changes in the prices of agricultural products relative to other prices.

3 Short-term fluctuations in agricultural prices

3.1

Many markets for agricultural products are notoriously unstable – that is, prices vary widely and erratically. In Figs. 3.3 and 3.4 price movements in two agricultural markets are shown, one a national market and the other an international one. During the period covered in Fig. 3.3 the UK market for eggs was more or less free from government interference and there were virtually no imports or exports. This particular price pattern therefore emerges from the interaction of egg supply and demand within the United Kingdom. Coffee, on the other hand, is, by value, one of the most important commodities traded internationally, and the prices quoted on the New York market for Brazilian coffee can be taken as representative of 'world' coffee prices.

There can be many causes of unstable prices in agricultural markets but two factors predominate – one is a supply characteristic, the other a characteristic of demand.

We have seen that an equilibrium price in a market will be maintained if there is no change in the conditions of demand and supply. However, the supply curve shows the quantity of a product which producers *plan* to supply to a market at alternative product prices. One of the features of agricultural supply discussed in the previous chapter was that the production of many agricultural products is subject to natural factors which cause unplanned variations in output. This means that, in an agricultural market, price must vary to equate quantity demanded with the actual (rather than the planned) quantity supplied. If we add to these supply fluctuations an observation made in Chapter 1 – that

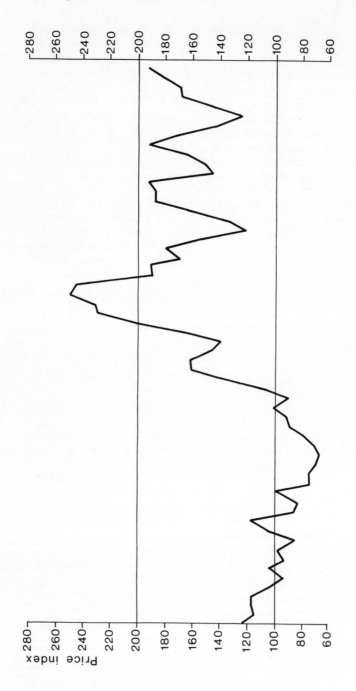

Figure 3.3   Monthly index of egg prices in the UK, 1971–75 (1968–72 = 100)
Source: MAFF statistics

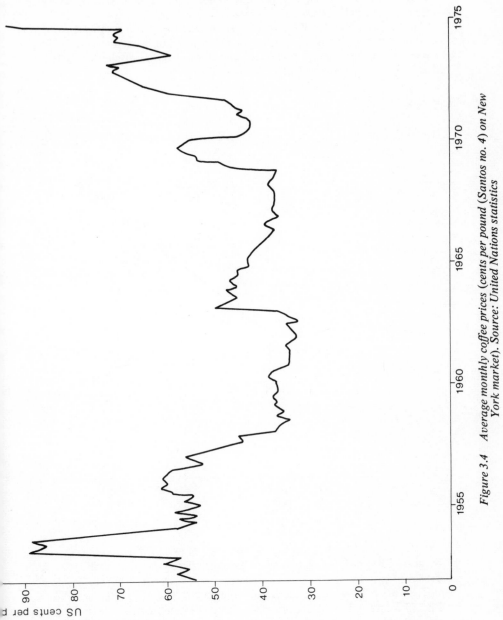

Figure 3.4   Average monthly coffee prices (cents per pound (Santos no. 4) on New York market). Source: United Nations statistics

most agricultural products have low price elasticities of demand, then market forces will tend to magnify the fluctuations in output into proportionately greater price fluctuations.

Figure 3.5 illustrates the impact upon market price of unplanned variations in output when demand is relatively price inelastic. If actual supply always equalled planned supply, market equilibrium would be established and main-

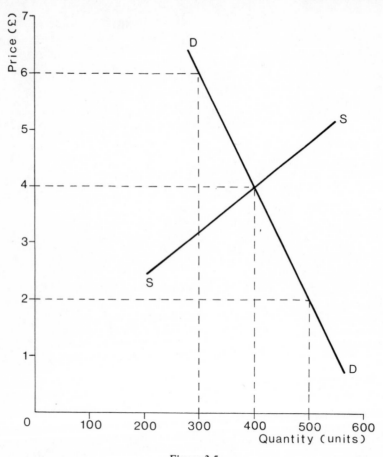

Figure 3.5

tained with 400 units sold at £4 per unit. Unplanned variations in output between 300 and 500 units lead to proportionately larger variations in price between £6 and £2.

The two markets for which the evolution of product prices are shown in Figs. 3.3 and 3.4 were chosen because one reflects a case where a very low price elasticity of demand is the major cause of price instability whereas in the other, unplanned variations in output are probably more important.

It is difficult to think of another food product so lacking in close substitutes as eggs. If we return to Table 1.2, we will see that the Ministry of Agriculture's estimate of the price elasticity of demand for eggs in the United Kingdom (−0·09) is, along with that for liquid milk, the lowest of those listed in the table. Egg production, however, is relatively stable; the average monthly variation in the quantity of eggs passing through UK packing stations in the period 1971– 75 was only about 3 per cent. (The generally higher level of egg prices from 1973 onwards was caused by a rise in feed costs.) On the other hand, the demand for coffee in most of the major importing countries is probably more price elastic (the value shown in Table 1.2 for the UK is −1·1). Against this, coffee is a crop which seems to be very susceptible to the natural factors which cause unplanned variations in output. In particular, the crop of the major producer – Brazil – is periodically devastated by frost. The average annual variation in total world production of coffee for export was approximately 20 per cent between 1953 and 1975.

One feature of an agricultural market, in which an inelastic demand translates given proportionate variations in quantity supplied into larger proportionate variations in price, is that revenue from the sale of the product will be inversely related to quantity supplied. This leads to the somewhat paradoxical development that what is a 'good' year for crop yields can turn out to be a 'poor' year for farm incomes. Not surprisingly, farmers can develop a cynical attitude to the operation of agricultural markets. The following is an excerpt from a newspaper article attempting to explain why farmers were not amongst those 'praying for rain in hundreds of little brown-washed clapboard churches here in Iowa on Sunday'.

A mahogany-tanned oldtimer who has farmed a section (640 acres) of corn and soya beans for the past twenty or so years just outside the village of Nevada, explains why he likes the weather just the way it is. 'The fact is we have more land under cultivation this year than ever before in our history, and all the forecasts put our yield per acre right up so we are expected to produce the biggest corn crop ever in 1975. That forecast kept the price I could get at the elevator way down this spring, and I don't like it. So if it keeps on being dry like this, and the crop is less, I'll get more money per bushel and have less work to do getting it in. I'll be a happier man. If it rains, fine, but if it doesn't, that's fine with me too' (1).

3.2

The price fluctuations shown in Figs. 3.3 and 3.4 are substantial but appear to be quite erratic. For many years, however, those studying the behaviour of agricultural markets have observed discernible patterns of a cyclical form – that is, regular movements in price and quantity which repeat themselves over a period of years. Examples of this kind of agricultural market are illustrated by Fig. 3.6, which shows the total number of pigs in Great Britain between 1865 and 1935, and by Fig. 3.7, which shows an index of potato prices in Belgium between 1960 and 1971.

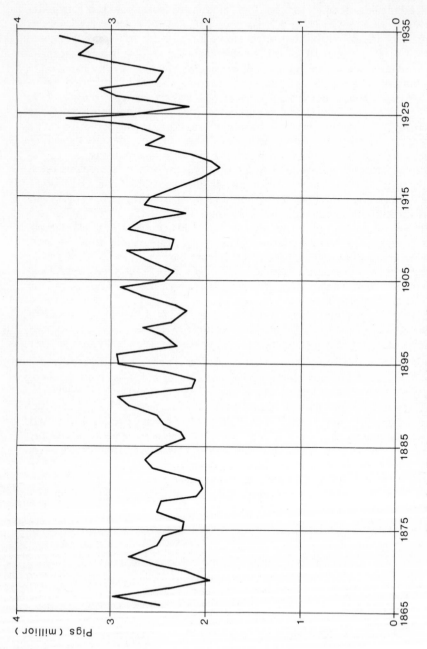

Figure 3.6   Total pigs in Great Britain (millions) 1865–1935. Source: MAFF (2)

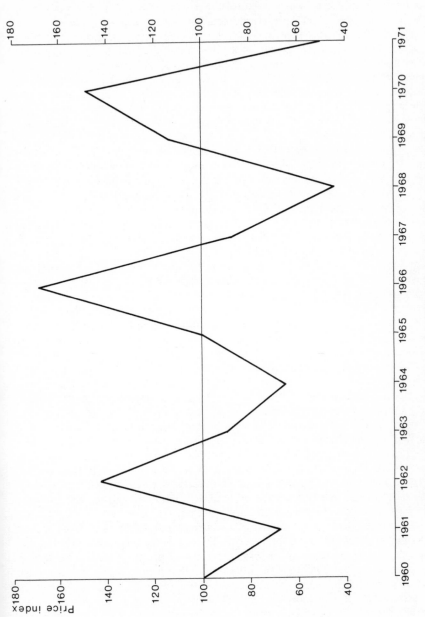

Figure 3.7   Index of potato prices in Belgium 1960–71 (1962–64 = 100). Source: OECD (3)

If we introduce one further characteristic of agricultural supply – the production time lag – we can construct a simple model of an agricultural market, called the *cobweb*, which predicts the development of a market cycle. In essence, the cobweb 'theorem' relates to a market for which the conditions of perfect competition apply with the incorporation of an additional assumption, that there is a time lag, of sufficient length to encompass the biological life cycle, between the decision to produce a certain level of output and the produce becoming available for supply to the market. Thus, in the cobweb, supply curves describe the relationship between output in the current time period and price in the previous time period – they are sometimes called *lagged output* curves.

In Fig. 3.8a, assume that there is some disturbance in time period T_1 which causes quantity supplied to be less than the planned amount of Q_p. Quantity supplied falls to Q_1 and the market price rises to P_1. At the higher market price of P_1, producers plan to supply quantity Q_2, and if on this occasion their plans are fulfilled, in time period T_2 price must fall to P_2 to clear the market. This reduces the quantity planned for T_3 to Q_3 units, which in turn means that price will rise to P_3. The quantity planned for period T_4 now rises to Q_4, and so output and price continue to oscillate.

In Fig. 3.8a the supply curve is steeper than the demand curve and this causes a *converging cobweb* – the oscillations in price and quantity get smaller and smaller in successive time periods so that, if there is no new disturbance in the market, equilibrium will eventually be re-established. Figure 3.8b shows the opposite case – a *diverging cobweb*, where the price and quantity fluctuations 'explode', and Fig. 3.8c is the special case where the slopes of both curves are the same, generating a *continuous cobweb*.

The first application of something resembling the cobweb model appears to have been made in 1917 when Moore (4) attempted to demonstrate that, whereas the current price of the cotton crop was determined by the size of output in the current year, output itself was influenced by the price in the previous year. There followed a number of similar applications to farm product markets in the United States, and also in Germany, where Arthur Hanau investigated the pig cycle. Kaldor (5) is credited with the coining of the word 'cobweb' to describe the typical diagram and, in the same year (1934), Leontief (6) used the rather engaging German equivalent, *spinnwebenbild*. The 'classic' article on the cobweb was written by Ezekiel (7) in 1938 and Waugh (8) gives an excellent review of more recent developments.

The cobweb theorem has therefore a relatively long history and it has proved extremely resilient in the face of criticism. It seems very probable that the cobweb model does capture the essence of the explanation of many cycles in agricultural markets. Perhaps its most fascinating aspect is that it shows how one very small disturbance can cause the development of a cycle which lasts in perpetuity. There are, however, two ways in which the basic cobweb model predicts market developments which are not consistent with many of the cycles observed to occur in agricultural markets. First, whereas the basic cobweb model suggests that one will usually find either converging or diverging oscilla-

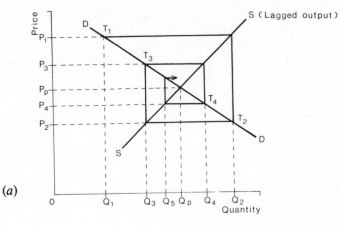

(a)

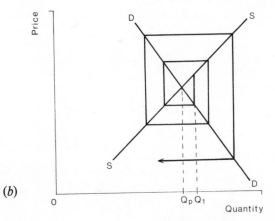

(b)

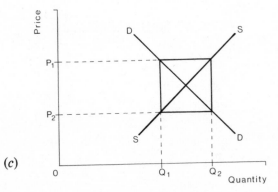

(c)

Figure 3.8

tions, the observed cycles are frequently astonishingly regular. Second, the basic cobweb model predicts a cycle for which the time between successive peaks or troughs would be double the production time lag, whereas many cycles appear to be longer than this – often about four times the production time lag. For example, on the basis of Fig. 3.6 the UK pig cycle appeared to last between three and four years, whereas pigs reach maturity in less than a year.

Taking the first of these points – the observed regularity of production cycles – it seems most unlikely that supply and demand curves would just happen to have the appropriate slopes to generate continuous cobwebs. Another possibility is that the conditions for a converging cobweb exist, but that a new disturbance is continually generating a fresh cycle. Again however, some sort of coincidental developments would be necessary to create quite the regularity of cycles shown in Figs. 3.6 and 3.7. The most likely explanation seems to lie in non-linear supply or demand curves. As Waugh points out (8), any cobweb will be continuous if it passes through the four corners of a rectangle, as in Fig. 3.9. The slopes at a, b, c and d need not be equal; if you start at a, you go

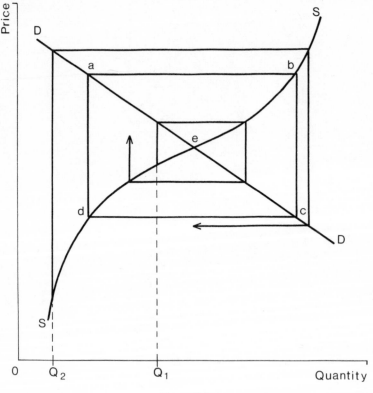

Figure 3.9

through b, c, d, and back to a. For such a solution to be stable, a further condition is required; the slopes of the curves must be such that any small deviation away from the path of the continuous oscillation takes the cobweb back to the rectangle, rather than away from it. This is what happens in Fig. 3.9. The equilibrium price and quantity is at point e. A small shortfall in production to Q_1 sets up a cobweb which diverges towards the rectangle $abcd$, where it becomes continuous. A large shortfall of production – to Q_2, say – sets up a converging cobweb which becomes continuous when it reaches the rectangle. Once the continuous cobweb is in existence, any deviation of planned output from actual output causes the oscillations to return to the continuous rectangle.

Is the shape of the supply curve in Fig. 3.9 a plausible one? A supply curve which is relatively elastic over a certain range but becomes increasingly inelastic at high prices, as producers find it more difficult to increase output further without investing in more fixed inputs, is certainly not unlikely. A supply curve which becomes inelastic at low prices is however contrary to the predictions of the theory of the farm firm. We must remember, however, that the curve in Fig. 3.9 is not a conventional short-run supply curve but is more correctly described as a lagged output curve. If we were to postulate a group of 'experienced' producers who had become more aware than others of the tendency for low prices to be followed by high prices, then the supply planned for the following time period might become relatively inelastic when price falls to low levels in the current time period.

Turning to the question of the length of the cycles, Larson (9) has put forward an alternative to the cobweb model, which he calls *harmonic motion*. This differs from the cobweb in that output is seen as a continuous process in which producers alter the rate of change of production, rather than take discreet production decisions. The rate at which they increase or decrease output depends on the relationship between current price and the trend of average prices. As a consequence, a price peak in time period T_1 leads to a peak in planned output in T_2 and a maximum in supply to the market (and thus a minimum price) in T_3. There is therefore a two-period lag between maximum price and maximum output, and cycles of four times the production lag result.

According to the cobweb theorem then, producers react immediately to price changes whereas with harmonic motion the change in the direction of the supply response only occurs after the price has passed above or below the trend of average prices.

However, it is not necessary to devise a model as sophisticated as harmonic motion to explain the occurrence of cycles which are longer than those implied by the relevant production time lag. It is rather unrealistic to expect producers to respond immediately to a price change when they are aware that the market which they supply is subject to price variation. If we were to incorporate in the cobweb model a *decision*, as well as a production, time lag, then this in itself would lead to the prediction of longer cycles. One way of doing so would be to assume, along the lines suggested in section 5 of the previous chapter, that production decisions are based on expected future, rather than current prices, and the Nerlove approach to supply response has in fact been used in connection with the cobweb phenomena (10, 11).

4 Longer term movements in agricultural prices

4.1 Agriculture's terms of trade

If one were to ask what was the most significant issue to which the principles of agricultural economics have been applied, then the answer must surely be connected in some way with long-term movements in the prices of farm products; either in attempting to understand the forces promoting such movements, predicting future price trends, or in analysing government policies designed to combat some of their effects.

When we talk about long-term movements in the prices of farm products we are usually concerned with the average price of all food or agricultural products taken together, rather than with price trends on individual agricultural product markets; and because we are looking at prices over a long period it is the movement of the general level of agricultural prices relative to all other prices which is important. However, it is not easy to determine precisely how the general level of agricultural prices has moved; to do so requires the construction of an index and weights must be attached to each individual agricultural product in order to assign the appropriate degree of influence of a change in the average price of that product on the estimated movement of the general agricultural or food price index. Usually the system of weights is derived from the relative values of products in some base year, and clearly the choice of base year will affect the weights attached to individual products and thus the way the general index is estimated to have moved. Given that a satisfactory index can be constructed, the relative movement of all farm prices can then be obtained by dividing the farm price index by a similar index constructed for non-farm products. The resulting set of numbers is usually referred to as agriculture's *terms of trade*. Figure 3.10 shows an estimate of movements in the terms of trade between food products and manufactured products on world markets between 1875 and 1975 and Fig. 3.11 shows an estimate of movements in the terms of trade for farm products in the United States (obtained by dividing a price index for farm products by a price index for non-farm products, both valued at the wholesale level). It is clear from these charts that the prices of agricultural products, relative to the prices of other products, do vary very substantially over long periods of time. There is, however, little evidence to suggest a secular trend in one direction or the other. (The data for Fig. 3.10 begin during the 'golden age of agriculture', a period of generally high food prices on world markets.) The impression is rather one of a gradual decline periodically offset by more rapid rises.

In spite of this historical evidence, there have grown up two schools of thought concerning longer term developments on agricultural markets, one of which argues that the forces of supply and demand are such that it 'is in the very nature of things' that agricultural prices should tend to decline relative to

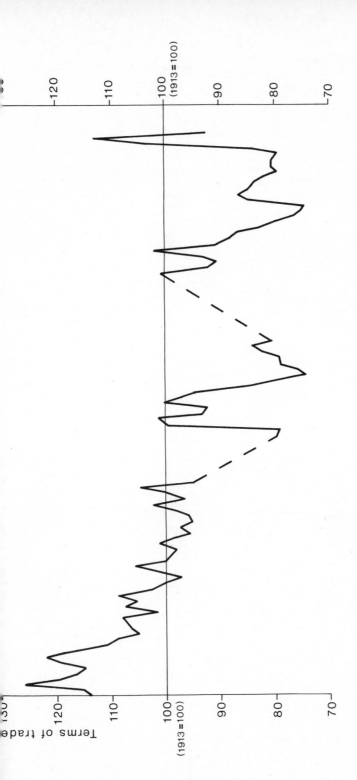

Figure 3.10   World terms of trade between food and manufactured products, 1875–1975 (1913 = 100). Source: 1875–1938 Lewis (12); 1950–75 estimated from United Nations statistics

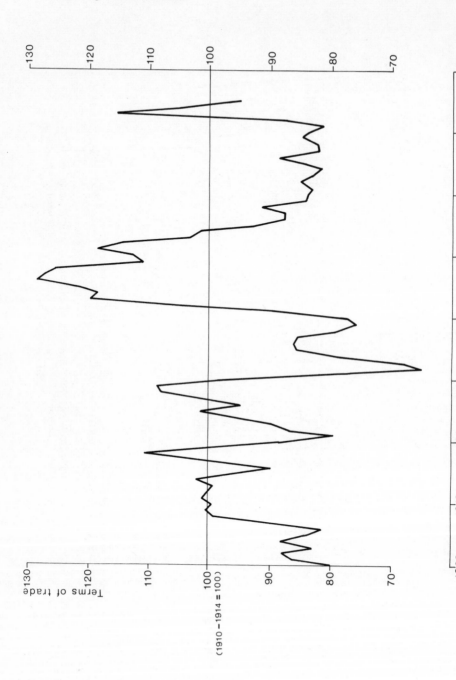

Figure 3.11   Terms of trade for farm products in the USA, 1900–75 (1910–14 ...

other prices, and the other which argues precisely the opposite. As it seems possible that the particular economic forces emphasised by each school of thought could take their turn at being the dominant force influencing longer term developments on agricultural markets, a sensible way to study how the characteristics of supply and demand for agricultural products can cause longer run price movements is to describe the argument of each school of thought in turn.

4.2 Declining agricultural prices: the economic origins of the 'farm problem'[3]

The thesis that farm product prices have an inherent tendency to decline relative to other prices was born out of events during the inter-war depression and was developed to explain the tendency for farm incomes to fail to keep pace with other incomes, in the context of the rapid economic growth experienced in the post-1945 period by the developed countries in North America and Western Europe. A similar argument has sometimes been put forward to explain a supposed decline in the terms of trade for low-income primary producing exporting countries.

The two most important factors affecting the prospects of farmers in advanced countries, it is said, are changes in the pattern of demand and technological improvement. The satisfaction derived from extra quantities of food falls rapidly once an adequate diet has been achieved. Because of this, as we saw in Chapter 1, families with low incomes spend a much larger proportion of their incomes on food than do the better off, and we find that income elasticities of both quantity demanded and expenditure tend to be very low and sometimes negative. The central feature of the demand for food products in a country in which average income levels are rising is therefore that the demand for food increases less rapidly than average incomes, and in the highest income countries, very little of extra income is spent on food products. Even where more is spent on food, it is often in pursuit of greater convenience, more prepared and processed types of food, rather than on greater quantity.

If the proportion of income saved by consumers remains constant as income rises, it follows that the income elasticity of expenditure for all products must equal unity – a given proportionate increase in income must bring forth the same proportionate increase in total expenditure. If, further, the relative prices of all products remain constant, the average income elasticity of quantity demanded (with individual products weighted by value) must also equal unity. The fact that in economically advanced countries income elasticities for food products are almost universally less than unity means that the income elasticities of demand for non-agricultural products must, on balance, exceed unity. Rising incomes will thus mean that the demand for non-farm products will tend to increase more rapidly than the demand for farm products.

We can illustrate this by constructing a diagram (Fig. 3.12) showing a market for a 'typical' agricultural product and the market for a 'typical' industrial product, and representing the different rates of increase in quantity

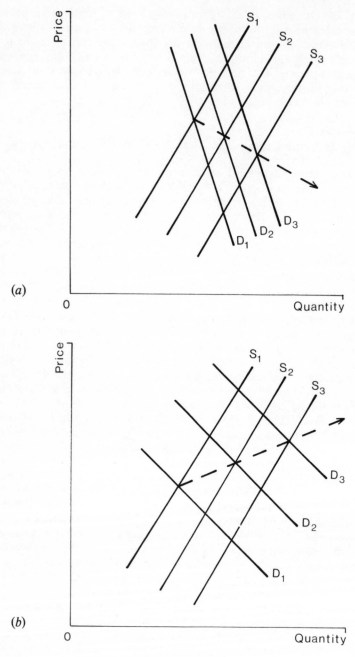

Figure 3.12   (a) Agricultural product, (b) Industrial product

demanded (at constant prices) by shifts in the demand curves, with the demand curve for the industrial product shifting more in proportion than the demand curve for the agricultural product.

Real incomes rise because output per head rises. Thus rising real incomes must mean shifts in supply curves as well as increases in demand. There are two interrelated factors which cause average real incomes and output in an economy to rise over time. They are:

(a) an increase in the economy's stock of capital resources, and
(b) the application of new, more productive, techniques of converting resources into goods and services.

In general, however, there is no reason to suppose that a more than proportionate quantity of new capital resources will go to non-agricultural activity unless there is some inducement or direction to do so. Similarly, we have seen that the impact of new technology can at times have a profound effect on agricultural supply. For these reasons, the supply curves for the agricultural and industrial products in Fig. 3.12 are shown as shifting at approximately the same rate.

Two major forces can therefore be seen to be operating upon the agricultural markets within economic systems in which average levels of incomes are rising. Output of agricultural products is tending to increase at a rate at least as rapid as output of other products. Consumers, on the other hand, wish to spend an increasing proportion of their growing incomes on non-agricultural products. These taken together would lead inevitably to a relative fall in the prices of farm products. Price instability in agricultural markets can mask the longer term developments, and cause the general tendency for relatively declining prices to be interrupted by shorter periods of sharply rising prices, but in the longer term, low price elasticity only increases the degree to which agricultural prices will need to fall to equate quantity supplied with quantity demanded in agricultural markets.

The relative fall in farm prices can therefore be thought of as a signal, the message being that because of overall rising income levels and improvements in agricultural productivity, consumers would benefit from a greater proportion of resources employed in non-agricultural activity. Our theory of the behaviour of a perfectly competitive market predicts that this is precisely what would happen when one industry experiences a fall in product prices relative to input prices. We would expect some farmers to give up production and sell their land to others who would enlarge their holdings, and we would expect part of the agricultural labour force to be able to obtain more remunerative employment outside agriculture. The rate of increase of farm output would be moderated, resources would be released to increase the production of non-farm products more rapidly, and the decline in farm product prices vis-à-vis other prices would be arrested.

It is our experience, however, that the agricultural industry does not respond quickly to market signals. Agricultural resources – particularly labour – are said to be *immobile*. A small relative decline in farm product prices is not sufficient to bring about a rapid adjustment in agricultural production and resource use, and there develops a *farm problem*, the most prominent symptom of which is a tendency for average incomes in farming to fall behind average incomes elsewhere in the economy. When the general rate of economic growth is rapid, and so pressures are placed upon agriculture to adjust very rapidly to changing economic conditions, a severe income problem can develop. Agriculture is thus said to have *an adjustment problem*:[4] the main problem of agriculture in developed countries is seen as the failure of the resource structure of the industry to adjust with sufficient rapidity in the face of the pressures brought about by improving technology and rising incomes, and governments are forced to become extensively involved in policies both to promote adjustment and to support agricultural prices.

What the argument of this section implies therefore is the development of a gap between incomes in agriculture and the incomes derived from 'comparable' occupations elsewhere in the economy, and this is something to which we return in Chapter 4. The argument does not necessarily imply an indefinite fall in the level of farm product prices relative to the level of non-farm product prices – though this is the conclusion which is often drawn. It would be possible for an economy to attain a position of *dynamic equilibrium* in which the rate of outflow of labour and other resources from farming was sufficient to maintain both a constant gap between farm and non-farm incomes and a constant level of farm product prices relative to the level of non-farm product prices. In terms of Fig. 3.12, a point would be reached where the relative fall in the price of agricultural products had opened up a gap between the earnings of resources employed in agriculture, compared with their earnings in industry, and this was stimulating a continual reallocation of the nation's resources between the two sectors. This reallocation of resources would cause the supply curves for industrial products to shift more and supply curves for agricultural products less, thereby stabilising the level of agricultural product prices relative to industrial product prices.

For a continual relative decline in farm product prices to occur it is necessary, not only that there should be a tendency, in the absence of resource adjustments, for the supply of farm products to increase more rapidly than demand, but that the extent to which supply tends to outpace demand should itself increase over time. Is such a view of longer term developments on agricultural product markets a plausible one? We will remember from Chapter 1 that there was considerable evidence suggesting that coefficients of income elasticity of demand for food products decline as the average income of a population increases. The implication of this for the above analysis is for a *decline* in the *rate of increase* of the demand for food products. If, together with this, the impact of technological advance in farming is such as to shift supply curves, in the absence of intersectoral resources adjustments, at a constant rate over time, then we might expect the result to be a perpetual relative fall in farm product prices.

4.3 Rising agricultural prices and the 'world food problem'

The second thesis concerning longer term developments on agricultural markets has a longer and perhaps more illustrious pedigree. In 1798, Thomas Malthus (16) warned that in his view the human race had a natural tendency to increase its numbers at a more rapid rate than man's capacity to increase food output. Subsequently, Malthus and some of his contemporaries were responsible for the subject of economics being labelled 'the dismal science' when they argued that a failure of food production to keep pace with a rapidly growing population would cause all economic systems to reach a 'stationary state', in which the majority of the population would exist at a barely subsistence standard of living. Malthus's doctrine has made such an impression upon the development of economic thought that many modern exponents of the view that the world's population will tend to rise more rapidly than food supplies would refer to themselves as 'neo-Malthusian'.[5]

The thesis of declining agricultural product prices and the development of a 'farm problem' has been very much the preserve of agricultural economists. On the other hand, the neo-Malthusian approach has been taken up by writers from many disciplines who have often seen the implications of their argument to be absolute food shortage at given levels of consumption, rather than in terms of the evolution of relative product prices and consequent resource adjustments. In essence however, the neo-Malthusian approach differs from the argument of the previous section only in the emphasis and relative values given to changes in the various factors underlying the supply and demand for agricultural products. The principles of agricultural economics can equally well be used to predict developments on agricultural product markets if we make a set of assumptions about the factors affecting supply and demand for agricultural products which correspond to the neo-Malthusian approach.

Since the end of the Second World War, the population of the world has been growing at a rate of about 2 per cent per annum, the rate of growth having increased steadily from that of about 0·5 per cent when Malthus was alive. At current rates of growth, the world's population will double every 37 years, with the major part of the increase concentrated in the less developed countries. Partly because of the opening up of new lands in North America and Australasia, but mainly because of technological innovation which improved the productivity of agricultural resources, food output has nevertheless tended to grow more rapidly than population. In the less developed parts of the world, increases in food production have just about been sufficient to meet the minimum requirements of a rapidly rising population. In the developed economies, however, increases in agricultural productivity have permitted a growth in food output well ahead of that needed to sustain a constant level of per caput food consumption. This has resulted in a prolonged period during which the terms of trade on world markets tended to move against food and agricultural products and it has allowed the proportion of productive resources employed in agriculture in the developed economies to decline, so that real incomes for about one in four of the world's population have risen above the basic necessities of food, clothing and shelter. The world market for most food products has been dominated by an international division of labour within the developed economies, with North America and Australasia generating a supply of food which exceeded the quantity demanded by their populations at existing world market prices, and Europe and Japan doing the reverse.

However, the neo-Malthusians would argue that it is not reasonable to expect past rates of technological advance in agriculture to continue indefinitely and, perhaps more critically, they have serious doubts as to whether the world possesses the political and institutional framework necessary to implement more widely existing knowledge concerning more productive techniques. Ultimately therefore, and probably sooner rather than later, they argue that population growth will overtake the rate at which improvements in productivity can increase food output in the less developed countries; unless there is to be a widespread development of the 'Malthusian population checks' of starvation and disease, the less developed countries must increase the proportion of their food supplies coming from world markets.

There is a second version of the argument which predicts rising food prices on world markets; one, however, which Malthus would not recognise. If we return to Table 1.5 we will see that income elasticities of demand for most food products in the low income countries are quite high. The fact that it has been *low* income elasticities of demand for agricultural products which has been credited as the significant factor influencing the evolution of prices on world markets is a reflection of the fact that, where average incomes have risen, these increases have been concentrated in those parts of the world where incomes were already quite high. One feature of agricultural demand discussed in Chapter 1 was the relationship between income distribution and the demand for agricultural products. It was suggested that, in general, we will find that a movement towards greater equality of income will increase the demand for a food product. Any significant movement towards greater equality in distribution of income, either within individual countries, or between rich and poorer nations, could therefore be expected to result in a substantial increase in the demand for food products. The success achieved by oil-producing countries in gaining a greater share of world income has led some experts to argue that a similar redistribution of income within the world economy could result if there were successful agreements to raise the price of some other primary commodities. Others discount this possibility (18).

In the world of the neo-Malthusian, therefore, the typical agricultural market will develop a tendency for demand curves to shift more rapidly than supply curves with the implication of a rise in agricultural product prices relative to other prices. This kind of market situation implies the opposite form of resource adjustment to that of a secular decline in agriculture's terms of trade. We will expect farm firms to become more profitable relative to non-farm firms and they will be induced to increase the quantity of fixed resources they employ. The decline in the proportion of resources employed in agriculture in the developed economies, and where feasible in the less developed economies, will be reversed. However, in this case we meet another kind of 'adjustment problem'. Agricultural production depends on the use of the so-called 'natural' group of resources and the facility with which output can be increased will be restricted by limits on the availability of extra quantities of such resources. The most obvious natural resources to which potential supply limits apply is of course land, but experts have also warned of limits to the availability of chemical fertiliser, water and fossil fuels.

What these resource limitations mean is that the supply of agricultural products can only be raised at increasing average cost. As farmers attempt to use more of these resources in limited supply, so the prices of these inputs will rise. In most cases output will be increased using more of those resources, the supply of which is not limited, in combination with little or no increase in the quantity of the limited resources. We know that, for given conditions of production, an increase in the use of one group of inputs, with all other inputs held constant, means diminishing returns. Thus because of both rising input prices and because it is not possible to increase the use of all inputs in proportion, agricultural supply increases will be associated with rising costs, and the prices of farm products will rise relative to other prices.

There are, moreover, two further views about the future course of agricultural production which mean that, in effect, an assumption that output can be increased with constant production functions is overoptimistic. First, there is an accumulation of evidence to suggest that the world might be entering a prolonged period of less favourable climatic conditions as far as agricultural production is concerned. Second, there is growing concern among ecologists that some modern farming techniques, such as the heavy use of pesticides and chemical fertilisers, may have such detrimental effects on the environment that their continued, or more widespread, use will be brought increasingly into question. If both of these views are correct, in formal terms, it means that in future agricultural production functions will reflect less favourable relationships between inputs and output than before.[6]

4.4 Longer term price movements in perspective

In this section we have described two alternative theses concerning the longer term evolution of agricultural product prices. One argument emphasises the impact of technological advance and the small proportion of extra income spent on food products. The other highlights the influence of rising population and the limits to resource supply. In both cases the way in which changes in the factors underlying the supply and demand for food and agricultural products are translated into longer term price movements can be thought of as an adjustment problem. In the first case, the failure of agricultural resources, particularly labour, to move with sufficient rapidity to alternative employment sustains the rate of increase of supply and tends to depress relative product prices. In the second case, limits to the availability of resources cause rising input prices and diminishing returns, thereby pushing up relative product prices.

These two ways of thinking about agricultural markets in the longer term are rarely found between the same covers, but they differ only in the assumptions made concerning what are thought likely to be the critical changes in the factors underlying the supply and demand for farm products. The principles of agricultural economics help us to understand what course of events on agricultural markets are likely to follow a particular assumed set of changes in supply and demand factors, and ultimately, how such changes will affect the problems and prospects of farmers and consumers. The incidence of these changes will vary both over time and between different agricultural markets. Table 3.2 summarises the main factors that have been postulated as likely to have a significant influence upon longer term developments on agricultural markets.

Table 3.2   A summary of the major factors which can influence the long-term evolution of agricultural product prices

	Factors affecting the demand for farm products	Factors affecting the supply of farm products
Factors tending to depress agricultural product prices	Low income elasticity of demand for agricultural products in advanced countries	Impact of technological advance in improving the productivity of agricultural resources
	Development of synthetic substitutes for farm products	Immobility of agricultural resources, particularly labour
Factors tending to raise agricultural product prices	High income elasticity of demand for farm products in less developed countries	Some agricultural resources in fixed supply
		Slow-down in technological advance, and failure to implement fully existing knowledge
	Population growth	Future period of less favourable climatic conditions for agricultural production
		'Environment hazards' of modern farming techniques

5 The food manufacturing and distributive industries

5.1

In many parts of the world the market for a food product is typically a traditional direct link between farmers and consumers where the price paid by the consumer is little in excess of that received by the farmer. In such circumstances the analysis of agricultural markets in terms of the interaction between farm supply and consumer demand is wholly realistic. However, for the majority of agricultural products in the developed economies, the directness of these traditional links has gradually been eroded with the result that the farmer is often no more than a supplier of a raw material to the food processing and distributive trades. Some indication of the extent to which final expenditure on food products can now exceed the equivalent value at the 'farm gate' is given in Figs. 3.13 and 3.14. In the United Kingdom, the farm value of food produce constitutes about one-half its estimated value when purchased by the final consumer and in the United States this proportion has declined to about one-third.

There are many reasons for the growth of the food manufacturing and distributive industries, but it is possible to isolate three main influences.

(a) As incomes rise, not only does the proportion of income spent on food products decline, but at high income levels consumers are prepared to pay for more variety in their diets and for more convenience in their food purchases.

The demand for a more varied diet has led to the same farm product being manufactured into contrasting consumer products. Consignments of grain which are more or less indistinguishable when they leave the farm sector reappear on supermarket shelves as bread, biscuits, breakfast cereals and (exercising a little imagination) eggs. The demand for convenience in food purchases is essentially a willingness on the part of consumers to pay for a saving in time. This involves such aspects as purchase at a convenient location and a preference for products which can be stored, which are easy to prepare, and which are quick to cook. The demand for variety and convenience in food purchases suggests that it may be helpful to make a notional distinction in the utility derived from food consumption between what we might call basic utility, where food performs the function of providing the sustenance necessary for life, and utility of form, time, and place created in the main by the processing and distributive sectors. The food manufacturer increases the utility derived from food consumption by changing the form in which the product is available for consumption, by altering the place where it is purchased, and by influencing the time when it must be consumed and the time taken by the consumer in preparing it for the table.

(b) The second reason for the growth of the food manufacturing and distributive trades is the change in settlement patterns which followed the industrial revolution. Large scale urban concentrations of population mean that the majority of food consumers do not live in farming localities. This population migration would not have been possible without the growth of organisations to perform the task of channelling farm output from localised rural markets to the urban centres.

(c) The third major influence has been technological improvements in the processing and distribution of food; many of these innovations have of course been induced by the changing patterns of demand associated with

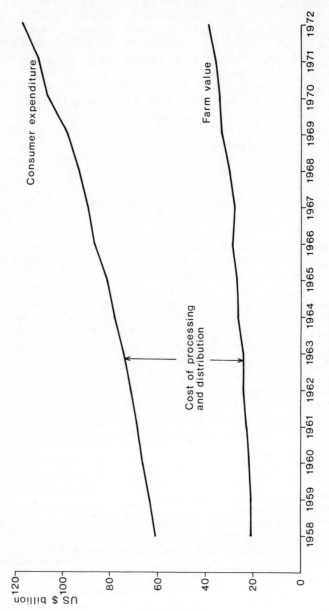

Figure 3.13   The cost of processing and distributing food in the USA, 1958–72.
Source: USDA statistics

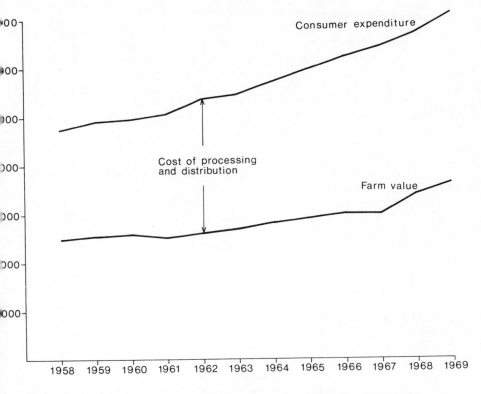

Figure 3.14   The cost of processing and distributing food in the UK, 1958–69. Based on Wollen & Turner (21) and Beaumont (22)

rising incomes and urban concentration. To illustrate how the food marketing process can be affected by technological change, we can cite two events which historically have perhaps been among the most significant, the development of railway transport and the introduction of refrigeration. The growth of an extensive railway network brought together localised agricultural markets which had previously been separated by the high cost and length of time taken to transport produce between the markets, and the railways were instrumental in allowing the rapidly growing populations in urban centres to be adequately fed. Refrigeration made intercontinental trade in meat possible and revolutionised the form in which much food was sold at retail level. Changes in consumer technology have also been important – particularly motor transport and domestic refrigerators, which have allowed consumers to purchase large quantities of food products at centralised locations and at less frequent intervals.[7]

5.2

In order to extend this chapter's discussion of agricultural markets to take account of the influence of the processing and distributive industries we will take, as a hypothetical example, one manufactured food product, canned peas. We use the term *market structure* to refer to the number and size distribution of the marketing firms through which a product passes before it reaches the final consumer and there are many alternative market structures that could apply to the supply of canned peas.

Let us assume first that there are a large number of both pea growers and pea canners, that the markets in which peas are sold to canners and canned peas sold to consumers are both perfectly competitive, and that peas are sold only in cans. There are two ways of viewing the supply of canned peas which, in effect, amount to the same thing. One approach is to assume that the manufacturer sells a product – canned peas – for which a major input is fresh peas. The alternative is to think of two industries producing individual products, peas and 'canning services', which are demanded jointly by consumers as canned peas. If we take the second approach, and make what is often a very reasonable assumption as far as the food manufacturing industry is concerned – that the two products must always be combined in the same proportion – then we can draw on the same diagram (Fig. 3.15), the demand curve for canned peas (D_{cp}), the supply curve of peas (S_p), and the supply curve of 'canning services' (S_c). Canners manufacture their own cans, which is their major production cost, and for convenience we will refer to the supply of canning services simply as the supply of cans. Because of the assumption of a fixed relationship between quantity of peas and quantity of cans, we can measure on the horizontal axis, quantity of peas, quantity of cans, or quantity of canned peas – which of them being implicit in the supply or demand curve under consideration.

The supply curve S_p and S_c show the relationship between market price and the quantity that will be supplied per time period of, respectively, peas and cans, both measured in pea/can units. The price required to bring forth a given quantity of canned peas must therefore be the sum of the prices required to bring forth the associated quantities of peas and cans, and the supply curve of canned peas is therefore the vertical addition of the individual supply curves for peas and cans. Equilibrium is established with Q_1 canned peas sold at price P_3. Pea producers receive price P_2 per can unit for their produce, and canners receive P_1 per can $(= P_2P_3)$ for their service.

Using the information contained in Fig. 3.15 we can derive the demand for peas. The price received for peas is the difference between the price paid for canned peas and the price received by canners for their contribution to the production of canned peas. The *derived demand curve* for peas (D_p) is therefore found by taking the vertical difference between the demand curve for canned peas and the supply curve of cans; it incorporates the decisions of both consumers of canned peas and producers of cans. For example, if a quantity of Q_2 canned peas are produced, the whole of this quantity will be purchased by

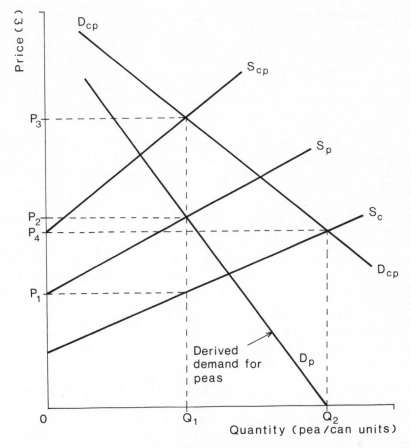

Figure 3.15

final consumers if the price of canned peas is P_4. But P_4 is the price per can necessary to induce canners to supply Q_2 cans. Thus Q_2 peas will only be demanded if the price of peas is zero and the derived demand curve for peas will meet the quantity axis at Q_2. (If we take the alternative way of viewing the marketing of canned peas mentioned earlier – that is, to assume that peas are one of many purchased inputs used by manufacturers of canned peas – then D_p shows the demand for peas by canners.)

The equilibrium price of peas is given by the intersection of the derived demand curve for peas with the supply curve of peas. As we have already seen this occurs when Q_1 peas are sold at price P_2. (We could equally well have shown the market equilibrium by deriving the demand curve for cans and equating it with the supply curve for cans.) The gap between the derived demand curve for peas and the demand curve for canned peas, which is P_2P_3

when the market is in equilibrium, is sometimes called a *marketing* or *distributive and processing margin* – or, colloquially, a 'mark-up'.

It is perhaps worth pointing out one practical application of the concept of derived demand which might not be generally realised – that the market analyst can use information relating to one stage in the marketing chain to throw light upon supply and demand relationships elsewhere in the chain. For example, it may be that it is difficult to obtain information regarding price or quantity at the 'farm gate'; knowledge of final demand and the conditions of supply for the marketing process will enable the demand curve for the product at the farm gate to be derived. Alternatively, it may be information concerning the operation of food manufacturers which is lacking. A certain amount might be deduced by deriving the supply and demand relationships for marketing services from information which may be available relating to the final product and to farm gate supplies.

The implication of the above analysis is that it is perfectly legitimate to represent the market for an agricultural product by the interaction of a single demand and single supply curve, as we did in the early part of this chapter, even when the farm product experiences a significant degree of processing before it reaches the final consumer. It is legitimate, that is, as long as we remember that the demand curve for the farm product is derived from the demand by the final consumer and that the *shape of the derived demand curve will be influenced by the conditions of supply of the manufacturing and distributive process.* This last point is important because a major cause of instability in farm product prices is thought to be the inelasticity of demand for food products. The table of price elasticities given in Chapter 1 was for the consumer products, but it is mainly price fluctuations to farmers that causes concern. Is, then, the derived demand for a farm product likely to be more or less elastic than the demand curve for the related consumer product?

Figure 3.16 shows the derived demand for peas (D_p) in three alternative cases, where the supply curve for cans (S_c) is, respectively, perfectly elastic, (Fig. 3.16a), very elastic (Fig. 3.16b), and moderately elastic (Fig. 3.16c). The demand curve for canned peas (D_{cp}) is the same in all three cases. We can see that when the supply curve for cans is perfectly elastic, the marketing margin remains constant at different quantities, and the derived demand curve for peas therefore has the same slope as the demand curve for canned peas. This means that a given change in the quantity supplied of peas will bring forth the same absolute change in the price of peas as of canned peas, and therefore that variations in the quantity supplied of peas will cause proportionately greater variations in the price of peas than in the price of canned peas. In other words, at any given quantity, the demand for peas is less price elastic than the demand for canned peas. If we look at Fig. 3.16b and c we will see that as the supply curve for cans becomes less elastic, so the *derived demand curve* for peas becomes increasingly less elastic than the *final demand curve* for canned peas.

We must conclude therefore that the conditions of supply within the processing and distributive industries can certainly influence the degree to

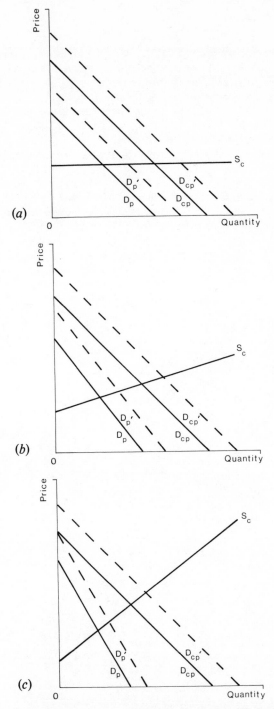

Figure 3.16 (a) Supply curve of cans perfectly elastic, (b) Supply curve of cans very elastic, (c) Supply curve of cans moderately elastic

which farm product prices are subject to instability and that, in general, where the marketing structure is a competitive one, it seems likely that unplanned variations in farm output will cause proportionately greater price fluctuations for farm products than for the associated consumer product.

This simple model of a market for canned peas can also be used to show that the conditions of supply in the marketing sector will influence the extent to which the farm sector is influenced by a change in consumer demand. The broken lines in Fig. 3.16 show the impact upon the derived demand for peas (D_p to D_p') of an increase in the demand for canned peas (D_{cp} to D_{cp}') under the three alternative supply conditions for cans. The derived demand for peas increases by the same quantity as the demand for canned peas when the supply of cans is perfectly elastic. The less elastic is the supply of cans, then the smaller is the increase in the demand for peas relative to the increase in the demand for canned peas.

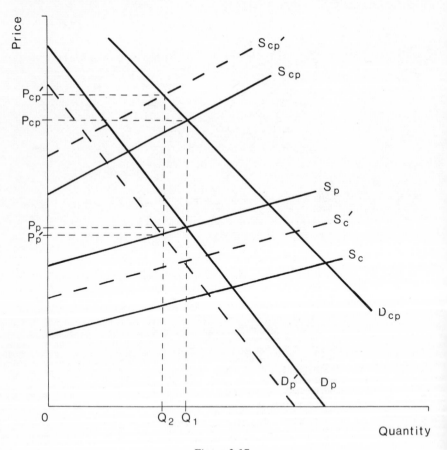

Figure 3.17

The model also indicates that the farm sector will be affected by any change in the supply conditions within the marketing sector. Suppose, for example, that there is an increase in the price of the metal used in the manufacture of cans. This causes the supply of cans shown in Fig. 3.17 to shift from S_c to S_c' and the supply of canned peas therefore shifts from S_{cp} to S_{cp}'. This leads, not only to an increase in the price of canned peas (from P_{cp} to P_{cp}'), but to a decrease in the demand for peas (D_p to D_p') and a fall in the price of peas from P_p to P_p'.

5.3

The foregoing discussion assumed perfectly competitive markets throughout. However, whereas an agricultural market which constitutes a more or less direct link between farmers and consumers is very likely to approximate quite closely to the perfectly competitive model, this is much less likely for markets containing substantial distributive and processing margins. It has been estimated, for example (24), that by 1968, in the United Kingdom, two firms supplied 80 per cent of potato crisps, that three firms virtually controlled the entire frozen food market, and that two-thirds of bread consumed was supplied by four firms. (By 1971, the bread market had concentrated to three firms controlling about three-quarters of supplies (25).) Similar conditions were reported for canned soups and instant coffee. The same author, commenting on food distribution, notes that 'some food companies report that as much as two-thirds of their business is now channelled through as few as fifteen major accounts'. Nearly 80 per cent of milk produced in England and Wales is sold to five companies. The firms engaged in retail milk distribution appear often to agree tacitly among themselves on dividing the market by areas (26). Many food manufacturers are multiproduct firms and decisions taken regarding price and quantity produced for several products may be interdependent. The sale of food products as 'branded' items means that the 'perfect market' assumption of an homogeneous product, which usually applies as far as farm gate supplies are concerned, may have to be abandoned by the time the product has passed through the food manufacturing process.

Once we make such radical departures from the assumptions of the perfectly competitive market, any attempt to predict market behaviour becomes a much more complex task; there are very many alternative market structures and each one may lead to different patterns of market behaviour. Even introductory economics textbooks usually describe several alternative models of 'imperfect competition', such as monopoly, where a market is supplied by one producer only, duopoly, where two firms supply a market, oligopoly, where a small number of firms supply a market, and monopolistic competition, described by Chamberlin (27) as 'a blend of monopoly and competition', where there are a large number of producers with freedom of entry to and exit from the industry, but in which each producer sells a product which is somewhat different from that sold by his competitors, usually because similar products are sold as 'branded' goods.[8] But postulating a model of non-perfect market behaviour is one thing, choosing the appropriate model for a particular agricultural product market is quite another. Our knowledge of the structure of 'imperfect' food markets is itself very imperfect. It is only quite recently that many agricultural economists in Western Europe have taken an interest in the economics of the food processing and distributive trades, though the interest is of a somewhat longer standing in the United States.

In the face of such a complex, and yet incomplete, picture of the structure of food markets, and in the context of the array of alternative models of market structure presented by economists, it is nevertheless easy to lose sight of the fact that there is one critical feature of a non-perfect competitive market which distinguishes it from the perfectly competitive market. This is that *there are buyers or sellers operating in the market who account for a sufficiently large proportion of total market demand or supply for the individual action of any such buyer or seller to have a perceptible impact upon the market*. We would normally gauge the strength of this impact in terms of the extent to which the action of any individual buyer or seller can alter price in the market. In a perfectly competitive market, no buyer or seller accounts for a large enough proportion of total supply or demand for his action alone to have a perceptible influence upon market price.

We use the term '*monopoly power*' to refer to the ability of a firm or individual to influence market price by altering the quantity offered for sale to the market, and a '*monopolist*' is a firm or individual who is the sole supplier to a market. The terms '*monopsony power*' and '*monopsonist*' are used in a similar way in connection with market demand. The term *market power* refers to a firm or individual having monopoly power, monopsony power, or both.

In the remainder of this section we will consider some of the implications of the exercise of market power in our example of the market for canned peas. First however, we must return to the theory of the firm and extend it to cover the behaviour of the firm which possesses market power.

Table 3.3 and Fig. 3.18 describe a numerical example of costs and revenue for a firm which possesses monopoly selling power. The relationship between costs and quantity produced is not in itself affected by the presence of monopoly power and the cost curves shown in Fig. 3.18 are of a similar form to those used to describe the cost structure of a farm firm in Chapter 2. The new element introduced in this example is that the price the firm receives per unit of product declines as the quantity produced increases. When, for example, 20 units are produced they sell at £8 per unit, but 30 units sell at only £7 per unit. For each additional 10 units of the product produced, the price received per unit declines by £1. As a result, total revenue cannot be increased indefinitely simply by increasing the level of output; total revenue increases at a decreasing rate as output is increased from 10 units to 50 units and declines when output is raised above 50 units. Marginal revenue – the rate of change of total revenue as output changes – declines throughout and takes negative values when the quantity produced exceeds 50 units.

However, the fact that the price of the product declines when more is produced in no way disturbs the procedure used in the previous chapter for

Table 3.3   A numerical example of profit maximisation by a firm possessing monopoly power

Quantity of product A produced		0	10	20	30	40	50	60	70	80
Variable cost	(VC)	0	2·5	10·0	22·5	40·0	62·5	90·0	122·5	160·0
Fixed cost	(FC)	100·0	100	100	100	100	100	100	100	100
Total cost	(TC)	100·0	102·5	110·0	122·5	140·0	162·5	190·0	222·5	260·0
Average total cost	(ATC)	—	10·25	5·5	4·08	3·5	3·25	3·17	3·18	3·25
Marginal cost	(MC)	—	0·5	1·0	1·5	2·0	2·5	3·0	3·5	4·0
Average revenue	(AR)	—	9	8	7	6	5	4	3	2
Total revenue	(TR)	—	90	160	210	240	250	240	210	160
Marginal revenue	(MR)	—	8	6	4	2	0	–2	–4	–6
Profit	(TR − TC)	–100·0	–12·5	50·0	97·5	100·0	97·5	50·0	–12·5	–100·0

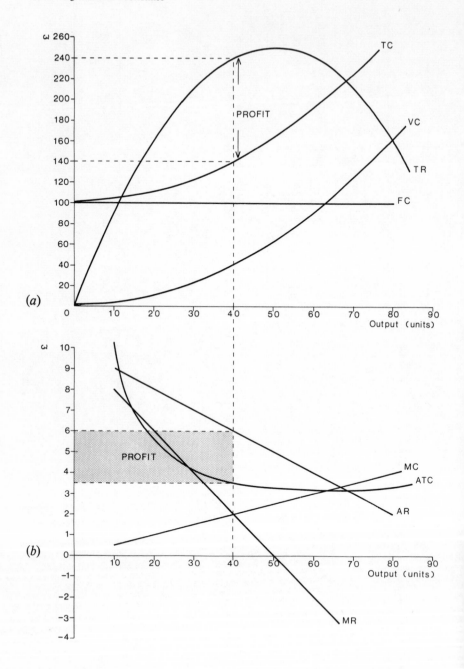

Figure 3.18

identifying the level of output which maximises profit. Maximum profit occurs when total revenue exceeds total cost by the greatest amount, and this is found by locating the level of output for which the slope of the total revenue curve equals the slope of the total cost curve, or in marginal terms, where marginal revenue – the rate of change of total revenue as output changes – equals marginal cost – the rate of change of total cost as output changes. In our example, profit is maximised at £100, when 40 units are produced.

Let us now look briefly at the optimum level of input application for a profit maximising firm which possesses monopsony buying power. In Fig. 3 19a the relationship between the quantity of input X used (all other inputs held constant) and revenue from the sale of the product is shown by the total value product (TVP) curve, and the rate of change of total revenue as the use of input X is changed, by the marginal value product (MVP) curve in Fig. 3.19b. The firm has monopsony buying power in the market for input X and therefore finds that the price per unit it must pay for input X – the average factor cost (AFC) – rises as more of input X is used. Total factor cost of input X (TFC) increases at an increasing rate, and marginal factor cost rises more rapidly than AFC.

The most profitable level of application of input X occurs when total value product exceeds total factor cost by the greatest amount – that is, when marginal value product equals marginal factor cost. The optimum level of application of input X for this firm is therefore Q_1 units and it must pay P_1 price per unit for this quantity of X.

In short then, the profit maximising firm will equate marginal cost of production with marginal revenue from the sale of the product and will equate marginal factor cost with marginal value product for each input, *whether or not it possesses market power*. But for the firm operating in perfect product and factor markets, decisions taken by it concerning how much to produce and what quantity of inputs to employ do not affect the price received for the product or the price paid for inputs. The marginal revenue from the sale of the product is therefore constant and equals the price of the product, and the marginal factor cost of any input remains constant and equals the price of the input.

The firm which possesses monopoly selling power, however, finds that each additional unit it sells of a product reduces the price received *for all its output*. When the firm produces extra units of a product, therefore, total revenue tends to increase because of the sale of the extra units, but this is offset to a greater or lesser extent because all its output sells at a slightly lower price. At any level of output, marginal revenue must therefore be less than the price of the product, and marginal revenue becomes negative when the loss of the revenue which is associated with the fall in product price exceeds the gain in revenue from the sale of extra units.

Similarly, the firm which possesses monopsony power in the market for a factor of production finds that when it employs additional units of that factor, the total cost of the factor increases, not only because of the purchases of the extra units of factor, but because the price paid per unit for the factor rises. For

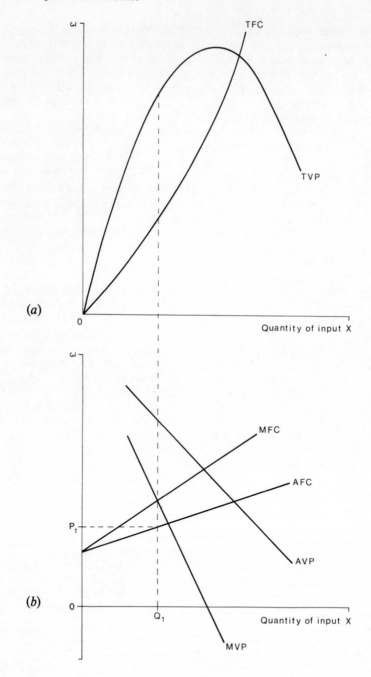

Figure 3.19

any level of factor use, therefore, marginal factor cost must exceed the price paid per unit of input.

A convenient method of measuring the monopoly power of a firm is to use the elasticity of its average revenue curve – in other words, the elasticity of demand for the *firm's* output. For the perfectly competitive firm, it is assumed that the firm can sell as much as it wishes without this affecting the price it receives for the product. Average revenue therefore remains constant as output changes, and the perfectly competitive firm faces a perfectly elastic demand curve for its output. Figure 3.20 illustrates the three factors that will determine the price elasticity of demand for the output of a firm possessing monopoly power. The three factors are:

(a) the response of other firms supplying the market to changes in market price;
(b) the price elasticity of demand for the product in the market;
(c) the proportion of total market sales accounted for by the firm.

(Similarly, the factors affecting monopsony buying power can be divided into:

(a) the demand response of other users of the input;
(b) the elasticity of supply of the input;
(c) the proportion of total input supplies employed by the firm.)

Consider the market demand curve (DD) shown in Fig. 3.20a. If the firm is a pure monopolist – that is, it is the only supplier of the product to this market, then the demand curve facing it will be this market demand curve, giving the average revenue curve AR in Fig. 3.20c. If there are other firms supplying the market, then we can expect the demand curve facing the firm possessing monopoly power ('firm 1') to be generally more elastic than the market demand curve. Suppose, for example, that there are ninety-nine other firms supplying the market, none of which however produces a sufficient proportion of total supply for its action alone to have perceptible impact upon market price. Figure 3.20b shows two curves, S_1 and S_2, representing alternative aggregate supply schedules for the remaining firms (firms '2–100'). The demand facing firm 1 will now be given by the difference between the quantity demanded in the market at any given price and the quantity supplied by firms 2–100 at that price. For example, when the market price is £7 per unit, 6000 units are demanded, and firms 2–100 are willing to supply 2000 units under supply condition S_1 and 5000 units under supply conditions S_2. The demand from firm 1 is therefore 4000 units in the first case (S_1) but only 1000 units in the second (S_2). Thus when market demand is DD and the supply of firms 2–100 is S_1, firm 1 faces a demand given by AR_1, and if the supply from firms 2–100 increases to S_2, the demand from firm 1 falls to AR_2.

With all three market situations for firm 1 (that is, (i) as a pure monopolist, (ii) when S_1 describes the supply from other firms, and (iii) when S_2 describes the supply from other firms) if market demand shifts to the generally more elastic relationship shown by the broken line $D'D'$ then so the demand facing the firm with monopoly power becomes generally more elastic. Third, the

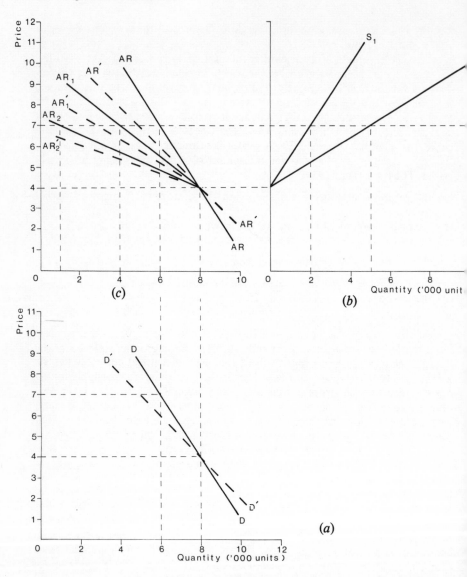

Figure 3.20   (a) Market demand, (b) Supply (firms 2–100), (c) Average revenue (firm 1)

elasticity of demand for the output from firm 1 will also be influenced by the proportion of the market which it supplies. In our example, with straight line demand curves, demand facing firm 1 becomes less price elastic as it increases its level of output.

5.4

Let us return now to the example of the market for canned peas. Figure 3.21 shows the same demand curve for canned peas (D_{cp}) and supply curves for cans (S_c) and peas (S_p) as in the basic model described earlier (Fig. 3.15). In Fig. 3.21, however, it is the demand curve for cans (D_c) which is derived rather than that for peas. If the conditions for a perfectly competitive market apply, equilibrium will be established as before, with Q_1 canned peas sold at price P_3, the price of peas being P_2, and of cans P_1. Consider, however, what might happen if one firm gains control of the entire pea canning industry. Since the supply curve for cans reflects the marginal cost curves of the individual firms supplying the market, if there is no reorganisation of the productive factors engaged in pea canning following the assumption of control of these factors by

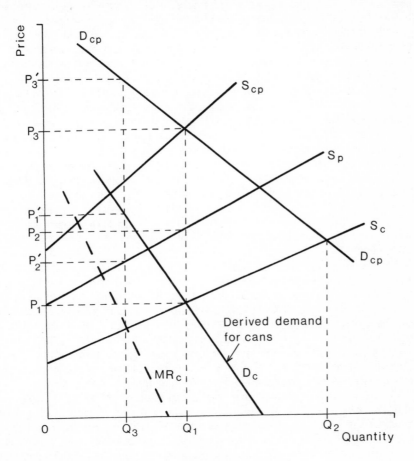

Figure 3.21

a single firm, the curve S_c will now represent the marginal cost curve of the single pea canning organisation. To find the 'level of canning' which will maximise this firm's profits, we must equate the marginal cost of cans with the *marginal revenue* derived from cans (MR_c). The marginal revenue from the production of cans relates to the derived demand curve for cans. Since this derived demand curve is found by taking the difference between the demand for canned peas and the supply of peas, it incorporates both the monopoly selling power of canned peas and the monopsony buying power of peas possessed by the pea canner. Compared with the equilibrium when the pea canning market was perfectly competitive, the quantity of canned peas produced falls from Q_1 to Q_3. The price of canned peas rises from P_3 to P_3', the price of cans from P_1 and P_1', and the price of peas falls from P_2 to P_2'. The rise in the price of cans equals the rise in the price of canned peas plus the fall in the price of peas. The pea canner has exercised both monopoly and monopsony power; he has pushed up the price of canned peas and forced down the price of peas.

Our conclusion is that, if a previously competitive marketing industry is taken over by a single, profit maximising, organisation, then the proportion of consumer expenditure on the product going to the marketing sector will increase, and the proportion received by the farm sector will decline.

As an alternative, consider the market implications of the formation by pea producers of a monopoly marketing agency whose function is to maximise the collective profits of the pea growers. If the pea canning industry remains competitive, then we find that the monopoly selling agency for peas has precisely the same market power as did the single canning firm. To see this, we only have to reverse the labels on the S_c and S_p curves in Fig. 3.21, so that the D_c curve now represents the demand for peas rather than cans, and we find that the pea selling agency will maximise the profits of the pea growers by curtailing pea production to Q_3 (in pea/can units). They will thereby force up the price of canned peas, all of which will be expressed as a rise in the price of peas, and they will force down the price of cans, which will be reflected as a further rise in the price of peas.

This is an interesting result, which illustrates once again how even very elementary models can give an insight into economic behaviour which is not attainable by a more intuitive approach. It seems 'intuitively' reasonable that a single firm, facing a large number of consumers and a large number of suppliers of an input could, by controlling the level of output of the industry, both force up the price of the product and force down the price of the input. It seems much less obvious that a single agency marketing a farm product could, by controlling the supply of that product, both force up the price of the consumer product and force down the marketing margin.

If we move in our example to a market structure where both pea producers and pea canners have market power, then our simple model of market behaviour is no longer able to provide a unique solution. Our model is able to predict the behaviour of the sector possessing market power only if there is a unique relationship between a quantity supplied and market price for the other sector. If both pea producers and pea canners take into account the effect of their output on market price, then neither will be able to arrive individually at a profit maximising solution, because they will not know the impact, upon the price of the other's product, of their own production decisions.

Although this kind of question therefore presents problems which are too complex for a basic textbook, the behaviour of a market in which more than one stage in a marketing chain possesses market power is nevertheless a most important one as far as agricultural economists are concerned. This is so, not only because the marketing process often does involve a series of stages, each one demonstrating some degree of industrial concentration, but because the channelling of farm produce through a central monopoly marketing agency is often advocated as a solution to the 'problem' of market power in the food processing and distributive trades. The implication is that, if producers are given 'countervailing market power', then the market is likely to reproduce something like a competitive solution, with the monopolist and monopsonist cancelling each other out. Our example of the pea canning industry suggests that this might very well be the case, as far as the market for peas sold to canners is concerned, but not in the market for canned peas. The likely outcome is that a quantity of canned peas will be produced which, with respect to Fig. 3.21, is less than Q_1 (and might be greater or less than Q_3). Consumers will pay a higher price for canned peas, the division of the excess of the price of canned peas over the competitive solution being distributed between canners and pea growers, the exact distribution probably depending on the respective power of the two sectors.

We have seen, then, that the exercise of market power by the food manufacturing and distributive industries can reduce the share of final consumer expenditure received by the farm sector, compared with the share the farm sector would be likely to receive with a perfectly competitive manufacturing and distributive sector. It is, however, possible to argue that an imperfectly competitive marketing sector will mean less instability in farm product prices, though our simple model of the pea canning industry does not provide us with any straightforward conclusions as to the behaviour of an imperfect market when there are unplanned variations in farm output. In our example the single pea canner paid a price for peas which was necessary to induce pea growers to supply the quantity required for maximum profits in the pea canning operation. But the supply curve for peas relates the quantity of peas producers *plan* to supply at alternative prices. Thus the model tells us nothing about how much the canner will pay for peas if there is an unplanned shortfall or excess of production. In principle, the monopsonist pea buyer can force the price of peas down to zero, once a particular crop has been harvested, *whether or not actual output equals planned output*. He does not do so because it is in his longer term interest to ensure that pea growers continue to plan to supply the quantity of peas which he requires. It is at least possible to argue therefore, that a monopsonist pea buyer might continue to pay the same price for peas, irrespective of what quantity is forthcoming in a particular season. In the perfect market, on the other hand, price must vary from year to year if there are unplanned variations in output.

The other action that pea canners might take in the face of an irregular supply of peas is to carry year-to-year stocks of peas, and it is with a discussion of the impact upon agricultural markets of the storage of commodities that we conclude this chapter. First, however, we must mention briefly three further aspects of the structure of agricultural markets, which lack of space prevents our covering in any detail.

First, it should be emphasised that there are circumstances in which the kind of comparison made in this chapter between the market affects of the exercise of market power vis-à-vis the perfectly competitive market will not be legitimate. To make these kinds of comparisons we must be able also to make a particularly bold assumption – that the average cost of producing the marketing service is not reduced when the number of firms supplying the service declines. Now, of course, one reason for the increased concentration of economic power in the food processing and distributive industries may have been the lower costs associated with larger scale units. It is not impossible that the sole manufacturer of a food product, exercising both monopoly selling power in the manufactured product, and monopsony buying power for the farm product, could nevertheless produce a greater quantity of the manufactured product, selling it at a lower price, and paying more for the farm product, than would a perfectly competitive, but higher cost, industry consisting of a large number of small firms. It is in the cases where market power is exercised by an agency which markets the produce of a large number of separate units, that the comparison is most likely to be realistic.

Second, it has not been possible in this chapter to consider the behaviour of agricultural markets where a major consideration of firms, when coming to production decisions, is the potential action that competitor firms might take in response to these decisions. Attempts to simulate behaviour in such 'oligopolistic' markets include the application of economic models, similar to those used in this chapter, to alternative approaches, such as the theory of games, mentioned in the previous chapter in connection with farm production.[9] One result of competition among a small number of firms in the food manufacturing and distributive trades has been the development of 'non-price' competition, with individual firms attempting to increase their sales by advertising, packaging, promotion campaigns, and so on.

Third, our knowledge of the structure of food marketing seems to improve as we consider stages nearer the point of final consumption. There have been a number of interesting studies made of price formulation at the retail level. To give just one example, an area which has attracted a lot of attention in the United Kingdom is the relationship between retail and wholesale meat prices.[10] It has been observed that retail meat margins are inversely related to wholesale prices – in other words, retail meat prices are more stable than wholesale prices. The issue has tended to be publicised when butchers have been observed to be sustaining retail price levels in the face of declining wholesale prices, but retail prices have also tended to remain stable when wholesale prices have risen.

Although it is not impossible to postulate market conditions that would result in the development of an inverse relationship between wholesale prices and retail margins (34), most writers appear to consider that retail butchers simply prefer stable selling prices, either because frequent price changes on a large number of items are costly, or because relations with customers are improved by the 'reliable' image given by stable prices. Meat retailers are able to absorb wholesale price variations into their margins either by 'averaging' or 'levelling'. Where prices of different meats do not move together, low margins on some products can be offset by high margins on others. Butchers may 'push' those meats which are in plentiful supply and for which wholesale prices are therefore relatively low – 'I can recommend the lamb this week, Mrs Jones' – rather than by attempting to increase sales by price cuts. In the case of levelling, wholesale prices are converted only gradually into price changes at the retail level, so that longer term wholesale price movements will be reflected in changes in retail prices, but shorter term fluctuations will not.

McClements (35) has shown that it is probably levelling that accounts for the greater proportion of the stability of retail meat prices relative to wholesale prices.

6 The role of storage

The ability to store agricultural commodities allows an irregular supply to match what is generally a more regular pattern of demand. This process of 'evening out' supply fluctuations reduces instability of agricultural prices in two ways. First, it means that those supply variations which can be predicted should cause price movements which reflect no more than the cost of storing the commodity. Most of the variation in supply which can be predicted is seasonal. A crop which is harvested over a period of one or two months is stored to meet a demand which exists throughout the year.

A good example of this kind of product is potatoes. Figure 3.22 shows the monthly variation in the price of maincrop potatoes in the United Kingdom between August 1970 and June 1974. The seasonal pattern is one of prices falling during August and September, when the crop is harvested, and then gradually rising until the following June. There is no price quotation for July, when the previous year's maincrop has been entirely replaced by the new season's early crop. The difference between the price in October and the price in June gives a rough indication of the cost of storing potatoes for nine months, relative to production costs. It is only a rough indication because the seasonal price pattern is disturbed by changing views on the adequacy of existing stocks, by the timing of the new season's supplies, by the gradual deterioration of the product from month to month and also by the operation of the *Potato Marketing Board*, which on occasions intervened to support market prices.

It is not possible to store potatoes for much more than a year and thus the average price between August and June is determined by one year's crop. This is one of the reasons why potato markets can demonstrate marked year-to-year cyclical price variations (see Fig. 3.7). The second stabilising effect of storage

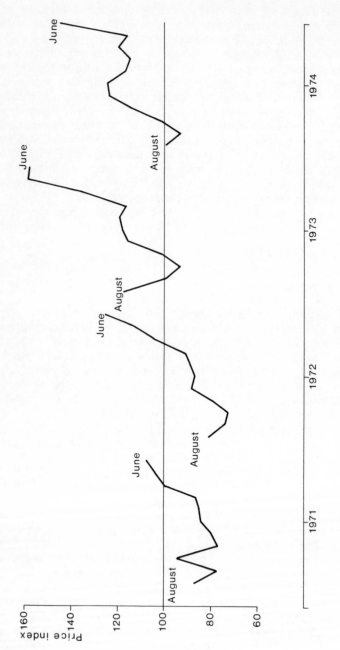

*Figure 3.22   Monthly index of maincrop potato prices in the UK, 1970–74
(1968–72 = 100). Source: MAFF statistics*

applies to products which can be stored for longer periods. It is to 'stretch' the market impact of those changes in supply and demand for a product which are less easy to predict. If, for example, supply is reduced in one year because of unfavourable weather conditions, information concerning the probability of a bad harvest usually becomes available before the impact is felt in reduced supplies. The existence of stocks means that this event can be reflected in market price movements prior to the lower level of supplies. Knowledge of the likelihood of a poor harvest will lead to the expectation of price rises in the future, which will increase the incentive to store the product. Some produce, which would have been sold on the market, will be retained in stocks, and this will tend to push up existing market prices. Alternatively, if a bumper harvest is expected, there will be a tendency to run down stocks, pushing down current prices. Once the supply shift is experienced, then the practice of holding stocks 'spreads' the price effect into future seasons. A bumper harvest in one year will cause stocks to be accumulated, reducing prices in subsequent years, while a poor harvest will mean that less than the normal amount is carried forward into the next year.

There are two main factors which determine how much of an agricultural commodity will be stored in a particular time period. The first factor is the cost of storage. Although very often the owner of a stock of a commodity will also possess the facilities for storing it, it is helpful when analysing the role of stocks to regard the owner of a stock as paying another merchant to store it for him. The lower the price that must then be paid to a merchant in return for his providing storage of the commodity, other things being equal, more of the commodity will be stored. The use of deep freezing techniques means that it is now possible to store virtually any agricultural commodity and when we say that a product cannot be stored, what we really mean is that the cost of storing it is too high to induce anyone to pay for storage when account is taken of the second factor affecting the quantity of stocks, namely expected future prices of the commodity relative to current prices. An individual will be prepared to pay a merchant to store a commodity for him if he believes that at some time in the future he will be able to sell the product at a gain over current market prices which will more than offset the price he pays for storage.

For some agricultural commodities there exists a market in *futures* and this provides a consensus of current expectations of future prices. A futures market[11] is part of a formally organised central market where contracts for the delivery of a commodity at some future date are bought and sold. There are two groups of individuals who operate on futures markets, known as *hedgers* and *speculators*, though a particular transaction can involve an element of both hedging and speculation. In essence, hedging in futures is a method of insurance against future price fluctuations by those who trade in the commodity. A merchant holding a stock of a commodity can contract to deliver a specific part of it at some future date, and at an agreed price, thus reducing the risk that a fall in the market price of the commodity will cause him to incur a loss. A firm which processes an agricultural product may contract to purchase some quantity of it in advance to reduce the risk of an adverse movement in the market price of the commodity.

The activity of speculation, on the other hand, involves no intention of ever dealing in the commodity as such. The speculator 'plays the market', buying and selling future contracts. A very simple speculative transaction would be for an individual to contract to deliver the commodity at some future date, and at some specific price, in the hope that the market price of the commodity would be lower than the contracted price when the date arrives. It will then be possible to find a merchant who will be prepared to pay for the contract to deliver the commodity because it will give him a better price for his produce than that currently ruling on the market. In practice, many speculators would never be involved in the establishment of contracts, nor would they be likely to hold futures when they matured. They would hope to make a profit by continually buying and selling futures, the prices of which vary over time as expectations of the future balance between supply and demand for the commodity alter.

The existence of a futures market means that we can relate the level of stocks to price expectations in a more formal way than is possible if the term 'future price expectations' implies no more than a mass of individual views. In Fig. 3.23 the level of stocks (Q) in time period T_0 is measured on the horizontal axes. The vertical axis in Fig. 3.23a measures the price per unit (P) paid for storing the commodity from time period T_0 to time period T_1 (we will restrict the analysis to two time periods). S_s is the supply curve of providing storage facilities, which is determined by the cost of storing the commodity from T_0 to T_1. It seems reasonable to suggest that over the range of stockholding which can be accommodated easily by existing capacity, the marginal cost of storage will rise only slowly as more is stored, and so the supply curve of storage might be quite elastic up to the limit of existing capacity. However, the marginal cost of storage will rise very rapidly once existing capacity is fully used, and so the supply curve S_s is shown as becoming very inelastic at higher levels of stockholding.

In Fig. 3.23b, the line W_s shows the relationship between the quantity of stocks which traders wish to hold from T_0 to T_1 and the expected 'reward' for holding stocks. The expected reward for stock holding (R) depends on both the price which must be paid for storage facilities (P) and the gap between the

---

Key to Fig. 3.23

Q is the quantity of stocks of the commodity (units) held from time period T_0 to time period T_1

P is the price (£ per unit) of storing the commodity from T_0 to T_1

E is the expected price (£ per unit) of the commodity in T_1 (the 'futures price') minus the current (T_0) price

R ($= E - P$) is the expected reward (£ per unit) for holding stocks of the commodity from T_0 to T_1

S_s is the supply curve of storage facilities

D_s ($E = 0$, $E = 5$, etc.) are demand curves for storage facilities, relating the demand for storage to the price of storage for alternative values of E

W_s relates the level of stocks to the expected reward for holding stocks from T_0 to T_1

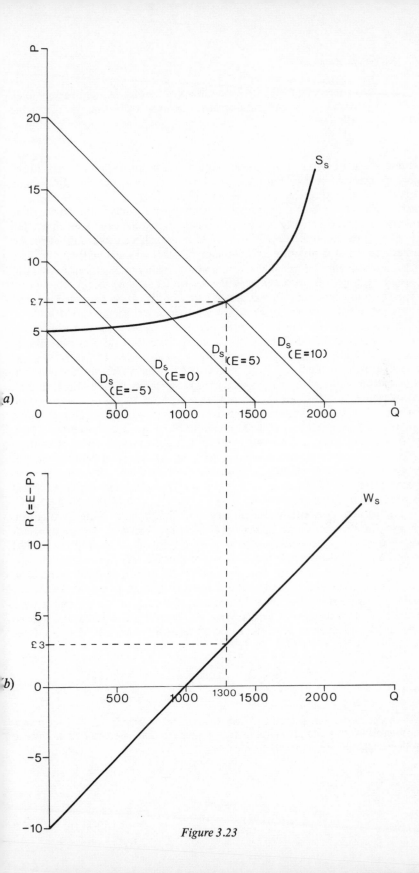

Figure 3.23

current price of the commodity in T_0 and the price traders expect to apply in T_1 (the 'futures' price). If we call the *excess* of the expected future price over the current price 'E', then

$$R = E - P$$

The line W_s slopes up to the right indicating that more stocks will be held the higher is the expected reward for stockholding. Some individuals are still prepared to store the commodity when the expected reward for doing so is negative. The futures market provides a consensus concerning future price movements for the commodity, but there will always be some who think that the price of the commodity will rise when most believe it will fall. Also, for marketing of the commodity to continue smoothly, traders will have to hold stocks, and therefore some of the commodity is likely to be stored from T_0 to T_1 even by traders who expect a negative reward for holding stocks.

The demand curves D_s ($E = 0$, $E = 5$, etc.) in Fig. 3.23a relate the demand for storage facilities to the price of storage. Since the demand for storage is influenced by future commodity price expectations as well as the price of storage, there will be a different demand curve for each level of price expectations. For example, suppose that the future expected price in T_1 is the same as the current price in T_0 (i.e. $E = 0$). Figure 3.23b tells us that traders will hold stocks of 1000 units when they expect a zero reward for stock holding, so that, if $R = 0$ and $E = 0$, then 1000 units will be stored if the price of storage is also zero – in other words, the demand curve for storage facilities, $D_s(E = 0)$, must intersect the horizontal axis at 1000 units. Similarly, we know from Fig. 3.23b that the expected reward for storage must fall to $-£10$ before no stocks will be held so, if the commodity price is expected to remain constant between the two time periods, the price of storage must rise to £10 per unit before the demand for storage facilities falls to zero (i.e. $D_s(E = 0)$ must intersect the vertical axis at a price of £10).

We are now in a position to identify in Fig. 3.23a the equilibrium quantity and price of storage for any given level of future commodity price expectations. For example, suppose the future price exceeds the current price by £10 per unit, i.e. $E = 10$. The demand curve for storage facilities is therefore D_s ($E = 10$), and the equilibrium level of stocks is 1300 at a price of £7 per unit paid for storage facilities. Traders therefore expect to make a profit of £3 per unit from storing the commodity (the excess of the future expected price over current price, less the cost of storage) and we see in Fig. 3.23b that the level of stocks will be 1300 units when the expected reward for stock holding is £3 per unit.

Notes

[1] The model is characterised rather differently by different writers.
[2] In many cases, of course, the observed price movements may also be consistent with an assumption of non-perfect markets.

3 A more detailed account of the economic forces behind the development of a 'farm problem' will be found in Chapter 2 of Marsh and Ritson (13).

4 The issue was seen clearly enough and thought sufficiently important in the mid-1960s for one American foundation to finance the establishment of centres in North America, Sweden and England with the objective of promoting 'agricultural adjustment'. See, for example, Aston and Rogers (14) and Rogers (15).

5 See, for example, G. R. Allen's review 'Agricultural Policies in the Shadow of Malthus' (17).

6 For a summary of each of these views, see G. R. Allen (19) and Ehrlich and Ehrlich (20).

7 Many of these developments in food processing and distribution are described in more detail in the OECD report 'Food Marketing and Economic Growth' (23).

8 For a particularly thorough treatment of alternative models of market behaviour, see Cole (28). The term 'imperfect competition' can be used in a more narrowly defined sense to mean roughly the same as 'monopolistic competition'.

9 Two of the earliest models of behaviour in an oligopolistic market were advanced by Hall and Hitch (29) and Sweezy (30). Cole (28) summarises several theories of oligopolistic market behaviour, and includes a short section on the 'Game Theory Approach'.

10 See, for example, Houston (31) and HMSO (32, 33).

11 For a detailed discussion of futures markets for agricultural commodities, see Tomek and Robinson (36) or a much earlier work, Waite and Trelogan (37).

References

(1) Winchester, S. 'Grain of controversy.' *The Guardian*, Wed., 6 Aug. 1975.

(2) Ministry of Agriculture, Fisheries and Food. *A Century of Agricultural Statistics*. London, HMSO, 1968.

(3) *Agricultural Policy in Belgium* Paris, OECD, 1974.

(4) Moore, H. L. *Forecasting the Yield and Price of Cotton*. New York, Macmillan, 1917.

(5) Kaldor, N. 'A classificatory note on the determinateness of equilibrium.' *Review of Economic Studies*, Vol. 1, Feb. 1934.

(6) Leontief, W. 'Verzögerte Angebotsanpassung und Partielles Gleichgewicht. *Zeitschrift für Nationalökonomie*, Vol. 5, 1934.

(7) Ezekiel, M. 'The cobweb theorem.' *Quarterly Journal of Economics*, Vol. 53, Feb. 1938.

(8) Waugh, F. V. 'Cobweb models.' *Journal of Farm Economics*, Vol. 46, No. 4, Nov. 1964. (Reprinted in *Readings in the Economics of Agriculture* (eds. K. A. Fox & D. G. Johnson), American Economic Association. London, Allen & Unwin, 1970.

(9) Larson, A. B. 'The hog cycle as harmonic motion.' *Journal of Farm Economics*, Vol. 46, No. 2, May 1964.

(10) Nerlove, M. 'Adaptive expectations and cobweb phenomena.' *Quarterly Journal of Economics*, Vol. 72, 1958.

(11) McClements, L. D. 'Note on harmonic motion and the cobweb theorem.' *Journal of Agricultural Economics*, Vol. XXI, No. 1, Jan. 1970.

(12) Lewis, W. A. 'World production, prices, and trade, 1880–1960.' *The Manchester School of Economics and Social Studies*, Vol. XX, No. 2, 1952.

(13) Marsh, J. & Ritson, C. *Agricultural policy and the Common Market.* PEP/Chatham House, London, 1971.
(14) Ashton, J. & Rogers, S. J. 'Agricultural adjustment – a challenge to economists.' *Journal of Agricultural Economics*, Vol. XVIII, No. 2, May 1967.
(15) Rogers, S. J. 'The elements of agricultural adjustment.' Bulletin No. 4. Agricultural Adjustment Unit, University of Newcastle upon Tyne, 1968.
(16) Malthus, T. R. *First Essay on Population, 1798.* London, Everyman Edition, 1958.
(17) Allen, G. R. 'Agricultural policies in the shadow of Malthus.' *Lloyds Bank Review*, No. 117, July 1975.
(18) 'Trade in primary commodities: conflict or co-operation? A Tripartite Report by Fifteen Economists from Japan, The European Community and North America.' The Brookings Institution, Washington, 1974.
(19) Allen, G. R. 'Some aspects of planning world food supplies.' *Journal of Agricultural Economics*, Vol. XXVI, No. 1, Jan. 1976.
(20) Ehrlich, P. R. & Erhlich, A. H. *Population, Resources, Environment: Issues in Human Ecology.* San Francisco, Freeman, 1970.
(21) Wollen, G. H. & Turner, G. 'The cost of food marketing.' *Journal of Agricultural Economics*, Vol. XXI, No. 1, Jan. 1970.
(22) Beaumont, J. A. 'The cost of processing and distributing food in the United Kingdom.' *Economic Trends*, No. 217, Nov. 1971.
(23) *Food Marketing and Economic Growth*, Paris, OECD, 1970.
(24) van Musschenbroek, K. 'Development in the food manufacturing and distributive industries.' *Journal of Agricultural Economics*, Vol. XXI, No. 3, Sept. 1970.
(25) Hart, P. E., Utton, M. A. & Walshe, G. *Mergers and Concentration in British Industry.* The National Institute of Economic and Social Research/Cambridge University Press, 1973.
(26) Mills, F. D. & Cook, R. S. 'Competition in milk retailing,' University of Reading, Department of Agricultural Economics and Management. Miscellaneous Study No. 54, Nov. 1972.
(27) Chamberlin, E. H. *Theory of Monopolistic Competition.* Harvard University Press, 1933.
(28) Cole, C. L. *Microeconomics: A Contemporary Approach.* New York, Harcourt Brace Jovanovich, 1973.
(29) Hall, R. L. & Hitch, C. J. 'Price theory and business behaviour.' *Oxford Economic Papers*, No. 2, May 1939.
(30) Sweezy, P. M. 'Demand under conditions of oligopoly.' *The Journal of Political Economy*, Vol. XLVII, Aug. 1939.
(31) Houston, G. 'Meat marketing margins in Britain.' *Journal of Agricultural Economics*, Vol. XV, No. 1, May 1962.
(32) 'Committee of Enquiry into Fatstock and Carcase Meat Marketing and Distribution.' (The 'Verdon-Smith Report'.) Cmnd. 2282. HMSO, 1964.
(33) 'Prices, profits and costs in food distribution.' National Board for Prices and Incomes, Report 165. Cmnd. 4645. HMSO, 1971.
(34) Parish, R. M. 'Price levelling and averaging.' *Farm Economist*, Vol. XI, No. 5, 1967.
(35) McClements, L. D. 'An analysis of retail meat pricing behaviour in Britain.' *Applied Economics*, Vol. 4, No. 4, Dec. 1972.
(36) Tomek, W. G. & Robinson, K. L. *Agricultural Product Prices.* Cornell University Press, 1972.
(37) Waite, C & Trelogan, H. C. *Agricultural Market Prices*, 2nd edn. New York, Wiley, 1951.

CHAPTER 4

Agricultural Resource Use

1 Introduction

In the final chapter of Part I of this book we complete our coverage of the basic principles of agricultural economics. The first three chapters have discussed demand, supply and markets for agricultural products. It remains to investigate more fully the use of resources in agricultural production.

Just as farm products are channelled from farmers to consumers via agricultural product markets, so productive resources are allocated to farms via *factor markets*, in which input prices are determined by the interaction of supply and demand for the factor. As with product markets, input markets can vary in their competitive structure, and as we shall see in Part II of the book, governments intervene to influence prices in factor as well as in product markets.

The first part of this chapter, therefore, discusses the theory of equilibrium in the market for a factor of production. This is followed by sections dealing with the markets for labour, 'capital' inputs, and land viewed in relation to their use in agricultural production. The chapter concludes with an analysis of the forces determining the size structure of an agricultural industry.

The argument is couched in terms of farm inputs, but much of the material is also relevant to the use of inputs by the firms providing agricultural marketing services.

2 The theory of equilibrium in factor markets

2.1 The demand for an input

We established in Chapter 2 that a profit maximising firm must equate the marginal value product (MVP) of an input with marginal factor cost (MFC). We have seen, further, that the main distinction between a firm operating in a perfectly, as opposed to an imperfectly, competitive factor market is that the firm which commands a significant proportion of market demand for an input takes account of the impact, on the market price of the input, of its own level of input use.

In order to consider the market demand for an input, let us first return to the simple example of production used in Chapter 2, and investigate in more detail the implications for the profit maximising firm of a change in the price of an input. We will remember that, with the price of product A (P_a) set at £20 per unit, and prices for inputs X and Y of £4 and £8 per unit, the firm maximised profit by producing 4 units of product A, using 8 units of input X and 4 units of input Y.

We found this position of profit maximisation by first locating the least cost combination of inputs to produce any level of output and then finding the level of output for which total revenue exceeded total (minimum) cost by the greatest amount.

We might equally well have expressed this profit maximising position by reference to the marginal value product of each input. When looking at the problem from this point of view we have so far only considered the optimum use of a single input, holding all other inputs fixed at some (arbitrary) levels. Under these circumstances, the optimum use of an input for the profit maximising firm was found to be that which satisfied the condition $MVP =$ input price. But to ensure that the firm is in a position of overall profit maximisation we need only generalise the argument and find levels of application for all inputs such that the marginal value products of all inputs are simultaneously equal to their respective prices.[1] This is shown for our production example in Fig. 4.1. We find that the marginal value product of input Y $(x = 8)$ equals the price of input Y when 4 units are applied, and we find correspondingly that the marginal value product of input X $(y = 4)$ equals the price of input X when 8 units of X are applied. In fact, it can be shown that, if the price of the product is £20 per unit, the price of input X is £4 per unit and the price of input Y is £8 per unit, then 8 units of X and 4 units of Y is the only combination of the inputs for which the marginal value product of both inputs simultaneously equals the respective input prices, and the use of this combination of inputs therefore maximises the profit from the production of product A − which confirms the result found in Chapter 2, section 3.1.

Now suppose the price of input Y falls to £6 per unit. If for some reason we cannot change the quantity of input X used, then the new optimum application of input Y will be found by equating MVP $(x = 8)$ with the lower price of Y, which occurs when 6.46^2 units of Y are applied. Therefore, when the use of only one input can be varied, the marginal value product curve for that input is the firm's demand curve for the input.

But it may well be the case that the use of inputs, other than the one which has changed in price, can be varied and in such cases the marginal value product curve will not be the firm's demand curve for the input. In our example, to obtain the firm's demand curve for input Y we must take account of the possibility of the firm adjusting the quantity it uses of both inputs. If we

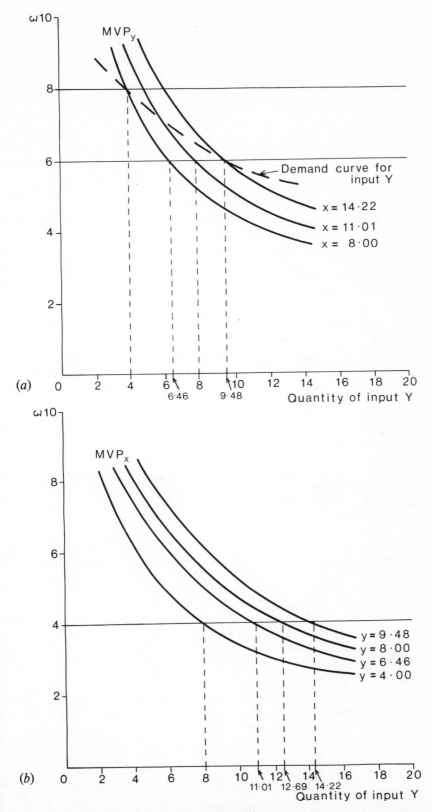

Figure 4.1

look at Fig. 4.1b we see that an increase in the use of input Y from 4 units to 6·46 units shifts the marginal value product curve for input X from MVP_x $(y = 4)$ to MVP_x $(y = 6·46)$ and it has become profitable to increase the use of input X beyond 8 units to 11·01 units. In turn however, such an increase in the use of input X increases the optimum application of input Y to 8·00 units. Each increase in the use of one of the inputs increases the optimum level of application of the other, but as we repeat the process we find that the steps get smaller and we gradually approach a new combination of inputs such that the marginal value products of both inputs are once again simultaneously equal to their respective input prices. This in fact happens in our example when y equals 9·48 units and x equals 14·22 units.

The new profit maximising position for the firm is shown in Fig. 4.2a. The fall in the price of input Y reduces the total cost of producing any level of output, so that the total cost curve shifts from TC_1 to TC_2 and the new profit maximising level of output is 7·11 units of product A. In Fig. 4.2b we see that the least cost combination of inputs to produce 7·11 units of product A (with the price of X being £4 per unit and the price of Y, £6 per unit) is 14·22 units of X and 9·48 units of Y.

In short then, the fall in the price of input Y from £8 per unit to £6 per unit has:

(a) Increased the quantity demanded by the firm of input Y from 4 units to 9·48 units. Thus, as shown in Fig. 4.1a, if adjustments in X are allowed, the firm's demand curve for Y will be modified to that indicated by the broken line.

(b) Increased the firm's output of product A from 4 units to 7·11 units, assuming that there is no change in product price. Thus a shift has occurred in the firm's supply curve for product A.

(c) Increased the quantity demanded by the firm of input X from 8 units to 14·22 units, assuming that there is no change in the price of X – the fall in the price of input Y has also caused a shift in the firm's demand curve for input X. The increase in the use of X is less in proportion than the increase in the use of Y, so the use of input Y has increased relative to the use of input X. We can divide the impact on the use of input X of the fall in the price of input Y into two kinds – the substitution effect, which reduces the quantity of input X contained in the least cost combination of the inputs required for any given level of output, and the effect of the fall in production costs which raises the level of output which maximises profit. In our example, the impact upon the use of input X of the increase in the profit maximising level of production of product A more than offsets the substitution effect of the change in relative input prices, but there are many production situations where the substitution effect could exceed the output effect so that a fall in the price of one input can reduce the firm's demand for another input.

In Fig. 4.3 we move from the firm's demand curve for input Y to a consideration of the demand for input Y by an industry comprising a large number

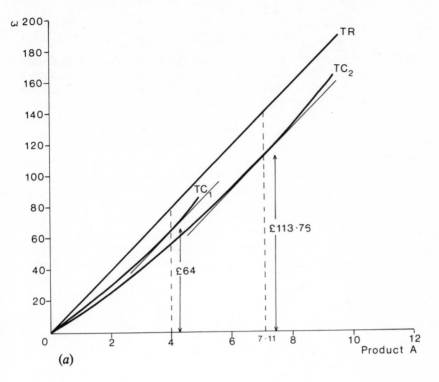

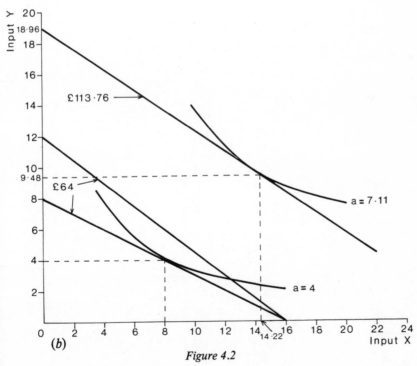

Figure 4.2

of firms. Clearly our starting point will be to aggregate the demand curves of all the firms comprising the industry, and let us suppose that this gives the curve D_1 in Fig. 4.3, showing an increase in aggregate demand for input Y from Q_1 to Q_3 units following the fall in market price of Y from £8 to £6. This industry demand response incorporates the impact of all firms adjusting the use of input X as well as input Y, but assumes that the price of product A and the price of input X both remain constant.

In the previous chapter it was mentioned that the response of market supply to a change in product price might be affected by subsequent price changes for inputs or other products. In our example, the fall in the price of input Y causes an increase in the quantity used of input X and an increase in the quantity produced of product A. However, the implications of the increase in product supply are different from those of the increase in demand for the other inputs. There may be many industries employing the same input and a single industry need not necessarily constitute a significant proportion of total input use. Let

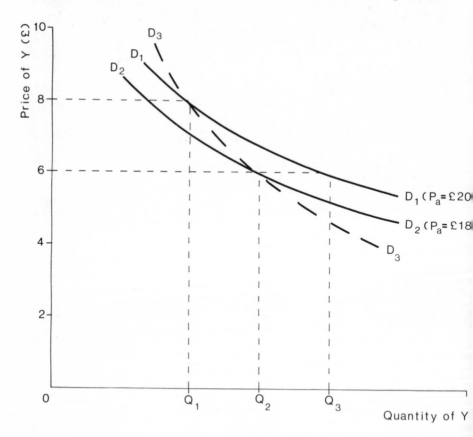

Figure 4.3

us assume that this is in fact the case with the use of input X by the industry producing product A, in which case we are able to assume no significant change in the price of input X.

In the case of a product, however, unless for some reason (such as international trade) we are concerned with the demand for an input from a group of firms which account for only a small proportion of supplies to the relevant product market, we must expect there to be a fall in product price as a result of the increase in quantity supplied following the fall in input price. For each product price there will be a demand curve for input Y, the lower the product price the nearer the input demand curve will be to the origin. The fall in the price of input Y increases output of product A, but this leads to a fall in the price of product A and a consequent fall in the demand for input Y. For equilibrium to be re-established, the industry must employ that quantity of input Y (say Q_2), which is associated with a market price of product A (say £18) which occasions the industry to demand Q_2 units of input Y when the price of Y is £6 per unit.

It is sometimes convenient to include the impact of the fall in product price within the form of the demand curve for the input, rather than by shifts in input demand curves defined for alternative products prices. This gives the curve D_3D_3, shown by the broken line in Fig. 4.3.

In Chapter 2 we saw that the identification of the marginal cost curve of a product for an individual firm facilitated the development of a theory of agricultural supply. We have now seen that another relationship identified in Chapter 2 – the marginal value product curve of an input – forms the basis of our theory of the demand for farm inputs. In the case of farm product supply it was thought generally reasonable to define the industry's short run supply curve as the sum of the individual firms' marginal cost curves for the product, but it was stressed that a firm's supply curve for the product would be more elastic than its marginal cost curve if there were opportunities for switching fixed factors between products within the firm in the short run. It was also pointed out that the industry supply curve would be less elastic than the sum of the individual firms' supply curves if input price changes followed a change in the industry's supply of the product. As far as farm input demand is concerned, it is thought that cases where the industry's demand curve for an input will be given by the sum of the individual firms' marginal value product curves for that input are more likely to be the exception than the rule. The *firm's demand* for an input will be more elastic than its marginal value product curve for the input because of the possibility of adjustments in the quantities used of all variable factors, but the *industry's demand* response will be less elastic than the sum of the individual firms' demand curves for the input because of price changes in the product market.

2.2 The supply of an input

Although there are some exceptions (see for example, Bottomley (1)), the supply curve of a factor to an industry will usually be positively related to the price paid for the factor by the firms in the industry. There are two ways in which the quantity supplied of a factor to an industry can be increased. There can be a movement of factors from employment in other industries (or a reduction in the quantity of 'new' inputs going to other industries), or there can be an increase in the total amount of the factor available for the use of all industries. The extent to which the quantity supplied of a factor can be changed in either of these ways varies considerably between different farm inputs. (The supply of land, labour and 'capital' inputs to agriculture is discussed in this context in the next three sections.)

In Fig. 4.4 we show three alternative supply curves for an input. The curve S_1 is perfectly inelastic, indicating that the factor is used only by this industry

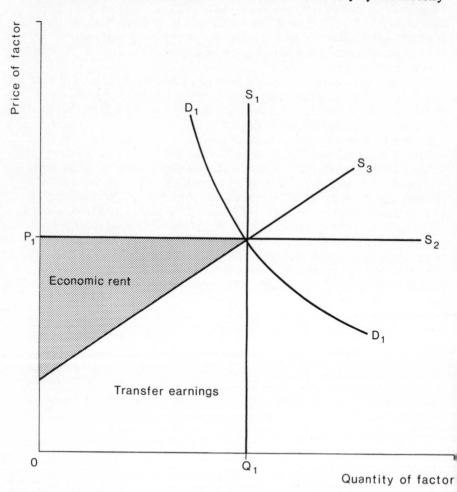

Figure 4.4

and that the amount of it available is fixed at Q_1 units. The curve S_2 is perfectly elastic, which implies that this industry does not account for a significant proportion of the total amount of the factor; as long as the firms in the industry are prepared to pay at least P_1 per unit for the factor, the industry may employ as much of it as it wishes. S_3 is the more typical case of an upward sloping input supply curve. The increase in the quantity supplied of the factor which follows an increase in its price may be caused by either or both of (i) an increase in the total amount of the factor, or (ii) the industry bidding supplies of the factor away from firms in other industries – the industry does account for a significant proportion of total factor use, so an increase in the quantity used of the input forces up the price paid by all the firms in all the industries employing the input.

If S_3 is the supply curve of the input, and D_1D_1 the industry's demand curve for the input, equilibrium is established in the industry's market for the input when the factor price is P_1 and Q_1 units are employed by the industry. The term *economic rent*[3] is used to refer to that part of the payment to a factor of production which is in excess of the minimum amount necessary to keep it in its present occupation, the remainder being called *transfer earnings*. If a factor is fixed in supply and used by only one industry (illustrated by the supply curve S_1 in Fig. 4.4) then the whole of the payment to the factor by the industry is economic rent. However, if the industry is faced by a perfectly elastic supply of the factor, then, as far as the industry is concerned, the entire payment to the factor is required to prevent it from moving to another industry (if S_2 is the factor supply curve, then a slight reduction beneath P_1 per unit in the price the industry is prepared to pay for the factor would mean that the industry could not employ any of the factor).

In the more usual case of an upward sloping supply curve, such as S_3, the amount that it is necessary to induce extra units of the factor into employment by this industry increases as more units are employed. The economic rent received by the nth unit of a factor employed by the industry is therefore the difference between the price paid for the factor and the price necessary to induce a factor supply of n units. The total economic rent received by the input in its employment by this industry is shown diagrammatically in Fig. 4.4 by the area bounded by the supply curve of the input and the price paid by the industry for the input.

3 Agricultural labour

3.1

There are three aspects of agricultural labour markets which have most attracted the attention of agricultural economists. These are:

(a) the impact of organised union activity;
(b) the factors influencing variations in the rate of outward migration of agricultural labour; and

(c) the persistence of a substantial gap between the average earnings of farm workers and the average earnings of workers in other occupations.

All three of these aspects can be illustrated by reference to the work of agricultural economists who have investigated the operation of the agricultural labour market in the United Kingdom.

The problems encountered in the organisation of a labour union in an industry in which there are many thousands of employers have been described by Self and Storing (2) and Mills (3). It appears that the National Union of Agricultural Workers (NUAW)[4] has probably never succeeded in achieving a membership comprising more than 30 per cent of the UK farm labour force. A few per cent of the rest are members of the giant Transport and General Workers Union (TGWU), but a substantial majority of the UK farm labour force do not belong to any trade union. Mills reported (in 1964) 3687 separate branches of the NUAW, with an average branch membership of only thirty-seven. The unions argue their wage claims, not directly with employers, but through the Agricultural Wages Board upon which independent members, in effect, conciliate and arbitrate between the farmers' and workers' unions. This Board establishes legal minimum wage rates including premia for responsibility, etc., but the average earnings of agricultural workers have tended to be 15 to 20 per cent in excess of the rates prescribed by the Board. In 1974 about 94 per cent of regular full-time agricultural workers received wages in excess of those implied by the prescribed basic and overtime rates (4).

We should not necessarily read into these figures that union activity has no significant influence upon agricultural wages. In an industry where the relationship between employer and employee is a close one, it may often be traditional to pay regular workers a little in excess of the required minimum, whatever that minimum may be. But it is equally possible that in many cases the premium over prescribed agricultural wage rates reflects a genuine interplay of supply and demand in an input market which is relatively free from the exercise of either monopsony buying power on the part of farmers, or monopoly selling power by labour.

This latter interpretation would resolve the apparent conflict between the statements of farmers, who persistently report that they are experiencing shortages of agricultural labour, and the writings of agricultural economists, who sometimes refer to a surplus. In the previous chapter it was mentioned that 'supply' could only exceed or be less than 'demand' *at some price*. A shortage was defined as the excess of quantity demanded over quantity supplied at any price lower than that required to bring the market into equilibrium, and a surplus defined as the excess of quantity supplied over quantity demanded at any price higher than the equilibrium. We have seen that agricultural wages in the United Kingdom have tended to exceed the prescribed minimum, but they have nevertheless been low in comparison with average industrial wages. Thus there may very well have been a shortage of agricultural labour, particularly of certain categories of labour, at prescribed minimum wages and a surplus at a wage comparable to average industrial wages.

3.2

The underlying causes of the decline in the relative size of the agricultural labour force in countries which have experienced sustained growth in average levels of income are well known and were outlined in the previous chapter (section 4.2). But the rate of outward migration does vary from year to year, and an investigation of the major factors affecting these variations can throw light on the operation of an agricultural labour market. The input demand curve which we derived in section 2 related the quantity demanded of an input to the price of the input, the prices of other inputs, the price of the product, and the relevant production function. On the supply side, as well as the level of agricultural wages, we might expect the prevailing level of wages in alternative occupations to be important. It would also seem probable that the rate of outward migration could be influenced by the number of job vacancies throughout the rest of the economy.

Cowling and Metcalf have published a number of studies of the UK agricultural labour market.[5] Whilst these studies produce somewhat differing results as to the relative importance of the variables influencing the rate of outward migration of agricultural labour, it does appear that changes on the supply side are more significant than changes in demand. Most studies confirm that the ratio of agricultural to industrial earnings, and the level of unemployment in the economy as a whole, influence migration. The outflow of labour also appears to respond to *changes* in the level of unemployment; when unemployment is rising, even if it is at a low level, the job expectations of potential migrants are adversely affected. In addition, there are significant regional variations in the influence of various factors.

3.3

Despite the persistent large outflow of labour from agriculture, earnings of farm workers in the United Kingdom in the post-1945 period have remained at approximately 70 per cent of average earnings in other industries (4). Estimates for other countries in Western Europe show a gap of a similar order of magnitude (6).

It is possible to postulate three kinds of explanation for these observed discrepancies between money wages in agriculture and in other industries. These may be summarised as:

(*a*) non-comparability;
(*b*) 'imperfections' in the labour market; and
(*c*) 'disequilibrium' in the labour market.

A discrepancy in earnings between two occupations can arise if either the job or the worker are not comparable. It is often claimed, for example, that there are substantial non-monetary rewards associated with agricultural employment, such as the benefits of living in a rural environment, a 'healthy' job, and perhaps, a lower cost of living. Economists refer to these aspects of employment as the *net advantages* of an occupation and variations in net advantages between occupations will lead differentials in money wages to persist when a labour market is in equilibrium. Wage differentials also persist if agricultural workers do not possess the same skills as those already working in industrial occupations.

On this last point, it is worth noting that this reason for the existence of money wage differentials does not necessarily imply that agricultural workers are, in some sense, less able than their industrial counterparts. It may well be that either group of workers will include a substantial proportion who are ill-equipped to take on the other group's occupations. The differential favours industrial workers because the pressure on the labour market is for a migration from agriculture to industry, rather than the reverse. Similarly, where there are significant costs associated with transferring between jobs the effect of these costs will be a wage differential in favour of industrial workers because of the direction of the migration which is taking place.

Money wage differentials on account of the factors mentioned above could occur in a perfectly competitive labour market but, in addition, differentials could arise because of imperfections in the labour market. The two most commonly mentioned imperfections are restrictions on labour supply and lack of perfect knowledge.

A powerful labour union in one industry may be able to sustain wages above the level applying to comparable, but less effectively organised, workers in another industry. It was suggested above that the agricultural labour market might be relatively free from the exercise of monopoly selling power when compared with the supply of labour to many other industries.

The second kind of imperfection is the possibility of ignorance on the part of agricultural workers, especially in the more remote regions, of the existence of opportunities for higher paid employment outside agriculture and, perhaps more significantly, a misconception, particularly among older workers, of the extent to which the non-monetary aspects of employment outside farming would, in the event of a move, offset the monetary benefits.

However, the importance of disequilibrium in the labour market as a cause of wage differentials between farm and other occupations has probably been overstated at times by agricultural economists. For example, referring to the United States, Hathaway and Perkins conclude:

> The belief that there is a serious malallocation of labour between farm and non-farm employment is hard to substantiate ... the earning capacity of farm people in non-farm employment may have been overestimated (7).

The third way in which money wage differentials could persist is if there is a significant adjustment time lag in the context of a situation where a continuous process of adjustment is required. Consider, for example, an economy in which there is, over a five-year period, both a substantial growth in average levels of household income and significant improvement in farming productivity. Assume that, at the start of this period the labour market is in equilibrium. Under these circumstances, the argument of the previous chapter (4.2) would be that a wage differential would develop between agricultural and non-agricultural occupations. It might well take a further five years for a sufficient degree of outward migration of the farm labour force to eliminate the differential and restore equilibrium in the labour market. (One reason for expecting this kind of time lag is that much of the adjustment takes place by an excess of the number of workers retiring over the level of recruitment.) If, however, during the second five-year period there has been a further growth in household income and more improvements in farm productivity, then the wage gap will not have been eliminated. The farm labour force finds that (like Alice in *Through the Looking Glass*) it has to run fast to stand still in terms of wage differentials. The persistence of money wage discrepancies between agricultural and other occupations could, therefore, in a growing economy, although not consistent with equilibrium in the labour market, nevertheless be consistent with a continuous movement towards an equilibrium in that market.

3.4

It is possible to find evidence to suggest that at some time, or in some country, all the factors mentioned above have contributed to the observed gap between money wages in farming and other occupations. Some years ago, an exhaustive enquiry was carried out at the Oxford Institute of Agricultural Economics into the extent and causes of the gap between agricultural and other earnings in a number of countries. This study concentrated on the incomes of farmers and family workers but much of its findings are relevant to wage labour. The report (8) of the study, which is still regarded in many ways as the 'classic' publication on this issue, eventually reached the conclusion that:

> The causes of the low supply price of agricultural enterprise in industrial nations where net migration is from agriculture, are, primarily (1) occupational immobility[6] outwards associated with mobility inwards, and (2) preference for farm life.

4 Capital inputs

If a major feature of the changing resource structure of agriculture in advanced countries has been the decline in the farm labour force, then another has been the increased use of capital[7] inputs, and particularly the increased use of inputs purchased from outside the agricultural sector. The kind of growth in the use of capital inputs which has taken place is illustrated by Table 4.1 which gives index numbers of major categories of farm inputs used in the United States between 1950 and 1973.

A growth in the quantity of capital inputs used in farming is a feature to be expected of an economy in which average levels of income are rising. In the previous chapter it was mentioned that there were two ways in which a nation could be successful in increasing average income levels, one of which was by

Table 4.1   Quantities of the main categories of farm inputs, USA 1950–73
(1950 = 100)

Year	Labour	Farm real estate	Mechanical power and machinery	Fertiliser and lime	All other inputs
1950	100	100	100	100	100
1955	85	100	115	140	110
1960	67	94	114	169	123
1965	55	94	118	249	139
1970	45	92	125	354	158
1973	45	91	130	388	161

Source: USDA.

the accumulation of its stock of capital resources. The increased use of capital items in farming, in one sense, *describes* part of agriculture's contribution to the rise in income levels.

The other way in which we said that average incomes were increased was by the introduction of new, more productive, methods of converting resources into products, and we have made reference on several occasions to the rapid improvements in agricultural productivity experienced in recent years.

The study of productivity improvement in farming is one area where the subject matter of agricultural economics and that of rural sociology tend to overlap.[8] The process whereby a more productive method is introduced into farming can in fact be viewed as a kind of *social change*, which Rogers and Shoemaker (11) define as 'the process by which alteration occurs in the structure and function of a social system'. They suggest three sequential stages in a social change: (i) *invention*, the process by which new ideas are created or developed, (ii) *diffusion*, the process by which new ideas are communicated to the members of a given social system, and (iii) *consequences*, the changes that occur within the social system as the result of the adoption or rejection of the innovation.

A social change can either emerge from within a social system or can be transmitted to it from outside, and when it does come about because of contact outside the system, it may be the incidental by-product of contact or it could be planned and directed by some outside agency. Now there have, of course, been many changes in farming practice which have occurred when one producer invents a more productive method and this method gradually spreads throughout the farming system, and it is not too difficult to cite productivity improvements that have not required the use of new inputs. But the major part of the improvement in farming productivity that has occurred in the twentieth century can be attributed to the directed introduction of new inputs – fertiliser, machinery and new breeds – following research at both government and commercial establishments.

Because the use of the new inputs has been planned, the process of adoption of an agricultural innovation has become the subject of widespread study by rural sociologists. A widely known study, which established a pattern for much subsequent work, was an investigation of the diffusion of hybrid maize in the United States during the 1930s. This study discerned a pattern in the adoption of the innovation which seems to be typical. If the percentage of farmers adopting the innovation is plotted against time, we get the bell-shaped frequency distribution shown in Fig. 4.5. The same data plotted cumulatively gives the 'S-shaped' curve, also shown in Fig. 4.5. Rogers (12) classified adopters in the bell-shaped frequency distribution into five groups: innovators, early adopters, early majority, late majority and laggards.

In Fig. 4.6 we plot the numbers of three kinds of agricultural machinery in England and Wales from 1935 to 1975. It can be seen that all display the 'S-shaped' pattern of adoption but the speed of adoption (or the breadth of the S) does vary a little. Jones (13) has suggested three broad groups of factors affecting the speed with which an innovation will be adopted within a group or diffused over a country. These are:

(a) the characteristics of the innovation;
(b) the media of communications; and
(c) the personal and sociological characteristics of the potential users.

The characteristics of the innovation he divides into economic and technical. The economic characteristics of a farming innovation include its operating costs, the rate at which an investment in it is recovered, and its net effect on farm income. However, there is little empirical evidence to support the *a priori* view that the lower the initial cost, and the higher the rate of return on capital and effect on farm income, the more rapidly the diffusion of the innovation.

The technical attributes of innovations which might bear on their speed of diffusion include the complexity, divisibility and conspicuousness of the innovation and their compatibility with existing practice. The more complex an innovation, the slower one might expect its diffusion to be. The divisibility of practice refers to the extent to which a farmer can try out an innovation before adopting it. Whereas this is clearly possible with seed and fertiliser, it is less possible with items of machinery. A conspicuous innovation is likely to be more quickly adopted than an inconspicuous one, both because the adopter may attain prestige from displaying his technical prowess and because other farmers will become aware of its introduction into the area more quickly. Finally, if a new practice is relatively easy to assimilate into an existing farm system it is more likely to be quickly adopted, both because it will be less unfamiliar to producers and because it is more likely immediately to be advantageous than something which does not fit in well with existing practice.

The pace at which an innovation is diffused is also a function of the existence of appropriate media of communication. One of the findings of the hybrid corn study mentioned earlier was that the time interval between first knowledge and the decision to adopt averaged about nine years. The most effective media of communication vary during this period, with the mass communication media

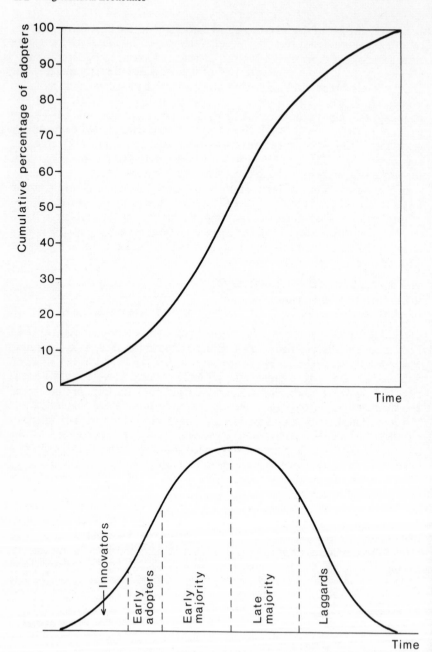

Figure 4.5   *S-shaped cumulative curve and bell-shaped frequency curve for adopter distribution*

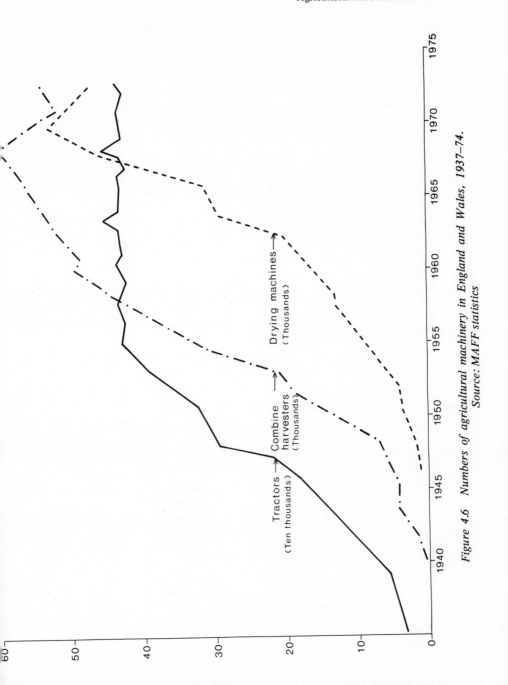

Figure 4.6 Numbers of agricultural machinery in England and Wales, 1937–74.
Source: MAFF statistics

of broadcasting and newspapers important at first, followed by contact with neighbours, agricultural advisory services and then merchants, dealers and salesmen. The extent to which a particular source of information is used varies not only for the individual at different stages in his adoption process, but also between individuals at different positions in the diffusion process. The innovator is more likely to read specialist journals and to have contact with advisory officers. In the hybrid corn case, salesmen were found to be the most important channel for early adopters but neighbours more important for the later adopters.

In the case of the personal and sociological characteristics of the adopters, as one might expect, relationships have been found between farm size, income, education and social origins of farmers on the one hand and whether they are early or late adopters on the other.

5 Land

5.1

Certain monosyllabic words have the emotional impact of a bullet, with the power to kill dead any rational discussion of the economics of the subject – and politicians, whose stock-in-trade is words, know well how to use them. One of these words is 'land'.

This is how Colin Clark begins his book *The Value of Agricultural Land* (14), and after referring to the widely differing personal associations that land can have and to the countless 'bloody wars' that have been fought over its ownership, he goes on:

But the existence of these terrible and overriding truths in no way absolves the economist from his duty of analysing the circumstances under which land is valuable, or less valuable, in the sense that people are or are not willing to pay high rents and prices for it.

This task is complicated, however, because much of the literature on 'land economics' is more orientated towards land than towards economics, probably for the reasons cited by Clark. Yet an understanding of the determination of agricultural land use and prices is no less dependent on an appreciation of the principles of agricultural economics as a whole than is – say – the determination of farm product prices. Many of the questions posed in agricultural land use studies can be resolved if we remember, first and foremost, that land is a resource used in farming which has much in common with other farm inputs. But, as with labour and capital inputs, there are certain features of land as a factor of production which distinguish the operation of markets for agricultural land from other input markets. In this section we discuss the implications of three such characteristics of land as a factor of production, namely that:

(*a*) the total supply of land available for all uses is more or less fixed in supply;

(b) in all economies there have developed a set of laws and customs regulating the control and use of land in agriculture; and
(c) land is peculiar as a factor of production in that every unit of it is somewhat different from every other, in particular, every unit of land is locationally unique.

5.2

It is usually said that land is fixed in supply and if by land we mean the surface area of the globe then this is of course correct. But when we refer to the supply of land we sometimes mean the supply of *agricultural land*, and the proportion of the earth's surface which can be cultivated is subject to fluctuations over time. By the use of labour and capital inputs, virgin land can be made suitable for cultivation, and it has even been possible to a limited extent to reclaim land from the sea. On the other hand, the quantity of land available for use by agriculture is gradually being reduced by urban development and, in spite of Ricardo's famous reference to the 'original and indestructible powers' of the soil (17) we now know that climatic changes, and some kinds of farming practice, can render once fertile land uncultivable. So the supply of *agricultural land* need not be fixed and can respond to changes in the amount paid by agriculture for its use.

Nevertheless, in most circumstances it is a useful approximation to regard the supply of agricultural land as fixed, and it is also helpful to begin by assuming that agriculture is the sole user of land. Under these assumptions, the same quantity of land will be made available for use by agriculture whatever its price, and the entire payment by agriculture for land will therefore come under our definition of economic rent. Rents will adjust to equate the quantity of land demanded with the (fixed) quantity supplied, and changes in land values or rents⁹ will take place as a result only of changes in the demand for land. Historically, the two longer term developments which we distinguished in the previous chapter as having a dominant, though contrasting, influence on the evolution of agricultural product prices – population growth and technological advance – have also probably had the major responsibility for changes in agricultural land values and rents.

If we assume first that there are no improvements in agricultural productivity, then population growth will increase the demand for agricultural products which will, in turn, increase the demand for farm inputs. The quantity supplied of labour and capital inputs can respond to this increase in demand, but the quantity of agricultural land supplied remains unchanged. The consequence would be a rise in land rents relative to prices of other farm inputs. It is this kind of picture that was, in fact, painted by Ricardo when he attempted to envisage the future course of economic development. He foresaw a gradual increase in the proportion of factor income accruing to landlords, an elimination of capitalist profits, and an end to economic growth. Population increases would be halted by the 'Malthusian checks' of famine and disease.

There is another way in which population growth could cause an increase in agricultural land values. If there is a tradition of small independent peasant farming in an area, a growth in population may cause an increase in the number of individuals willing to control agricultural land at any given level of rents. Clark (14) cites evidence of an association between density of agricultural population and land values in a number of countries. It is, however, difficult to establish the reason for such an association. It may simply be that good agricultural land is associated with both a large farming population and high rents. Alternatively, where transport costs are significant, we would expect the increase in the demand for food associated with rising population to cause higher rents in the more densely populated areas.

Clark (14) has assembled information from all over the world concerning agricultural rents and land prices in different time periods. In general, we find that real farm rents have tended to rise more or less continuously, but in many cases, particularly in the twentieth century, the proportion of total factor income received by landlords has fallen. The explanation for this is undoubtedly to be found in the impact of technological advance.

In the previous section we noted that many improvements in agricultural productivity have been associated with the introduction of new capital inputs. But a productivity improvement need not necessarily mean a relative increase in the use of capital inputs. A *neutral innovation* may be described as a change in the production function which, if there were no change in input or product prices, would be likely to increase the demand for all inputs in the same proportion. If an innovation is biased, the demand for one or more inputs is likely to increase more in proportion than the demand for the other inputs, and when account is taken of any decline in product prices because of the increase in supply which could follow the productivity improvement, the demand for some inputs may decline.

Another way of describing the kind of productivity improvements that have been adopted by agriculture, then, is to say that they have been biased towards capital inputs ('capital using') and have been land (and labour) saving. These land-saving innovations have counteracted the impact of population growth on land values.

5.3

It is probably still correct to say that, in most parts of the world, the market for agricultural land is not significantly affected by a demand for land in non-agricultural use. But in those countries which have experienced substantial industrialisation and which are also relatively densely populated, increasing attention is being directed towards the competition for land between agricultural and other uses. Table 4.2 gives some statistics of changes in the use of land in the United Kingdom between 1950 and 1970.

In view of the publicity which is given to the 'relentless urban encroachment on the countryside' the rate of transfer of land from agriculture to urban use may, at less than 0.1 per cent per annum, seem relatively modest. (The rate of transfer to urban use has quickened a little since 1970.)

Table 4.2   Land-use changes in the United Kingdom, 1950–70

	Agriculture	Forest and woodland	Urban	Other	Total
Land area in 1950 (thousand hectares)	20 255	1532	1652	653	24 092
Land area in 1965 (thousand hectares)	19 624	1817	1912	739	24 092
Percentage of total land area in 1950	84·1	6·4	6·8	2·7	100
Percentage of total land area in 1965	81·5	7·5	7·9	3·1	100
Annual average rate of land transfer 1960–70 (thousand hectares)	−47·6	+26·3	+19·7	+1·6	—
Annual average rate of land transfer 1960–70 (percentage of total land area)	−0·20	+0·11	+0·08	+0·01	—

Source: Champion (18).

Government restrictions on the use of land for urban development have created two separate land markets in the United Kingdom. The supply of land for urban use is restricted and such land has a much higher marginal value product than land in agricultural use. The marginal value product of land in farming has virtually no influence on which land is allocated to urban use, except in as much as planning permission is more readily given when poorer quality farming land is involved. As Michael Boddington puts it:

Land which is worth between £125 per hectare and £2500 per hectare in farming may achieve a value of £10 000 to £100 000 per hectare with the simple passage of planning consent. Hence, any variability in fertility is immediately obliterated by the value of situation and the right to build: most farmers would be glad of the opportunity to sell their very best land at the lowest price for development land (19).

In Table 4.2 we can see that in recent years more land in the United Kingdom has in fact been lost by agriculture to forestry than to urban use; after centuries of felling trees for fuel and timber, and clearing for agricultural use, the trend has been reversed. Most new tree planting is by the Government Forestry Commission, which has bought agricultural land on the open market at a price reflecting its value in agricultural use. It is, however, mainly 'poor' agricultural land which has been transferred to forestry whereas a large (and increasing) proportion of agricultural land transferred to urban use is regarded as 'good' agricultural land. A measure has been devised by Stamp (20) to express land transfers from agriculture in terms of production potential units.

Using the Stamp classification, Champion (18) concludes that between 1950 and 1965, although forestry accounted for slightly more of the land transferred from agriculture than did urban development, this represented a loss in the country's agricultural production potential of only 0·7 per cent compared to one of 2·9 per cent resulting from urban expansion. To put this loss in perspective it is worth noting that improvements in productivity and the increased use of capital inputs were sufficient during this period to offset in one average year the total losses in output resulting from ten years of land transfers from agriculture.

Rising income levels have recently been associated with another source of competition for the use of agricultural land (apart from that for urban growth) – that derived from the desire for the pursuit of recreational activities in the countryside. In part this development represents merely another source of demand for land in non-agricultural use, but many recreational activities are peculiar in that they do not require exclusive use of land. We thus have the development of dual (and even multi-) land use, with the factor of production land simultaneously being used to fulfil consumer wants in the form of both agricultural output and various recreational activities. It is perhaps surprising that recreation in the countryside and agricultural production can, in most cases, coexist without interfering too much with each other and indeed sometimes complementing one another. But there are, of course, many ways in which farming practice can be disturbed by recreational activity and conversely a modern, technically efficient and highly specialised farming industry is not always consistent with the visual amenity of rural areas (21).

There is, then, increasing competition for the use of the factor of production land between agriculture on the one hand, and forestry, urban development and countryside recreation on the other, and there are correspondingly increasing Government attempts to influence on a national scale the allocation of land between these competing uses. The reasons for such Government involvement, and the contribution that the subject matter of economics can make to public decision-making in land use, is something to which we return in Part II of this book.

5.4

The pattern of land ownership at any time reflects events which stretch well back in history and in each country there have grown up a set of laws and customs governing the transfer of land between owners and regulating the allocation of land to producers. We use the term *agricultural land tenure* to refer to the economic, legal and political arrangements regarding the ownership and management of agricultural land. There is a wide diversity of land tenure systems throughout the world[10] but, for the developed market economies, it is helpful to distinguish two broad categories, *owner-occupiership* and *tenancy*.

If a farmer is an owner-occupier he owns the land which he farms and is responsible for its maintenance. The tenant pays a (usually) annual rent to a landowner for the use of the land he farms. It is rather difficult to separate the ownership of agricultural land from the ownership of certain capital items – such as drainage, roads, and buildings, as all of these must be connected with a particular land area. For this reason it is usual in a tenancy system for the landlord to own these items of capital – known collectively as *landlord's capital* – and to hire them to the tenant. All other capital inputs are referred to as *tenant's capital*. Tenancy systems vary as to the exact division in the provision of capital inputs between tenant and landlord, but in general all those inputs which could, if necessary, be moved to another farm will be part of tenant's capital.

It is payment by the tenant for those inputs categorised as landlord's capital which leads to the confusion between the common use of the word 'rent' in farming, and the economist's definition of 'economic rent'. The total payment by a tenant to a landlord – agricultural rent – may now be divided into three parts, namely,

(*a*) a payment for those inputs known collectively as landlord's capital;
(*b*) transfer earnings;
(*c*) economic rent.

The division between (*b*) and (*c*) will vary depending upon whether we are considering transfer earnings from the point of view of the allocation of land to a single farming enterprise, to agriculture as a whole, or land in any use.

5.5

There are two main reasons why agricultural land cannot be regarded as a homogeneous factor of production. First, the productive potential of land varies, principally because of variations in soil type, but also because of local differences in climate and topography. We refer to these differences as *variations in land quality*. Second, the 'farm gate' prices of inputs and products vary on account of proximity to product and factor markets and this causes *locational variations* in agricultural land. The first of these features was included in Ricardo's theory of rents. A nineteenth century German landowner called von Thünen is usually credited as being the first writer to recognise the implications for land use of location in relation to agricultural markets. We may conveniently use the term '*economic potential*' to refer to variations in land as a factor of production in agriculture on account of differences in quality and location.

We can illustrate the relationship between the economic potential of land and agricultural rents by the use of a simplified example in which we assume that all land is divided into similar sized units and let to tenant farmers, that product and purchased input prices remain constant, and that rents are determined on a free market. In Fig. 4.7 the land area of a country is classified according to its economic potential on the horizontal axis in units numbered 1 to 100, with unit 1 being the most profitable land and unit 100 the least. The line R_1R_1 shows the excess of revenue over the cost of labour and other current costs which can be earned on land of different quality by a farmer of 'average' ability. We will refer, for convenience, to this excess as *net revenue* per hectare.

Out of net revenue the tenant must earn an income from farming. Farmers of course differ in ability, but there is no strong reason to believe that the difference between net revenue earned by a 'good' farmer and that earned by a 'poor' farmer will vary significantly with soil quality.

Thus if landlords accept as tenant the highest credible bidder, farm rents will equal the net revenue that can be earned by a farmer of 'average' ability less the income required by the 'average' tenant to prevent him from moving to another occupation. Farm rents will include payment for the use of items of landlord's capital, and the remainder will come under our definition of 'economic rent', since the land has no alternative use. The division of farm rent into economic rent and payment for use of landlord's capital is a notional one; landlords will continue to add capital inputs as long as the addition of such inputs results in an increase in the net revenue earned on the land exceeding the cost of supplying the capital inputs. To keep the example as simple as possible, the payment for landlord's capital is shown in Fig. 4.7 as constant over land of different economic potential.

In Fig. 4.7, then, land which is shown by the 20th unit on the horizontal axis will earn an average net revenue of £100 per hectare per annum. Of this the 'normal' farming income equals £30 per hectare and £70 per hectare is paid to landlords in farm rent. The cost to the landlord of supplying landlord's capital is shown as £30 per hectare, and economic rent is £40 per hectare. In our example, unit 80 would earn no economic rent, and units 81–100 would not be cultivated.

Ricardo's interest in the determination of agricultural rents arose out of a controversy over the high price of corn in Britain during the Napoleonic wars. On one side it was contended that prices were high because landlords were charging high rents. Ricardo, however, was one of a group which argued that the price of corn had been forced up by a shortage because of the disruption of the wars. This had increased the profitability of growing corn in Britain and competition by farmers had bid up land rents. Thus rents were high because the price of corn was high and not vice versa.

We can show the impact upon rents of a rise in grain prices in Fig. 4.7 by a rise in the net revenue line (to R_2R_2). Such a price rise would cause an increase in the net revenue that can be earned on all qualities of land. How will this increase in net revenue be distributed between farm income and farm rents? If there is a plentiful supply of prospective tenants of similar ability and income expectations to existing farmers there is no reason to expect average farm incomes to rise. Farm rents will be bid up and absorb the entire increase in net revenue and some poorer land will be brought into cultivation. (And, indeed, the plough did 'advance up the hillside' in Britain during the Napoleonic wars.)

However, if new entrants are less able or have higher income requirements than existing farmers, the rise in corn prices will cause the incomes of existing farmers to rise and not all the increase in net revenue per hectare will be absorbed in farm rents. Since this increase in the amount earned by existing

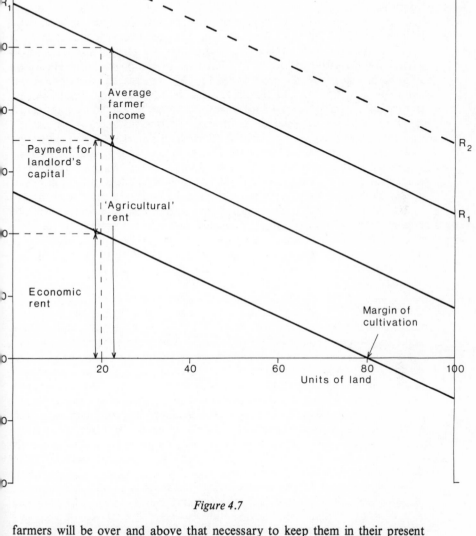

Figure 4.7

farmers will be over and above that necessary to keep them in their present occupation, it is itself a form of economic rent. It may be that there is a time interval before a sufficient number of new entrants of similar ability and income requirements to existing farmers become available, in which case the economic rent earned by existing farmers will be temporary. Some economists use the term *quasi rent* to refer to a payment to a factor of production which occurs because there is an increase in the demand for the factor which is fixed in supply in the short run, but for which there is a more elastic supply in the long run.

A few years after Ricardo had developed his theory of agricultural rents, von Thünen published a book called *The Isolated State* (23) in which he pointed out that transport costs to a market could be a source of important differences in land rents and land use. We can illustrate von Thünen's argument by a diagram similar to Fig. 4.7 except, in this case, we assume land of a single quality and classify land according to distance from a product market. In Fig. 4.8a the distance from the product market (M) is measured on the horizontal axis. The lines R_a, R_b, and R_c indicate the net revenue less 'normal' farmer income and payment for landlord's capital that can be earned by a farmer of average ability in the production of three alternative crops, A, B and C, assuming given prices for the three products at the market M. The lines slope down reflecting the cost of transporting the crop for sale in the market. Product A is a high value crop but costly to transport – either because it is bulky in relation to value or because it is perishable. Product C does not sell at a high enough price to be able to compete with product A for land near to the market centre, but it has much lower transport costs and is therefore competitive with product A at a distance from the market. Product B is competitive in an intermediate distance from M. The theory therefore predicts the emergence of product zones surrounding a market centre. These are shown in Fig. 4.8b and it is sometimes possible to detect such circular areas of land use around market centres.

Von Thünen discussed other locational aspects of land use in addition to the simple impact of product transport costs, and subsequent writers such as Lösch (24), Dunn (25) and Chisholm (26) have extended and developed the argument. But as agricultural location theory has become more sophisticated, the importance of location in relation to factor and product markets has declined due to a fall in transport costs relative to other agricultural production costs. A modern theory of the free market determination of farm rents must incorporate both the locational and quality characteristics of agricultural land.

We have referred to the 'margin of cultivation' in connection with both quality and locational aspects of agricultural land. However, economists sometimes talk about two kinds of cultivation margins – the *extensive margin* of cultivation and the *intensive margin* of cultivation. The extensive margin is the one referred to above. It indicates that, for some given set of economic circumstances, land of poor quality or land distant from markets might not be brought into cultivation. It is called the extensive margin because the cultivated land of poorest quality or least desirable location is likely to be used less intensively – that is, a smaller quantity of labour and capital inputs used per unit of land – than land of better quality and/or more desirable location. The intensive margin describes the quantity of labour and capital per hectare used on land of the highest economic potential.

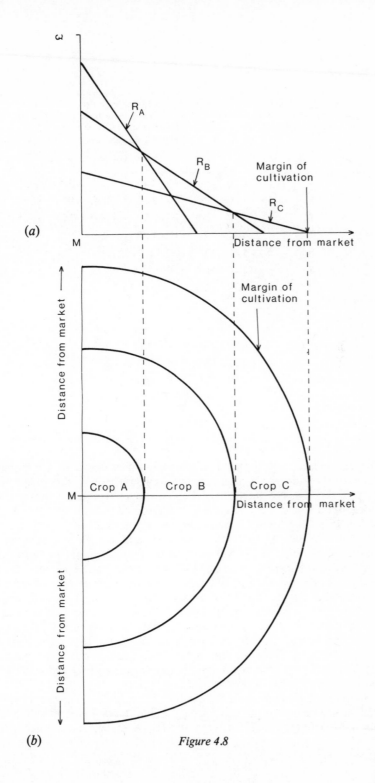

(a)

(b)

Figure 4.8

Table 4.3

Bundles of labour and capital inputs (Value £100)	Increase in total revenue (£ per hectare per annum) resulting from the application of each additional bundle of labour and capital on land of quality grade:							
	A	B	C	D	E	F	G	H
1	160	150	140	130	120	110	100	(90)
2	150	140	130	120	110	100	(90)	
3	140	130	120	110	100	(90)		
4	130	120	110	100	(90)			
5	120	110	100	(90)				
6	110	100	(90)					
7	100	(90)						
Intensive margin of cultivation								
8	(90)							
Total revenue (£)	910	750	600	460	330	210	100	–
Total cost (£)	700	600	500	400	300	200	100	–
Net revenue (£)	210	150	100	60	30	10	0	–
'Normal' farmer income (£60, say)	60	60	60	60	60	60	60	–
Economic rent (£)	150	90	40	0	–	–	–	–

(Columns D and E are separated by the vertical label: *Extensive margin of cultivation*)

The distinction is illustrated in Table 4.3, which describes a hypothetical example of the increase in total revenue brought about by the application of successive 'bundles' of labour and capital inputs (combined in some fixed proportion) on land of varying quality. It is assumed that all agricultural land is divided into holdings of equal area and the holdings ranked according to land quality, with grade 'A' being the best land, and grade 'H' the worst. For example, the first bundle of £100 worth of labour and capital applied to grade B land results in a total revenue of £150, the second bundle increases the total revenue by £140, and so on. The intensive margin is the number of bundles of labour and capital which reduces the revenue added by the last bundle on grade A land to £100 – in the case of Table 4.3, this is the seventh bundle. The extensive margin is given by the poorest quality land which is just capable of providing an acceptable income from farming (and which therefore earns no economic rent). In Table 4.3 this is 'grade D' land. We would expect both margins to vary with general advances in farming technology and with changes in the relationship between product and input prices.

A simplifying assumption in the example illustrated by Table 4.3 is that all land is farmed in holdings of equal area. Land of 'grade E and F' quality might still be capable of generating an acceptable farmer income if combined in larger units, and it is of course common to find poorer quality (or poorly located) land combined in much larger holdings than good quality land (or land located close to markets). There is, however, more to the determination of farm size than land quality, and it is on the question of the forces determining the size structure of the farming sector that we conclude the present chapter.

6 The economics of size in farming

6.1

This chapter has been concerned so far with the operation of factor markets viewed as the mechanism by which quantities of individual inputs are allocated to agricultural production. The remainder of the chapter is devoted to a consideration of the forces determining the distribution of resources of all kinds among different farm firms within the farming industry, or to put it more crudely, the determination of the size distribution of farm firms.

There are two problems which must be overcome if we are to develop a theory of the determination of the firm size distribution within agriculture. The first of these can be stated quite simply: What do we mean by farm size? The second is that the implications of the conventional theory of the farm firm, as expounded in Chapter 2 of this book, seem to be the emergence of a much more uniform pattern of farm size (however measured) than the pattern observed in most advanced economies.

6.2

Most authorities would agree that 'farm size' is something to do with the quantity of productive resources controlled by the farm firm. The most common measure of size has always been land area, but this suffers from the obvious disadvantage that the proportion of land to other farm inputs varies considerably between different farm types. Other measures have been invented, usually in order to assist in the administration of government policies relating to farm size. In the United Kingdom, the term *standard man days* (SMD) has been used as a measure to distinguish those farms which can be regarded as 'viable' for assistance from those which cannot be so regarded. (A 'full-time farm' is defined as one which is thought, on average, likely to require at least 275 SMDs per year.) But none of these measures can be acceptable in a theory of farm size, as they either attempt to measure size by reference to one resource only, or they reflect a normative view of resource requirements based on averaged input–output data.[11]

We know that when a producer takes decisions concerning a change in what he regards as his size of business, he talks in terms of gaining control of more 'capital'. What he is referring to would be more correctly described as *money capital* and access to increased quantities of money capital enables him to increase the quantity of physical capital inputs which he controls. Now, in the last resort, agriculture's capital stock is a collection of physical inputs and a fundamental measurement of a farm's capital stock must be in a multiplicity of physical units. Nevertheless, we are very well aware that there is a strong link between the use of money capital and the stock of capital inputs on a farm.

For most statistical and administrative purposes, a monetary valuation of farm capital is probably the most helpful representation of farm size, and changes in a farm's control of money capital is the best indication of growth in farm size. But can money capital also provide the requisite measure in a theory of farm size distribution? The answer is that it can, but that it is not entirely satisfactory. To value a farm capital stock we must not only arrive at a satisfactory set of prices in order to bring together dissimilar inputs in a common monetary valuation – a problem which is, of course, encountered whenever we wish to aggregate two or more inputs or products – we must have some procedure for dealing with the dimension of time.

The reflection of value over time is one of the strengths of farm capital as an indicator of farm size and in particular of growth in farm size. But the time dimension means that, if we take an item of farm capital such as, for example, a tractor, there are three alternative methods of valuing it. In order to illustrate this problem, a brief excursion into the principles of discounting and compounding is required.

The central notion in capital valuation is that time has a price. When a producer purchases an item of capital equipment he could as an alternative have loaned the same sum of money and received a return on it in the form of a 'rate of interest'. If he borrows the sum required to purchase the input, he must pay interest on that amount as long as the loan is outstanding. Consider, for example, the purchase of an item of farm capital equipment which, for given product prices and technical conditions of production, is expected to increase farm revenue by £100 per annum for six years (whereupon the equipment is worn out and has no productive potential on this or any other farm). This net revenue stream is shown in the second column of Table 4.4. The first increase in revenue occurs at the end of the first year, whereas the input is purchased at the beginning of year 1 (which in the Table 4.4 is called the end of 'year 0').

Now, assume that the producer is able to borrow or lend funds at an interest rate of 10 per cent per annum. Column 3 of Table 4.4 shows the way a sum of money of £400, invested at the end of year 0, will accumulate if it receives a rate of interest of 10 per cent per annum compound. At the end of one year it has accumulated to $(£400) + (0 \cdot 1 \times £400) = £440$, at the end of two years the accumulated sum will be $(£440) + (0 \cdot 1 \times £440) = £484$, and so on.

Column 4 of Table 4.4 shows the similar accumulation of a sum of £435·53 (the reason for the choice of this odd figure will emerge in due course). Thus, in our example, columns 3 and 4 show the financial return foregone when a capital input, the purchase price of which is respectively £400 and £435·53, is added to the farm capital stock, given a rate of interest of 10 per cent per annum.

In column 5 of Table 4.4 we apply the same compounding procedure to the stream of net revenue generated by the addition of the item of fixed equipment to the capital stock; it shows the sum that past instalments of net revenue will

Table 4.4

1	2	3	4	5	6	7	8
Year end		Compounded value of £400 at end year 0	Compounded value of £435·53 at end year 0	Compounded value of £100 per annum	Discounted (present) value of £100 per annum	3–5	4–5
0	—	400·00	435·53	—	435·53	400·00	435·53
1	100	440·00	479·08	100·00	379·08	340·00	379·08
2	100	484·00	526·99	210·00	316·99	274·00	316·99
3	100	532·40	579·68	331·00	248·68	201·40	248·68
4	100	585·64	637·65	464·10	173·55	121·54	173·55
5	100	644·20	701·42	610·51	90·91	33·69	90·91
6	100	708·62	771·56	771·56	—	-62·94	—

have accumulated to if each instalment is invested at a rate of 10 per cent when it is received. For example, at the end of the second year the past value of net revenue compounded to the present (end year 2) is £100 + (£100 × 1·1) = £210, and at the end of three years it is £100 + (£210 × 1·1) = £331, and so on.

In column 6 of Table 4.4 we answer a different question: What is the present value at the beginning of each year of the remainder of the stream of net revenue? Consider, for example, the equipment at the end of the fifth year of its life, when there is to come only one further sum of £100. We ask, 'What is the sum of money which, if invested now at a rate of 10 per cent per annum, will accumulate to £100 one year hence?' (End year 6.) The answer is £90·91 (= £100/1·1) and we call this the *present value* of £100 one year in the future. At the end of the fourth year, then, the present value of the future revenue stream (£100 in one year's time and a further £100 in two years' time) is

$$\frac{£100}{1·1} + \frac{£100}{(1·1) \times (1·1)} = £173·55$$

The present value of the future stream of £100 per annum for six years is, at the end of year 0, £435·53.

Now, using the information in the Table 4.4, there are two alternative methods of valuing the capital item in any particular year of its life. On the one hand we could regard its value simply as the present value of its future stream of net revenue – that is, the figures in column 6 of the table. Alternatively, we could take a historic view of its value and take the purchase price of the capital item less the amount it is estimated to have earned in the past, both compounded to the present. This method of valuation is found by taking column 5 from column 3 (when the purchase price is £400) and column 5 from column 4 when the purchase price is £435·53. The two methods of valuation correspond if (and only if) the purchase price of the input is the same as the present value of the net revenue stream it generates. (Thus, in our example, the figures in column 8 are the same as those in column 6.)

The occurrence of equality between the purchase price of an input and the sum of the net revenue stream it generates, discounted to the time the input is purchased, may not require such an extraordinary coincidence as might seem at first. We know that the profit maximising firm must equate the marginal value product of an input with its price. If we extend this principle to take into account the price of time for a durable input, then we would expect the profit maximising firm to employ units of capital as long as the present (discounted) value of the net revenue stream (or stream of future marginal value products) of the input exceeds its price per unit.

Thus, for profit to be maximised over time, if we take any capital input which can be divided into reasonably small units, the present value of an additional unit of the input at the time of its purchase will equal the cost of an additional unit of the input. The conclusion is that, for the profit maximising firm which achieves equilibrium in a world of unchanging input prices, product prices, and technology, our measures will coincide. But the world does change, and changes in prices and technology will cause the measures to diverge and perhaps more importantly, will mean that the capital valuation of a farm will vary not only as a result of changes in the quantity of inputs controlled by the firm over time but because of changes in the underlying prices which enable us to value them. That, in essence, is the problem of measuring size in terms of capital valuation.[12]

Earlier we mentioned that there were three alternative methods of valuing an item of farm capital and so far we have mentioned only two. The third is its off-farm value. It is reasonable to presume that an item of farm capital could be sold at a price which corresponds to the discounted value of the net revenue it can generate on a typical farm, if the cost of transferring it between farms is insignificant – an example might be a tractor. However, a feature of many agricultural inputs (we noted this in Chapter 2, section 5) was that their off-farm salvage value is thought to be significantly less than their value in current use – in which case the present value method of valuation will exceed the sale value.

Finally, we should note that the accounting convention of valuing an asset by regularly depreciating it over its lifetime will give a capital valuation which will not normally correspond with any of these three measures.

6.3

The second problem which arises in connection with the size distribution of farm firms is that the conventional theory of the farm firm appears to suggest a much more uniform pattern of size than is observed to apply. The term 'increase in scale' was used in Chapter 2 to refer to an increase in a firm's use of all inputs in some fixed proportion. There is, however, no reason why, for any set of input prices, the ratio of inputs in the least cost combination should remain constant as output rises. This is why changes in the use of inputs in some fixed proportion cannot form a measure of business size. It is nevertheless the nature of returns to scale which is mainly responsible for the varying relationship between profit and business size.

In Fig. 2.12 we drew a 'long run average cost curve for a firm' which enveloped a series of short run average cost curves – the assumption being that 'for a given set of input prices, the quantity of fixed factors of production used in each case is such as to minimise the average cost of producing Q_1, Q_2 and Q_3 units of output'. The decline and subsequent rise of the long run average cost curve was said to reflect increasing and then decreasing returns to scale. We noted that most economists took 'the view that, if it really were possible to increase the use of all resources in some fixed proportion, constant returns to scale would ensue.' However, because there are some inputs which cannot be split into small units it was likely that, initially, increasing returns to scale would apply to those inputs, the quantity used of which can be varied. 'Just which inputs will be included in returns to scale will depend on the size of farm – and thus whether or not a particular resource has to be regarded as indivisible or not – and the time period under consideration, which affects which factors can be varied.' The elimination of wastage in the use of inputs which cannot be broken down into small units should therefore cause the long run average cost curve to decline as output increases. However, as long as the quantities available of one or more inputs are fixed for the farm, the long run average cost curve will eventually begin to rise as decreasing returns will begin to operate to those inputs which can be increased. In this context, then, an industry, operating in a perfect market, will be in long run equilibrium when the typical firm is producing at the minimum point on its long run average cost curve.

Now, there are two points which arise over this treatment of the forces determining the size of farm firms. First, the implications of relating the determination of the size distribution of farm firm to the minimum point on the long run average cost curve are that, for a similar type of farming, the optimum size of farm will be much the same for all producers. In the short run, different firms will find themselves with different bundles of fixed factors, but in the long run, all are free to choose whichever combination of inputs they wish, including fixed factors. Yet we find a very wide range of business size to exist and it is difficult to explain this variation on the basis of imperfections in the system, or indeed by differences in the 'objectives' of producers. Nor does it seem possible that such a wide diversity of farm size could merely be the result of a perpetual state of disequilibrium, with firms continually adjusting to the same optimum size (which is itself continually changing as the economic environment evolves).

The second question mark over this approach to farm size is why there should necessarily be any constraint on the ability of the farm firm to increase the quantities used of all resources, if we are prepared, that is, to take a long enough view of the decision making process, as we must when we are considering the factors influencing the long-term growth of farm firms. If there are no such constraints, then we would expect average cost to decline as the benefits of economies of scale were felt. Eventually perhaps all possibilities for economies might be exhausted and extra output would be obtained at a constant rather than declining average cost. This would remove some of the impetus to increasing firm size but would still not impose a constraint on continuing growth of farm firms and one would have thought that a firm would need to grow very large relative to the observed size of farm firms before all possibilities for reducing economies of scale had disappeared. But we find that the agricultural sectors of market economies normally comprise many hundreds of thousands of farm firms. Clearly there must be some constraint on growth of farm size to prevent the kind of growth and reduction in numbers of firms that has taken place in many other industries.

The conventional theory of the farm firm, therefore, when applied to the determination of the size structure of the agricultural industry, runs into two related problems since it appears to predict the emergence of (i) fewer farm firms and (ii) farms of a more uniform size, than is observed in practice. In relation to these problems, there has grown up at the University of Reading a set of ideas, originated by Tuck (29, 30, 31) and developed and applied by

Ritson (32) and Upton (33), which attempt to explain the determination of the pattern of farm business size in relation to variations in managerial ability. The theory is an extremely effective one in that:

(*a*) it has intuitive appeal because it uses the idea of return to money capital employed in the farm business, and we know that, in a practical context, it is access to and return on capital which seems to control the growth of farm firms; and

(*b*) it is successful in predicting the emergence of just the variety and fluctuating pattern of farm business size that has been observed by many researchers, including for example, Harrison (34, 35) in parallel work, also carried out at Reading University.

The theory nevertheless does possess the drawback of some uncertainty over the measurement of 'size', a problem that seems likely to be present in any theory of the determination of farm business size.

There follows a brief outline of this approach to the pattern of farm business size. Readers may look at the references cited for a more detailed coverage.

6.4

We referred at the beginning of this section to the rate of interest on loanable funds as 'the price of time'. The 'time' which must be paid for in the context of agricultural production is the interval between the payment for the use of resources and the sale of the resulting output. The conventional treatment of the theory of the farm firm, which is in terms of relationships between cost and revenue, ignores this question of time in the sense that any problem associated with the requirement to purchase inputs prior to the receipt of revenue from the sale of output is assumed away. It is the provision of money capital which allows this time interval to be bridged. In order to appreciate the process by which money capital is provided for an agricultural industry it is necessary to consider, briefly, the aggregate composition of a nation's output and income.

In any time period, the output of an economy can conveniently be divided into two categories: output consumed within that time period (or added to stocks while its equivalent is removed from stocks for consumption), which we call *consumption* (*C*); and output not consumed within the time period, which includes net changes in stocks of goods for consumption but which consists in the main of capital goods, which we call *investment* (*I*). Thus we have the identity

$$\text{National output} \equiv C + I$$

For simplicity, we ignore international trade transactions and government transactions, which would have to appear in more elaborate equations of this kind. We also ignore the distinction between planned and unplanned investment.

The total income earned by factors of production in any time period can similarly be divided into two categories, income spent on consumption and income not so spent, known as savings. Thus

$$\text{National income} \equiv C + S$$

The fact that national output has a value and sells at a price is directly related to the payments to factors of production in the production process. In fact the sale of output provides the funds out of which such payments are made (here taken to include 'payments' of profit). So that, in value terms, national output must equal national income, and hence saving must equal investment.

Another way of putting this is to say that, if all income was spent by consumers as soon as it was received, then the whole of national output would have to be of consumer goods. It follows that, in order to enable the economy to produce products which will subsequently be used further in the production process, someone somewhere in the economy must be prepared to withhold income from consumption. In this respect the time interval between the generation of national income by the production of capital goods, and the eventual embodiment of such goods in final consumption, is vital. The longer this time interval, other things being equal, the greater is the current sacrifice made by the community in the form of income being withheld from consumption.

In the case of agriculture, the farmer is often the individual who withholds income from consumption expenditure (i.e. saves it) and then invests his own savings in his own business. In the economy as a whole, however, those individuals and institutions which are willing and able to withhold income from consumption expenditure are often different from those who control the use of resources in production. It is the function of the *credit institutions* to transfer what is, in reality, an option to commit a certain quantity of resources to the production process, created by the individual who withholds income from consumption ('the saver') to the individual who commits resources to production ('the producer'). It is usually the case that individuals who wish to be producers are prepared to pay for the option to commit resources to the production process. Similarly, individuals who withhold income from consumption expect to receive a price for so doing. This price is the rate of interest on loanable funds.

(More correctly, it is known as 'pure interest' to distinguish it from market interest rates which can include elements attributable to such things as administrative costs, an allowance for risk, and inflationary expectations.)

The individual producer must therefore have control of money capital in order to be able to use capital inputs, and he must not only pay a price for capital inputs, he must pay a premium, in the form of the rate of interest on money capital. This will be paid to credit institutions, when money capital is borrowed; when a producer supplies his own money capital, its price is an opportunity cost, represented by the rate of interest it could earn if lent to a credit institution.

Every item of money capital employed in the business will have its physical counterpart in productive resources.

Where money capital is used to finance payments to labour or land, the physical counterpart of the money capital comprises the goods which can be purchased by workers or landowners with rent or wages. (When rent and wages are paid in kind prior to the production of produce, then it is not difficult to view such goods as part of the capital inputs required by the farm.)

However, a unit of capital which is needed for the use of a particular resource will not normally correspond to the cost of that resource which would appear in an annual account. This will only be the case when the full cost of the resource must be paid at the beginning of the production period and the full return from the use of the resource occurs at the end of the production period, whereupon the resource has no further production potential. More commonly, the cost of production attributed to a particular input and the amount of money capital required for its use will differ. When there is a flow of output during the production period under consideration, and when all of an input need not be purchased at the onset of the production period, the money capital required will be less than the cost of production. For those capital inputs which contribute to output for a period in excess of one production period, the quantity of money capital tied up in the input will exceed the cost attributed to the input in an annual account. This variation in the relationship between the cost attributable to an input and the quantity of money capital required for its use is related to a distinction commonly made between *working* (or *circulating*) *capital* and *fixed capital*. Roughly, we could say that working capital is the name given to the money capital associated with those inputs which require a quantity of money capital which is less than the annual sum paid for the inputs, and fixed capital refers to those inputs which require more money capital for their use than the cost usually attributed to them in an annual account.

The fact that money capital is required for the use of all productive resources, and that a price, in the form of the rate of interest on loanable funds, must be paid for the use of every unit of money capital, means that we can view the financial relationships between inputs and outputs in the production process in terms of the relationship between the cost of extra units of money capital and the return from the use of money capital. We define *marginal return to money capital* (which may be negative) as the excess of the additional (annual) revenue over the additional (annual) cost derived from the use of one extra unit of money capital in the firm. The extra unit of money capital might be used to purchase any combination of inputs, which might in turn be used to produce any product. The use of extra units of money capital in a business will continue to add to profit as long as the marginal return to money capital exceeds the marginal cost of money capital (the rate of interest). Restated in terms which take account of the use of money capital (and therefore including the price which must be paid to bridge the time interval between the payment for inputs and the sale of produce), the position of profit maximisation for a firm will occur when the marginal return to money capital, wherever and however it is allocated within the farm business, equals the marginal cost of money capital.

If we return to the example of the purchase of an item of capital equipment used in section 5.2 we can reformulate the approach taken in Table 4.4 to be in terms of marginal return and marginal cost of money capital. To do so we must transform the six-year example into annual terms by assuming a succession of six-year cycles, with the cost of the machine being the depreciation bill over six years. If then we take the case where the machine costs £435·53, the marginal return to the money capital required for its use will be the difference between the extra revenue brought in from the use of the machine less the extra costs incurred as a result of the purchase of the machine. Over six years, this is £600·00 − £435·53 = £164·47 − an average annual flow of £27·41. If we take as the amount of money capital tied up in the machine the average capital valuation of the machine during its life, then the average money capital required in any one year will be one-sixth of the sum of the amounts in either column 6 or 8 in Table 4.4, i.e. £274·1. With the rate of interest on borrowed funds equal to 10 per cent per annum, the annual cost of using this capital is £27·41. Thus, in this example, if the price of the input is £435·53 and the rate of interest is 10 per cent, the marginal return to money capital employed in this use equals the marginal cost of capital. This is the result we would expect, since previously we discovered that the price of the input equalled the discounted stream of net revenue it generated.

If, alternatively, the machine is priced at £400·00, the marginal return to money capital increases to £33·33 per annum, but we now have the problem that the two different methods of valuing the machine differ and therefore we have two alternative methods of estimating the quantity of money capital tied up in this item of capital equipment during its life. In both cases, however, the marginal return to money capital now exceeds its marginal cost.

If we take one of the possible measures of capital value − accepting that this may be an arbitrary choice − we can illustrate the idea of optimum farm business size as in Fig. 4.9. The horizontal axis measures the prospective increment in money capital allocated to a farm business for the coming time period. The line *MTP* described the relationship between increase in farm business size and marginal return to money capital for a profit maximising firm assuming that all output technically possible with any given quantity of inputs is successfully achieved − it has been referred to by Tuck as the *maximum technical potential*. The maximum technical potential is shown as rising as business size is increased and possibilities for economies of scale are exploited,[13] and gradually levelling off as further possibilities for scale economies diminish. Small positive increments in money capital imply a decline in the capital valuation (i.e. the 'size') of the farm, since some new capital will be required to offset the depreciation of the existing capital stock. A negative increment in money capital invested in the business implies the sale of some existing assets.

In practice, the presence of uncertainty over the outcome of future events, and the fallibility of farmers and farm managers in identifying and maintaining appropriate resource combinations, will mean that the maximum technical potential will rarely, if ever, be attained. The marginal return to money capital

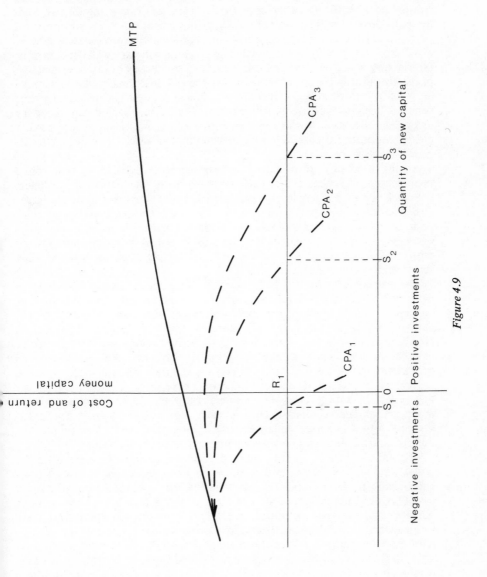

Figure 4.9

must therefore be risk discounted. In agriculture, the management function is traditionally associated with one person, or with a single identifiable group, and it is not possible to isolate the appropriate degree of discounting for risk from the individual or individuals within which the management function resides. For this reason, the extent to which any particular farm business might be expected to attain its maximum technical potential will vary with the farmer or farm manager in question, and it is central to our theory of the determination of the size distribution of farm firms that the risk that a particular farm business will fail to achieve its maximum technical potential in the coming time period is likely to increase as the quantity of additional capital considered for immediate allocation to the firm becomes greater and therefore represents a greater proportional change in scale beyond that at which an individual's past performance is known.

As the absolute size of farm business increases, it is likely that actual performance will depart more substantially from the maximum technical potential due to the problems of ensuring adequate supervision of the larger business. Thus in formal terms it can be argued that diseconomies of scale begin to operate as farm business size becomes relatively large because there is one factor of production which cannot be increased in proportion with all others, even in the long run – the factor of production which aims at providing supervision and management.

The marginal return to money capital, discounted for the risk that the individual in question will not attain the maximum technical potential for that business, is called by Tuck the *credible prospective achievement*. In Fig. 4.9, the curves CAP_1, CAP_2 and CAP_3 represent (for three different hypothetical farm firms possessing the same kind of productive process and for a particular moment in time when all are operating at the same scale), the credible prospective achievement of three individuals, and these differ on account of the assessment of managerial ability and farming experience. The optimum allocation of new capital (i.e. change in business size when the increment in capital is made net of depreciation) occurs in each case where the risk discounted marginal return to capital equals the rate of interest, R_1. At a later moment of time, of course, the situation will very probably have changed again.

The interest rate R_1 is that charged or received (ignoring administration costs) on risk free loans, and is therefore only applicable where all risks connected with the farm business are taken by the producer. Although it is the case that a substantial proportion of farm capital is privately owned by farm families (34), the credit institutions are the principal providers of capital funds for growth. For this reason, Tuck stresses the significant role of the agricultural credit institutions in identifying those producers with *proven managerial ability* and thus determining the pattern of growth in farm businesses. If credit institutions take a similar view to that taken by individuals '2' and '3' of their prospective achievement, then the institutions will limit the quantity of extra capital they provide to that necessary, in the coming time period, to achieve the business size implied by points S_2 and S_3 respectively, and they will charge a rate of interest in excess of R_1 to take account of whatever proportion of production risks they themselves bear (the division of risks depending on what security is attached to the loan). In the case of individual '1' the optimum amount of new capital is negative – in other words, if the individual takes a credible view of his prospective future achievement in the light of past performance, he can expect a higher return if he sells some items of capital equipment or land, and invests a quantity of money capital S_1O at interest rate R_1.

Thus it is argued that the optimum size of farm business is a balance between the economies of size in farming and the risk that an individual will fail to achieve the maximum potential return to increments of money capital in his

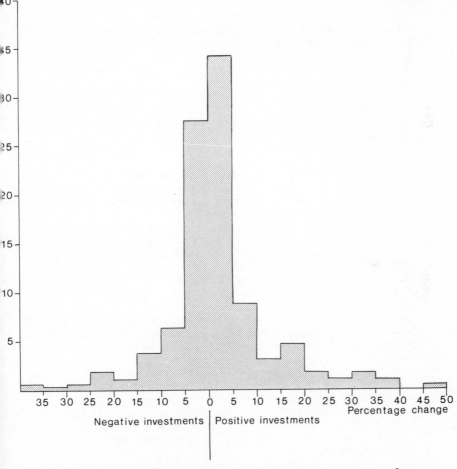

Figure 4.10   Distribution of farms according to investment as a percentage of assets (England, 1969). Source: Harrison (35)

business. The existence of a farming industry which continues to comprise many hundreds of thousands of farm businesses can be explained as a result of the incidence of this balance, and the theory predicts the emergence of a wide variety of size of business in farming. Furthermore, it will be a size pattern which is in a constant state of flux, as farmers gain experience on the one hand, or on the other prove that they are not capable of providing adequate management on the larger farm. Indeed, it is a picture that one would have expected would look rather like that illustrated in Fig. 4.10, which is taken from Harrison's study of farm businesses in England (35).

Notes

[1] The appendix to Chapter 2 does cover this approach to the profit maximising solution for our simple production example, although the text of the chapter does not.

[2] This and subsequent values for x, y, and a in this example have been rounded to two decimal places.

[3] The term 'economic rent' is a rather unfortunate one. The word 'economic' is often omitted and economists refer just to 'factor rents'. It can easily be confused with the alternative meaning of 'a payment to landlords for the use of land and buildings'.

[4] Since 1966, the National Union of Agricultural and Allied Workers (NUAAW).

[5] A summary of this research is given in Chapter 3 of Cowling, Metcalf and Rayner (5).

[6] The term *immobility* of agricultural labour is used in a rather imprecise way to refer to many of the reasons postulated for the failure of agricultural workers (as well as farmers and family workers) to respond to wage differentials. See, for example, Newby (9).

[7] The word 'capital' can have a much deeper meaning than its use in this section where it simply describes items of machinery, buildings, fertiliser, and so on. The idea of the allocation of 'capital' to farm businesses as the force determining their pattern of growth is discussed in section 6.

[8] Another area already encountered is in the study of the occupational immobility of farmers and farm workers (9). For a discussion of the use of sociology in agricultural economics, see Gasson (10).

[9] Although there are reasons why land prices and rents need not always move in accord, we should remember that, in essence, 'land has value because it can earn rent' (14) and we are here considering factors which will influence both agricultural land prices and land rents.

[10] One system which has received a lot of attention from agricultural economists, is that of *share cropping*, where the payment for land is a proportion of output. For a recent contribution, plus a list of the principal references, see Sutinen (22).

[11] At the time of writing, the European Community appears to be moving towards a farm size classification system loosely based on the value added concept. Value added is the total value of farm sales per time period less the value of inputs purchased from other firms.

[12] For a number of years now, there has raged a controversy over the interpretation of 'money capital' as an aggregation of a national capital stock. The major question to which this debate has been directed is the distribution of the national product

between capital and labour and this does not concern us here. However, it is likely that one side of the debate would readily accept the idea of a theory of the determination of size structure of the agricultural industry based on the concept of money capital, and the other would not. For an account of the 'capital controversy' see Harcourt (27). Some of the implications for farm planning are discussed by Upton (28).

[13] For a contemporary analysis of the evidence concerning economies of size in farming, see Britton and Hill (36) and Madden (37).

References

(1) Bottomley, J. A. 'The paradox of factor–pricing in underdeveloped rural areas.' *Journal of Agricultural Economics*, Vol. XXIV, No. 3, Sept. 1973.

(2) Self, P. & Storing, H. *The State and the Farmer*, Chap. VII. London, Allen & Unwin, 1962.

(3) Mills, F. D. 'The National Union of Agricultural Workers.' *Journal of Agricultural Economics*, Vol. XVI, No. 2, Dec. 1964.

(4) Ministry of Agriculture, Fisheries and Food. *Agricultural Labour in England and Wales*. London, 1975.

(5) Cowling, K., Metcalf, D. & Rayner, A. J. *Resource Structure of Agriculture: An Economic Analysis*. Oxford, Pergamon, 1970.

(6) Marsh, J. & Ritson, C. *Agricultural policy and the Common Market*. Chatham House/PEP, London, 1971.

(7) Hathaway, D. E. & Perkins, B. 'Farm labour mobility, migration and income distribution.' *American Journal of Agricultural Economics*, Vol. 50, No. 2, May 1968.

(8) Bellerby, J. R. *et al*. *Agriculture and Industry: Relative Income*. London, Macmillan, 1956.

(9) Newby, H. 'The low earnings of agricultural workers: a sociological approach.' *Journal of Agricultural Economics*, Vol. XXIII, No. 1, Jan. 1972.

(10) Gasson, R. 'Use of sociology in agricultural economics.' *Journal of Agricultural Economics*, Vol. XXII, No. 1, Jan. 1971.

(11) Rogers, E. M. & Shoemaker, F. E. *Communications of Innovations: A Cross-cultural Approach*. New York, Free Press, 1971. (Revised edition of (12).)

(12) Rogers, E. M. *Diffusion of Innovations*. New York, Free Press, 1962.

(13) Jones, G. E. 'The diffusion of agricultural innovations.' *Journal of Agricultural Economics*, Vol. XV, No. 3, June 1963.

(14) Clark, C. 'The value of agricultural land.' Oxford, Pergamon, 1973. (This is basically an enlarged version of (15).) (Including, as chapter 2, (16).)

(15) Clark, C. 'The value of agricultural land.' *Journal of Agricultural Economics*, Vol. XX, No. 1, Jan. 1969.

(16) Clark, C. 'Von Thünen's "Isolated State".' *Oxford Economic Papers*, Nov. 1967.

(17) Ricardo, D. Vol. 1: *Works and Correspondence. On the Principles of Political Economy and Taxation* (ed. P. Sraffa). Cambridge University Press, 1951.

(18) Champion, A. G. 'Competition for agricultural land.' In *Agricultural Resources* (eds. A. Edwards & A. Rogers). London, Faber, 1974.

(19) Boddington, M. A. B. 'The assessment of agricultural land.' In *Agricultural Resources* (eds. A. Edwards & A. Rogers). London, Faber, 1974.

(20) Stamp, L. D. *Applied Geography*, London, Penguin, 1960.
(21) Westmacott, R. & Worthington, T. 'New Agricultural Landscapes.' Countryside Commission, London, HMSO, 1974.
(22) Sutinen, J. G. 'The rational choice of share leasing and implications for efficiency.' *American Journal of Agricultural Economics*, Vol. 57, No. 4, Nov. 1975.
(23) Hall, P. (ed.) 'Von Thünen's "Isolated State".' Oxford University Press, 1966.
(24) Lösch, A. *The Economics of Location*. New Haven, 1954.
(25) Dunn, E. S. *The Location of Agricultural Production*. Gainesville, University of Florida Press. 1954.
(26) Chisholm, M. *Rural Settlement and Land Use: an Essay in Location*. London, Hutchinson, 1962.
(27) Harcourt, G. C. *Some Cambridge Controversies in the Theory of Capital*. Cambridge University Press, 1972.
(28) Upton, M. 'Capital theory and farm production economics.' *Journal of Agricultural Economics*, Vol. XXVII, No. 3, Sept. 1976.
(29) Tuck, R. H. *An Introduction to the Principles of Agricultural Economics*, Chaps. 7 & 8. Longman, 1961.
(30) Tuck, R. H. 'A reconsideration of the theory of agricultural credit.' *Journal of Agricultural Economics*, Vol. VII, No. 1, Jan. 1956.
(31) Tuck, R. H. *An Essay on the Economic Theory of Rank*. Oxford, Blackwell, 1954.
(32) Ritson, C. 'Economic growth and the optimum scale of enterprise in farming.' *Journal of Agricultural Economics*, Vol. XXIII, No. 3, Sept. 1972.
(33) Upton, M. *Farm Production Economics and Resource Use*, Chap. 8. Oxford University Press, 1976.
(34) Harrison, A. 'The Financial Structure of Farm Businesses.' University of Reading, Department of Agricultural Economics and Management. Miscellaneous Study No. 53, 1972.
(35) Harrison, A. 'Farmers and Farm Businesses in England.' University of Reading, Department of Agricultural Economics and Management. Miscellaneous Study No. 62, 1975.
(36) Britton, D. K. & Hill, B. *Size and Efficiency in Farming*. Saxon House, 1975.
(37) Madden, J. P. 'Economies of Size in Farming: Theory, Analytical Procedures, and a Review of Selected Studies.' Economic Research Service, USDA, Washington, 1967.

Appendix

Interaction among markets: a note on partial and general equilibrium analysis

The phrase 'assuming all other factors remain constant' (and variants on it) has been used many times in the first four chapters of this book, but a major problem in both theoretical and empirical work in agricultural economics is to know which things it is reasonable to assume do remain constant and in which circumstances. The difficulty arises because what we are often doing is applying a cut-off point in our analysis and saying in effect that reactions beyond this point are sufficiently small to be ignored. Consider for example the effect of a substantial increase in consumer 'taste' for a food product (A) in an economy where initially all factor and product markets are in equilibrium. Our approach to this kind of question in any of the previous chapters would have been to note that the change in tastes would involve a shift in the demand curve for product A and that this would tend to force up market price. There would then be a supply response to this rise in price and a new equilibrium would be established in the market for product A. In estimating supply response we would very probably have taken account of some induced changes in the prices of the inputs used to produce product A, but otherwise we would have assumed that factor and product prices throughout the economy remained unaffected. But of course a more thorough investigation of the market implications of this change in consumer tastes would reveal many other price adjustments throughout the economy. Without attempting to detail all such repercussions, we can note the probability of some change in the conditions of supply for those products which use significant quantities of the same kind of productive resources as are used in the production of product A, and a strict application of our basic theory of consumer demand would lead us also to expect some change in the conditions of demand for other products as a necessary consequence of the initial change in taste for product A. There would thus be adjustments in many other prices. Some of these price changes will in fact influence the market demand or supply for product A – in other words, there will be a feedback effect in the market for product A.

Nevertheless, we might be quite justified in ignoring these feedback effects on the grounds that their impact upon the new equilibrium price for product A will be relatively small. The approach to market equilibrium which restricts the investigation of price and quantity adjustments to one market, or to a group of closely related markets, is called *partial equilibrium analysis*. In contrast *general equilibrium analysis* is concerned with the economy as a complete system of interacting markets and the general equilibrium approach encompasses the totality of market adjustments throughout the economy.

Now, by its very nature, agricultural economics is well suited to partial equilibrium analysis, since it is concerned with the application of economic principles to one (fairly well defined) part of an economic system – though relatively strong interdependencies among agricultural products in both production and consumption may mean that 'partial' needs sometimes to be interpreted to include the entire agricultural and food sector. Sometimes also it may be the case that the actions and reactions of some change in the agricultural sector, while going beyond the agricultural sector in a way which cannot be ignored, may be concentrated on some relatively restricted area of non-agricultural activities (e.g. rubber and plastics, vegetable and synthetic fibres). In such cases a partial equilibrium analysis may still be appropriate but it would need to go beyond the agricultural sector itself. The advantage of partial equilibrium analysis is the wholly practical one of enabling us to deal with many questions drawing on less information, and utilising much less time, than would be necessary if we always took the general equilibrium approach. There are, however, two areas within the broad subject matter of agricultural economics where a general equilibrium approach may be necessary. First, there are cases where the repercussions throughout the economy as a whole of some change within the agricultural sector may be too substantial to ignore. This situation is most likely to arise when a substantial proportion of total economic activity is accounted for by the agricultural sector. Thus, for example, in the case of many low income countries, we might find that a rise in income levels in farming would markedly alter the national distribution of income, with important implications for the pattern of demand throughout the economy.

Second, there is the relationship between government and agriculture. Many aspects of government policy towards agriculture are founded upon national policies towards such things as incomes, employment, efficiency, and so on. This means that often it is only by viewing the agricultural sector as a component of a complete economic system that we can understand the rationale behind many of the ways governments attempt to influence the operation of the agricultural sector. The next chapter introduces, in an elementary and limited manner, one approach to general equilibrium analysis and we use this in Part II of the book as a basis for the application of agricultural economic principles to the analysis of government agricultural policies.

Policy

CHAPTER 5

The Economics of Welfare and Policy

1 Introduction

Most applications of agricultural economic principles take a particular economic system as given and attempt to predict some aspect of the future course of economic events within that system. Such applications can for example range from a consideration of the impact upon the farm firm of some change in the use of inputs, to much broader questions concerning agricultural production and consumption at a national and international level, and many examples of this kind of approach were given in Part I of this book. The part of agricultural economics known as *agricultural policy* differs from other applications of agricultural economic principles in that it is concerned with an attempt to comprehend what might constitute an improvement in the operation of an economic system.

Governments develop agricultural policies in order to make what they see as improvements in the agricultural aspects of the economic system under their jurisdiction. They do this in the main by influencing agricultural factor and product prices with the effect of altering the allocation of resources and the distribution of income throughout the economy. A study of agricultural policy therefore requires that we should consider the problem of ranking the alternative economic situations open to a society into categories of 'better' and 'worse'. It is this which distinguishes the subject matter of Part II of this book. In Part I no attempt was made to comment upon the merits, from the point of view of society as a whole, of the various resource and product allocations discussed. The branch of general economics which provides the basic theory for much of what agricultural economics has to offer as a discipline to the study of agricultural policy is called *welfare economics*. That the economist's study of agricultural policy has its foundations in welfare economics is made clear if we quote some definitions of welfare economics:

Welfare economics is the study of the well-being of the members of a society as a group, in so far as it is affected by decisions and actions of its members and agencies concerning economic variables. . . . Welfare economics differs from the economics of individual behaviour and behaviour of the firm, being concerned with the extent to which the objectives of the society as a whole are fulfilled rather than the private objectives of its members. (D. M. Winch (1).)

Welfare economics analyses criteria for the maximisation of individual and collective welfare or utility. (Maurice Dobb (2).)

Theoretical welfare economics is ... that branch of study which endeavours to formulate propositions by which we may rank, on a scale of better or worse, alternative situations open to a society. (E. J. Mishan (3).)

Welfare economics is the theory of how and by what criteria economists and policy-makers make or ought to make their choice between alternative policies and between good and bad institutions. (Arrow and Scitovsky (4).)

In spite of the evident link between agricultural policy and welfare economics, agricultural economists have not always recognised the part that welfare economics can play in their analysis of agricultural policies. There are probably two reasons for this. First, the policy message of welfare economics can be annoyingly elusive to discover. Very often the subject seems to tell the economist that what he thought was a perfectly straightforward remark about – say – the 'economic' merits of a particular policy, cannot in fact be justified. The tendency has been to use a much simpler approach based on a single hypothesis that goes something like this:

The allocation of resources and distribution of produce associated with competitive conditions is 'economically efficient'; Governments will cause departures from competitively determined resource allocations and product distributions when implementing policies, but it is the function of the economist to draw attention to the 'economic costs' associated with such policies, as well as to indicate the various market effects that a policy is likely to have.

A second reason for the partial eclipse of welfare economics as a basis for agricultural policy analysis is that the writings of welfare economists are, frankly, often pretty tough going. Much of the material is very esoteric – written by professional economists for other professional economists. There is scarcity of the kind of sound basic introductory texts which abound in other branches of economics.[1] It is nevertheless the belief of the present author that an introductory chapter on welfare economics is an essential basis for a text-book discussion of the economics of agricultural policy. However, space must limit what can be included of an extremely extensive subject. The scope of this chapter is limited in the main, therefore, to examining two aspects of welfare economics of particular relevance to the work of agricultural economists in the field of agricultural policy. These are:

(a) The sense in which an allocation of resources and distribution of products which emerges from a perfect market economy can be regarded as economically efficient. (And thus, by implication, the extent to which a government policy which leads to a departure from these conditions can be regarded as 'economically inefficient'.)

(b) The sense in which it might be possible to measure the welfare effects of a particular policy change.

It must be emphasised that what follows is not intended as an elaborately rigorous exposition of welfare economics. It is, rather, an attempt to make accessible to students of agricultural economics those aspects of welfare economics which have important implications for the economist's study of agricultural policy.

2 A simple model of welfare maximisation

2.1 The nature of economic welfare

If a person says that he undertakes to look after the welfare of a child, then he takes it upon himself to be concerned with everything which may affect the well-being of the child. . . . There is no part of well-being called 'economic well-being'. The word 'economic' qualifies not well-being, but the causes of well-being or changes in it. If I am interested only in someone's economic welfare, then I interest myself only in the economic things which may affect his well-being. (Little (7).)

Little describes 'well-being' as 'happiness', and both these words are virtually interchangeable with two words that were used in Chapter 1 in connection with the theory of consumer behaviour — 'utility' and 'satisfaction'. It is the view that the welfare of a society is, in part, dependent upon the utility derived by its members through consumption that enables the economic principles described in Part I of this book to be applied to the analysis of government agricultural policies. This approach to policy necessitates three assumptions about the kind of society under consideration, namely:

(a) that the Government has the well-being of its people at the centre of policy formulation;

(b) that the Government is, in general, prepared to regard the individual as the best judge of at least most aspects of his own welfare; and

(c) that the individual demonstrates his preferences by the action he takes in the market.

These assumptions do not mean that the Government has no role in the economic affairs of a nation. Many important functions remain, and one which is especially important in the context of this chapter is for some agency to act as the representative of society (or, to put it another way, the 'collective will of the people') to arbitrate when a particular economic event leads to an increase in the welfare of one individual (as he sees it) but to a decrease in the welfare of another individual (again as viewed by himself). It is an unfortunate fact of life that many economic actions are of this form. To take a very simple example, if the economy performs in such a way as to allocate an apple to me (and I eat it) then this means that the apple cannot be consumed by anyone else. Unless there are so many apples available that everyone can have as many as he wants, the consumption of the apple by me (which increases my welfare according to assumptions (b) and (c) above) must by necessity imply that someone else's welfare is lower than it could otherwise have been.

2.2 Characteristics of the model

The fundamental question to which we now turn is 'what economic order (i.e. what allocation of resources and distribution of commodities) would lead to the maximisation of the collective welfare of society?' To assist an attempt to answer this question we will use a very simple model of an economy which contains only:

Two kinds of productive resource, which we will call X and Y
Two products, A and B
Two individuals, U and V

We retain the practice introduced in Chapter 2 of using lower case letters to indicate quantities (so that, for example, x represents quantity of input X, b represents quantity of product B, and u represents level of utility attained by individual U). Our objective is to find the allocation of the resources X and Y between the production of the products A and B, and the distribution of the products A and B between the individuals U and V, which maximises the collective satisfaction of U and V. We will refer to the collective satisfaction of U and V as the *welfare of society* (W), and to the individual satisfactions of U and V as *utilities*. We make a number of assumptions concerning the operation of this simplified economy and its relation to the welfare of society. These are as follows:

(a) That the welfare of society is increased if one person is made better off and no-one made worse off. This is known as the *Paretian value judgement.*[2] To be precise, we should extend this assumption to include: that welfare is decreased if one person is made worse off without someone else being made better off, and that welfare is unchanged if no one is made either better or worse off.

(b) That an individual's welfare is deemed to have increased if he chooses to move to a new position. This assumption relates the Paretian value judgement directly to the utility function of demand theory which was discussed in Chapter 1. There we assumed that the individual consumer acted in such a way as to maximise his satisfaction. An increase in utility can thus be regarded as synonymous with the individual being better off, and the welfare of society becomes dependent solely upon the levels of utility experienced by the individuals comprising society:

$$w = f(u, v)$$

We preclude the possibility that someone other than the individual himself (for example, the Government) might be better placed to decide whether a particular action will in fact increase the individual's welfare. (Clearly, in practice there are circumstances when a government does take this view about the consumption of individuals, for example by making the use of certain narcotics illegal.)

(c) That the individual's utility depends entirely upon the goods and services that he consumes and that he will always prefer more of a good to less. This means that we have implicitly assumed that individual utility functions are independent of one another, i.e. individual U can neither gain nor lose satisfaction merely as a result of observing some change in the quantity of goods consumed by V. It also means that utility is not affected by the provision of factor services – there is no 'disutility' attached to work (or, at least, we are ruling out variations in this element).

(d) All goods are private. A private good is one such that its consumption by one individual precludes its consumption by someone else. By contrast, a collective good is one which, by its very nature, is simultaneously available to a group of consumers.

(e) There are no production externalities. A production externality is where one productive activity affects the productivity of another.

(f) The state of technology and quantity of resources available remain constant for the economy and there are no economies of large-scale production.

These assumptions are clearly very restrictive but some have been included merely so that we can have as simple an example as possible and can be relaxed without causing too many complications. Similarly, the choice of a two-factor/two-product/two-person model is for simplicity and similar conclusions can be derived for a multifactor/multiproduct/multiperson model. Finally, it should be pointed out that we are avoiding those questions which involve a choice between consumption in different time periods, although this problem is touched upon in the next chapter.

2.3 The concept of a social welfare function

The identification of the collective welfare of society as being related to individual utilities means that we can represent welfare by a diagram which shows the individual levels of utility experienced by U and V. In Fig. 5.1 any point between the axes represents a combination of levels of utility for U and V and thus a specific level of welfare for society. For example, point R represents a level of utility of u_2 for U and v_1 for V, and we will call the level of social welfare associated with this pair of individual utilities w_1. The Paretian value judgement means that any point above and to the right of R will represent a higher level of welfare than w_1 since all such points represent higher levels of utility for both U and V. Similarly, point R is associated with a higher level of welfare than any point located in the quadrant below and to the left of R.

The question now arises as to whether we can say anything about R in relation to points located in the remaining two quadrants. A movement from R

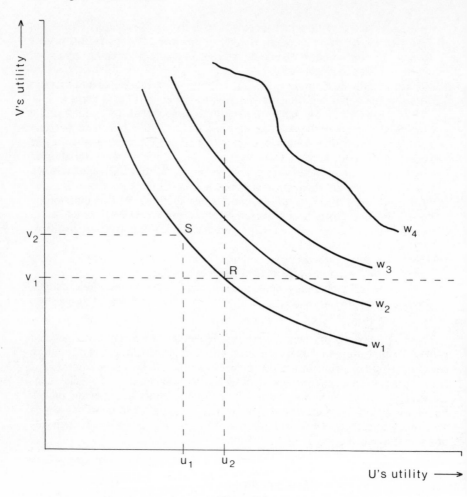

Figure 5.1

into either of these quadrants represents an increase in utility for one individual and a decrease for the other. A movement to point S, for example, represents an increase in V's utility to v_2 but a decrease for U to u_1. To rank two configurations of the economy, R and S, when individual U is better off at R than S, but individual V is better off at S than R involves some judgement as to whether the improvement in V's utility between S and R does or does not outweigh the worsening of U's welfare with the same change. Such a ranking involves what are known as *interpersonal comparisons* and the role that such judgements can play in welfare economics has probably caused more headaches for welfare economists than anything else.

A reluctance to become involved in interpersonal comparisons means that we will always go as far as we can in categorising alternative economic situations into better and worse by restricting the economy to changes where the new position is a Paretian improvement upon the old. However, so many policy changes are of the kind where some individuals are made better off and some made worse off that it is foolish to pretend that economic policy is restricted to situations where Pareto improvements are possible.

The fact of the matter is that government policy frequently *seeks* to take from some and give to others. A government policy to raise the income of hill farmers, financing the subsidy by income tax, implies that society regards the improvement in the welfare of hill farmers as outweighing the loss of utility by those paying higher taxes. If society were able to rank every possible configuration of the economy we would have what is known as a *social welfare function* relating individual utilities to community welfare.[3] This can be represented in Fig. 5.1 by a set of welfare contours joining pairs of utilities for U and V which are associated with the same level of welfare for society. Any contour must slope down continually from left to right. At no stage can a welfare contour become vertical or horizontal, since this would imply that the same level of social welfare was generated when the utility of one individual was increased but the other remained unchanged; we have specifically defined this as representing an improvement in society's welfare by virtue of the Paretian value judgement.

Can we say anything further about the likely shape of welfare contours? This depends on the view we take of consumer utilities. In Chapter 1 we distinguished indifference curve theory from measurable utility and said that it was necessary to assume only that each indifference curve represented a series of combinations of commodities which were preferred by the consumer to all combinations lying on lower indifference curves. This would mean that all that could be said about the axes in Fig. 5.1 would be that any point on an axis is preferred to all lower points. No precise meaning would be attached to the distance between two points on one of the axes, and there would be no significance in the slope of any welfare contour. (To emphasise this, welfare contours are sometimes drawn as irregular lines, such as w_4.)

However, if we were to allow ourselves the luxury of an assumption that consumer utility was quantitatively measurable, then a specific distance along one of the axes would represent a specific change in utility for U or V. If we were further to suggest that an important feature of the social welfare function might be equality in one form or another, then any welfare contour would be likely to be shaped convex to the origin which would mean that, as we gradually reduce the utility of one individual by successively equal amounts, it would require increasing increments of the other individual's utility to leave social welfare unchanged.

A social welfare function, giving a complete ranking of all alternative configurations of an economy, is a useful theoretical tool which helps us to understand the way in which certain economic changes can be regarded as representing an improvement for society as a whole. In practice, it is not possible for a Government to establish such a complete statement about relative values in society but governments nevertheless do formulate often quite complex policies relating to interpersonal comparisons. These can include specific objectives with respect to various groups in society. For example, in Fig. 5.1, we could specify certain minimum levels of living for U and V implying that beyond a certain point social welfare cannot be increased by improving the position of one individual if it means the other individual falling below the minimum standard. Superimposed upon specific objectives, government policies, such as a progressive taxation system, give a crude indication of the kind of improvement in the position of one group of individuals required to offset a given reduction in the position of others. The combined implications of such policies can amount to a statement about interpersonal comparisons which is not all that far removed from the complete picture provided by the theoretical concept of a social welfare function.

2.4 The optimum conditions

In our simple two-factor/two-product/two-person economy the level of welfare that can be attained is constrained by:

(a) the quantities of the resources X and Y which are available;
(b) the existing state of knowledge concerning the way in which the resources can be converted into the products A and B (the production functions of A and B);
(c) the relationship between consumption of A and B and utility for U and V (the utility functions of U and V).

Three conditions are necessary for the attainment of what is known as a *Pareto optimum* for this simple economy – that is, a position where it is not possible to make one individual better off without making the other worse off. These three conditions are as follows:

Condition 1　That the two factors X and Y should be allocated between the production of the two products A and B in such a way that it is not possible, by some alternative allocation, to increase the output of one of the products without reducing the output of the other. This we shall call the *production efficiency condition*.

2　That the two products A and B should be distributed between the two individuals U and V in such a way that it is not possible, by some alternative distribution, to increase the utility of one individual without reducing the utility of the other – the *exchange efficiency condition*.

3　That the combination of output of A and B in the economy should be such that it is not possible, by choosing some other combination of output, to increase the utility of one individual without decreasing the utility of the other – the *output efficiency condition*.

A further condition is necessary for *welfare maximisation*. This is that the Pareto optimum achieved should lie on the highest attainable social welfare contour.

2.5 Production efficiency

In Fig. 5.2, the quantity of input X available is given by the length of the horizontal axis AC and the quantity of input Y available by the vertical axis AD. The conditions of production for product A are given by the set of iso-product curves labelled a_1, a_2, etc. giving the alternative combinations of the two inputs X and Y which can be used to obtain specific levels of output of A. (The subscripts in Fig. 5.2 are labels – they do not represent units of product – but a higher number in the subscript does always indicate a greater quantity.)

If we now measure the quantities of X and Y available from an origin located at B, we can show the conditions of production for product B on the same diagram by the set of iso-product curves labelled b_1, b_2, etc. Any point inside the box $ACBD$ now represents a unique allocation of the available quantities of factors X and Y between the production of the products A and B. For example, point R shows an allocation of AE of X and AH of Y to the production of product A. EC $(= BG)$ of X and HD $(= BF)$ of Y is left unallocated to the production of A and is available for the production of B. The iso-product curves upon which point R lies $(a_2$ and $b_2)$ give us the total production of the two products with this particular allocation of the factors of production.

A feature of point R is that there are other possible allocations of X and Y between the production of A and B which will give higher levels of output for both A and B. All points within the shaded area lie on higher iso-product curves for both A and B. Only those points where two iso-product curves are tangential to one another represent allocations of X and Y such that it is not possible to produce more of one product without reducing the output of the other. At these points of tangency the marginal rate of substitution between X and Y will be the same for the production of A and B. The line joining these points is known as a *contract curve* and gives us our condition for production efficiency: the factors of production X and Y will be allocated between the production of A and B in such a way that it is not possible, by some alternative allocation, to increase the output of one product without reducing the output of the other if the marginal rate of substitution between the inputs is the same in the production of both products.

2.6 Exchange efficiency

The quantities produced of A and B generate utility for individuals U and V through the process of consumption. Our second efficiency condition for the attainment of a Pareto optimum is that the available quantities of A and B should, during the time period under consideration, be distributed between U and V in such a way that it is not possible, by some alternative distribution, to

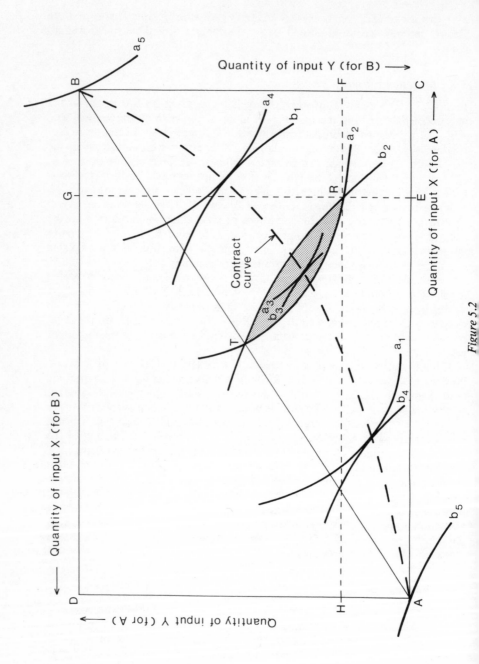

Figure 5.2

increase the utility of one individual without reducing the utility of the other. We can show the exchange efficiency condition by the same box diagram technique as used in Fig. 5.2. In Fig. 5.3 the quantity of product A available is measured by the horizontal axis UC ($= VD$) and the quantity available of product B by the vertical axis UD ($= VC$). The preferences of U and V concerning the consumption of alternative combinations of A and B are given by the two sets of indifference curves labelled u_1, u_2, etc. and v_1, v_2, etc. U's indifference curves relate to an origin located at the bottom left-hand corner of the box and V's indifference curves to an origin located at the top right-hand corner of the box. Any point within the box represents a specific distribution of the available quantities of A and B between individuals U and V, but only those points lying on the contract curve[4] represent distributions which are consistent with exchange efficiency. The points are characterised by the fact that they represent distributions of A and B where the marginal rate of subsitution between A and B is the same for U and V. The exchange efficiency condition is therefore: that the two products A and B will be distributed between the two individuals U and V in such a way that it is not possible, by some alternative distribution, to increase the utility of one individual without reducing the utility of the other, if the marginal rate of substitution between the products is the same for both individuals.

2.7 Output efficiency

In Fig. 5.4 the information contained in Fig. 5.2 concerning the maximum possible combinations of output of A and B that can be produced from the given quantities of X and Y are shown in the form of a *production possibility curve* or *product transformation curve*, with quantity of product A measured on the horizontal axis and quantity of product B on the vertical axis. The word 'transformation' refers to the fact that the curve shows the way in which output of one product can be 'transformed' into the other product by reallocating factors of production. The slope of the curve is therefore sometimes called the *marginal rate of transformation (MRT)* between the products.

The production possibility curve in Fig. 5.4 differs from that shown for an individual farm firm in Fig. 2.5 in that we are now considering various allocations of *two* inputs between two products. There will normally be many different ways in which some of X and some of Y could be taken away from the production of A and bring about the same reduction in the output of A (e.g. one could take away a lot of X and a little of Y, or the other way round, and both could have the same effect on A's output). There is the implicit assumption in the product transformation curve that transformation is in fact effected in the most favourable possible way, i.e. the resources transferred are chosen in such a way as to yield the maximum extra output of B consistent with given loss of output A.

The production possibility curve in Fig. 5.4 is shown shaped concave to the origin. If we return to Fig. 5.2 we can see the reason for this. If all the economy's resources are allocated to the production of A then the resulting

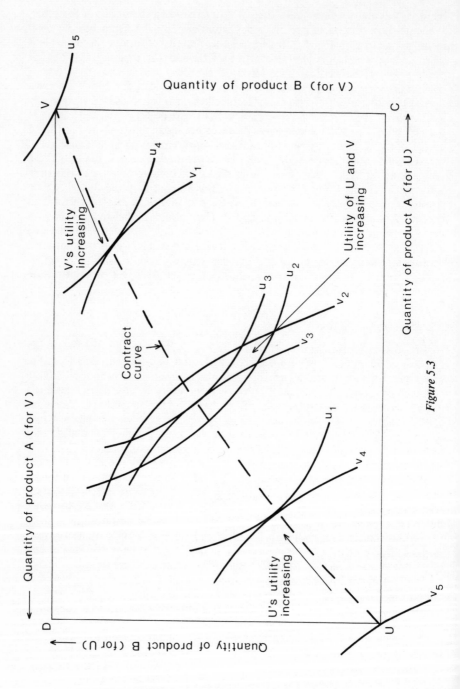

Figure 5.3

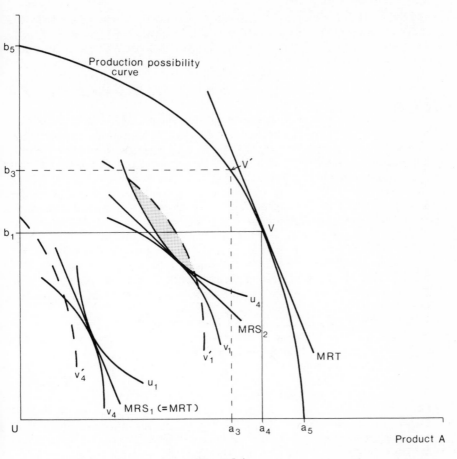

Figure 5.4

output is a_5 (and no B). Similarly, b_5 is the maximum quantity of B that can be produced. Clearly therefore, the production possibility curve in Fig. 5.4 must intersect the A and B axes at a level of output of a_5 of A and b_5 of B.

Consider now the diagonal AB in Fig. 5.2, and assume that the production functions for both A and B demonstrate constant returns to scale. Any movement along this diagonal will imply a certain proportionate change in the use of both factors in the production of A which must, because of the assumption of constant returns to scale, result in the same proportionate change in the output of A. At the same time, this movement along the diagonal will imply a certain proportional change in the use of both factors in the production of B which again must result in the same proportionate change in the output of B. For example, if point T represents one-half the available quantities of X and Y being allocated to A and B, the output combination at T

(a_2 and b_2) will be equal to one-half a_5 and one-half b_5. If, for some reason, the only permitted allocations of X and Y to the production of A and B were those shown by the diagonal, then a straight line production possibility curve would result. The fact that all allocations along the diagonal (apart from those at A and B) can be improved upon by moving towards the contract curve is the reason why the production possibility curve in Fig. 5.4 is shaped concave to the origin.

With constant returns to scale, the production possibility curve could only become a straight line if all the points of tangency for the iso-product curves in Fig. 5.2 were located on the diagonal – a possible but improbable event; improbable because the 'intensity' of factor use varies between different production processes – some products are land intensive, some labour intensive, and so on. It is only when the factor intensities of X and Y are the same for A and B that the iso-product curve pattern of the two products would be identical with the result that the points of tangency would be on the diagonal.

If decreasing returns to scale apply, this will emphasise the curvature of the production possibility curve. (With increasing returns to scale, however, it is possible that a production possibility curve could become convex to the origin. This is why we assumed earlier that there were no economies of large-scale production in our simple economy.)

Any combination of output given by the production possibility curve is consistent with the first (production) efficiency condition. If we ensure that any such combination is distributed so as to be consistent with exchange efficiency, then our first two conditions for obtaining a Pareto optimum will both apply. For example, take the combination of output of a_4 of A and b_1 of B, given by point V on the production possibility curve in Fig. 5.4. We can show the alternative distributions of these quantities of A and B by constructing the box Ua_4Vb_1 (let us call it box 1). Once we have chosen the output combination a_4 and b_1, all other points on the production possibility curve can be ignored, and the levels of utilities derived by U and V from the consumption of alternative distributions of a_4 and b_1 can be shown by indifference curves, with the origin for U at the bottom left-hand corner of the box, and the origin for V at the top right-hand corner of the box, as we did in Fig. 5.3. Two pairs of utilities for U and V which cannot be improved upon in a Pareto sense by any other distribution of a_4 and b_1 are u_4 and v_1, and u_1 and v_4. Since the combination of output, a_4 and b_1, is derived from the production possibility curve, the allocation which yields these pairs of utilities for U and V must be consistent with both production and exchange efficiency. There can therefore be only one way in which it might be possible to make a Pareto improvement upon either u_4 and v_1 or u_1 and v_4, and that is by the choice of an alternative combination of output for the economy. In other words, is there another box which can do better?

Consider the alternative feasible output combination for the economy, a_3 and b_3, given by the point V' on the production possibility curve. The levels of utility for U and V which can be derived from this alternative combination of output, can similarly be shown by the box diagram technique – in this case, box $Ua_3V'b_3$ (say box 2). The origin for V's indifference curves moves to V', U's origin remaining located at U. Thus U's indifference curves are unaffected, but V's indifference curves are all shifted bodily by the same distance, and in the same direction, as a movement from V to V'. v_1 and v_4 are now shown by the broken lines v'_1 and v'_4. In this case, box 2 can improve upon u_4 and v_1 – all those allocations of a_3 and b_3 which lie in the shaded area give higher levels of utility for U than u_4 and higher levels of utility for V than v_1. On the other hand, there is no distribution within the second box which can even just attain u_1 and v_4.

If we take any pair of utilities which is derived from an *efficient distribution* of an *efficiently produced* combination of output, whether or not it will be possible to make a Pareto improvement upon that pair of utilities by the choice of an alternative combination of output for the economy will depend upon the relationship between the marginal rate of transformation for the economy, and the marginal rate of substitution for the individuals. The marginal rate of transformation determines the rate at which it is possible to transform output of one product into output of the other, and thus the way in which the shape of the boxes can be altered. The marginal rate of substitution determines the rate at which it is possible for U and V to increase the consumption of one product and reduce the consumption of the other but remain indifferent concerning the change. Briefly, if the marginal rate of transformation for the economy exceeds the common marginal rate of substitution then, in terms of Fig. 5.4, there will be other boxes containing more B and less A which will allow a Pareto improvement to be made. Thus, in Fig. 5.4, box 2 can improve upon u_4 and v_1. Conversely, if the marginal rate of transformation for the economy is less than the common marginal rate of substitution for the individuals, there will be boxes containing more A and less B which will allow a Pareto improvement to be made. Only if the marginal rate of transformation for the economy is the *same* as the marginal rate of substitution for the individuals will it not be possible to improve the position of one individual without reducing the utility of the other individual by the choice of another box. (This condition applies for the distribution of a_4 of A and b_1 of B (box 1) which yields u_1 and v_4.) The third condition for the attainment of a Pareto optimum (that the combination of output for the economy will be such that it is not possible, by choosing some other combination, to increase the utility of one individual without reducing the utility of the other) will therefore be met if the common marginal rate of substitution between A and B for U and V is the same as the marginal rate of transformation between A and B for the economy.

2.8 From a Pareto optimum to welfare maximisation

The three conditions for the attainment of a Pareto optimum can be generalised to apply to a multiresource/multiproduct/multiperson economy, in which case they become:

Condition 1 Production efficiency: the marginal rate of substitution between any two inputs must be the same in the production of any two products.

        2 Exchange efficiency: the marginal rate of substitution between any two products must be the same for any two individuals.

        3 Output efficiency: the marginal rate of transformation between any two products for the economy should be the same as the marginal rate of substitution between the products for all individuals.

The concept of a Pareto optimum can be illustrated for the two-person case by the *welfare frontier* in Fig. 5.5. Any point on the frontier is derived from a

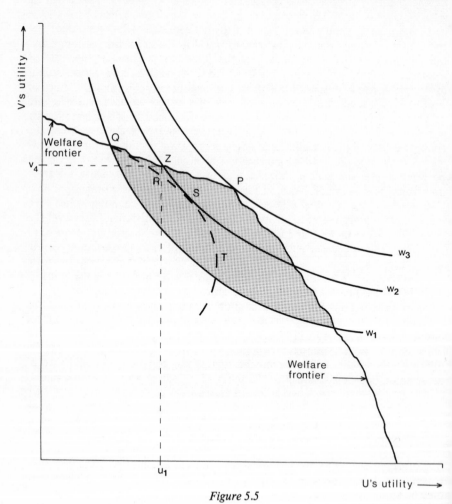

Figure 5.5

conformation of the economy which satisfies the three conditions. For example, we know from Fig. 5.4 that one such point will be u_1 and v_4 – point z in Fig. 5.5. All points inside the frontier fail to satisfy one or more of the conditions and for any such point an appropriate movement towards the frontier can increase the utility of one individual without reducing the utility of the other. If we add to Fig. 5.5 the concept of the social welfare function, illustrated by Fig. 5.1, the overall position of welfare maximisation for the economy will be given by the point (or points) on the welfare frontier which is associated with the highest attainable welfare contour – in Fig. 5.5 this is w_3 at point P.

3 Welfare and competition

3.1 The perfect market equilibrium

Nothing was said in the previous section about the method by which resources are allocated and products distributed. The purpose of this section is to examine the allocative implications of a particular system of markets in equilibrium known as a perfect market economy – in other words, an economy in which all factor and product markets are perfectly competitive and in general equilibrium. The reason for this examination is that the theoretical model of a perfect market economy has often been used by agricultural economists as a benchmark for judging the economic efficiency of agricultural policies.

We will take the conditions for the attainment of a Pareto optimum in turn. First, we know from Chapter 2 that producers exercising least-cost criteria must choose quantities of inputs such that the marginal rate of substitution between each pair of inputs is equal to the inverse ratio of their prices. Thus the allocation of resources between alternative products will be efficient (i.e. the production efficiency condition will be met) if all producers are free to buy inputs without limit at prices which are common to all. This is the case in a perfect market economy.

Second, under the theory of household behaviour discussed in Chapter 1, consumers freely exercising their preferences subject to a budget constraint and facing fixed prices will maximise their satisfactions by choosing combinations of products such that the marginal rate of substitution between any two products is equal to the inverse ratio of their prices. The distribution of products among consumers will therefore be efficient (i.e. the exchange efficiency condition will be met) if all consumers can exercise free choice, subject to a budget constraint, at prices which are the same for all. Again, this applies in the case of a perfect market economy.

The consistency of perfect competition with the third condition is somewhat more difficult to show. Consider first the case of a two-product firm. For any given allocation of resources to that firm there will be a production possibility curve relating to the firm, such as the one shown in Fig. 5.6. In order to maximise profits the firm must maximise the joint revenue from the sale of the

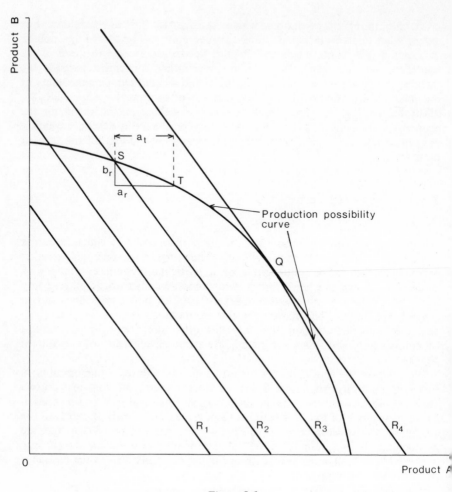

Figure 5.6

two products for whatever quantity of resources it opts to employ. We can show the total revenue associated with any combination of products by the iso-revenue lines R_1, R_2, etc. Any iso-revenue line represents different combinations of the two products which, when sold, yield the same revenue. The slope of any iso-revenue line will therefore be given by the inverse ratio of product prices. Maximum revenue occurs when the firm chooses a combination of A and B such that the marginal rate of transformation for the firm is equal to the inverse ratio of product prices (point Q in Fig. 5.6). Thus the profit maximising two-product firm will choose an output plan which is consistent with the third condition for the attainment of a Pareto optimum, and, by aggregation, so will an economy of two-product firms.

For an economy consisting of single product perfectly competitive firms, it is not difficult formally to prove (though we do not do so here) that the equality of product price with marginal cost of production leads the economy to an equilibrium which satisfies the third condition (see, for example, Lancaster (5)). For our purpose, a more intuitive explanation extending the argument relating to Fig. 5.6 will suffice. Let the production possibility curve in Fig. 5.6 now relate to the whole economy. Suppose the economy is located initially on the production possibility curve at point S and consider a small transfer of resources from B production to A production which moves the output combination for the economy to point T on the production possibility curve. The slope of the iso-revenue line passing through S (R_3) tells us how much extra A must be produced (a_r) if total revenue is to remain unchanged (at R_3) following a fall in B production of b_r. The slope of the production possibility curve between S and T indicates how much extra A can be produced (a_t) if the resources released when B production is reduced by b_r are used in A production. Thus if the economy is located at S and the price of products A and B are those indicated by the slopes of the iso-revenue lines R_1, R_2, etc., it is possible, by a suitable transfer of resources from B production to A production, to obtain an increase in the monetary value of output of product A which exceeds the consequent reduction in the monetary value of output of product B.

If input prices are such that the price of B is equal to the marginal cost of producing B at point T the price of A must exceed the marginal cost of producing A. It will be profitable for A firms to increase output, bidding away factors from B output, until price equals marginal cost in the production of both products (at Q, in Fig. 5.6). (This assumes no change in the relative prices of A and B; if the price relationship between A and B indicated by the iso-revenue line R_1, R_2, etc. applies when the economy is located at point S, then an increase in the output of product A and a reduction in the output of product B associated with a movement along the production possibility curve towards Q would be likely to mean (in a perfect market economy) a fall in the price of A relative to B and an equilibrium position somewhere between S and Q.

The perfect market economy thus maximises the value of output that can be produced per time period if output is valued at prevailing market prices. It thereby satisfies the third efficiency condition for the attainment of a Pareto optimum.

3.2 The conflict between efficiency and distribution

We have shown that a perfect market economy will achieve a Pareto optimum – a position on the welfare frontier – if the assumptions made concerning our simple model of welfare maximisation are applicable. It is this characteristic of the perfect market economy which lies at the heart of the identification of competition with 'economic efficiency' and it must be considered a remarkable result.

In view of the immense quantity of individual economic decisions required in respect of resource allocation and product distribution, it is most unlikely that any other conceivable economic system could achieve a Pareto optimum. And though the perfect market economy is not an existing real world phenomenon, it is at least feasible in the sense that a Government could attempt, and probably come reasonably close to maintaining, the conditions necessary for its operation. The association between competition and efficiency was indicated 200 years ago when Adam Smith said that 'in pursueing his own advantage' every individual was 'led by an invisible hand to promote an end which was no part of his intention', namely to 'render the annual revenue of the society as great as he can' (10). This conclusion was elaborated by later writers such as Walras, who said, 'The consequences of free competition ... may be summed up as the attainment, within certain limits, of maximum utility. Hence free competition becomes a principle or a rule of practical significance, so that it only remains to extend the detailed application of this rule to agriculture, industry and trade' (11). Subsequently economists made a distinction between 'free' and 'perfect' competition to draw attention to the fact that a Government policy of 'laissez-faire' would not necessarily result in a perfect market economy. But it was not until well into the twentieth century that Western economists formulated serious objections to competition as a 'rule of practical significance' for guiding the allocation of factors and the distribution of products.

These objections can be grouped into two categories. First, there is the problem that if we relax some of the assumptions made at the beginning of this chapter concerning the kind of simple economy to be examined, then it no longer follows that the perfect market economy will attain a Pareto optimum. The assumptions relating to the absence of (i) increasing returns to large-scale production, (ii) collective goods, and (iii) production externalities, are particularly important in this respect. The theoretical issues raised by variations in these assumptions are usually very complicated and great care is required when attempting to interpret the welfare implications in any individual case. Much of the subject matter of *cost–benefit analysis* is concerned with an attempt to establish appropriate allocative rules for the provision of collective goods for industries where increasing returns to large-scale production are present, and where production externalities are significant, and some of these issues are discussed in the next chapter. For the remainder of this chapter we will concentrate upon the second kind of objection to the perfect market economy. This is of more immediate relevance to the subject matter of agricultural policy; it is the apparent conflict between economic efficiency and an equitable income distribution, a problem which would still be very much present in an economy which did meet the stringent assumptions of our simple model.

The first thing to note is that there is no reason why a perfect market equilibrium should correspond to the position of overall welfare maximisation for Society. Indeed, we could go further and argue that any perfect market equilibrium would almost certainly not correspond to a welfare maximisation position. This is because it seems reasonable to assume that a social welfare function would normally incorporate some considerations of equality, and it is our experience that competitive economies tend to be associated with inequality in income distribution. In these circumstances we can make a second observation – that there will be numerous economic situations which, although not Pareto optima (because they depart from one or more of the efficiency conditions), will nevertheless be preferred on welfare grounds to the perfect market solution when the distributional question is taken into account. Illustrating this for the two-person economy in Fig. 5.5, assume that the point Q is a position on the welfare frontier associated with a perfect market equilibrium. By reference to the social welfare function – represented by the welfare contours w_1, w_2, etc. – all those positions within the shaded area are preferred to the Pareto optimum at Q because they lie on higher welfare contours than w_1.

In the perfect market economy, the same set of prices is responsible for both the allocation of resources and the distribution of income. All income in the perfect market economy is derived from the ownership of productive factors and as already mentioned the price mechanism therefore maximises the value of output that can be produced per time period – the valuation of products being relative to a distribution of income which has itself been thrown up by the maximisation process. This means that there will not be one, but many, alternative perfect competition equilibrium positions all of which will be Pareto optima.

Suppose, for example, that a government imposes a once and for all programme of income redistribution and that having done so it makes no further attempt to influence the distribution of income. With the change in the distribution of income is likely to come a change in aggregate demand. (For instance we saw in Chapter 1 that a more equal distribution of income would probably result in an increase in the demand for most food products.) The competitive system therefore begins to adjust to a different composition of output and allocation of resources. The changes in output composition and resource allocation are brought about by relative movements in product and input prices. These price movements will themselves influence the evolution of a new pattern of income distribution. Gradually the economy adjusts to a new perfectly competitive equilibrium with the price system maximising the value of output as viewed by the income distribution thrown up by the maximisation procedure. But there is no reason why the new equilibrium should imply the same composition of output, allocation of resources, or distribution of income as that pertaining prior to the government redistribution programme. The implication is that there is no such thing as a uniquely efficient allocation of resources for an economy, nor a correspondingly uniquely efficient set of product and input prices.

In the above example, what was an efficient allocation of resources prior to a temporary interference in the economy by the Government is no longer so after the effect of the redistribution has worked itself through the economy.

We can summarise the argument of this section so far as follows:

(a) A perfect market economy will attain a Pareto optimum position if the economy conforms to the assumptions listed at the beginning of this chapter.

(b) There will be many alternative perfect market Pareto optima – each one maximising the value of output as viewed by the accompanying income distribution, but none of them is inherently likely to correspond to an overall position of welfare maximisation for society.

(c) There will be many non-Pareto optimum positions which will be preferred to many (and perhaps all) perfect market equilibrium positions because of the distributional question.

These considerations lead to the view that a Government will seek some permanent involvement in policies to influence the distribution of income. Unfortunately, as we shall see, any attempt by a Government to depart substantially from the distribution of income thrown up by the perfect market economy will simultaneously imply the non-fulfilment of the Pareto conditions. There is thus an inevitable conflict between economic efficiency and the pursuit of a more equal distribution of income. In the above example the Government distribution programme was limited to a temporary event with a perfect market equilibrium being allowed to re-establish itself. Suppose alternatively that the Government introduces a permanent income distribution policy. This would involve some combination of taxes and subsidies on factor and product prices. As before we might expect a new pattern of final demand to emerge with the implication that, if the economy is to return to a Pareto optimum, there must be a change in the composition of output and allocation of resources. However, a government policy which results in the owner of a factor receiving a different sum from the price paid for the resource by the producer, or a consumer paying a different price for a product than that received by the producer, means the non-fulfilment of the Pareto conditions.[5] *Such a departure from the Pareto conditions may be termed a loss in economic efficiency.*

The fact that a policy of income redistribution does imply a loss of economic efficiency is not in itself any criticism of such policies. We can emphasise this by returning to the two-person case of Fig. 5.5. The broken line might represent a feasible redistribution path for the economy away from a perfect market equilibrium at Q. For a small, and perhaps even moderate degree of income redistribution, the loss of economic efficiency may be relatively unimportant but the magnitude of the loss will increase as the Government seeks further and further to depart from the kind of income distribution implied by a perfectly competitive economy. The redistribution path is therefore shown to move gradually away from the welfare frontier as U's position is improved at the expense of V. The postulation of a social welfare function suggests that redistribution from U to V should proceed to position S, since this is the highest welfare contour reached along the redistribution path. In practical terms, the position of overall welfare maximisation at P is unattainable and improvements in social welfare can only be obtained by accepting some loss in economic efficiency.

The social welfare function, when precisely defined, is only a hypothetical concept. An actual income distribution policy may be related to relatively straightforward objectives, and bearing in mind the conflict between distribution and efficiency, it is possible to postulate alternative forms that the distribution objective might take. One possibility would be the establishment of some minimum level of living in the economy. This minimum would be specified in terms of a minimum consumption level and would be reflected in Fig. 5.5 by associated minimum levels of utility for U and V. For example, if V is well above the minimum level and the minimum for U is represented by u_1, this would imply redistribution to point R. Combined with the minimum standard of living there could be a maximum. At R, V might still be above the maximum, and thus further redistribution would be required.

In his article 'An Examination of Some Main Objectives in Agricultural Economic Policy' (13), Tuck postulates an alternative feasible objective which might be applied to policy decisions about personal income distribution. The objective is postulated in the form of the slogan 'The highest attainable lowest standards of living' ('The greatest good of the least fortunate' is an alternative form). The slogan refers to 'absolute' and not relative standards and Tuck argues that a policy designed to benefit the least well-off (who might, for the purposes of argument, be small farmers) would eventually reach the point at which further changes in their favour would adversely affect their absolute position. The reason is the conflict between efficiency and distribution. At some point a policy of redistribution designed to increase the relative share of the least well-off will cause a reduction in their absolute standards because of the efficiency losses of the redistribution policy. According to Tuck, 'The exact position of this point would depend upon the factors included in our measure of living standards but it is evident that it would be reached long before incomes in general were remotely approaching universal equality.' Translating these remarks into the context of the two-person Fig. 5.5, point T is the maximum attainable lowest standard of living; it is the position where it is no longer possible to increase further the utility level of U by making V worse off.

3.3 Second best optima

An appropriate policy designed to achieve an overall optimum position for an economy, then, would seem likely to include considerations of both equity and efficiency. Distributional objectives may well be specified in such a way that the benefits from economic efficiency will be derived from a course of action which amounts to making Pareto improvements wherever possible, subject to the attainment of certain objectives with respect to personal incomes. For example, in the case of the minimum standard of living specified for U in Fig. 5.5 maximising the benefits of economic efficiency would involve 'doing the best one can' for V, subject to the requirement that U's utility does not fall below u_1. Viewed in this way, the best solution would be if the economy could attain a position on the welfare frontier at Z. However, we know that, because a policy of redistributing income to U involves a departure from the Pareto conditions, point Z is unattainable. The best that can be achieved is a second best optimum, which might be position R. Less efficient methods of meeting the minimum objective for U would generate lower levels of utility for V than that experienced at R.

A real world situation is bound to include government-imposed constraints upon resource allocation and product distribution, in order to fulfil objectives with respect to the distribution of personal incomes, as well as for other reasons, and of course it is not just government policies which cause departures from the Pareto conditions – for example, there is the case of monopoly pricing. Thus economic efficiency becomes the attainment of a second best optimum, which can be defined as a position where it is not possible to make one person better off without making someone else worse off, given the existence of certain immovable constraints upon resource allocation and product distribution within the economy.

Now, it would be most convenient if the attainment of a second best optimum required the application, wherever possible, of the same optimising rules with respect to production, distribution and output efficiency as those required for a first best optimum. These rules are fairly straightforward, easily translated into terms of market prices, and known to be associated with competitive markets. However, in a now famous article entitled 'The General Theory of Second Best', Lipsey and Lancaster (14) argued otherwise. Generalising a conclusion that had been arrived at independently by several authors, they first pointed out what we have already established – that the attainment of a Pareto optimum requires the simultaneous fulfilment of all the conditions. Given that one of these conditions cannot be fulfilled somewhere in the economy, it is no longer possible for the economy to attain a Pareto optimum – the best that can be attained is a so-called second best optimum. However, they then went on to argue that the attainment of a second best optimum will require a departure from other conditions as well. 'The belief that it is better to fulfil some of the conditions rather than none is false' (14).

Consider for example an economy which produces two groups of products only, agricultural goods and manufactured goods. Agricultural goods are produced under competitive conditions but manufacturing industry is controlled by monopolists. (There are no large-scale economies in either sector.) Price therefore exceeds marginal cost for manufactured goods but equals marginal cost for agricultural products. The economy fails to attain a (first best) Pareto optimum because the appropriate condition with respect to output efficiency is not met. (We will assume that the conditions relating to production and distributional efficiency are met.) A movement towards competitive pricing in the manufacturing sector would lead to an increase in the output of manufactured products. Some resources would be bid away from the agricultural sector, reducing output of agricultural products. Compared to the composition of output with a Pareto optimum, the presence of monopoly pricing in the manufactured sector leads the economy to produce too few manufactured products and too many agricultural goods.

The Government now decides to introduce a policy to support agricultural incomes. As we shall see in Chapter 8, a frequent method of agricultural income support is a policy designed to increase the prices received by farmers for their produce, and two alternative methods of raising farm prices are production quotas and product subsidies. Quotas restrict quantity of produce coming onto the market thereby pushing up market prices. In the case of product subsidies the Government supplements the price received by the farmer from the market.

What comment can the economist make concerning the implications for economic efficiency of these alternative methods of increasing agricultural prices? If we assume that farmers continue to attempt to maximise profits by equating marginal cost of production with the price *they* receive for their produce, then in the case of product subsidies, the marginal cost of production will exceed the price actually paid by the consumers (ignoring distributional margins). With production quotas, farmers are prevented from increasing output to the level at which marginal cost equals the price paid by the consumer. In terms of conventional economic criteria therefore, both policies would be regarded as representing departures from an efficient allocation of resources. But this is in fact only the case if the agricultural policy is introduced into an otherwise perfectly competitive world. When we take into account the existence of monopoly pricing in the manufacturing sector, one of the policies – the quota system – which restricts agricultural output thus releasing resources for use in manufacturing industry – takes the economy towards a second best optimum. The alternative policy of subsidising agricultural products leads to an increase in agricultural output, taking the economy further away from a second best solution.

At first sight the implications of the theory of second best are, to say the least, somewhat disquieting. Lipsey and Lancaster certainly took a very pessimistic view of the opportunities for deriving rules for judging the relative efficiencies of alternative economic situations. Subsequent writers (15) have been more optimistic. An investigation of their work on the theory of second best would take us well beyond the scope of a basic textbook, but three main points seem to have emerged.

First, it appears that the attainment of a second best optimum need not require a universal departure from the familiar optimising rules discussed in this chapter. In particular, there are likely to be circumstances where the fulfilment, wherever possible, of the production and exchange conditions will be what is required. The main culprit (as in our example) seems to be the output composition condition, but this does mean that equating marginal cost with price will not always lead to an increase in economic efficiency.

Second, it is argued that it may not be too difficult to apply a rule-of-thumb judgement to discover whether or not the application of the familiar optimising rules are likely to produce a movement towards a second best optimum.

'It would be very reasonable,' says Mishan, 'to believe that (i) the smaller are the constrained sectors relative to the remaining ones, and (ii) the larger are the initial price-marginal cost ratios of the free sectors as compared with the constrained sectors, the surer we are to improve matters by optimising in the free sector alone than by standing and sadly sucking our thumbs under the sign of second best' (16).

Third, it is suggested that it will sometimes be possible, on a case-by-case basis, to establish at least approximate optimising rules for the attainment of a second best optimum. (For example, much of the theory of customs union (17) is really an exercise in second best optimising.)

The theory of second best appears to leave three courses of action open to the economist who is interested in making observations concerning the relative economic efficiency of alternative agricultural policy devices. These are:

(a) To decide instead to make observations about something else.
(b) To attempt to derive second best optimising rules for whatever policy measure is under consideration.
(c) To take the view that the application of conventional economic efficiency criteria, although not always leading to a second best optimum, will nevertheless be likely to get a lot closer to it than applying no efficiency criteria at all. After all, as Mishan has argued, '[If we] descend for a moment to the exigencies of the real world, since time is taken to adjust the sizes of industries in response to continual changes in the overall pattern of demand, it is unlikely that at any instant of time we shall, even in the absence of all such constraints, attain a Pareto optimum, much less that we should for long maintain it. We can only hope to be moving in that direction most of the time and not too far away from an optimum for any prolonged period. It should not bother us too much then if we cannot pick out exact second best solutions provided that we are able to adjust frequently towards positions which are fairly close to optimal' (16).

A combination of (b) and (c) is of course also possible. One could apply the conventional efficiency criteria unless there is some fairly straightforward argument (as there was in the case of our agriculture/industry example) for suggesting that this would take us away from a second best position. 'If second best theory has a positive contribution to make it is of serving notice that, in the presence of constraints, slap-dash optimising, wherever one can, may not improve matters; one has in that case to proceed cautiously – which is rather different from not proceeding at all.' (Mishan again (16).)

With the theory of second best, there is a clear danger of throwing the baby out with the bath water. Although the search for second best optimising rules has many attractions, it has the disadvantage of making the policy message more difficult to comprehend. The economist can have some hope that the policy-maker will take account of questions of economic efficiency when recommendations are based on conventional efficiency criteria. In contrast, and to quote one of the Author's colleagues (who has experience as a government adviser), 'The trouble with the theory of second best is that if you ever once dare even to hint at its existence when in conversation with a policy-maker he immediately loses interest in *any* advice on agricultural policy which is based on economic analysis.' And on that note, we proceed to the next section, which examines the possibility of measuring welfare effects, and for which course of action (c) is required.

4 The measurement of welfare changes

4.1 Economic surplus

In the previous section we examined the relationship between welfare and competition. It was discovered that, given certain restrictive assumptions about the economy under consideration, a perfectly competitive equilibrium would lead to a Pareto optimum for society. This is why a competitively determined allocation of resources and distribution of products can be described as 'economically efficient'. It was further argued, however, that Governments would be most unlikely to accept the perfect market solution as an overall optimum for society when questions of distribution are taken into consideration. Governments formulate policies which seek to redistribute income among the population, and it is argued later that the distributional question has had a dominant influence upon the development of agricultural policies. The extent to which a Government will pursue distributional policies depends upon its view of when, and when not, the improvement in the position of one group of individuals more than offsets a worsening in the position of another group of individuals, or in more formal terms, it depends upon its view of the nature of the social welfare function.

Redistributional policies will mean a departure from competitively determined Pareto optimum. But there is no point in an economist criticising a government policy as 'economically inefficient' simply because of this. Some loss of economic efficiency is probably an inevitable consequence of a policy which is seen as improving social welfare. Similarly, there are other accepted objectives of government (lying outside the scope of the simple approach to social welfare adopted in this chapter) which may also imply departures from a competitively determined allocation of resources and distribution of products. A legitimate critique of the efficiency of a government policy must therefore take the form: 'Of two or more alternative methods of achieving a particular objective (an objective, say, of ensuring some minimum income level for a section of society), has the Government chosen a method which is economically less efficient than an alternative, in the sense that the choice of the alternative would represent a Pareto improvement for the economy?'

In order to be able to compare policies in this way we must have some measure of the welfare effects of alternative policy devices. For example, at the end of Chapter 8 a comparison in terms of economic efficiency is made between two alternative agricultural policy devices under the assumption that both achieve a specific income objective. The measurement technique used is known as *economic surplus*, which can refer to either consumer utility or factor income. In this chapter we restrict our investigation to the consumer measure. A discussion of the parallel measure relating to the ownership of factors of production will be found in Mishan (18), and we show how both measures can be applied to particular policy problems in the next chapter. A survey article in the *Economic Journal* (19) provides a comprehensive and readable background to the whole question of the concept of economic surplus and its use in economic analysis.

The concept of consumers' surplus (sometimes referred to as just 'consumer surplus') was first postulated by Marshall. He explained it as follows:

> The price which a person pays for a thing can never exceed, and seldom comes up to that which he would be willing to pay rather than go without it: so that the satisfaction which he gets from its purchase generally exceeds that which he gives up in paying away its price; and he thus derives from the purchase a surplus of satisfaction. The excess of the price which he would be willing to pay rather than go without the thing over that which he actually does pay, is the economic measure of this surplus satisfaction. It may be called consumers' surplus (20).

The value of this idea is that it can be expressed in terms of something which *is* measurable (or at least can be estimated) – the area under a demand curve. Suppose for example that a man is found to be purchasing eight loaves of bread per month and paying 20p per loaf (Fig. 5.7a). The price of bread falls successively to 19p and 18p per loaf and our consumer is found to be purchasing successively nine and ten loaves per month. It can be argued that he has enjoyed a net increase in satisfaction, an approximate measure of which is 17p, that is 2p on each loaf he would have bought if the price had remained at 20p per loaf, 1p on the loaf he would have been induced to buy if the price had fallen only to 19p per loaf, and nothing on the loaf he has just been induced to buy when the price fell to 18p.

Extending the concept to the market demand curve shown in Fig. 5.7b, if the price of a product falls from P_2 to P_1, a measure of the aggregate benefit to consumers of the price fall is the area P_2ABP_1, being the increase in consumers' surplus consequent upon the price fall.

Two major question marks have been raised over the use of consumers' surplus as a measure of changes in welfare. The first refers to the income effect of a price change. The second has provoked a debate over whether it is legitimate to use the technique if some individuals are made worse off as the result of the implementation of a policy.

4.2 The income effect[6]

Marshall eventually became dissatisfied with the consumer surplus measure because he was aware that a fall in the price of a good would make the consumer better off (i.e. would increase his real income) and that this in itself would affect what 'he would be willing to pay rather than go without the thing'. However, it was not until the development of indifference curve analysis allowed a more precise distinction to be made between the income and substitution effects of a price change (see Chapter 1, section 1.5) that a clear interpretation was possible of the welfare effects of measuring the area under a demand curve. Using indifference curve techniques, Hicks (21) in his own words 'rehabilitated' consumers' surplus and defined a measure of it which he called the *compensating variation* (*CV*). For the privilege of being able to buy a good at its existing price the consumer is willing to pay some maximum sum,

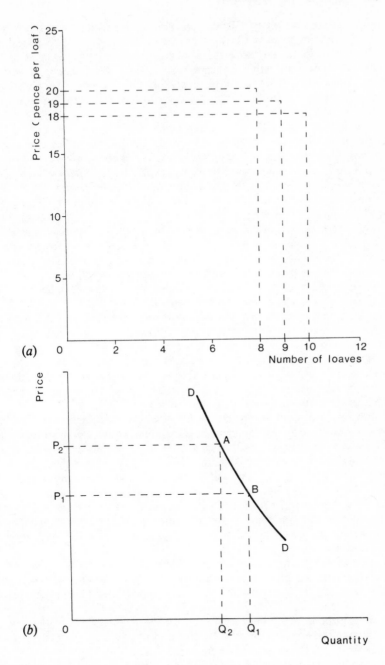

Figure 5.7

his compensating variation. Henderson (22) pointed out an alternative measure, the minimum sum the consumer would be prepared to accept to compensate him for abandoning the opportunity of buying the good at its existing price. The alternative measure was called the *equivalent variation* (*EV*) by Hicks (23). The two measures differ in that one (the *CV*) is a monetary valuation of the benefit to the consumer of the introduction of the good viewed from the level of utility he experiences in the absence of the good. On the other hand, the *EV* measure represents a monetary valuation of the benefit of the introduction of the good viewed from the higher level of utility experienced when the good is being purchased. If the consumer buys more of the good as his income increases then we will expect his monetary valuation of the benefit of being able to buy the good to increase with his income.

The distinction is illustrated in Fig. 5.8a (which is similar to Fig. 1.5). Quantity of good A is measured on the horizontal axis and the consumer's remaining money income on the vertical axis. Income is Y_0, and when the good is not available the level of utility is I_0, as the indifference curve I_0 intersects the Y axis at Y_0. However, when the good becomes available at price P_1 ($= Y_0/Q_0$) the consumer is able to achieve utility level I_1 by purchasing Q_1 of A.

The welfare gain to the consumer of the introduction of the good is unambiguous – it is the difference between the utility levels I_1 and I_0. The problem arises because we wish to find a monetary expression of this welfare gain. The *CV* measure asks the question: 'What is the maximum sum the consumer would be prepared to pay for the privilege of being able to buy the good?' The answer is Y_0Y_1 because, if we reduce the consumer's income to Y_1, by purchasing Q_2 of the good he is just able to achieve the same level of utility (I_0) when buying the good as he was experiencing with the higher level of income I_0 in the absence of the opportunity to buy the good.

Alternatively, we could ask the question: 'What is the minimum sum that the consumer would accept as compensation for abandoning the opportunity to buy the good at its existing price?' The answer is Y_2Y_0, since his income must be raised to Y_2 if he is to achieve the same level of utility without the good as he experiences with income Y_0 plus the opportunity to buy the good. The *CV* measure thus represents a monetary valuation of the introduction of the good viewed from the lower level of utility (I_0) experienced in the absence of the good, and the *EV* measure represents the monetary valuation of the introduction of the good viewed from the higher level of utility experienced after the introduction of the good.

If instead of examining the introduction of the good we were to consider the effect of the removal of the good, the *CV* question becomes, 'What is the minimum sum the consumer would accept as compensation for the removal of the good?' (The answer is Y_2Y_0.) And the *EV* question (which views the loss of the good from the level of utility received in its absence) becomes, 'What is the maximum sum the consumer would be prepared to pay to retain the privilege of being able to buy the good?'. (The answer is Y_0Y_1.)

The introduction or removal of a good is a special case of a price rise or price fall. More generally, therefore, the definition of *CV* is: the sum of money,

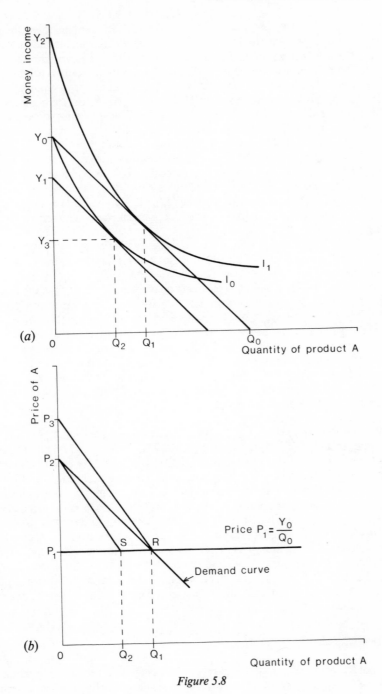

Figure 5.8

paid by the consumer when the price falls (or received by him when the price rises), which, following the change in price, leaves him at his initial level of utility. The EV is the sum of money, received by the consumer when the price falls (or paid by him when the price rises), which, if there were no price change, would nevertheless give him the same level of utility as the price change.

In Fig. 5.8b these measures are shown on a price/quantity diagram. The individual's demand curve for product A is defined by the points of tangency of budget lines and indifference curves. The budget line for income Y_0 and price P_1 is Y_0Q_0 in Fig. 5.8a giving a consumption of the product of Q_1. The individual's demand curve for the product must therefore pass through point R in Fig. 5.8b, where Q_1 is purchased at price P_1. Now let P_2 be the price which reduces the consumption of A to zero. This price would be given in Fig. 5.8a by the slope of a budget line tangential to I_0 at Y_0. We now have two points on the individual's demand curve, which, for convenience, is assumed to be a straight line in Fig. 5.8b.

We now construct in Fig. 5.8b two lines which represent measures of, respectively, the slopes of I_0 and I_1 at various levels of consumption. We have already defined the slope of I_0 at Y_0 as being equal to P_2, and we know that the slope of I_0 is equal to P_1 when Q_2 is being consumed. We thus have the line P_2S (like the demand curve it is assumed for convenience to be a straight line) which traces out the slope of I_0 at different levels of consumption of A. By a similar argument, if we define the slope of I_1 at its intersection with the Y axis (in Fig. 5.8a) as being equal to P_3, the line P_3R traces out the slope of I_1 at different levels of consumption of product A. The lines P_2S and P_3R are sometimes known as *compensated demand curves* since they show how much the individual will purchase of product A at different prices if his money income is continuously adjusted so as to leave his real income constant (at I_0 for P_2S, and at I_1 for P_3R).

We can now state that area P_1P_2S in Fig. 5.8b is equal to Y_0Y_1 in Fig. 5.8a, and that area P_1P_3R in Fig. 5.8b is equal to Y_2Y_0 in Fig. 5.8a.[7] The area under the demand curve P_1P_2R is an approximation to either of the exact measures of the consumer's surplus, and differs from them because of the income effect of a price change. If there were no income effect, the consumer would purchase the same quantities of good A at different income levels for any given price of good A. Geometrically, this requires the indifference curves to have the same slope for any given quantity of A. If I_0 and I_1 in Fig. 5.8a possessed this property, Q_2 would be the same quantity as Q_1, the two indifference curves would intersect the Y axis with the same slope, and the three measures of consumers' surplus would coincide. For most practical purposes the area under the individual's demand curve is a perfectly acceptable approximation to either of the exact measures.

4.3 The compensation principle

It would appear therefore that we can proceed with a certain amount of confidence on the basis that the area under a demand curve provides a realistic aggregate monetary measure of the welfare effects of a price change. This means that a policy which results in a net increase in consumer surplus for one or more individuals, and no reduction in consumer surplus for any other individuals, can be taken as representing a Pareto improvement for the society. But what happens if a calculation shows a net increase in consumers' surplus, but involves some individuals being made worse off? In 1939, Kaldor (24) argued that if a change in policy resulted in some persons being made better off and some worse off, but that the gainers could compensate the losers and still be better off themselves, then one had an objective criterion for recommending the policy because of the implied improvement in economic efficiency. This is precisely the situation that results if a particular policy produces a net gain in consumers' surplus – those that gain as a result of the policy could compensate those that lose and still be better off themselves. This argument has become known as the *compensation principle* and refers to hypothetical compensation, that is, the criterion was supposed to remain valid whether or not compensation takes place.

The simple kind of welfare maximisation model described earlier in this chapter had not been fully developed at the time Kaldor was writing. Its application to the compensation principle clarifies one point immediately. If compensation does not take place, the fact that some individuals are made worse off means that a Pareto improvement is not involved, and whether or not the policy represents an improvement can only be decided by reference to a social welfare function.

For example, suppose the Government introduces a policy which has the effect of increasing the price of bread and reducing the price of champagne, and it is found that the gain in consumers' surplus on champagne exceeds the loss on bread. Since it is probable that champagne will be purchased by only a small proportion of the population who have relatively high incomes, the poorer sections of society will be made worse off. If this kind of redistribution is regarded as undesirable, it is irrelevant that champagne drinkers could compensate the remainder of the population and still be better off themselves – irrelevant, that is, unless compensation does take place, in which case a Pareto improvement is involved (assuming the process of compensation to be costless). We must conclude therefore that the calculation of a net increase in economic surplus following the implementation of a government policy cannot provide a clear justification for the policy if a redistribution of income is involved which the Government regards as undesirable. But what if the policy implies a redistribution which the Government favours (or at least towards which it is neutral)? Shortly after the postulation by Kaldor of the compensation principle, Scitovsky (25) pointed out an ambiguity in its application when a policy involves redistribution, an ambiguity which applies irrespective of whether or not the redistribution is regarded as desirable or undesirable. This in its turn became known as 'Scitovsky's paradox' and was succinctly summarised by Robertson as follows:

> Mr Kaldor suggested that, if there occurred a structural economic change from B to A, say the imposition or removal of a tariff, then general ecfare

[Robertson's name for economic welfare] can truthfully be said to have been increased if it turns out that those whose ecfare has been increased by the change could compensate in money those whose ecfare has been diminished, and still find their ecfare increased. . . . It was pointed out by Professor Scitovsky that the distribution of income may be so altered by the change from B to A that it would now be possible, if the change back to B were made, for those whose ecfare would be increased by this reverse change to compensate those whose ecfare would be diminished, and still find their own ecfare increased. In this case we would have to say that general ecfare was both greater at A than B and greater at B than A, which does not seem a very sensible thing to say (26).

The nature of the Scitovsky paradox can best be understood by the use of an analytical device – the *community indifference curve* – which has found most of its applications in international trade theory and which in any case, we will need for our discussion of international trade policy in Chapter 7. For illustrative purposes, we return to a two-commodity/two-person world.

Take any pair of utility levels of individuals U and V, say those labelled u_3 and v_6 at point c_1 in Fig. 5.9a. In Fig. 5.9b, one combination of the two products A and B which is able, by an appropriate efficient distribution to achieve the utility levels u_3 and v_6 is Oa of A and Ob of B. By constructing the box $OaRb$ and, as before, locating the origin for U at O, and the origin for V at R, any point within the box can represent a specific allocation of the available quantities of A and B to U and V. By choosing the allocation of A and B given by the point of tangency of indifference curves u_3 and v_6, it is just possible to attain utility levels u_3 and v_6.

There are, however, many other combinations of the products A and B which can attain u_3 for U together with v_6 for V. The community indifference curve, C_1 is a line joining different combinations of the products A and B which, while maintaining an efficient distribution of the products, can, if appropriately allocated between U and V, just attain the pair of utilities u_3 and v_6.

Consider another pair of utilities, u_4 and v_8 (point c_2 in Fig. 5.9a). We know that none of the combinations of products lying on community indifference curve C_1 will be able to attain u_4 and v_8; all these combinations possess the property that, by a suitably efficient distribution, it is just possible to attain u_3 and v_6, but not a Pareto improvement upon u_3 and v_6 such as u_4 and v_8. Every point on community indifference curve C_2 must therefore contain more of both A and B than some point on C_1, and thus these two community indifference curves cannot intersect.

Now take a third pair of utilities, u_6 and v_4 (point c_2' in Fig. 5.9a). Compared with both points c_1 and c_2, c_2' represents an improvement for U but a deterioration for V – i.e. not a Pareto improvement. It is now quite possible that one of the combinations of A and B which can achieve u_6 and v_4 might also be able to achieve either u_4 and v_8 or u_3 and v_6. In Fig. 5.9b, a redistribution from V to U along the contract curve in box $OaRb$ could in fact cause a movement from u_3 and v_6 to u_6 and v_4. If therefore we trace out a

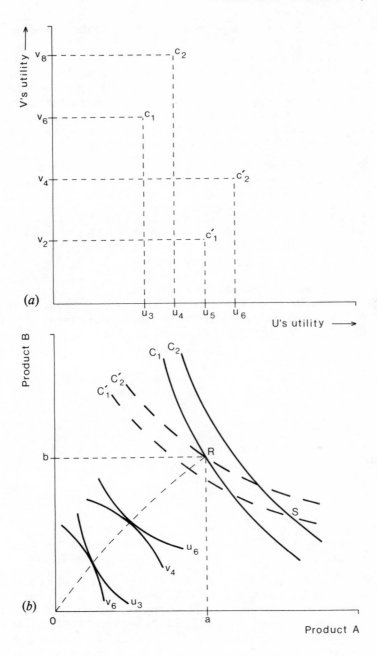

Figure 5.9

community indifference curve for u_6 and v_4 (shown by the broken line, C_2') it will intersect C_1 at point R.

Two community indifference curves which relate to two different levels of welfare in society, neither of which is a Pareto improvement upon the other, thus have the disturbing property that they can cross. This means that if we postulate a set of non-intersecting community indifference curves (as we do in Chapter 7) and use them to illustrate how a government policy (such as the removal or imposition of a tariff) can improve the position of a country, the technique is only valid if either:

(a) no member of society is made worse off by the policy change, or
(b) compensation takes place to ensure that no member of society is worse off as a result of the change in policy.

Returning now to the Scitovsky paradox, suppose that a particular policy changes the output composition of the economy from position R to position S in Fig. 5.9b. The original distribution of products at R generates utility levels u_3 and v_6 and the new distribution at S gives u_5 and v_2. The fact that S lies above and to the right of part of indifference curve C_1 means simply that it is possible to find a distribution of the quantities of A and B available at S which is a Pareto improvement upon u_3 and v_6. In other words, it would be possible for the gainers from the policy change (in this case U) to compensate the losers (V) and still be better off themselves. Indeed, we know from the diagram, that since point S lies on community indifference curve C_2, compensation could take place so as to achieve u_4 and v_8.

If, however, compensation does not take place we find that precisely the same comments can be made about the reverse move; there is a distribution at R (for example, u_6 and v_4) which is a Pareto improvement upon the actual distribution at S (u_5 and v_2). The paradox arises because compensation is hypothetical. If compensation does take place following the move from R to S, then a Pareto improvement is made. Similarly, if compensation takes place following the reverse move from S to R (with initial distribution at S being u_5 and v_2), then a Pareto improvement is made.

Where then does this leave the compensation principle? To quote Robertson again:

> The plain man's difficulty with it is that it seems to make what *does* happen to general ecfare depend on what *might* happen, but doesn't and very likely for practical reasons couldn't in the way of compensation (26).

The policy message is that distributional questions cannot be ignored. A calculation which shows that a particular policy change would lead to a net increase in economic surplus is of little value if nothing is known of the distribution of the various costs and benefits involved. A calculation which shows a net increase in economic surplus and identifies the extent to which various sections of society are affected by the policy change can be extremely useful. Recent work by agricultural economists has tended to move in this direction – taking a particular policy device and both analysing its effect in terms of efficiency criteria and estimating the extent to which the various groups in society – e.g. producers, taxpayers and consumers – are either net gainers or net losers of the policy.

Given that a reliable estimate of the extent and distribution of the change in economic surplus likely to follow the introduction of a particular policy can be made, the task of assessing the merits of the policy is still by no means straightforward. Even if we restrict judgement upon the policy to questions of efficiency and distribution, a calculation which shows a net increase in economic surplus would only appear to imply an unambiguous improvement if either:

(a) no one is made worse off as a result of the policy; or
(b) all those who are made worse off are compensated by those who are made better off.

Where it is inevitable that some people will be made worse off by the policy, then a judgement is only possible in the context of some distributional objective.

(a) If a policy change shows a net loss in economic surplus and involves a redistribution which is regarded as undesirable, the policy can be rejected on both distributional and efficiency grounds.
(b) If, however, a policy change implies a desirable redistribution then it is the reverse (Scitovsky) criterion which is relevant from the point of view of economic efficiency.

In practical terms, (b) means that the supply and demand curves used for estimating changes in economic surplus ought to be those relating to the distribution of income which follows the policy change rather than those existing before the change. Though not an impossible task, this is clearly much more difficult than to make estimates based on existing relationships, and in practice it is usual to assume (probably quite reasonably) that the Scitovsky paradox does not apply. (An example of the kind of policy change which might lead to the occurrence of the Scitovsky paradox is given in the next chapter.)

Where there is a conflict between the efficiency and distributional aspects of a policy change, a judgement upon whether or not an improvement is involved can only be made by reference to a social welfare function. Since social welfare functions (though imprecisely formulated) are part of the business of government, when an economist is unable to make a recommendation himself, the Government will (or at least should) nevertheless be interested in his calculations of the efficiency and distributional impact of a particular policy.

5 Conclusion

In the remainder of this book we consider the application of economic principles to three broad areas of interaction between government policy and agriculture. First, we look at the appraisal of large-scale public investment projects. This area of government policy frequently impinges upon agriculture – particularly in the context of land use – but is not normally regarded as part of agricultural policy as such. Next, we investigate various aspects of the relationship between government policies and international trade in agricultural products. Finally, we attempt a more systematic approach to the analysis of agricultural policies, examining various policy instruments primarily in relation to the one objective which seems to have been predominant in the post-1945 period – agricultural income support.

We will find that the ideas developed in this chapter concerning the conventional meaning of economic efficiency, its relation to income distribution, and the possibility of measuring the welfare effects of economic changes, are central to the way economic principles have been applied to the study of agricultural policy.

Notes

[1] This lack is beginning to be remedied by the appearance of chapters on welfare economics in some modern microeconomic textbooks. Kelvin Lancaster's book (5) and the Open University's *Second Level Course* (6) are noteworthy in this respect.

[2] After the Italian-born economist who worked at Lausanne, Vilfredo Pareto (1848–1923).

[3] The concept of a social welfare function was originated by Bergson (8). Arrow (9) explored some of the complexities involved in deriving, in a free society, a social welfare function based on individual preference patterns.

[4] There is an implicit assumption here that the utility functions for U and V are of such a form as to prevent the contract curve going off the edge of the box. A similar assumption applies to the production functions in Fig. 5.2.

[5] The way in which Government distribution policy will lead to a departure from the Pareto conditions is of course a complex affair. The matter is dealt with in some detail by Peter Bohm in *Social Efficiency: A Concise Introduction to Welfare Economics* (Chapter 3 – 'Efficiency aspects of employment and distribution policy') (12).

[6] Section 4.2 is difficult and may be omitted on first reading. It shows that the area under an individual's demand curve for a product is an approximate measure of the change in utility he experiences as a consequence of a change in the price of the product. It therefore relates the consumer surplus measure to a welfare change for society, as illustrated, for example, by a movement from S to P in Fig. 5.5.

[7] This is not difficult to prove but requires the use of calculus. P_2S in Fig. 5.8b is the first differential of the indifference curve I_0. By integration, therefore, area OP_2SQ_2 in Fig. 5.8b is equal to Y_0Y_3 in Fig. 5.8a. But OP_1SQ_2 (Fig. 5.8b) equals Y_1Y_3 (Fig. 5.8a) being the amount spent on the product when money income is Y_1. Thus Y_0Y_1 equals area P_1P_2S. Similarly, Y_2Y_0 equals area P_1P_3R.

References

(1) Winch, D. M. *Analytical Welfare Economics*. London, Penguin, 1971.

(2) Dobb, M. *Welfare Economics and Economics of Socialism*. Cambridge University Press, 1969.

(3) Mishan, E. J. 'A survey of welfare economics, 1939–59.' *Economic Journal*, Vol. LXX, No. 278, June 1960.

(4) Arrow, K. J. & Scitovsky, T. (eds.). *Readings in Welfare Economics*. American Economic Association. London, Allen & Unwin, 1969.

(5) Lancaster, K. *An Introduction to Modern Microeconomics*. Chicago, Rand McNally, 1969. (Read (6) in conjunction with the relevant chapter of this book.)

(6) *Income Distribution and Welfare*. Social Sciences: a second level course, Microeconomics Units 13–14. Open University Press, 1974.

(7) Little, I. M. D. *A Critique of Welfare Economics*, 2nd edn. Oxford University Press, 1957.

(8) Bergson, A. 'A reformulation of certain aspects of welfare economics.' *Quarterly Journal of Economics*, Vol. LII, No. 4, Feb. 1938. (The article is under the name of Birk.)

(9) Arrow, K. J. *Social Choice and Individual Values*. New York, 1951.

(10) Smith, Adam. *An Enquiry into the Nature and Causes of the Wealth of Nations*, 4th edn. 1826.

(11) Walras, L. *Elements of Pure Economics*, 1926. (Translated by W. Jaffe, 1954.)

(12) Bohm, P. *Social Efficiency: A Concise Introduction to Welfare Economics*. London, Macmillan, 1973.

(13) Tuck, R. H. 'An examination of some main objectives in agricultural economic policy.' *Journal of Agricultural Economics*, Vol. XVIII, No. 1, Jan. 1967.

(14) Lipsey, R. G. & Lancaster, K. 'The general theory of second best.' *Review of Economic Studies*, Vol. XXIV, 1957.

(15) Some contributions to the second best debate, plus references to others, are collected in 'The Theory of Second Best.' *Review of Economic Studies*, Vol. XXIV, July 1967.

(16) Mishan, E. J. 'Second thoughts on second best.' *Oxford Economic Papers*, N.S., Oct. 1962.

(17) Lipsey, R. G. 'The theory of customs union: a general survey.' *Economic Journal*, Vol. LXX, Sept. 1960.

(18) Mishan, E. J. 'What is producer's surplus?' *American Economic Review*, 1968.

(19) Currie, J. M., Murphy, J. A. & Schmitz, A. 'The concept of economic surplus and its use in economic analysis.' *Economic Journal*, Vol. LXXXI, Dec. 1971.

(20) Marshall, A. *Principles of Economics*, 8th edn. London, Macmillan, 1920.

(21) Hicks, J. R. 'The rehabilitation of consumers' surplus.' *Review of Economic Studies*, Vol. VIII, 1941.

(22) Henderson, A. M. 'Consumers' surplus and the compensating variation.' *Review of Economic Studies*, Vol. VIII, 1941.

(23) Hicks, J. R. 'Consumers' surplus and index numbers.' *Review of Economic Studies*, Vol. IX, 1941.

(24) Kaldor, N. 'Welfare propositions in economics.' *Economic Journal*, 1939.

(25) Scitovsky, T. 'A note on welfare propositions in economics.' *Review of Economic Studies*, Vol. IX, 1941.

(26) Robertson, Sir Dennis. 'Utility and All That.' The Manchester School, May 1951.

CHAPTER 6

Social Cost–Benefit Analysis (with Special Reference to the Appraisal of Agricultural Projects)

1 Introduction

Cost–benefit analysis is the name given to the process of assessing the merit, from the point of view of the community as a whole, of the allocation of investment funds to a particular project or between competing projects. The procedure is also applicable to many aspects of government policy not directly involving the investment of public funds and the term is sometimes used in this context as well. (For example, one might reasonably describe an attempt to assess the merits of a set of government policies designed to stimulate domestic farm output as 'a social cost–benefit analysis of domestic agricultural expansion'. Similarly, one could describe an attempt to evaluate the consequences, from the point of view of the country as a whole, of a government decision to introduce a system of levies on imported agricultural products as a 'cost–benefit analysis of the new policy'.)

In this chapter we concentrate on the problems associated with the appraisal of public investment projects (or, as will sometimes be required, the public appraisal of private investment schemes) giving special attention to those kinds of projects which involve, directly or indirectly, agricultural production. Some examples of the application of cost–benefit techniques in the broader context of overall agricultural policy will be found in Chapters 7 and 8.

The starting point for any cost–benefit analysis is the compilation of a list (or diary) of all the extra costs and benefits foreseen as the result of the project, and attaching to these costs and benefits the date or dates to which they are applicable. Thus:

Time period	Cost	Benefit
1	C_{11}, C_{12}, C_{13}, etc.	B_{11}, B_{12}, B_{13}, etc.
2	C_{21}, C_{22}, C_{23}, etc.	B_{21}, B_{22}, B_{23}, etc.
3	C_{31}, C_{32}, C_{33}, etc.	B_{31}, B_{32}, B_{33}, etc.
etc.	etc.	etc.

At this stage, costs and benefits would be listed in terms of their own units, for example, 200 tons of wheat; five tractors; 7000 gallons of petrol; six semi-detached houses; 4000 jobs; and so on.

We may divide the problems connected with compiling and interpreting such a list into three groups.

(a) The process of compiling a correct list, i.e. achieving a good diary as above, including all the items that it should, and none that it should not.

(b) The process of attaching the correct 'price tags' to the various costs and benefits so that they can be aggregated to form a monetary valuation.

(c) The process of reducing costs and benefits which occur in dissimilar time periods to a common base for comparison (i.e. some form of discounting procedure).

These three groups of problems connected with compiling and interpreting a list of costs and benefits might equally well apply to the analysis of any project, whether public or private. When considered from the point of view of the individual firm, questions relating to large-scale investment projects differ only in degree from other management decisions. The overall business objectives of the firm, and many of the tools of analysis used as aids to decision-making, will be the same. The large-scale nature of the project will require an extension of techniques to deal with costs and returns occurring over a longer time period, and some systematic method of making provision for risk and uncertainty (which tends to increase as the time horizon is lengthened) may need to be introduced.

The crucial distinction between the 'private' appraisal which might be undertaken on behalf of the individual firm responsible for a project, and a social cost–benefit analysis of the same project concerns the *objectives* to which the appraisal will be related. In principle, costs and benefits falling upon any member of society[1] may be included in a social cost–benefit analysis – although ethical distributional judgements may rule out the interests of certain individuals. In other words, in the language of the previous chapter, a social cost–benefit analysis views the merits of a project on the basis of its impact upon *social welfare* and in the context of a view of the relevant *social welfare function*. It is this which makes welfare economics the foundation upon which cost–benefit analysis must be built, and indeed some writers refer to cost–benefit analysis simply as 'applied welfare economics'. In contrast, private project appraisal is concerned only with the interests of a specific group of individuals responsible for a project, and the subject matter of welfare economics is of no relevance to the choice of an appropriate decision from their point of view, except inasmuch as some large-scale private investment projects may require government approval. In such circumstances, the firm involved may think it wise to point out to the Government some of the 'social' benefits of the project.

This does not of course necessarily mean that many individuals in an economy, apart from the shareholders (or whatever), will not benefit from a privately funded project (as they can, for example, via employment or tax revenue) nor indeed that, under certain circumstances, private and social objectives might not lead to identical (or at least very similar) decisions concerning a particular project. In the previous chapter it was shown that, if we make certain assumptions about the kind of economy under consideration, then the pursuit of private objectives (consumers acting so as to maximise utility and producers so as to maximise profits) would lead the economy to a Pareto optimum position. This position, it was argued, could be described as representing an 'efficient' allocation of resources in the sense that it gave the maximum value of goods and services that the economy was capable of producing, if output was valued at prevailing market prices. It was further pointed out that equilibrium prices in a perfect market economy would reflect the relative values placed by consumers on alternative quantities of different goods, but that this consumer valuation was related to the distribution of income which was itself solely determined by the equilibrium prices of factors of production in the perfect market economy.

Now, the implication of this argument for cost–benefit analysis is that the simple pursuit of private objectives will serve the public interest (or to put it another way, a private project appraisal should lead to the same decision as would a social cost–benefit analysis) if three sets of requirements are met:

(a) A set of assumptions, similar to those made with respect to the simple model of an economy used in the previous chapter, must apply to the economy now under consideration.
(b) The economy must be in perfect market equilibrium.
(c) We must accept the prevailing income distribution as being appropriate from the point of view of valuing costs and benefits.

In spite of the fact that in any real world situation these requirements will not be met, economists nevertheless regard the argument that it is possible to stipulate a set of conditions which, if met, would result in the pursuit of private objectives also meeting social objectives as being particularly significant for cost–benefit analysis. Because of it they are able to justify a cost–benefit procedure in which (i) the project is evaluated in the same way as it would be in private project appraisal – i.e. the question is asked, 'Is it profitable?', but in addition, (ii) an attempt is made to adjust this evaluation of costs and benefits where there appears to be a significant departure for the conditions required for the pursuit of private objectives to be consistent with social objectives.

Because the cost–benefit procedure is typically of this form, we shall find it convenient in this chapter to take the three groups of problems mentioned earlier, i.e. compiling a correct list of costs and benefits, valuing costs and benefits, and discounting for time, and consider how in each case the appraisal of a project from the point of view of social objectives might lead to a different approach than would be the case if the project was appraised on the basis of private objectives.

2 Identifying costs and benefits

Three main areas appear to be involved when considering the effect of social rather than private objectives on the problem of compiling a correct list of costs and benefits. These refer to the *number of individuals* it is necessary to consider, the *kinds of things* which might qualify as costs and benefits, and cases where there are costs and benefits which '*spill over*' the boundaries of the project itself.

As already mentioned, typically the range of individuals whose costs and benefits 'count' will be greater in the case of social cost–benefit analysis. It may include all the members of society, whereas, for the purpose of decision-making anyway, the range of individuals to be considered for a private project may be restricted to a very few. It is possible, however, that the range will be narrower if income distribution considerations entirely rule out costs and benefits falling upon certain individuals who would figure largely in the tabulation of costs and benefits for the same or similar project evaluated under private objectives.

Social objectives may lead to a whole range of effects being regarded as costs and benefits which one would not normally find entered in private accounting – for example, the provision of employment, saving foreign exchange, affecting the amenity value of the countryside, and so on. A study of polder development in the Netherlands (1) takes crop output as the primary benefit, but lists a whole range of other benefits, including:

More space for housing
Wider facilities for recreation
The stimulating effect on scientific theory and practice
Better food supplies in times of need
Reorganisation of land
Contributions towards the goodwill and reputation of the Netherlands abroad
A sense of achievement
A contribution to healthy social development

It may be that some of these kinds of costs and benefits do not readily lend themselves to this kind of analysis at all – it may be very difficult to go much beyond identifying them. This leads to a frequent dilemma in cost–benefit analysis – whether or not to attempt some sort of valuation of these less tangible costs and benefits. The danger of doing so is that the estimated value may be wildly inaccurate; the danger of not doing so is that the policy-maker may ignore an important welfare effect of a project simply because it is not included in the formal addition of costs or benefits.

Perhaps the most obvious situation in which social cost–benefit analysis will require the identification of effects that would often not be included in private project appraisal concerns those costs and benefits which are said to *spill over* the natural boundaries of a project. An *external effect* (or an *externality*) is defined as a direct effect on someone's profit or welfare arising as an incidental by-product of some other firm's or person's activity. The most commonly cited externalities tend to be environmental (e.g. water, air and noise pollution) and the main problem here is not so much identifying them as evaluating them. However, it is not necessarily the case that all externalities should be included in a cost–benefit analysis. To help to identify those which should, a distinction has been made (2) between *technological* and *pecuniary* spillovers. A technological spillover occurs when an external effect of a project alters the physical production possibilities open to other producers or the satisfaction possibilities open to consumers. A pecuniary spillover, on the other hand, involves a monetary transfer within the economy. (In the language of the previous chapter, a technological spillover involves an outward movement of the welfare frontier and a pecuniary spillover does not.)

We can illustrate the distinction by the use of an example of a simple project, which is to construct a road from an area where an agricultural product is cultivated to a market centre. Prior to the building of the road, communications between the production area and the market centre were not good enough to make the marketing of the product worthwhile. The benefit of the project is the net profit from extra sales of the product and the cost is that of constructing the road, but these do not concern us here.

Now, suppose the road just happens to pass by a small local petrol station and that, as a result, the proprietor of the petrol station benefits from a substantial increase in his profit. This would be of no concern to a private project appraisal, but should the benefit be included in a social cost–benefit analysis of such a project?

The extra profit for the filling station may have arisen in a number of different ways. The source of the extra profit might be increased operational efficiency, increased sales, a higher price per unit of sales, or some combination of the three.

(a) The simplest to deal with is increased operational efficiency, which results as an incidental by-product of the road. This represents a true technological spillover – the physical production possibilities of the economy have been enlarged and the increased profit is associated with a net gain to the economy. Part of the benefits of increased operational efficiency may have been passed on to petrol users in the form of lower price; in this case some of the benefit may already have been included if the project (itself perhaps one of these petrol users) had correctly anticipated the price of petrol applicable to it, but an allowance should also be made where it involves non-project petrol users.

(b) Increased sales may be to project or non-project users. The extra petrol may be diverted from other petrol stations or be imported, but only in the case where the source of petrol was – say – an oil well in the back garden of the filling station, which was gushing forth previously unused supplies, would it seem legitimate to include extra profit from increased sales as an external benefit.

(c) If the extra profit is derived from an increase in the price of petrol sold by the station because of a semimonopolistic position in the face of increased demand, then the benefit is a transfer from petrol users to the filling station proprietor, and should not be included. (This is the kind of effect which often results in higher rent values adjacent to new roads.) However, if purchases of this petrol were an element in the original list of costs of the project and if the monopoly price was used when pricing these, the part of the filling station's extra profit derived from sales to the project would need to be included to offset the element of the cost of the project which represents only a transfer payment within the economy.

Alternatively, when the project was costed, a 'shadow' price, which was lower than the market price actually paid for the petrol, could have been used. See section 3.4 below.

If petrol is higher priced here than elsewhere in the economy because of cost of transport to this point of delivery, then no extra profit would be involved. If the price of petrol in the economy as a whole rises due to the operation of the project, then we are in the realms of a deeper problem, which is dealt with in the next section.

This simple example illustrates what is, perhaps, the one golden rule of cost–benefit analysis – that it is an exercise in the application of economic logic and not an exercise in the application of a set of rules. We have justified the inclusion, as a benefit, of an externality which increases the productive capacity of the economy, in this case expressed as a reduction in the quantity of resources per unit of output required by the filling station, on the grounds that the community would regard extra goods a benefit. We have argued that an externality which constitutes a transfer within the economy should not be included – but it might very well figure as a benefit if it involves a transfer within the economy that we are able to regard as beneficial, in the sense that it is consistent with some government objective towards income distribution (see section 3.3 below). Similarly, we have argued that a pecuniary spillover might need to be included as a benefit if the method of costing the project has included transfer payments.

3 Measuring costs and benefits

3.1 The use of market prices

The great attribute of market prices, with all their shortcomings, is that they provide an enormous amount of information concerning production possibilities, consumer preferences, and sometimes government objectives, which is available to the economist at relatively low cost. One might go further: cost–benefit analysis, as presently understood, would be unlikely to exist if price data were not available to provide a basis for valuing costs and benefits. Otherwise, resources and products could have whatever values decision-makers required them to have in order to be able to deem a project worthwhile (or not). Equally however, if market prices always provided a perfect valuation of all relevant costs and benefits there would be no need for cost–benefit analysis to exist as a distinct technique since private initiative and conventional financial assessment could be relied upon to meet social objectives.

In this section, circumstances in which a valuation of costs and benefits at market prices might be regarded as inappropriate in a social cost–benefit analysis are considered under four headings – non-marginal changes, income distribution, shadow prices, and non-traded items.

3.2 Valuing non-marginal changes

When a project has a significant effect on the market price of some product or factor we must resort to the relevant supply or demand curve in order to attach an appropriate 'social' valuation of the extra output produced or the extra inputs used. Figure 6.1 depicts the market for some food product (A). DD is the demand curve and SS the supply curve. Equilibrium is attained with 200 units sold at a price of P_2 per unit.

Now consider a project which produces a fixed quantity of 100 units of product A per time period. The impact of this on the market for product A will be to force down market price, increasing consumption but reducing the quantity supplied by existing (non-project) producers. A new equilibrium will

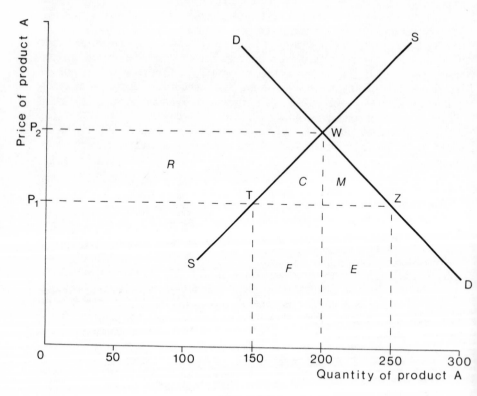

Figure 6.1

be established, with 250 units sold at price P_1; 150 units are supplied by existing producers and 100 units by the project.

We will assume that the project is costed separately; our task is to estimate the benefit of the 100 units of product A produced by the project.

Even if we are content to value the output of the project at market prices, we have in this case a problem – which price? Should it be P_1 or P_2? Consider first that part of the output of the project which constitutes increased consumption. Consumers could have been induced to pay almost price P_2 for 201st unit consumed but are only prepared to pay price P_1 for the 250th unit consumed. Thus it is argued that the demand curve between W and Z indicates the marginal valuation of an extra quantity of 50 units of product A when 200 units are already being consumed. The value of the extra 50 units is therefore the area under this section of the demand curve (area M + area E).

The remaining 50 units produced by the project displace supplies by existing producers. If non-project producers of product A supply under conditions of perfect competition (a very important if), the supply curve between T and W will indicate the marginal cost of producing extra units of product A between a total supply of 150 and a total supply of 200 units. Thus if existing producers reduce their supply from 200 units to 150 units the value of resources released will be indicated by the area under the supply curve between W and T, i.e. area C + area F.

In aggregate, then, the benefit to the economy of the project's output of 100 units of product A per time period is area $C + F + M + E$. Note that this 'social' valuation of the output of the project exceeds the valuation it would be given in a private project appraisal by an amount $C + M$, since the relevant valuation by a private project would be the revenue from the sale of the produce, which is 100 units at price P_1, i.e. area $F + E$.

3.3 Distribution

Cost–benefit studies have often ignored distributional questions, so that the philosophy of the practice becomes 'if total benefits, to whomsoever they accrue, exceed by some suitable margin total costs, upon whomsoever they fall, then in principle the project is deemed worthwhile'. There are two basic objections to this approach.

First, it is in fact impossible to ignore distributional questions entirely. If for example we value products and resources at prevailing market prices then this valuation is not independent of income distribution – it is a valuation which is related to the existing income distribution. In Chapter 1 we discussed how a change in the distribution of income might be expected to bring a new pattern of demand. Purchasing patterns differ for a wide variety of reasons – because of age, sex, education, etc., but more than anything else because of income itself. If we take £10 000 from a rich man and distribute it among the poor it will most probably be spent on very different products and this would, in turn, imply adjustments in the equilibrium level of market prices.

The second objection to the view that distributional questions can be ignored is that, since cost–benefit analysis is ultimately concerned with the levels of welfare attained by individuals, unless one takes the view that the consumption of a particular product contributes equally to social welfare irrespective of which member of society consumes it, then it must matter how the costs and benefits of a project are distributed. Any project is likely to have some redistributive effect – it is virtually inconceivable that net benefits will be distributed precisely in relation to the existing income distribution. A significant degree of redistribution may occur where, for example, the project is financed from a progressive tax system, where the output of the project is purchased mainly by high or low income groups, where a project draws substantially upon a particular resource, thus forcing up its price, and where externalities are involved (since these are often associated with a comparatively small number of individuals).

The dangers inherent in attempting to ignore distributional effects were stressed by the Reading University research team who are monitoring the impact on agriculture of the new city of Milton Keynes:

> It is clear … that the costs associated with the impact upon the agri-cultural industry of the new city of Milton Keynes (with the possible exception of rural visual amenity) are very small in relation to the overall balance between costs and benefits. However, these costs possess in common the feature of being associated with a small number of individuals. The practice of judging the merit of a development project upon the basis of the relationship between overall costs and benefits to society as a whole breaks down if certain individuals in society are obliged, personally, to bear a disproportionate share of the costs. For example, society is unlikely to tolerate a situation which results in 4000 individuals being £1 per annum better off at the expense of one individual losing the whole of his income of, say, £2000 per annum – although the crude cost benefit ratio to society as a whole shows an excess of benefit over cost of 100 per cent. It is for this reason that the practice of compensation is of great importance. If costs to individuals are correctly assessed, and compensation is paid in full, then these items of costs will be distributed throughout the community in line with general taxation policy (3).

This kind of argument stresses the importance in cost–benefit analysis of not only attempting a general valuation of project output and resources used, but also of identifying the impact upon different sections of society. If, for example, we return to Fig. 6.1 we can see that, whereas consumers of product A benefit from the project, existing producers of product A are made worse off. The economic surplus measurement technique (described in the previous chapter) enables us to assess the impact of the project on producers and consumers of product A. Consumers benefit by the gain in consumers' surplus ($R + C + M$). Producers previously sold 200 units at price P_2, but in the new equilibrium situation they sell 150 units at price P_1 – there is therefore a fall in revenue received by existing producers of $R + C + F$. However, in reducing their output by 50 units, existing producers reduce their costs by $C + F$, so that they suffer a net loss of area R, and we usually refer to this as a reduction in *producers' surplus*.

Note that we can also obtain the estimated overall benefit of the project output using the economic surplus technique. (Remember, we have left aside the cost of the project itself.) We have:

Benefit to consumers (increase in consumers' surplus) $= R + C + M$
Cost to producers (reduction in producers' surplus) $\quad = -R$
Revenue received by project $\qquad\qquad\qquad\qquad\qquad\quad = F + E$
Therefore net benefit of project output $\qquad\qquad\quad = C + M + F + E$

We would expect this result to be the same as that obtained in the previous section since we are only adding up the same information in a different way. But the economic surplus technique has the clear advantage over a valuation of output and resources in that it gives both an overall comparison of costs and benefits *and* identifies the major components of the distributional impact of the project.

When a project does seriously disadvantage a group in society then this seems to be in general a problem for the policy-maker rather than for the project appraiser. Perhaps the most satisfactory answer (as suggested in the quotation from the Milton Keynes investigation) is compensation. In fact, we can use Fig. 6.1 to illustrate the compensation principle, which we met in the previous chapter (section 4.3). Let us assume that the cost of the resources used by the project is covered by the revenue from the sale of the product ($F + E$) and we are concerned here only with the impact of project output on producers and consumers. Since the gain in consumers' surplus ($R + C + M$) exceeds the loss in producers' surplus (R) it *would* be possible, in principle, for consumers to compensate producers and still be better off themselves. If therefore compensation does take place (and it is not too costly) then a Pareto improvement is involved.

If compensation is not possible, then a judgement must be made by the policy-maker as to whether the benefit to those who are made better off is sufficient to outweigh the loss to those who are made worse off. In the case of the example illustrated by Fig. 6.1, such a decision might not be too difficult, but where a project affects a number of different groups in society, making some better off and others worse off, then there is a danger that the policy-maker will simply ignore the distributional impact (because of its complexity). For this reason, some writers have suggested (4) that a cost–benefit analysis might go beyond merely identifying the impact of a project on different groups in society; the project appraiser might attach weights to the various costs and benefits, the weights depending upon which group is affected. The weights would be derived from past decision by policy-makers and would be, in effect, an attempt to interpret from the observed action of Government an approximate view of the relevant social welfare function.

When compensation does not take place, either because it is not possible or because the distributional effect of the project is consistent with some overall government policy towards redistribution within the economy, then another problem arises. A project for which, on the basis of prevailing market prices, benefits exceed costs, might conceivably so alter the distribution of income, that costs exceed benefits when valued on the basis of equilibrium prices in the post-project situation. This is what we referred to in the previous chapter (section 4.3) as 'Scitovsky's paradox'.

For example, take a society where the general level of income is relatively low, but within which there is a rich élite. There is a rare fungus growing wild, which is much prized locally as a delicacy, and which fetches a high price in the market. The Government decides to set up a project to cultivate the fungus. The project is costly, particularly because of the amount of labour required. Nevertheless, on the basis of current demand (i.e. taking into account the fact that market price is likely to fall as a result of increased supply) an excess of benefit over cost is shown and the project goes ahead. It is financed by taxation of the wealthy and much of the cost is devoted to wage labour, thus leading to a general rise in wage levels throughout the economy.

The fall in the post-tax incomes of the very rich leads them to reduce their purchases of the fungus, but the working population spend their extra income on basic goods such as food and clothing. The price of the fungus therefore falls relative to the prices of many other products in the economy, and it is quite possible that an appraisal of the project, valuing costs and benefits at the new levels of market prices, might show an excess of cost over benefit. The new procedure for aggregating individual consumer preferences no longer leads to the conclusion that it is appropriate to devote so many of the nation's resources to the production of this particular product.

In truth, for most projects it does seem rather unlikely that this kind of situation could arise. But the Scitovsky paradox is important because it underlines most dramatically that the valuation of costs and benefits which is provided by market prices is dependent upon the income distribution to which this particular set of market prices relates.

To sum up then, the possible justification for disregarding distribution effects are as follows:

(a) The effect of any one project on the distribution of income is considered inconsequential, or the overall distributional effects of all projects are thought to be neutral and may therefore be disregarded.

Where these conditions are met, this view could only be objected to if the Government were experiencing difficulty in fulfilling, by conventional means, a particular distributional objective. Large direct transfers might be less politically feasible, and perhaps more administratively costly, than transfers that occur as a byproduct of government investment projects – in which case the overall distributional effect of government projects should not be neutral.

(b) A given unit of a good or service has the same incremental impact upon welfare in society, irrespective of who consumes it.

It seems likely that the definition of 'welfare in society' implied by this approach would usually not be acceptable.

(c) It is not the job of economists to make judgements about the relative worthiness of different individuals in society.

This is a common view, but is quite untenable in the context of cost–benefit analysis. It is the project appraiser who is best placed to discover when and what redistribution is likely to occur. He should at least provide information on this aspect of a project, even if it is left to others to translate government objectives towards distribution into the overall comparison between benefits and costs of a project. In any case, as we have seen, he cannot ignore distribution. He must make some distributional judgement when valuing costs and benefits, even if it is the common one that costs and benefits are valued relative to the existing distribution of income (the judgement which is made when values are based on market prices).

(d) Questions of income distribution can be disregarded because, if a crude calculation shows total benefits to exceed total costs, this would mean that it would be possible for those who benefit to compensate those who lose, and still be better off.

This is a restatement of the *compensation principle* introduced in the previous chapter. There we came to the conclusion that, if compensation does not take place, it is not possible to say whether an improvement is involved without making some judgement concerning relative values in society.

(e) This leaves us with the possibility that:

Distributional questions can be ignored on the grounds that the Government will ensure that full compensation takes place.

With respect to this, we should first note that full compensation will be difficult to achieve unless the project appraisers give detailed information regarding the distributional consequences of the project. Second, such a redistribution may not be costless – the cost of 'putting right' any distributional wrong of the project should perhaps be included as a cost in the analysis. Third, as mentioned already, large direct transfers of income might not be politically feasible, whereas transfers as byproducts of projects may.

There is, thus, an overwhelming case for explicit recognition of the income distribution implications of a project. Costs and benefits need not only to be identified and valued, they must be attached to the individuals or groups they affect. Where a major redistribution is caused by a project the effects of the redistribution on market demand should in principle be taken into account, so that if the redistribution is in accord with government objectives, the project can be assessed in relation to the new income distribution.

3.4. The use of shadow prices

3.4.1

A *shadow price* may be defined as a price which an economist attributes to a good or factor on the grounds that it provides a more appropriate indication of the value to the community as a whole of this good or factor than do prevailing market prices. The term is also sometimes used in cost–benefit analysis when notional prices are attached to those welfare effects of a project which are not priced through the market at all.[2]

We have seen that if we make certain assumptions about the kind of economy under consideration, and we leave aside questions of income distribution, then the prices at which the output of a project sells can be taken as a true reflection of the marginal value of this output to society. Correspondingly, the price which must be paid for the inputs used in a project reflect the value of output foregone as a consequence of the employment by the project of these resources. Shadow prices are therefore used in cost–benefit analysis when, in the context of a particular project, there appears to be a serious departure from one or more of the conditions required for market prices to reflect 'social' values. In this section we look at three of the kinds of situations which have led to the use of shadow prices in cost–benefit analysis.

3.4.2

Suppose a project uses an input which is produced by a monopolist. We know that a profit maximising monopolist will sell his product at a price which exceeds its marginal cost of production (Chapter 3, section 5.3). Should the input be valued at the price paid by the project, or should a shadow price relating to the marginal cost of producing the input be used?

Figure 6.2 depicts the market for an input (X) which is produced by a monopolist. The demand curve of non-project users of the input is D_1. The marginal cost curve of X is MC – this would be the supply curve of the input if the industry was organised under conditions of perfect competition and operating under identical cost conditions to the monopolist. The profit maximising level of output for the monopolist is 150 units of X selling at a price of P_1 per unit – given by the point of intersection of his marginal revenue curve (MR_1) with his marginal cost curve.

The project requires a fixed quantity of 100 units of X per time period. The demand curve for X will therefore shift horizontally by 100 units to D_2. The new equilibrium price for X is P_2 with a quantity of 190 units supplied by the monopolist.

The answer to the question 'Should the project value the input at its marginal cost of production or at its market price?' depends on whether and to what extent the monopolist increases his output in response to the increase in demand.

Our basis for attaching a value to the quantity of X used by the project is the value of alternative output foregone. Forty of the 100 units of X used by the project are provided by an increase in output by the monopolist and the remaining 60 units are bid away from existing users. The 40 units which represent increased output should therefore be valued at marginal cost (i.e. a *shadow price* should be used), on the grounds that this measures the value of inputs – and thus the value of alternative output foregone – required to increase output of input X from 150 to 190 units. The remaining 60 units, it is

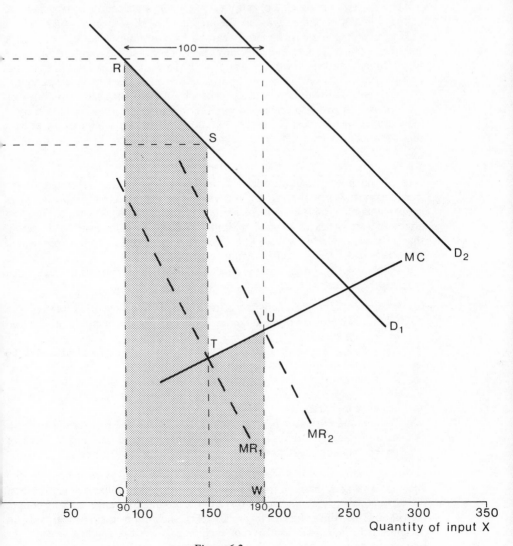

Figure 6.2

argued, should be valued at market price. Existing users of input X were prepared to pay price P_1 per unit when 150 units were offered for sale but are prepared to pay the higher price P_2 for only 90 units. Consequently, the area under the demand curve (D_1) between S and R indicates the value of output foregone when the quantity of X employed by existing users is reduced from 150 to 90 units.

Thus the estimated value of output foregone as a consequence of using 100 units of input X per time period by the project is the shaded area *QRSTUW*.

Note that the increase in profit earned by the monopolist is a pecuniary spillover of the project which may need to be taken into account for distributional reasons. Also, the use of a shadow price reflecting the marginal cost of producing X will only be appropriate if other markets in the economy are competitive. If the inputs used to produce X are themselves supplied by monopolists, or are also employed by other monopolists, then we are firmly in the world of second best (Chapter 5, section 3.3) and the choice of the correct shadow price becomes a much more difficult task.

3.4.3

One of the most common uses of shadow prices concerns internationally traded goods. When the output of a project is exported, or the project uses imported inputs, *shadow exchange rates* are sometimes used for translating prices in foreign currency into a domestic currency equivalent. The use of shadow exchange rates is thought to be particularly relevant to the appraisal of projects in many less developed countries.

The theory of exchange rates is developed in the next chapter. Let us for the moment take it that:

(a) A currency rate of exchange is determined, like any other price, by a balance between supply and demand – in this case the supply and demand for 'foreign exchange'.

(b) The supply of foreign exchange is generated by a country's exports and the demand for foreign exchange depends on its imports.

(c) The supply curve of foreign exchange is upward sloping to the right, i.e. the quantity supplied of foreign exchange increases as the price of foreign exchange increases, and

(d) The demand curve for foreign exchange is downward sloping to the right, i.e. the quantity demand of foreign exchange increases as the price of foreign exchange decreases.

In Fig. 6.3, quantity of foreign exchange (in dollars) is measured on the horizontal axis and price of foreign exchange (pence per dollar) is measured on the vertical axis. (It is more common to quote sterling exchange rates as dollars per pound, so this reverse formulation is shown on the vertical axis in parenthesis.) The equilibrium rate of exchange, where the quantity supplied of foreign exchange is equal to the quantity demanded, is 50p per dollar (two dollars = one pound).

Consider a project which requires an imported tractor selling on world markets at, say, $6000. The cost to the project of the tractor in terms of domestic currency is therefore £3000. With free exchange rates, £3000 is also the estimated value of the other goods foregone (by the importing country) as a result of importing the tractor. Goods will be imported as long as they can be sold at a price which when converted from dollars into pounds, is less than the domestic cost of producing similar goods. With an exchange rate of $2 = £1

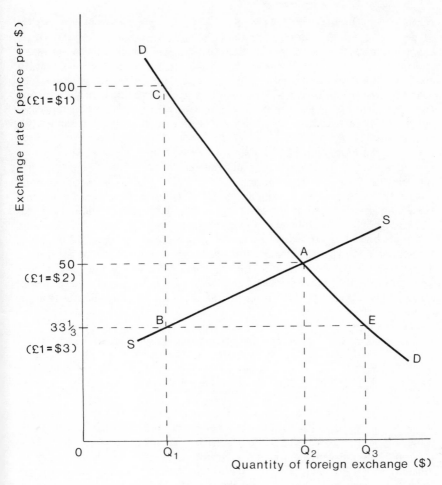

Figure 6.3

therefore it will just be possible profitably to import a product which sells for – say – $20 on world markets and costs £10 to produce domestically, though a slight movement of the exchange rate which increases the price of foreign exchange above 50p per dollar will render the imported product uncompetitive. Thus the $6000 of foreign exchange required by the project means that the economy sacrifices alternative imported goods which cost approximately £3000 to produce domestically.

Alternatively, we could regard the cost to the economy of importing the tractor as the output foregone in order to provide $6000 extra foreign exchange. When the equilibrium exchange rate is $2 = £1, it will just be profitable to export a good which costs – say – £10 to produce domestically if it can be sold on world markets for $20. At the margin therefore, it is possible to provide a small additional amount of foreign exchange (of $6000) by exporting goods which require about £3000 of domestic resources to produce.

Suppose now that the Government fixes the exchange rate at £1 = $3. There are a number of reasons which might induce a government to do this, which need not concern us here, and a number of ways of sustaining (what is called) an overvalued rate – evidence that the rate was overvalued would be provided by a persistent balance of payments deficit and/or government trade restrictions.

One of the more common mechanisms for sustaining an overvalued rate is *exchange control*. In terms of Fig. 6.3 this means that, at the fixed exchange rate, the supply of foreign currency falls to Q_1. Demand on the other hand increases to Q_3 and the Government is forced to ration Q_1 foreign exchange in some way among the total demand of Q_3 – usually by granting import licences for imports up to the total value of Q_1 per time period.

We are now charged with the task of placing a social cost upon the import of a tractor required by the project and selling on world markets at $6000. An import licence has been granted for the tractor, for which the project pays (when converted at the official exchange rate) £2000. Is there, however, a case for applying a higher shadow price for the tractor in the cost–benefit analysis of the project?

The relevant consideration is again the goods foregone as a result of importing the tractor. This may vary depending on whether the extra foreign exchange required is generated by increased exports or released by reducing other imports. At the official exchange rate, Q_1 is the maximum amount of foreign exchange that is likely to be generated in the absence of government assistance so the only justification for the project appraisers to regard increased exports as the source of foreign exchange would be if it were known to be the Government's intention to finance the import requirements of the project by increased exports. If the new exports are of products which could be sold profitably on world markets if the price of foreign exchange was allowed to rise only a little above $33\frac{1}{3}$p per dollar (relating to a position on the supply curve SS marginally above B) then the shadow price of the tractor need not exceed £2000 by very much. If, on the other hand, the project appraisers were aware that the Government was likely to subsidise the export of products that appeared much less commercially viable, then a higher shadow exchange rate might be called for.

More commonly, it will be appropriate to regard foreign exchange required by a project as displacing other imports – the project is granted an import licence which prevents licences being granted to other potential importers. Some economists suggest, therefore, that a shadow exchange rate should be used which is equivalent to the rate that would apply if the current amount of available foreign exchange were allowed to find its own price in the market (i.e. £1 = $1, when Q_1 is supplied). The justification is that, since Q_1 currency is demanded at rate £1 = $1, at the margin of current imports a product selling for $1 on world markets will cost £1 to produce domestically. This, however, would unequivocally be the appropriate shadow exchange rate only if foreign exchange had been rationed on the basis of ability to pay – by an auction of licences, say, or perhaps an ad valorem tax on all imports. This would lead to Q_1 being distributed to those imports which correspond to the part of the demand curve above C. Where import licences are distributed by government decision, one could be less certain that the cost, in terms of value of goods foregone, of importing the tractor was, in fact, as much as £6000, which is the price in terms of domestic currency implied by the shadow exchange rate of £1 = \$1 (or, for that matter, that it was not more than £6000).

A similar argument can be applied to the valuing of the exports of a project – the relevant shadow price being the domestic value of the extra imported goods made possible by the foreign exchange earnings of the project. Again, however, one must be cautious about automatically applying a high shadow price. To quote Mishan, 'The calculation of the expected benefits, arising from the project's exports, must depend on the economist's judgement of the additional imports the Government will actually allow' (5).

This section again illustrates the difficulty of devising generally applicable rules in cost–benefit analysis. In answer to the question 'How should we value traded goods when exchange rates are thought to be overvalued?', we have progressed little beyond 'Well, it all depends'. We have, however, linked the answer to domestic valuation of consumption foregone as a consequence of the imports or made possible by the exports. This value will vary, not only with the extent to which the currency is overvalued, but with the method of sustaining the rate (whether by exchange control, import tariffs, export subsidies, or whatever).

3.4.4

Unemployment provides another argument for the use of shadow prices. If a project draws on previously unemployed labour, then there is no output foregone as a consequence of the project employing labour. Apparently labour should therefore be valued using a zero *shadow wage rate*.

However, this approach views employment solely in terms of the potential contribution of labour to national output. If we take account of the fact that the individual worker may not be indifferent, for some given income level, between employment and unemployment, different considerations may apply. On the one hand, a reduction in unemployment means a loss of leisure time. For example, it may be necessary to pay a wage of £40 per week for labour when unemployment benefit is £30 per week. From this we could deduce that leisure is valued at £10 per week, and the shadow wage rate becomes £10. On the other hand, many regard unemployment as a 'social evil' and would view the provision of employment by a project as representing a benefit independent of the contribution made by labour to project output. For this reason it is possible that, in some circumstances, a negative shadow wage rate could be used in cost–benefit analysis. (There is also of course the problem that a reduction in the overall level of unemployment in a country might have adverse macro-implications, particularly for the rate of inflation.)

Like shadow exchange rates, shadow wage rates have been most commonly used in the appraisal of projects in less developed countries. Here the matter is complicated because the distinction between employed and unemployed labour is much less clear-cut than it is in advanced countries, and the extent to which there does exist a pool of so-called surplus labour in such economies is a matter of great contention.

Briefly however, first it is contended that in heavily populated rural areas it is likely that the marginal product of labour will be very low. Where agriculture is organised on the basis of small family farms the real income of family workers is likely to be based on a share of total output. In order to attract labour from traditional agriculture, a wage will need to be paid which is at least comparable with the existing real income, but the marginal product of labour (and thus the loss in output if the labour leaves traditional agriculture) may be much less than this. Second, prevailing wage rates very often (for what are loosely termed 'institutional reasons') exceed by a substantial margin the income levels of non-wage labour. This latter aspect is important because it implies that if a project employs labour at prevailing wage rates this will involve a significant increase in the spending power of part of the nation's work force. It is this latter point which has led to the use of quite complicated formulae to arrive at shadow wage rates for some projects in less developed countries.[3] For example, let:

M be the marginal product of labour in its previous employment
Y be the income of labour in its previous employment
W be the wage paid by the project

If all markets are perfectly competitive and in equilibrium, then wages will equal marginal products in all occupations. For the reasons cited above, however, in less developed economies Y may exceed M and W exceed Y. If the project is viewed solely in terms of its contribution to the output of the economy then a shadow wage rate of M should be used (reflecting the output lost as a consequence of the employment of labour by the project). The problem arises when the Government concerned places a higher priority on the production of investment goods than it does on the production of consumption goods. The workers employed on the project have an increase in income equal in each case to:

$$W - Y$$

The members of each worker's family have an increase in income equal to:

$$Y - M$$

In total therefore, there is an increase in purchasing power within the economy for each worker employed by the project of:

$$(W - Y) + (Y - M) = W - M$$

If a proportion c of extra income is spent on consumer goods, then the project will increase consumption in the economy by:

$$c(W - M)$$

If the value attached to increased consumption is regarded as some proportion (say λ) of the value of increased output of investment goods, then the shadow wage rate becomes:

$$M + c(W - M)(1 - \lambda)$$

This is, of course, only an illustrative example of one possible way in which a special formula upon which to base a shadow wage rate could arise; what is appropriate will vary with the circumstances of the economy concerned.

3.5 Valuing non-traded items

Prices emerge because of interdependence among the consumption actions of individuals. If I eat an apple this precludes its consumption by anyone else so that, unless there are so many apples that everyone can have as many as he wishes, there will be a market for the purchase and sale of apples. If there is an overabundance of apples – as can occur in some areas in late summer – apples may have zero price. No particular problem exists for valuing non-scarce goods therefore – they do not lack a market price, they have zero price. It could be perfectly proper, in the case of a project which produced as an incidental by-product, a surplus of water, to give this zero value (assuming no cost of disposal) in one part of the world but to value it as an external benefit in another. But we are concerned here not with cases of zero prices, but with cases where a market price does not exist.

There are two reasons why something which affects the welfare of an individual may not be priced through the market. First, there are those welfare effects experienced by an individual which cannot be brought about by deliberate action. If no one is able, by a conscious action, to bring about what is required then it cannot have a price – 'the things money cannot buy'. These kinds of welfare effects, however, need not detain us. Cost–benefit analysis is not concerned with the things money cannot buy. If the welfare of an individual is affected by a project then the effect can be 'bought' by implementing the project.

The other important category of welfare effects derived from items which are not priced through a market concerns those effects which are enjoyed (or suffered) collectively by a group of individuals. A collective good is one which, if it provides a benefit to any one person, necessarily provides a similar benefit to a group of people. Collective goods will lack markets when the cost of ensuring that only those who pay, benefit, is too high in relation to the benefit involved. Many collective goods are of this form. If I employ the British army to defend the United Kingdom against some foreign power they will find it difficult to avoid defending the rest of the UK population at the same time. There is no way that a market price for the defence of Britain can develop because once one person pays up, the country is defended and that is that. The quantity of national defence must be decided collectively and the cost allocated by central decision. Another common example of a collective good is public health measures. A programme of vaccination may be seen initially as protecting the individuals who are vaccinated – in which case it is a private good – but ultimately, the main benefit of the programme will be in reducing throughout the population the chances of contracting the disease.

By their very nature, therefore, the provision of these kinds of effects – such as defence and public health programmes – will not offer to private firms a commercial inducement commensurate with their benefits; they are sometimes called *public goods*. But many of the externalities of private projects are also collective goods. Since these effects will usually not be priced, they will not feature in a private project appraisal.

In social cost–benefit analysis, then, the welfare effects for which there will be no existing market price to provide a basis for valuation are:

(a) The provision by Government of public goods.
(b) Those externalities which are collective goods and for which it is not possible to prevent those who do not pay from receiving the same benefit as those who do.

To clarify the issue of externalities, consider the following example.

Farmer Giles plans to erect a rather unsightly building. The only other person likely to view this building, apart from members of the Giles family, is the local squire who resides in a large house overlooking the proposed site of the building. The squire approaches farmer Giles and offers him a sum of money to erect the building in a more concealed (but less convenient) position. Once farmer Giles has been approached, the potential impact on the squire of siting the building in an alternative position becomes something that can be bought by the squire and sold by the farmer. It enters the farmer's decision-making process as an item affecting profit. A market price has appeared for the relocation of the building, whether or not farmer Giles's estimate of the cost to his business of choosing the less convenient position exceeds the maximum amount the squire is prepared to pay.

The problem arises when several thousand local residents are affected by the siting of the building, but no one is distressed sufficiently to pay the sum required by farmer Giles. Now it is, of course, possible that the local residents will get together and collectively pay farmer Giles. But such a situation would seem to require a rather small, closely knit community with each individual being affected in much the same way. Otherwise, the costs of achieving unanimity and the problems over ensuring that everyone paid their 'fair share' would make it unlikely that a market system could provide a solution.

It is this kind of situation which leads to the requirement that planning permission should be obtained for the erection of buildings. In principle, each planning decision represents a mini-cost–benefit analysis. However difficult the task, the planning authorities are comparing the collective disutility of the farm building with the cost to the nation of siting it in a less convenient location.

In the case of collective benefits, similar considerations apply. Perhaps the wife of farmer Giles maintains a beautiful garden which provides much pleasure to all who pass nearby. No market price is paid for the incidental viewing of this kind of garden because it is too costly, in relation to the amount of benefit, to find a system of charging. The erection of a large wall and the installation of a man with a ticket machine might, in any case, reduce the enjoyment received by the Giles family from their garden. But if enough people enjoy viewing the garden, then very probably it will not be long before an enormous wall does appear round the grounds – and the beauty of the garden enters the market system.

So much for explaining the nature of non-traded items. How does one set about attaching a value to them? Since these items usually have to be compared with a preponderance of costs and benefits which derive from the market system, the procedure is to ascribe to them the price that it seems would apply if it were possible for an individual to purchase his own portion of a collective good – either by relating the effect to a similar item which is priced by the market, or by attempting to discover what monetary valuation an individual would be prepared to pay for a benefit, or accept as compensation for a cost.

The 'amenity value' of rural areas represents a good example of a situation where decisions over the use of a nation's resources affect the welfare of the population by the provision of a collective benefit which usually cannot be priced through the market. In recent years there have been a large number of cost–benefit studies of recreational facilities, and the literature is surveyed by Sinden (7) and Burton and Fulcher (8). Most studies have attempted to measure the benefits of public investment in recreational facilities – such as, for example, the establishment and maintenance of national parks – so that benefits can be compared with the government expenditure involved. Arguably however, it is in the context of public policy over alternative uses of land – whether by private or public bodies – where the practice may be of most use in the future, as it is contended that the income elasticity of demand for recreational facilities is much higher than that for food, and that the competition for land between agriculture and recreation will gradually move in favour of the latter (9). Estimating recreational benefits in a way which allows them to be compared with traded items, such as crop output, is of course extremely difficult. The most promising development, in which the work of Clawson (10) has been prominent, is to attempt to estimate the demand curve for a particular amenity by investigating the relationship between the number of journeys undertaken per 1000 population, and the distance travelled. It would be misleading to suggest that this technique is completely satisfactory, but if an implicit demand curve is derived in this way, the amenity benefit of a particular area or facility can be estimated using the consumer surplus technique.

Another effect which often works out as a collective benefit not priced through the market is the saving of time. If, for example, we return to the road project discussed in section 2, it may be that the road is available for use by non-project traffic, but that it is not possible to charge such users. The benefit to incidental road users will most probably be a saving of time over the alternative routes.

There may be information concerning the price people have been prepared to pay to use similar roads elsewhere. If not, the value of the time saved must be valued directly. It is usual to distinguish two kinds of time-saving – work time and leisure time. For work time it is reasonable to take the gross wage per hour as an estimate of the value of working time gained, since this is the amount the employer is prepared to pay for the services of labour time. For leisure time, the starting point is the net wage received by the individual, since if the individual is free to vary his working time, he is indifferent at the margin to work or leisure.

Three problems are attached to this way of valuing leisure time. First, for many individuals, employment is offered in the form of a package payment for a specified length of working week. Given the choice, the individual might opt for more work or more leisure at the going wage rate. Second, there is usually a disutility attached to work, so that at the margin, the value of leisure is the wage less the disutility of working. Third, travelling cannot always be regarded as lost leisure time – it may be one way of spending leisure and one must compare it with the value attached to alternative uses of leisure.

The Roskill Commission investigation into the siting of a proposed third London airport (11) approached the valuation of time by separating it into business and leisure time. Business time was related to salary levels plus overheads. Leisure time was estimated from the results of a substantial number of empirical studies into the choices of travellers when free to choose alternative means of transport, i.e. where they could choose to pay more in return for a more rapid means of transport. Both business and leisure time valuations were criticised (12): The valuation of business time on the grounds that travel time saved would not, in fact, be spent on productive work; leisure time was thought by some not to be relevant to air travellers for whom travel time should be regarded as part of the holiday.

4 The problem of time

4.1

We have already encountered the problem of making a comparison between costs and benefits which occur in different time periods in Chapter 4 (section 6) in connection with the factors affecting the growth in farm business size, and it was suggested that future revenue would need to be discounted for comparison with current costs. But the choice of an appropriate rate of discount poses no serious conceptual problems for private project appraisal. Funds invested can, as an alternative, be invested on the capital market at a (usually) known rate of interest. Similarly, borrowed funds must be repaid with interest. The private decision-maker will therefore discount future costs or benefits on the basis of whatever rate of interest on loanable funds is applicable to his business; just as market prices provide the basis of valuing costs and benefits for private project appraisal, so market rates of interest on borrowed capital provide the basis for comparing costs and benefits over time.

Why should future costs and benefits be discounted at all when a project is being assessed from the point of view of its effect upon society as a whole? Or why, for that matter, should a discount rate be used in connection with those agricultural policy decisions which are concerned with planning a nation's agriculture in anticipation of expected future requirements? The answer is simply that, for any individual, consumption in one time period is not the same as consumption in another time period. If we are presented with the opportunity of consuming an extra unit of a product in one of two time periods, in most cases we will not be indifferent as to which it is, and in particular we will be influenced by how much in total we expect will be available for consumption in each of the time periods. We can illustrate this with the use of a very simple two-period/one-product example.

In Fig. 6.4 (Fig. 6.5 magnifies the relevant part of Fig. 6.4) the horizontal axis measures quantity of good A available for consumption in time period T_0 and the vertical axis shows quantity of good A available for consumption in time period T_1. Given the productive capacity of the economy in T_0, the maximum quantity of good A that can be produced is 100 units. The consumption of 100 units of A in time period T_0, however, would mean no allowance for the depreciation of the economy's capital stock, so that the maximum quantity of good A which could in that case be produced in time period T_1 would be 70 units. (We assume that storage of product A between the two time periods is not possible.) If the consumption of good A in time period T_0 is reduced to 90 units, this releases part of productive capacity for the production of investment goods so that the capital stock of the economy is kept intact and the maximum production of good A in time period T_1 is now 100 units (point R). The sacrifice of a further 10 units of product A in T_0, by allowing part of the output of the economy in T_0 to be used to increase productive capacity, increases the amount of good A available for consumption in time period T_1 to 120 units, and a reduction of consumption in T_0 to 70 units allows a maximum production of 130 units in T_1. The line $PQRS$ therefore relates consumption in time period T_0 to consumption in time period T_1 – we might call it a *consumption possibility curve* (*CPC*) between the two time periods. A choice exists of any combination of consumption on (or within) the line.

In practice, a similar decision with respect to saving and consumption must be made in T_1. We will find it easier, however, if we disregard the existence of future time periods after T_1 and assume that all of output in T_1 is consumed in that time period.

The declining slope[5] of the *CPC* curve from S to P indicates that the most productive investments are chosen first. If, for example, the economy opts to consume 80 units of product A in T_0, it obtains 120 units in T_1. This means a return of 20 units of A in T_1 for investment, net of the allowance for depreciation, of 10 units of A in T_0 – an average rate of return on net investment of 100 per cent. The marginal rate of return on investment is indicated by the slope of the consumption possibility curve. This suggests that, at point Q, the last investments to be implemented are yielding a return of 1·5

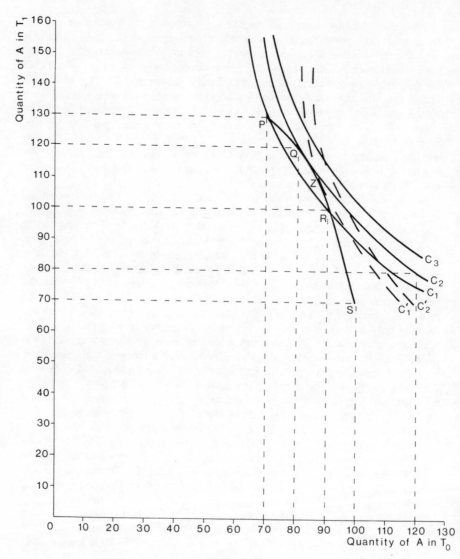

Figure 6.4

units of A in T_1 for every one unit sacrificed in T_0 – a marginal rate of return of 50 per cent. Thus the marginal rate of return on investment is: (slope of *CPC* curve – 1) × 100, and when the slope of the *CPC* curve declines to 1, the marginal rate of return on investment is zero.

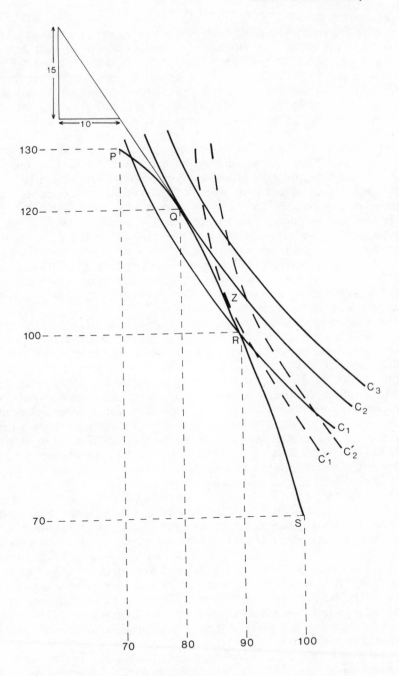

Figure 6.5

To decide upon an optimum policy towards saving in T_0 we must have some statement about the way society values consumption of product A in T_0 relative to consumption of product A in T_1. In Figs. 6.4 and 6.5 this relationship is shown by the set of *intertemporal community indifference curves* C_1, C_2 and C_3. Each curve joins different combinations of quantity consumed of product A in T_0 and T_1 which are equally preferred by society for some given distribution of income. The curves are shaped convex to the origin indicating that, as the quantity consumed in one time period is reduced by equal amounts, it requires increasing quantities of consumption in the other time period to leave society indifferent concerning the change. Extra saving in T_0 will lead to higher levels of social welfare, when welfare is viewed over the two time periods, as long as the slope of the *CPC* curve – the marginal rate of transformation between consumption in T_0 and T_1 is greater than the slope of the relevant community indifference curve – society's marginal rate of substitution between consumption in T_0 and consumption in T_1. The optimum amount of saving for this economy in T_0 will be that which takes it onto its highest possible intertemporal community indifference curve. This occurs at point Q, where the *CPC* curve is tangential to community indifference curve C_2. (Thus we can add to the list of *optimum conditions*, derived in the previous chapter, a condition for optimising over time.)

The rate of substitution between consumption in T_0 and T_1 at point Q we call the *social time preference rate*. It is that rate of return which, in the light of (i) the possibilities open to the economy for transforming a consumption sacrifice in T_0 into extra consumption in T_1, and (ii) society's pattern of preference for consumption in T_0 compared with consumption in T_1, distinguishes those investments in T_0 which take the economy towards a higher intertemporal community indifference curve, and which therefore improve social welfare over the two time periods, from those which take the economy onto a lower community indifference curve and reduce social welfare. Thus in social cost–benefit analysis, the concept of a social time preference rate provides us with a way of comparing costs and benefits which occur in dissimilar time periods.

Two methods of discounting are in common use. One, the *net present value* (*NPV*) method we met in Chapter 4. This method discounts, at the social time preference rate, all future costs and benefits to present values. If the present value of all benefits exceeds the present value of all costs, then in principle the project is deemed worthwhile from society's point of view. A second approach is to calculate the *internal rate of return* (*IRR*). This is the rate which makes the present value of all benefits exactly equal to the present value of all costs. Since we will generally be comparing future benefits with present costs, the more benefits exceed costs, the higher will be the rate of discount necessary to make the present value of benefits equal the present value of costs. The decision criteria in this case is therefore that the internal rate of return should exceed the social time preference rate.

There are certain inconsistencies in the *IRR* method and the *NPV* method is regarded as theoretically preferable. Policy-makers do, however, sometimes like to work with rates of return. The *IRR* method has the added advantage that it puts off, and may even avoid altogether, the often contentious question of what social discount rate to use.[6]

4.2

So much, then, for the logic of why a discount rate should be used in the appraisal of a public project or policy. But how do we decide what this rate should be? Discussion concerning the choice of a social time preference rate has revolved around the issue of whether or not, and to what extent and why, this rate should differ from prevailing market rates on loanable funds.

In a perfect market economy, it can be argued that long-term interest rates will equate the supply and demand for loanable funds.[7] A supply of funds is generated by saving and must reflect individual time preference rates. The demand for funds comes from investment and must reflect the rate of return on investment. Savers can be expected to withhold from present consumption as long as the rate of interest they receive enables them to consume a quantity in the future which exceeds that quantity which would leave them indifferent between present and future consumption. Those who invest can be expected to borrow as long as the return on their investment exceeds the amount they pay in interest.

Thus the free actions of borrowers and lenders should lead to a market rate of interest which equates the marginal rate of return on capital with the community's marginal rate of substitution between present and future consumption for some given income distribution. For the example illustrated by Fig. 6.5, this would be the rate of interest associated with the common slope of community indifference curve C_2 and the consumption possibility curve at Q. (But remember that an investment will normally generate a flow of consumption over several time periods, and that society's preferences for consumption in sequential time periods will reflect the necessity for saving in future periods as well as the present – both factors that can be ignored in our simplified two-period example.)

There is, however, a general consensus among economists that the social time preference rate should be below market rates of interest. There are a number of justifications for this view. First, uncertainty concerning the outcome of future events leads to a multiplicity of interest rates depending on the credit risks involved. It would be possible to vary the social discount rate in response to the degree of risk attached to individual projects, or even to vary the rate applied to different costs or benefits within a single project, but it is usually found convenient to express costs and benefits in their certainty equivalents. The relevant market rate of interest should therefore ideally be risk free, and the most commonly used is the rate on long-term Government bonds.

The techniques used for dealing with risk and uncertainty do not differ markedly between a private or a social appraisal of a project. There is, however, one aspect of decision-making underuncertainty which may cause private and social decisions to diverge. For public projects costs and benefits

292   Agricultural Economics

will frequently be spread over many thousands or millions of people, many of whom may be affected by several projects, so that the risk involved for any one individual is very small. It is less likely therefore that social cost–benefit analysis will need to take account of risk aversion when valuing costs and benefits. (See Chapter 2, section 4.3.)

One point upon which everyone seems to be in agreement is that the rate of discount used should be adjusted to make an allowance for the expected rate of change in the general level of prices. When inflation is expected, market rates link the monetary valuation of goods and services in different time periods. If for example prices are expected to rise by 5 per cent between T_0 and T_1, a premium of 5 per cent would need to be subtracted from market rates to obtain the 'real' social time preference rate.

Note that it is the *expected* rate of inflation which is important. If expected rates of inflation in the United Kingdom during the mid-1970s had been as high as actual rates, then (even) higher interest rates would seem likely to have applied. Nevertheless, when the rate of inflation exceeds market rates of interest on loanable funds the message could be that a negative social time preference rate is justified. In these circumstances, individual savers appear prepared to exchange a quantity of present consumption for a smaller quantity of future consumption.

In principle, of course, a rate of discount incorporating inflation could be used in conjunction with a valuation of future costs and benefits at 'inflated' prices. The normal practice, however, is to value costs and benefits at present 'today's' prices, which is why 'real' interest rates must be used.

A third problem with market rates of interest is the tendency for the monetary authorities of a country to manipulate them for reasons of short run economic expediency. For a private project the fact that it is the Government which is forcing up interest rates is irrelevant – the high rates are still the ones which apply to the project. In social cost–benefit analysis, however, it may be quite justified to take a longer term view and discount at the estimated long-term rate in the absence of official manipulation, because it is this, and not the contrived rate, which reflects social time preference. (On the other hand, if a Government perpetually attempts to influence rates in one direction, this might be taken as evidence of a government policy directed towards longer term investment in the economy.)

4.3

The above arguments for choosing a social time preference rate which is less than market rates may well cause practical difficulties for the project appraiser, but they do not present any really serious conceptual problems. However, the main area of discussion on social time preference rates concerns much more debatable matters. In short, the argument is that individuals, when taking decisions which involve a choice between present and future consumption, attach less value to future consumption than is optimal from the point of view of society as a whole.

In 1920 Pigou (16) claimed that people had a 'deficiency of the telescopic faculty'. By this he meant that before the event people underestimated the amount of satisfaction they would ultimately derive from future consumption. We can illustrate the Pigou argument by referring again to Figs. 6.4 and 6.5. The intertemporal indifference curves C_1, C_2 and C_3 have been drawn *neutral to time* – that is, any curve which passes through a particular combination of consumption in T_0 and T_1 must also pass through the reverse combination – C_2 passes through a combination of 80 in T_0 and 120 in T_1, so it must also pass through 120 in T_0 and 80 in T_1. All the indifference curves are therefore symmetrical about a line drawn at an angle of 45 degrees to the origin, and the time preference rate is zero (a marginal rate of substitution between consumption in T_0 and T_1 of 1) when consumption in the two time periods is equal.

Note that we end up with a positive social time preference rate in our example, not because people are assumed to be biased towards present consumption but because of the assumed path of the consumption possibility curve. This indicates that, by a suitable saving in T_0, a growth in total output over time is possible. If alternatively we took a 'limits to growth' view of the future in which large quantities of saving might be necessary in T_0 if the level of output in T_1 is to be sustained, then the *CPC* curve would be flatter, and start from a lower point, we could well have a negative social time preference rate.

According to the Pigou argument, although the set of indifference curves C_1, C_2, etc would correctly represent a population's ex post valuation of consumption, ex ante each individual possesses *pure time preference* for consumption in T_0 as opposed to T_1. This would imply a set of community indifference curves which were 'biased' in favour of T_0, such as those shown by the broken lines C_1' and C_2'. The outcome is a lower amount of saving and investment in T_0 (at point Z) and higher market rates of interest.

If we accept that Pigou was correct about people having pure time preference for current consumption, it does not follow that we should automatically adjust discount rates so as to equate them with ex post satisfactions. This is because there may be a very good reason for an individual to have pure time preference – he cannot be certain that he will be alive in future time periods. He may be discounting future consumption for the risk that he will not be alive to enjoy it. So if we take the step of reducing the social discount rate on the grounds that market rates reflect people's pure time preferences, and if this preference is because of uncertainty over future consumption, rather than an incorrect ex ante valuation, we are introducing an important new element into cost–benefit analysis; we are redefining welfare to refer to an immortal society, rather than in terms of the preferences of those alive at the onset of the project. And one wonders what meaning can be attached to a decision which takes into account the welfare of unborn individuals *in any way other than the collective concern of the present generation for the welfare of future generations* (which can be thought of as welfare enjoyed by the present generation because of knowledge that future generations will receive some expected degree of satisfaction). Is there, then, any case for the project appraiser's taking a view of the importance of future generations which is more generous than that expressed by private individuals through their current saving decisions?

Marglin (17) has postulated an argument which goes some way to providing an answer to this dilemma. He suggests that an individual would be willing to save more in the interests of future generations if he knew that others would do likewise. Although an individual might save to provide for his own descendants, the major part of welfare of future generations is dependent upon the overall economic environment within which they exist. The argument is that most people would be happy to see society make a substantial provision for future generations, but that such a provision must be made by public authority – it is a form of collective good – and will not emerge from the aggregate of private decision. Thus the interests of future generations can be recognised by the use of a social time preference rate which is lower than market rates, and which reflects the present generation's collective view of the needs of unborn generations.

Others argue that Governments should go further than this, that they should make a provision for the future which exceeds that desired by current generation – the Government should be 'the trustee for unborn generations as well as for its present citizens' (Pigou (16)).

4.4

In spite of the abstract and philosophical issues involved, discussion on the appropriate discount rate is not merely part of an arid academic debate. The question of whether one can justify the use of a social discount rate which is substantially less than market rates on borrowed capital is of vital practical importance to the evaluation of Government projects and policies. If a high rate is used, it is most unlikely that a public investment project, for which most of the benefits occur in fifteen to twenty years time, will appear viable.

As Price pointed out (18) when discussing the use by the UK Treasury of a 10 per cent rate of discount for land use studies, '[This] would seem, temporarily at least, to end the British forester's hope of an economic rationale for upland afforestation. No matter how many social benefits were dragged into the analysis, the study team found it impossible to achieve a positive net present worth for new planting.' (The net present value of a benefit of £1 occurring in twenty-five years time is 9p when discounted at 10 per cent per annum.)

Nevertheless, some do hold the view that the social time preference rate is just 'theory' and not important as far as the practitioner is concerned. For example, the author of a book on the economic analysis of agricultural projects dismisses the social time preference rate as follows:

> A third rate sometimes suggested is the social rate of return, a rate which, it is suggested, more adequately reflects the time preference of the society

as a whole than does the opportunity cost of capital. Although interesting in theory, it is too difficult to identify in practice to be commonly used for agricultural project analysis (19).

The use of the internal rate of return procedure may avoid the difficult task of choosing a precise social discount rate. A decision on the appropriate rate is postponed until after cost–benefit calculations have been made. Some decision, of course, must eventually be taken, for a decision to implement the project implies that the relevant social time preference rate is below the internal rate of return; but how much below need never be specified if the internal rate of return is obviously high. Similarly, if the internal rate of return is low, and the project rejected, all that is implied is that, whatever the relevant social discount rate is, it is not as low as the internal rate of return of the project under consideration. However, if the internal rate is neither obviously high nor low, the contentious issue of what is the social time preference rate must be faced, though not necessarily by those performing the appraisal.

Unfortunately, the internal rate of return techniques has certain shortcomings when the issue is which project to undertake or when to implement it (5). The net present value method overcomes these problems but only, of course, if the appropriate social discount rate is known. It may therefore not be possible to avoid the requirement to specify a social time preference rate. The weight of the argument in this section has been that the social discount rate should be below (and probably substantially below) market rates on borrowed capital, but no neat formula exists to determine how far below. This is ultimately the decision of someone who must apply the kind of arguments contained in this section to the economic and political environment within which the project is to operate. Peters quotes Wibberly and Ward's choice of a social discount rate:

The ingenious argument is advanced that an indicator of such a rate might be derived from:

(a) The Dutch experience in reclamation work where the selling value of reclaimed farms is roughly one-half of the capital cost involved. Since reclamation is undertaken on the basis of democratic, elective, decisions the inference is that Dutch society has implicitly chosen a 'social' discount rate equal to one-half the market rate.

(b) The British experience, documented by Wibberly himself, which suggests that we [the British] also are prepared to spend sums, notably on hill farming improvement, and in other measures which can be represented as an attempt to replace food lost from urbanised acres, which are roughly double the observed agricultural market values of land taken for urban use. This also means that an appropriate adjustment may imply working on the basis of a social rate of discount which is one half the market rate.

These are potent arguments precisely because they attempt not only to make the case for the use of a low discount rate but also provide some indicator of how it might stand in relation to market rates. The very simplicity of the ideas involved provides the decision maker, at the very least, with a rough guide, and affords a welcome relief from the maze of imponderables which surrounds the more sophisticated theoretical formulations associated with the notion of social time preference. One has some basis for a rough cut value judgement (20).

5 Conclusion

The techniques of social cost–benefit analysis are often imprecise and the answers unsatisfactory. For a subject whose end product is the very practical consideration of passing judgement upon a potential item of public expenditure, its subject matter appears to delve into irritatingly abstract and philosophical arguments. This is inevitable. The formulation of decisions aimed at an optimum allocation of productive resources from the point of view of society as a whole is a most complex affair and it would be dangerous to pretend otherwise.

As Prest and Turvey remark, 'The truth of the matter is that, whatever one does, one is trying to unscramble an omelette, and no one has yet invented a uniquely superior way of doing this' (2).

Winch adds, 'For all its imperfections, imprecision and scope for controversy, cost–benefit analysis remains the most useful technique we have for focusing attention on the crucial issues involved in making decisions that must be made somehow' (21).

This is the crux of the matter. It is not the omnipotence of the techniques used that gives cost–benefit analysis its importance, but that decisions on public investment must be taken *somehow*. The term 'cost–benefit analysis' simply describes what the subject of economics has to offer as an aid to the taking of decisions on the allocations of public investment funds or to the evaluation of public policies.

It is not, however, so much that the imprecision and abstraction are problems in themselves, but that these characteristics may lead to only a partial application of cost–benefit analysis. This danger is referred to by Mishan (5) as 'horse and rabbit stew', the recipe for which starts 'take one horse and one rabbit'. One then does all manner of exotic culinary things to the rabbit, all of which more or less fail to affect the inevitable horsy taste of the stew.

Suppose, for example, we are considering a choice of open-cast coal mining or afforestation on a particular piece of land. In this case, the rabbit in the cost–benefit analysis is the cost of mining or planting and the revenue from coal or timber sales. The horse is the social costs derived from the unsightliness of open cast mining or the social benefits of the amenity use of woodland. In reality, these latter two factors may have a much larger impact upon the aggregate welfare of the population, but because cost–benefit analysis cannot provide simple, undisputed rules for valuing amenity, it is the more measurable items of coal and timber costs and revenue that the impatient practitioner devotes most of his attention to and which dominate the final answer. Coal is favoured, therefore, because too little weight is attached to the items which are difficult to value. (An answer, incidentally, which is likely to be reinforced if neither the appraiser nor the decision-maker is prepared to become involved in the 'abstract' idea of using a social time preference, rather than a market rate of discount.)

'It is better,' says Mishan, 'to know what it is one should know, even if one cannot know it, than to know something that is irrelevant.' (5)

Cost–benefit analysis should not therefore be regarded as a set of rules (invented by someone else, who has done all the hard work) that can be plugged into a problem to come up with the right answer. Admirable as they are in many ways, manuals of project appraisal (22, 23) tend to encourage this approach, as the term 'manual' implies that one can teach people what to do, without paying all that much attention to why they are doing it. It is much more likely that the 'right' answer will come from a good economist who has never studied cost–benefit analysis as such rather than a poor economist clutching a manual in either hand whose head is full of ideas of shadow prices, internal rates of return and sensitivity analysis. The techniques are not really all that important. It is the rationale that counts.

Notes

[1] The definition of 'society' must be a political one, but broadly defined it might be taken to include the world rather than a national population. 'Society' may include future societies.

[2] The term is also used in mathematical programming with an analogous but more precisely defined and therefore different meaning.

[3] For example, see a much referred to OECD study 'A Social Cost–Benefit Analysis of the Kulai Oil Palm Estate' (6).

[4] An alternative approach, which incorporates the influence of all future time periods is to regard the vertical axis as measuring quantity potentially available in T_1 (rather than quantity actually consumed).

[5] It is the *absolute value* of the slope which is referred to throughout this section.

[6] There are numerous publications dealing with discounting procedures which include comparisons of the *NPV* and *IRR* methods – see, for example, Mishan (5), Carr (13), Merret and Sykes (14) and Jenson (15).

[7] This is something else which would be disputed by one-half of the protagonists in the 'capital controversy' mentioned in Chapter 4 (section 6).

References

(1) *An Assessment of Investments in Land Reclamation.* International Institute for Land Reclamation and Improvement, Publication No. 7. Wageningen, Veenman, 1960.

(2) Prest, A. R. & Turvey, R. 'Cost–benefit analysis: a survey.' *Economic Journal,* Vol. LXXV, No. 300, Dec. 1965.

(3) Various, 'Milton Keynes Revisited, 1971.' University of Reading, Department of Agricultural Economics and Management, Miscellaneous Study No. 51, June 1972.

(4) Weisbrod, B. A. 'Income redistribution effects and cost–benefit analysis.' In *Problems in Public Expenditure Analysis* (ed. S. B. Chase, Jr.). The Brookings Institution, 1968. (Reprinted in *Cost–Benefit Analysis*. (ed. R. Layard). Penguin, 1972.)

(5) Mishan, E. J. *Cost–Benefit Analysis*. London, Allen & Unwin, 1971.

(6) Little, I. M. D. & Tipping. D. G. 'A social cost–benefit analysis of the Kulai Oil Palm Estate, West Malaysia.' Development Centre Series on Cost–Benefit Analysis. Case Study No. 3. Paris, OECD, 1972.

(7) Sinden, J. A. 'The evaluation of extra-market benefits: a critical review.' *World Agricultural Economics and Rural Sociology Abstracts*, Vol. IX, No. 4, Dec. 1967.

(8) Burton, T. L. & Fulcher, M. N. 'Measurement of recreation benefits – a survey.' *Journal of Economic Studies*, Vol. III, No. 2, July 1968.

(9) Thomson, K. J. & Whitby, M. C. 'The economics of public access in the countryside.' *Journal of Agricultural Economics*, Vol. XXVII, No. 3, Sept. 1976.

(10) Clawson, M. & Knetsch, J. L. *Economics of Outdoor Recreation*. Baltimore, Johns Hopkins University Press, 1969.

(11) Flowerdew, A. D. J. 'Choosing a site for the Third London Airport: the Roskill Commission's Approach.' In Layard (4).

(12) Mishan, E. J. 'What is wrong with Roskill?' *Journal of Transport Economics and Policy*, Vol. IV, No. 3, 1970. (Reprinted in Layard (4).)

(13) Carr, J. L. *Investment Economics*. London, Routledge & Kegan Paul, 1969.

(14) Merrett, A. J. & Sykes, A. *The Finance and Analysis of Capital Projects*, 2nd edn. London, Longman, 1973.

(15) Jenson, R. C. 'Some characteristics of investment criteria.' *Journal of Agricultural Economics*, Vol. XX, No. 2, May 1969.

(16) Pigou, A. C. *The Economics of Welfare*. London, Macmillan, 1920.

(17) Marglin, S. 'The social rate of discount and the optimal rate of investment.' *Quarterly Journal of Economics*, Vol. LXXVII, 1963.

(18) Price, C. 'To the future: With indifference or concern? The social discount rate and its implications in land use.' *Journal of Agricultural Economics*, Vol. XXIV, May 1973.

(19) Gittinger, J. P. *Economic Analysis of Agricultural Projects*. Baltimore, Johns Hopkins University Press, 1972.

(20) Peters, G. H. 'Land use studies in Britain: a review of the literature with special reference to applications of cost–benefit analysis.' *Journal of Agricultural Economics*, Vol. XXI, No. 2, May 1970.

(21) Winch, D. M. *Analytical Welfare Economics*. London, Penguin, 1971.

(22) Little, I. M. D. & Mirrlees, J. A. *Manual of Industrial Project Analysis, in Developing Countries*. Vol. II: *Social Cost–Benefit Analysis*. Paris, OECD, 1968.

(23) Overseas Development Administration. *A Guide to Project Appraisal in Developing Countries*. London, HMSO, 1972.

CHAPTER 7

Agricultural Trade Policy

1 Introduction

We can conveniently divide the economic transactions which cross state boundaries into three kinds, namely:

(a) The international movement of products.
(b) The international movement of factors of production.
(c) The international movement of money capital.

The distinction between (a) and (b) is not clear-cut. Of the three broad groups of factors which we distinguished earlier, land cannot cross state boundaries. Labour can, and does, but international migration of labour is now so severely curtailed by government regulations that it is usually appropriate to assume that labour is completely immobile between countries. This leaves 'capital' inputs, but the capital input of one firm will often be the product of another. Thus in international trade theory, what is regarded as a product and what as an input is largely a matter of convention and the term 'international commodity trade' is sometimes used to refer to all international economic transactions excluding those which are transfers of money capital. In the case of agricultural economics, however, the convention is a fairly straightforward one. Anything which is normally the product of a farm firm is regarded as an agricultural product and continues to be so called as long as its farm gate value represents a significant proportion of its traded value – imports of rubber are regarded as part of agricultural trade, imports of automobiles are not.

The study of international trade exists as a branch of economics[1] because of the action of Governments. If it were not for the implementation of government economic policies which impose restrictions on the free movement between countries of factors and products, there would be no need to distinguish between 'domestic' and 'international' trade when investigating the operation of agricultural product and factor markets. Once we accept the fact that markets develop because individuals find that they can consume a greater quantity and greater variety of goods if they specialise in one productive activity and exchange part of their output for other goods and services, then it is perfectly natural to expect this principle to imply an international division of labour and, as a consequence, to mean some movement of factors and products across state boundaries. In the absence of government intervention, therefore, the focus of attention when attempting to understand the process of production, marketing and consumption of agricultural products would be a partial (and where appropriate a general) equilibrium solution for the world economy. Interest in spatial aspects would be restricted to such matters as the impact of transport costs on the location of production and the origin of regional disparities in levels of income and growth.

It has, however, taken economic thought rather a long time to come round to this point of view. Most introductory economics textbooks introduce questions of international trade in the context of a theory known as the doctrine (or principle) of *comparative advantage* (or costs). This was developed in the early nineteenth century and its starting point is a world of complete national autarky in which there is no international movement of products or factors. This position is then compared with one in which trade in products is permitted. Perfect mobility of factors within countries, but complete immobility between countries is assumed. Its simplest version is a two-country/two-product model with no transport costs and a constant marginal rate of transformation between the products (i.e. straight line production possibility curves). Using this model it is possible to demonstrate the rather unremarkable result that trade, by allowing each country to specialise in one of the products, will mean that in total more of both products can be produced (except in the special case where the marginal rate of transformation between the products is the same in both countries). The theory, which can easily be generalised for the multiproduct, multifactor case, is therefore no more than an international extension of the familiar argument encountered in Chapter 3, concerning the origin and development of commodity markets.

The great defect of the comparative advantage argument, or at least of the way the argument is often presented, is that it fails to distinguish, and sometimes horribly confuses, the positive effects of trade – i.e. what exchange of goods will take place, what are the implications for product and factor prices etc., and the welfare effects – i.e. the extent to which individuals are made better or worse off as a result of international trade. During the first half of the twentieth century the positive aspects were developed in the so-called 'Heckscher–Ohlin' theory (6, 7), which investigated the reasons for the existence of national comparative advantages and explored the implications of product trade for factor prices. The central proposition of the Heckscher–Ohlin theory is that a country will tend to export those goods which use intensively its abundant factor, and import goods which use intensively the country's scarce factor.

Shortly after World War II Samuelson (8) proved that, subject to certain very restrictive assumptions, free trade would lead to the equalisation of factor prices even without free international movement of factors. Because the assumptions are so restrictive, what Samuelson in effect showed was that, in the absence of free international movement of factors, what one would normally expect to find is considerable variations between countries in factor prices. However, his work did emphasise that the study of international trade is the study of the implications of government restrictions on free intercountry movement of products and factors, and this left subsequent writers free to view trade policy as a part of general economic policy, and often as an exercise in applied welfare economics. Indeed, much of the work on the welfare aspects of trade theory, particularly the work of Meade (9), has led rather than followed the advance of welfare economics.

The other twentieth-century development of international economics has been the study of international financial movements, but it is contemporary trade theory which has found most applications in agricultural economics.

2 Trade theory

2.1 The 'gains' from trade

We can illustrate the welfare gains from trade by a simple application of the production possibility–community indifference curve method of analysis developed in Chapter 5. Figure 7.1 shows production possibility curves for two products, A and B, in countries 1 and 2. The set of community indifference curves I_0, I_1 and I_2 represent, for some given distribution of income in country 1, different combinations of the two products which are equally preferred by the inhabitants of country 1. In the absence of trade, therefore, country 1 maximises welfare, subject to the fixed distribution from which community indifference curves I_0, I_1, etc. are derived, by producing and consuming 8 units of product A and 7 units of product B (at point R in Fig. 7.1a). By a similar argument, the preferred production and consumption of country 2 is 8 units of product A and 10 units of product B (at point S in Fig. 7.1b).

There are two ways in which countries 1 and 2 may gain from trade. First, it is probable that the inhabitants of both countries could be made better off by some exchange of their existing output of A and B. Second, it is likely that they could enhance these gains by altering the quantities they produce of A and B.

In Fig. 7.2 the production of products A and B in countries 1 and 2 has been aggregated to form a 'box'. Any point within the box now represents a specific distribution of 16 units of product A and 17 units of product B between the two countries, with the consumption of country 1 measured from an origin located at the bottom left-hand corner of the box and that of country 2 measured from an origin located at the top right-hand corner of the box. Point T represents the 'no-trade' distribution, where countries 1 and 2 achieve welfare levels I_0 and J_0 respectively. There are, however, ways of distributing 16 units of product A and 17 units of product B between countries 1 and 2 (shown by the shaded area in Fig. 7.2) which can yield higher levels of welfare than I_0 for country 1 and J_0 for country 2. If, for example, country 1 exchanges 3 units of product A for 4 units of product B from country 2, country 1 can attain welfare level I_1 and country 2 attain welfare level J_1. Since I_1 is tangential with J_1 at point U,

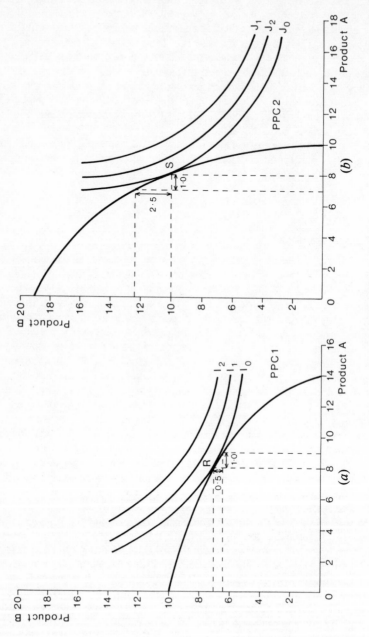

Figure 7.1 (a) Country 1, (b) Country 2

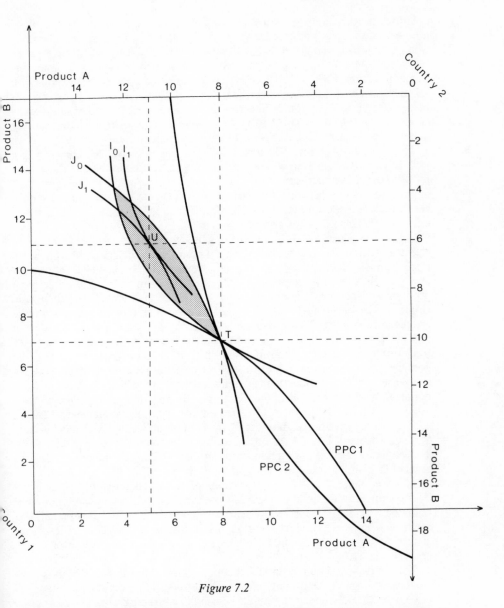

Figure 7.2

this distribution of the products between the countries represents a position where it is not possible, by some further trade, to improve the welfare of one of the countries without reducing the welfare of the other.

It should be emphasised that the movement from T to U in Fig. 7.2 represents a potential and not necessarily an actual gain in welfare for the countries concerned. In section 4.3 of Chapter 5 we argued that a movement to a higher community indifference curve could only constitute an unambiguous welfare gain if no individual was made worse off as a result of the change. In the remainder of this chapter we shall make several references to countries attaining a 'higher level of welfare' as a result of some aspect of trade policy. In all cases where this is not further qualified, it will be a *potential gain* which is being referred to – i.e. a movement to a position where, if compensation were costless, it *would* be possible to make at least one inhabitant of the country better off without making any other inhabitant worse off.

The implication of Fig. 7.2, then, is that two countries will be able to make a welfare gain by trade even without making any alteration in the quantities they produce of the products involved. This will be the case unless the marginal rate of transformation between the products happens to be the same in both countries whereupon, in terms of Fig. 7.2, indifference curves I_0 and J_0 would have been tangential to one another at point T.

Figure 7.3 illustrates the additional gains from trade that can accrue to countries 1 and 2 if they do alter their patterns of production. The marginal rate of transformation between the products is greater in country 2 (at point S in Fig. 7.1b) than it is in country 1 (at point R in Fig. 7.1a). If the output of product A in country 1 is increased by 1 unit and the output of product A in country 2 decreased by 1 unit, this enables an extra amount of product B to be produced in country 2 (approximately $2\frac{1}{2}$ units) which exceeds the amount of product B lost from country 1 (about $\frac{1}{2}$ unit). As long as the marginal rates of transformation between the products is different in countries 1 and 2, it will be possible to increase the aggregate output of both products if each country specialises in the production of the product for which it has a lower opportunity cost than the other country. By exploiting their *comparative advantages* to the full, country 1 increases its output of product A to 12 units and reduces its output of product B to 4 units, and country 2 increases its output of product B to 14 units and reduces its output of product A to 6 units. This results in a total production from both countries of 18 units of A and 18 units of B, giving us the second bigger 'box' shown in Fig. 7.3. The shaded area identifies all those distributions of 18 units of A and 18 units of B which allow both countries to attain higher levels of welfare than when they traded at point U in Fig. 7.2 but did not specialise in production. If, for example, country 1 exchanges 5 units of product A for 6 units of product B from country 2, to give a distribution at point W in Fig. 7.3, country 1 attains welfare level I_2 and country 2 level J_2.

The simple two-country model therefore shows how trade can make the inhabitants of both the trading partners better off. Any individual country will of course normally be faced with the possibility of trading with a large number of other countries and it is often convenient, when considering a single country, to view trade as an opportunity to exchange produce with 'the rest of the world' at given terms on 'world markets'.

This is the approach taken in Fig. 7.4. In the absence of international trade, country 1 maximises welfare by producing a_3 of A and b_2 of B at point R on its

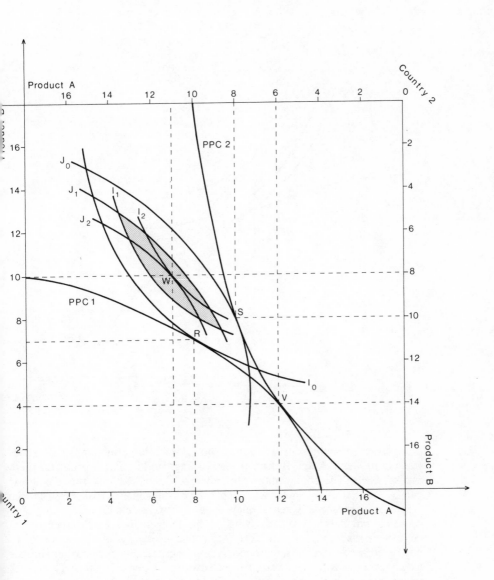

Figure 7.3

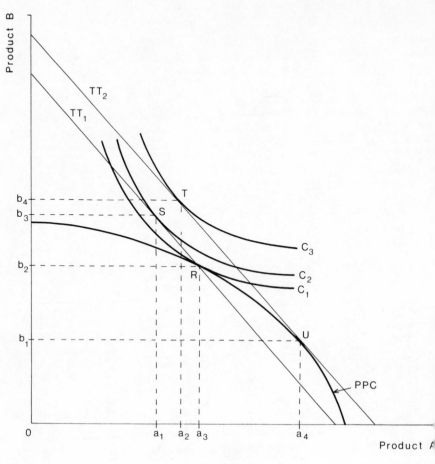

Figure 7.4

production possibility curve. Suppose now that a large number of countries trade in products A and B thereby establishing 'world' market prices for these two products. The opportunities presented to country 1 by international trade can be thought of as similar to the position of the consumer (depicted in Fig. 1.5) who, for some given money income, has a choice of buying any combination of two products lying on his budget line. The income of the country is determined by the fact that it produces a_3 of A and b_2 of B but having done so can then sell product A on world markets and use the proceeds to buy product B (or vice versa). If we now draw a line (TT_1) through point R which joins different combinations of product A and B which would have the same total value, if sold on world markets, as does a_3 of A and b_2 of B, we have in effect the country's budget line. The rate at which the country can exchange product A for product B – or the country's *terms of trade* – will be determined by the world prices of A and B and is therefore indicated by the slope of the line TT_1. (We assume, for the moment, that imports or exports by country 1 do not influence the country's terms of trade.) The country can raise its level of welfare from C_1 to C_2 by exchanging a_1a_3 of A for b_2b_3 of B on world markets.

The consumption possibilities open to country 1, which are shown by the terms of trade line TT_1, relate to the output combinations a_3 of A and b_2 of B. However, for the given terms of trade shown by the slope of the line TT_1, it is possible for the country to increase its 'income' by producing more of A and less of B, since the marginal rate of transformation between A and B at R indicates that the country can increase its output of A and exchange it on world markets for a quantity of B which exceeds the reduction in the output of B caused by the transfer of resources to A production. By moving along the production possibility curve towards U, the country, in effect, pushes out its 'budget' line and can continue to do so until the marginal rate of transformation in the economy is the same as the rate at which A can be exchanged for B on world markets (at point U). The welfare maximising position for the country is therefore to produce a_4 of A and b_1 of B, and to exchange a_2a_4 of A for b_1b_4 of B to attain welfare level C_3 at point T.

Finally, we can use Fig. 7.4 to illustrate an extension of the argument concerning the relationship between welfare and competition to include international trade. We will remember that in Chapter 5 (section 3) we concluded that producers equating marginal costs with marginal revenue would lead the two product perfect market economy to a position on its production possibility curve such that the marginal rate transformation (MRT) for the economy equalled the inverse ratio of product prices. Similarly, we concluded that consumers maximising utility would purchase quantities of the two products such that their marginal rates of substitutions (MRS) between the products also equalled the inverse ratio of product prices. Thus to be in equilibrium the perfect market economy must be located at a point on its production possibility curve such that the MRT for the economy is the same as the MRS for all consumers – or, in other words, at point R for the economy depicted in Fig. 7.4.

If we now allow free trade in products A and B between country 1 and the rest of the world, it will be profitable for traders to export product A and import product B, since the price of A, relative to that of B on world markets (shown by the slope of line TT_1 or TT_2) is greater than it is in the domestic economy (the common slope of the PPC curve and C_1 at R) when no trade takes place. The equilibrium quantity of trade will be that which makes the relative prices of A and B in the domestic market the same as in world markets. Thus to be in both domestic and international equilibrium, the perfect market economy must be located at a position on its PPC curve such that the MRT between the products equals the inverse ratio of prices on world markets (at point U), and the quantity of trade must be such as to make the MRS between the products for all consumers also equal to the inverse ratio of world prices (at point T, for the distribution of income indicated by the community indifference curves C_1, C_2, etc.)

2.2 The market effects of trade

The impact of international trade upon a commodity market can be analysed if that part of the supply and demand for the commodity originating in one country is separated from the supply and demand originating elsewhere in the world. A comparison can then be made of the two markets in partial equilibrium first when the country market is isolated from the world market and second when free trade is permitted. It is also helpful to distinguish between the product for which a country is a potential importer (which we will call product A) and the product for which a country is a potential exporter (product B), and between the cases where production and consumption of the product within a country is significant relative to the quantity of the product which is traded internationally (country 2) and when it is not (country 1). This gives us four alternative market situations and these are illustrated in Figs. 7.5–7.8.

These four market models have been used extensively by agricultural economists when illustrating aspects of agricultural trade policy, and the student will therefore find it extremely useful if he can fully master the relationships involved in each of the diagrams. He will then find that he is well equipped to tackle the argument in a wide variety of journal articles, as well as subsequently in this book, when one or more of the basic models are used to illustrate the impact of some agricultural policy device on trade and welfare.

In Fig. 7.5a the supply curve S_h shows the quantity of product A supplied per time period at different product prices by producers in country 1. Similarly the demand curve D_h shows the quantity of product A demanded per time period at different product prices by consumers in country 1. If the market for product A in country 1 is isolated from the rest of the world, equilibrium will be established with q_p units sold at a price of P_p per unit.

In Fig. 7.5b, the supply curve S_w represents the total quantity which will be supplied to world markets (i.e. exported) per time period at different product prices by all other countries. Similarly, the demand curve D_w represents the quantity which will be demanded from world markets (i.e. imported) by all other countries. Equilibrium is established in the world market with a quantity of Q_w thousand units traded internationally at a price of P_w per unit.

Let us now permit traders in country 1 to buy or sell product A freely on world markets. Since the production and consumption of product A in country 1 is very small in comparison to the quantity traded internationally, we can regard as imperceptible any effect on the world price of country 1's market becoming integrated with the world trading system. In country 1, however, the market price of product A will fall from the protected level P_p to the world level P_w, assuming that transport costs are negligible. (If necessary, transport costs can be included in this kind of analysis by adding a margin when projecting the world price into country 1's domestic market.) Domestic consumption increases from q_p to q_e, domestic production falls from q_p to q_h, and a quantity of $q_h q_e$ of product A is imported from world markets.[2]

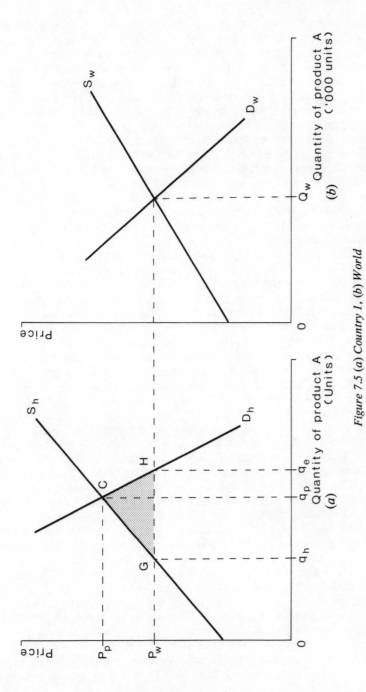

Figure 7.5 (a) Country 1, (b) World

Figure 7.6 illustrates the second market situation, where a country's production and consumption of a product is still regarded as insignificant in world terms (we sometimes refer to this as the 'small country assumption') but where the country is now a potential exporter of the product. When the domestic market is isolated from the world market, q_p of product B is sold in country 1 at price P_p. With free trade between country 1 and the rest of the world, domestic consumption decreases to q_h, domestic production increases to q_e, and a quantity of $q_h q_e$ units is exported to other countries.

In Fig. 7.7 we drop the small country assumption and now use the same scale for the quantity axis in Figs. 7.7a and b. As before, S_h, D_h, S_w and D_w are the domestic supply curve, the domestic demand curve, the supply curve of exports to world markets, and the demand curve for imports from world markets. When the market for product A in country 2 is isolated from the rest of the world, the domestic market will be in equilibrium with q_p sold at price P_p and the world market will be in equilibrium with a quantity of Q_p traded internationally at price P_w.

If we now wish to consider the implications of allowing free trade in product A between country 2 and the rest of the world, the problem that confronts us is that any imports or exports by country 2 *will have* a perceptible impact upon the world market equilibrium price. We can identify this free trade world equilibrium price if we either transfer the information from the domestic diagram (Fig. 7.7a) onto the world diagram (Fig. 7.7b) or if we transfer the information from the world diagram onto the domestic diagram.

Taking the former course of action, we can derive from Fig. 7.7a the quantity of product A which will be exported from, or imported into, country 2 at any given price by taking the difference between domestic supply and domestic demand at that price. For example, at any price above P_p, producers in country 2 will supply a greater quantity than will be consumed domestically, and this excess of production over consumption gives us the supply curve of exports from country 2, shown by the curve S_x in Fig. 7.7b. Similarly, at any price less than P_p, consumption of product A in country 2 will exceed domestic production, and this gives us the demand curve for imports of product A by country 2, shown by the curve D_m in Fig. 7.7b. To find the free trade equilibrium price on world markets we must equate the supply of exports by all countries (including country 2) with the demand for imports from all countries (again including country 2). The total supply curve of exports to world markets (S_T) is obtained by adding the supply of exports from country 2 (S_x) to world supply (S_w), and the total demand from world markets (D_T) by adding the demand for imports by country 2 (D_m) to world demand (D_w). The free trade equilibrium in world markets therefore occurs with a quantity Q_e of product A traded internationally at price P_e. Country 2 imports a quantity Q_m ($= Q_w Q_e$).

The free trade equilibrium price can alternatively be identified in Fig. 7.7a by deriving the supply curve of imports to country 2 and the demand curve for exports from country 2. At any price above P_w there is an excess of exports supplied to world markets (by all countries excluding country 2) over imports demanded from world markets (again by all countries except country 2),

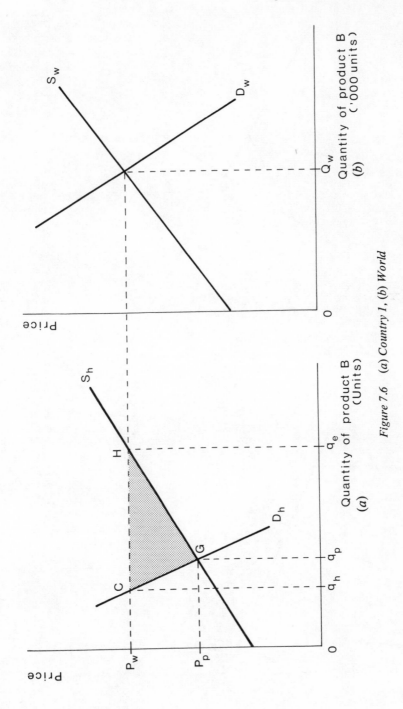

Figure 7.6   (a) Country 1, (b) World

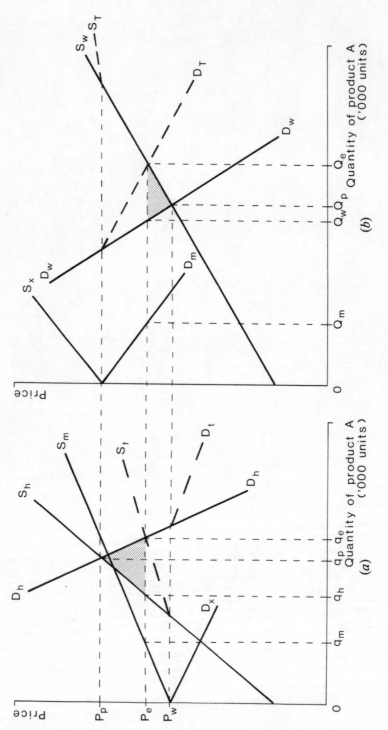

Figure 7.7 (a) Country 2, (b) World

and this excess constitutes the supply of imports to country 2's market (S_m). Similarly, the demand curve for exports from country 2 (D_x) is derived from the excess of world demand for product A over world supply of product A at all prices less than P_w. To find the total quantity supplied to country 2's market (S_t) we add the supply of imports, S_m, to the domestic supply S_h, and to find the total quantity demanded from country 2's market (D_t) we add the demand for exports D_x to the domestic demand, D_h. The free trade equilibrium price P_e is found by equating the total quantity supplied to country 2's market with the total quantity demanded from country 2's market. Compared with the protected domestic market equilibrium, consumption of product A in country 2 increases from q_p to q_e, the quantity supplied by producers in country 2 falls from q_p to q_h, and $q_m\ (=q_hq_e = Q_m = Q_wQ_e)$ is imported from world markets.

Figure 7.8 illustrates the fourth market situation, where country 2 is a potential exporter of product B and where production of product B in country 2 is significant in world terms. The curves S_m, D_x, S_x, and D_m have been derived as in Fig. 7.7. Compared with the no-trade equilibrium, if the market for product B in country 2 becomes integrated with the world trading system, consumption in country 2 decreases from q_p to q_h, the quantity supplied by country 2's producers increases from q_p to q_e, and a quantity of $q_x\ (=q_hq_e = Q_x = Q_wQ_e)$ is exported from country 2.

In the previous two chapters we have seen how, with the aid of the concept of economic surplus, it might be possible to measure the welfare gains and losses resulting from some change in government policy. Applying this technique to the market models shown in Figs. 7.5–7.8, we can demonstrate not only that trade will provide a net gain in economic surplus for countries 1 and 2, but that free trade will maximise the welfare gains from trade. In Fig. 7.5a, therefore, the welfare gains from free trade in product A, compared with the situation where country 1's market is isolated from the rest of the world, are represented by the excess of the gain in consumer surplus P_pCHP_w over the loss in producer surplus P_pCGP_w (shown by the shaded area), and in Fig. 7.6a by the excess in the gain in producer surplus P_wHGP_p over the loss in consumer surplus P_wCGP_p. Similarly, in Fig. 7.7a the shaded area represents the excess of the gain in consumer surplus over loss in producer surplus, and in Fig. 7.8a the excess of gain in producer surplus over loss in consumer surplus.

Furthermore, in all four cases we can see that if we gradually increase the quantity of imports or exports from zero upwards, this net gain in economic surplus will be at a maximum when the quantity of imports or exports reaches its free trade level. Taking the example of country 1 importing product A in Fig. 7.5, as long as the quantity of imports is less than q_hq_e, extra imports which either replace domestic production (q_p towards q_h) or add to domestic consumption (q_p towards q_e) will do so at an import cost which is either less than the cost of producing the domestic units replaced or less than the marginal valuation placed by consumers on the extra units they purchase. However, once the imported quantity exceeds q_hq_e, extra imports will cost more (at price P_w) than either the valuation of extra units by consumers in country 1 or the domestic cost of production of units replaced in country 1.

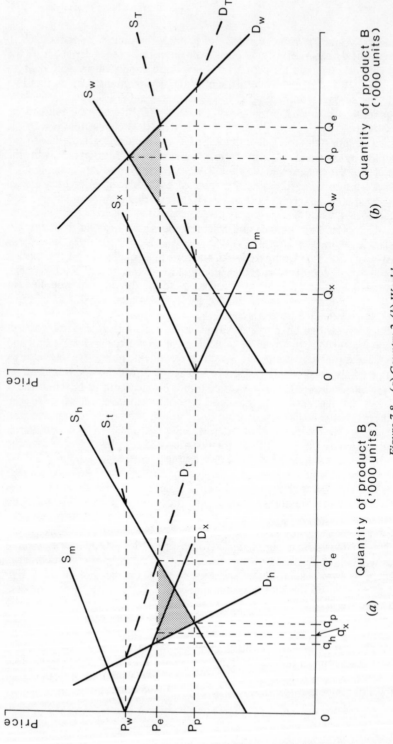

Figure 7.8   (a) Country 2, (b) World

Figures 7.7 and 7.8 depict a market situation where the adoption of a free trade policy by country 2 does have a perceptible impact upon the world equilibrium price. In this case there is therefore also a potential welfare gain to be made by the rest of the world, shown by the shaded areas in Figs. 7.7b and 7.8b.

2.3 The theory of exchange rates

In addition to those government policies which are designed with the specific intention of influencing the movement of goods between countries, there is one aspect of general economic policy which has important implications for all international economic transactions. This is that individual states possess their own currencies, that national governments have control over the supply of money and can thus influence the general level of prices when these are expressed in terms of domestic currency, and that governments exercise control over the rate at which their own currency can be exchanged for foreign currency. In section 2.1 of this chapter we were concerned only with the way two countries *could* improve their levels of welfare by trade, not with the mechanisms by which trade might take place. Section 2.2 examined international trade in the context of the commodity market mechanism, but the implicit assumption in Figs. 7.5–7.8 was that there was a fixed rate at which prices in the currency of country 1 or country 2 were converted into foreign currency and that the vertical axes were aligned accordingly. The 'partial' nature of the analysis meant that we could ignore any impact, on this rate of exchange, of variations in imports of product A or exports of product B.

We can see the relationship between international commodity trade and international exchange of currencies if we drop the 'partial' assumption and now assume country 2 exports only product B and imports only product A. We will call country 2's currency the pound (£) and assume that the dollar ($) is used in world trade. Traders who wish to import product A into country 2 must convert pounds into dollars if they are to be able to purchase product A on world markets. World traders who wish to purchase product B from suppliers in country 2 will need to exchange dollars into pounds. There will thus emerge a *supply* of pounds to be converted into dollars and a *demand* for pounds to be exchanged for dollars. In Fig. 7.9 this supply and demand for pounds is related to the exchange rate. The quantity of pounds to be exchanged for dollars per time period is measured on the horizontal axis and the price of pounds, in dollars per pound, is measured on the vertical axis.

To find what quantity of pounds will be demanded at alternative exchange rates we must examine the market for exports of product B. Let us assume that the currency exchange rate is initially set at $2 to £1. In Fig. 7.10 the curves S_x and D_x show the supply and demand for exports of product B from country 2, in Fig. 7.10a in terms of pounds and in Fig. 7.10b in terms of dollars. The vertical axes have been aligned, with the same length measuring £1 in Fig. 7.10a and $2 in Fig. 7.10b. (The supply and demand for exports have been derived from domestic and world supply and demand relationships in a similar way to S_x and D_x in Fig. 7.8.) In equilibrium, 100 units of product B will be exported per time period at a price of £1 (or $2) per unit. Thus when the exchange rate is $2 to £1, there will be a demand for £100 to be exchanged for $200 and this gives us one point on the demand curve for pounds shown in Fig. 7.9.

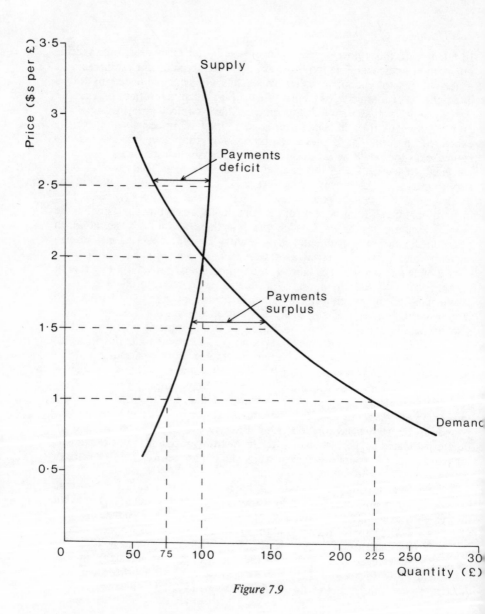

Figure 7.9

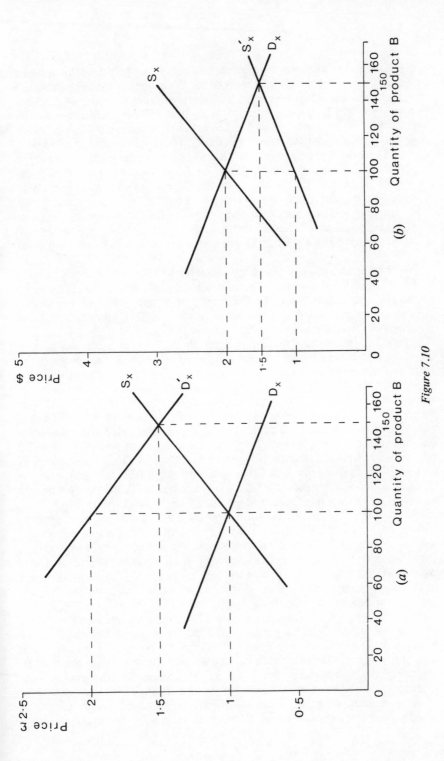

Figure 7.10

Suppose that the exchange rate falls to one dollar for one pound (known as a *depreciation* or *devaluation* of the pound). What impact will this have on exports of product B? The new exchange rate will not alter the demand for exports of product B by world traders *when this demand is expressed in dollars* (Fig. 7.10b) but will alter this demand when it is converted into pounds (Fig. 7.10a). For example, where previously 100 units were demanded at a price of $2 per unit or £1 per unit, 100 units will now be demanded at a price of $2 per unit or £2 per unit. The demand curve for exports of product B, in terms of pounds, therefore shifts to D'_x. Similarly, the supply curve of exports of product B from country 2 remains unaffected by the fall in the exchange rate when this supply is expressed in relation to prices quoted in pounds, but shifts to S'_x when prices are quoted in dollars. For example, where previously 100 units were supplied at a price of $2 per unit, 100 units are now supplied at $1 per unit.

The equilibrium quantity of exports increases to 150 units, selling at a price of £1·50 (or $1·50) per unit. There is therefore a demand for £225 to be exchanged into dollars when the exchange rate is one pound for one dollar. Repeating this process for other exchange rates, we build up the demand curve for pounds to be converted into dollars, shown in Fig. 7.9.

Figure 7.11 shows how we can similarly obtain the supply curve of pounds to be converted into dollars by analysing the impact of alternative exchange rates on the market for imports of product A into country 2. S_m is the supply curve of imports and D_m the demand curve for imports. With the exchange rate set at two dollars to the pound, the equilibrium quantity of imports is 50 units purchased at a price of £2 ($4) per unit. Thus the quantity supplied of pounds to be converted into dollars is £100. A fall in the exchange rate to one dollar for one pound shifts the supply curve of imports in terms of pounds to S'_m, and the demand curve for imports in terms of dollars to D'_m. The quantity of imports falls to 30 units at a price of £2·50 (or $2·50) per unit, and the quantity supplied of pounds to be converted into dollars falls from £100 to £75 as a result of the fall in the value of the pound from £1 = $2 to £1 = $1.

We can see from Fig. 7.10a that, unless the demand for exports of product B from country 2 is perfectly inelastic, a devaluation of the pound will always lead to an increase in the demand for pounds. The demand curve for pounds in Fig. 7.9 therefore slopes downward continually. However, a fall in the value of the pound on foreign exchange markets will not necessarily lead to a decrease in the supply of pounds to be converted into dollars. It will only do so if the elasticity of demand for imports is greater than unity. In our example, the fall in the value of the pound from £1 = $2 to £1 = $1 is associated with an elastic part of the import demand curve – a 25 per cent increase in the price of product A (from £2 to £2·50) brings forth a 40 per cent decrease in the quantity of imports demanded (from 50 units to 30 units). As we move down the straight line demand curve, however, the demand for imports becomes more inelastic and when the absolute value of the coefficient of elasticity is less than −1, a given percentage change in the price of product A will bring forth a smaller percentage change in the quantity of imports. A fall in the exchange

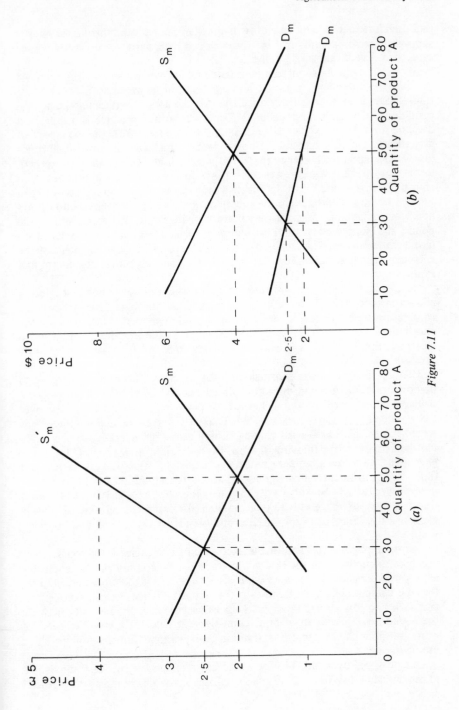

Figure 7.11

rate therefore increases the quantity supplied of pounds, and for this reason the supply curve for pounds in Fig. 7.9 becomes backward sloping at exchange rates in excess of (about) $3 to the £.

In our example the equilibrium exchange rate is two dollars to one pound. At this rate the conditions of supply and demand for the imported product A are such as to lead to a supply of £100 for exchange into dollars, and the conditions of supply and demand for the exported product B result in a demand for £100 in exchange for dollars. It is also clear from our example that a change in the conditions of supply or demand for product A or B will result in adjustments in the currency market as well as in the commodity markets. If, for example, there were to be an increase in the demand for product A in country 2, this would imply an outward movement of the demand curve D_m in Fig. 7.11a, and an increase in the supply of pounds to be converted into dollars at all exchange rates. At the prevailing exchange rate of two dollars to the pound the supply of pounds would now exceed demand on the currency market and for equilibrium to be restored there must be adjustment in the currency exchange rate as well as in the prices and quantities of imports and exports.

Note that, by using the information concerning the dollar value of imports and exports in Figs. 7.10b and 7.11b, we could equally well have shown the equilibrium exchange rate in terms of supply and demand for 'foreign' currency and indeed it was this formulation which we found more convenient to illustrate the idea of a shadow exchange rate in the previous chapter (section 3.4.3).

The possibility of a backward sloping supply curve of domestic currency to be converted into foreign currency, which occurs when there is an inelastic demand for imported products, has led to speculation among economists over the possibility of a free market in exchange rates being destabilising. This would happen if a backward sloping supply curve for the domestic currency cut the demand curve (moving upward) from the right. In this case a fall in the exchange rate below its equilibrium level would cause supply to exceed demand thus leading to further currency depreciation. The condition for a free market in exchange rates to be stabilising (known as the *Marshall–Lerner condition*) is that the sum of the elasticities of demand for imports and exports should exceed unity. (See, for example, Kindleberger (10) pp. 166–168 and pp. 656–658.)

Our example of a market for the exchange of currencies is, of course, very much oversimplified. In the real world trade involves many products and the supply and demand for pounds exchanged into dollars is therefore derived from the aggregate value of all imports or all exports. Trade also involves many currencies so foreign exchange markets will establish exchange rates between the pound and the currencies of all countries with which country 2 trades. But it is not difficult to generalise this kind of example for the multiproduct, multicurrency case.

Our principal oversimplification has been to ignore international movement of money capital. When we include the effects of such movements, the value of imports of goods and services per time period need not equal the value of exports during the same time period. A net inflow of money capital allows a country to import a greater value of goods than it exports by, in effect, borrowing from residents in foreign countries. Certain categories of international movements of money capital are deliberately engineered by national monetary authorities when governments wish to establish currency rates of exchange which are different from free market equilibrium rates.

Suppose, for example, that the Government of country 2 decides to aim for an exchange rate of $2·5 to the £, which is in excess of the free market equilibrium rate of $2 = £1. At this higher rate the supply of pounds for exchange into dollars exceeds the demand. In order to sustain the rate the Government must bridge the gap (which is known as a *balance of payments deficit*). It can do this by drawing on the nation's stock of gold and foreign currency reserves, by official overseas borrowing from foreign governments or international institutions, or by manipulating domestic rates of interest on money capital so as to attract more funds from overseas. Similarly, if the Government of country 2 decides to aim for an exchange rate below the free market equilibrium level – say one of $1·5 to the £ – the excess of demand for pounds over supply of pounds to be exchanged for foreign currency is called a *balance of payments surplus*, and the gap is bridged by an accumulation of stocks of gold and foreign currency, and by lending abroad. Just which kinds of international capital flows are regarded as autonomous, and thus consistent with balance of payments and exchange rate equilibrium, and which are regarded as Government inspired, is partly a matter of convention, a convention which varies from country to country.

3 Agriculture and trade policy

3.1 Trade and distribution

Several references have been made in this chapter to government regulation of the free international movement of goods and services. In this section we discuss some of the reasons for the implementation by governments of policies which influence the level of trade in agricultural products.

We have seen how a country can improve its welfare by trade and how free trade can maximise welfare. In spite of this, Governments have rarely been prepared to allow anything like free international trade. Sometimes this has been because of a misunderstanding of the relationship between trade and welfare, but often it is because, by a departure from free trade, a government can attain an improvement in (what it sees as) the welfare of its people.

One way in which a departure from free trade could be associated with an improvement in welfare will be obvious to anyone who has studied the previous two chapters. It has long been recognised that tariffs affect the distribution of income and, in 1948, Samuelson and Stopler (11) showed formally how one section of the community could be made absolutely worse off by trade. But the contention of economists prior to the second half of the twentieth century was that, although one section of the community could lose relatively, and perhaps even absolutely, by trade 'the community as a whole would be better off'. It was only with the clarification of the relationship between welfare and distribution which was introduced by post-war economists that it has become widely accepted that 'the community as a whole' can only be regarded as better off if either:

(a) no member of the community is made worse off and at least one person is made better off, or
(b) some kind of value judgement is made as to the extent to which the benefit to those who are made better off can be regarded as offsetting the loss to those who are made worse off – in other words a statement about the relevant social welfare function.

In Chapter 5 it was argued that government policies aimed at redistribution are not costless. Apart from the fact that resources are required to administer such policies, they inevitably imply some departure from the Pareto optimum conditions. The income distribution associated with free trade might be regarded as unacceptable by Government and a departure from free trade may lead to a more acceptable distribution. Such a departure from free trade will involve a reduction in the potential level of welfare for the economy but it is by no means necessarily the case that this loss will be greater than the one which would be experienced if the Government maintained a policy of free trade and attempted to improve the distribution of income by some other means.

As it happens, it *has* been questions of income distribution which, more often than not, have been behind the formulation of government policies which have caused significant departures from free trade in agricultural products. There have been cases when such policies have tended to increase the quantity of agricultural products traded internationally and it has not always been an agricultural interest to which the policies have been directed. For example, in 1974 the British Government introduced a policy which aimed to assist food consumers and which led to increased imports of some of the subsidised products, particularly butter and cheese (12). But in the majority of cases government policies have tended, either directly or indirectly, to restrict agricultural trade, and the principal aim of such policies has been the support of agricultural incomes.

The final chapter surveys in some detail the various methods open to governments to support agricultural incomes and discusses, among other things, the implications of the various mechanisms for agricultural trade. In the remainder of section 3 of the present chapter, we consider some other reasons for agricultural trade policy. None of these has had such widespread implications for agricultural trade as has the desire on the part of governments to increase agricultural incomes, but nevertheless each one has been influential at some time in some country, and it is not inconceivable that any one could become more important than agricultural income support at some time in the future.

3.2 Agricultural self-sufficiency

Arguments in support of policies to restrict food imports appear from time to time in countries for which free agricultural trade would imply a substantial proportion of the nation's supply of food imported from world markets. Two distinct arguments are involved, which we can label the *terms of trade* and the *security* arguments. These are, however, nearly always presented in a most confused and imprecise manner, and commonly expressed in the form of a general call for greater agricultural self-sufficiency (or a defence of the existing degree of agricultural self-sufficiency) 'because no country should rely on the world market for its supply of food'. In this section we attempt to disentangle, and present in a rational manner, these two strands of the 'self-sufficiency' argument for the restriction of agricultural trade.

It is usual to represent the relationship between a country's food consumption and production in the form of a *self-sufficiency ratio*. This is a country's production of a product during a particular time period expressed as a percentage of its consumption of the product during the same time period. Self-sufficiency ratios can give a misleading impression of a lack of dependence on imported supplies because of the use of imported inputs in domestic agriculture. The self-sufficiency argument therefore involves not only the proportion of the consumption of a particular product which is domestically produced, but also the proportion of the inputs used in the production of the product which are themselves domestically produced. Even more ambiguous can be estimates of 'overall self-sufficiency'. Some way has to be found of bringing different products together in a common measure. With most published estimates of overall self-sufficiency, the weights used are market prices but an alternative is to use calories or a composite nutritional index. A calorie calculation is likely to give a higher self-sufficiency estimate than prices because most countries import a lower proportion of basic and cheaper (per calorie) food products than they do of the more 'exotic' and higher priced products. (A discussion of the use of the agricultural self-sufficiency concept will be found in one of the series of studies produced by FAO on agricultural adjustment (13).)

Here we start from a standpoint which accepts the conventional welfare merits of free trade but add to it a firm belief in the second (neo-Malthusian) of the two alternative theses concerning longer term movements in world food prices discussed in Chapter 3. The welfare implications for a food importing country of a rise in world agricultural terms of trade are illustrated, using the simple two-product example, in Fig. 7.12. The curve *PPC* is the country's production possibility curve between the (food) product A and the (manufactured) product M. The world terms of trade between manufactured and food products are represented in the initial time period by the slope of the line A_1M_1, which indicates that OA_1 of the agricultural product can be exchanged on world markets for OM_1 of manufactures. In our example, because only two products are involved, the world terms of trade between food and manufactures also happen to be the country's terms of trade, which are usually defined

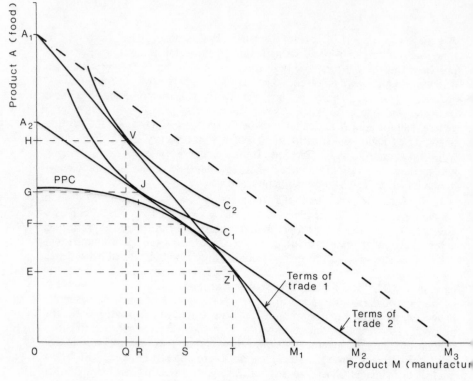

Figure 7.12

as the prices of the products the country exports divided by the prices of the products the country imports. The country maximises welfare (subject to the usual distributional qualifications) by producing OT manufactures and OE agricultural produce, and exchanging QT of its manufactured output for EH imports of food.

Suppose now that the terms of trade between food and manufactures on world markets shift to those represented by the slope of the line M_2A_2, (which is the same as the slope of the line A_1M_3) indicating that OM_3 manufactures are now required to purchase OA_1 agricultural produce. As we would expect, this development in the world economy reduces the maximum level of welfare attainable by the food-importing country (from C_2 to C_1) – the terms of trade are said to have moved against it – and to maximise welfare in the second time period the country must increase its output of agricultural produce from OE to OF and reduce its agricultural imports from EH to FG.

This part of the argument is fairly straightforward. The difficulty arises when we ask, 'Should the Government of a food-importing country, which expects a substantial rise in world agricultural terms of trade, introduce policies in preparation for the future?' One school of thought would answer 'yes' – the

Government should adopt measures to stimulate domestic agricultural output and to restrict imports. In reply, however, it can be pointed out that a policy of free trade will itself bring about the appropriate resource adjustments, as it gradually allows the impact of rising world food prices to be experienced by domestic producers and consumers. The reply is a convincing one simply because the view that it is in the country's interest to reduce food imports *is* a free trade argument. It is based on the hypothesis that a country should allocate its productive resources so as to equate marginal costs with world prices. As we have seen, 'the welfare merits of free trade' represents no more than a simple extension of the argument encountered in Chapter 5 concerning the welfare merits of the resource allocation brought about by perfectly competitive markets.

The possibility that government policies to promote an adjustment to the new free trade equilibrium might be justified emerges only when we remember that the process of adjustment will not be instantaneous. When viewed against a changing world market, welfare in any given time period will depend on some decisions concerning resource allocation taken in previous time periods. If the policy-maker takes a different view from private decision-makers in agriculture concerning the expected future trend of prices on world markets, he may feel that the only way he can precipitate the resource allocation decisions which he thinks are required is to anticipate the future trend of world prices, restrict imports, and raise domestic agricultural prices above those applying on world markets.

Another possible justification for government intervention in agricultural markets in anticipation of rising world food prices concerns those allocative decisions which involve a future benefit in return for a current cost. The most important of these are decisions regarding land use.

The transfer of land from agricultural to urban use is widely regarded as a 'one-way option' – land cannot easily be switched back and forth from agricultural to urban use in response to movements in agriculture's terms of trade on world markets. If the proportion of the nation's land devoted to agriculture is to be optimum in some future time period (when agricultural product prices are expected to be higher than at present relative to other product prices) then the proportion of land devoted to agriculture is unlikely to be optimum in relation to present world food prices. Thus decisions which relate the pattern of land use in a particular economy to the future expected balance of prices on world markets must involve a comparison of current costs with future benefits.

As we saw in Chapter 4, private decisions concerning the comparison of costs and returns over time are linked by market rates of interest on money capital. But in the previous chapter we suggested that there was a convincing set of ideas which suggest that market rates of interest undervalue future benefits from society's point of view. If this is correct, then private decision-makers would not be expected to take 'correct' resource allocation decisions in the light of expected rises in world food prices, even if their expectations of price changes were identical to those of the policy-maker. Clearly then, the question of what rate of interest to use when comparing present costs with future benefits is an important one from the point of view of many agricultural policy decisions (as well as for project appraisal).

The 'terms of trade' argument for a degree of agricultural self-sufficiency in excess of that which would emerge from free trade therefore requires more than merely a prediction of a long-term rise in world agricultural terms of trade. Either:

(a) There must be a divergence of view between the policy-maker and private decision-makers within the domestic economy concerning future movements in world food prices; there must be reason to believe that the policy-maker is a better forecaster of prices than are private decision-makers; and we must be satisfied that the policy-maker is only able to persuade the domestic agricultural industry to accept his view of future conditions of world markets by the imposition of a policy which anticipates, in the domestic market, his forecast of rising world prices.

Or:

(b) There must be grounds for believing that private decision-makers undervalue, from society's point of view, future benefits in relation to present costs.

We should also note that although the terms of trade argument for the imposition of government measures to restrict agricultural trade always seems to be linked to a forecast of rising world agricultural prices, a similar argument could be used to justify the depression of agricultural prices on domestic markets if a long-term decline in world agricultural terms of trade was forecast.

The second strand of the self-sufficiency argument concerns food security. Whatever predictions are made with respect to future trends in world food prices, there is a risk that the forecast will turn out to be badly off target. Irrespective of whether the forecast turns out to have been too high or too low, this means a welfare loss relative to the outcome if a correct forecast had been made and allocative decisions taken accordingly. There is, however, a sense in which a country is in a worse position if it fails to foresee an upward movement in world agricultural terms of trade than if it overestimates the future level of world food prices. Partly this is because world food prices do tend to rise more rapidly than they fall (which means less time to adjust to an unpredicted price) but mainly it arises because of the crucial role of food as the most basic of all man's consumption requirements. To compare the extreme cases, a large food importer, which finds that it is unable to obtain any supplies from world markets (however unlikely this might be) is in a worse position than a country which finds that it is unable to sell, at any price, its export surplus on world markets (again however unlikely this might be). The food security argument for agricultural self-sufficiency therefore represents a kind of insurance policy; a country can opt to pay a little more each year for its food (foregoing some of the benefits from trade) in return for increased security of supplies.

Sweden presents perhaps the best example of a country for which considerations of food security have had an important influence upon the formulation of agricultural trade policy.

For centuries Sweden has adopted a position of 'extreme' international neutrality. Because of this, the Swedish people have readily accepted the need to maintain a minimum level of domestic agricultural production, and agricultural product prices in Sweden, for both producers and consumers, have been among the highest in Europe. During the post-1945 period, however, the Swedish Government has taken the view that the level of agricultural self-sufficiency exceeded that required to fulful the nation's food requirements in the event of an emergency and that part of the cost of the self-sufficiency policy was therefore unnecessary. Partly in order to lessen the political opposition to a policy to contract domestic agricultural output, guidelines were established in 1947 and revised in 1967 (14) which included an attempt to calculate the productive capacity required to ensure that the country's food requirements could be met during an emergency. An 'emergency' was defined as 'a period of up to three years during which Sweden would, for any reason, be cut off from imported supplies' (15). According to the 1967 guidelines, the appropriate minimum productive capacity was 80 per cent of consumption. Both production and consumption were expressed in terms of calories, and production was normalised with respect to yield. It was calculated that to become 100 per cent self-sufficient there could, first, be a 10 per cent cut in calorie consumption. The remaining 10 per cent gap could be closed by a shift in production from livestock to arable products. The increase in calorie output that would result would more than offset the reduction in output due to the elimination of imported agricultural inputs.

3.3 The theory of tariffs and the balance of payments

In this section we consider two further arguments which have been advanced in support of government measures to influence the level of agricultural trade. The two arguments, like those concerning food security and long-term movements in the terms of trade, have sometimes been confused in public debate.

The *theory of tariffs* is the name given to the economic analysis which seeks to show in what circumstances a country can, by exploiting monopoly or monopsony power on world markets, make a welfare gain by a policy of trade restriction. The notion that an important trading nation might gain an advantage by restricting its trade had been hinted at by some nineteenth-century economists. The first formal treatment of the theory was provided in 1906 by Bickerdike (16), who applied Marshall's (then) recently developed concept of consumer surplus. Subsequently, the production possibility–community indifference curve technique was used to develop the theory for the general equilibrium case (17, 18).

Figure 7.13 illustrates the same kind of market situation as Fig. 7.7 – that is, a country (we called it 'country 2') which is a potential importer of a product and for which imports represent a significant proportion of the total quantity of

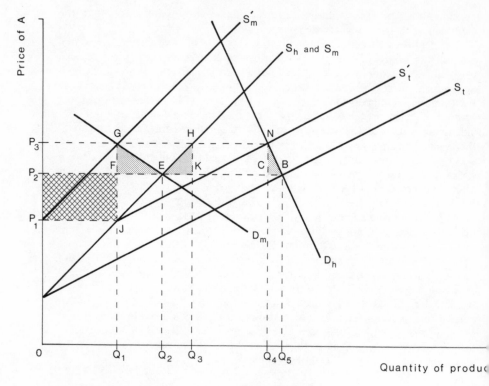

Figure 7.13

the product traded internationally. On this occasion, to simplify the diagram imported and domestic supply response are shown to be identical so that the supply curves S_h and S_m lie on top of each other. The free trade equilibrium price is P_2 with Q_5 units of product A consumed in country 2 per time period. The quantities of imported and domestic supplies are the same at Q_2 $(= Q_2Q_5)$ units.

The Government of country 2 now imposes a tariff of P_1P_3 per unit on imports of product A. The effect of the tariff is to shift the supply curve of imports upward by the amount of the tariff (to S'_m). (For example, foreign suppliers were prepared to supply Q_1 units to country 2's market when they received price P_1 per unit. Following the imposition of the tariff, therefore, Q_1 will be supplied at a market price of P_3, with P_1 received by foreign suppliers and P_1P_3 pocketed by the Exchequer in country 2.) The new equilibrium market price in country 2 is P_3. Imports fall to Q_1 units and domestic production increases to Q_3.

Using the economic surplus technique of welfare measurement, consumers can be seen to be worse off by an amount P_2P_3NB but domestic producers gain by P_2P_3HE. The Government collects the tariff revenue P_1P_3GJ. A welfare gain is made by country 2 if this tariff revenue exceeds the net loss in economic surplus $EHNB$. Since OQ_1 equals Q_3Q_4 (the quantity of product A imported), area P_2P_3GF equals area $KHNC$. A welfare gain accrues therefore if P_1P_2FJ exceeds the sum of the triangles EHK and NBC.

In his presentation of the argument, Bickerdike (16) used only the supply and demand for imports. If in Fig. 7.13 we derive the demand curve for imports, D_m, the consumer loss on imported produce following the imposition of the tariff is P_2P_3GE, so a net gain in welfare accrues if area P_1P_2FJ exceeds the triangle FGE. This result is the same as that given above, since, by geometry, the area of triangle GFE must equal the sum of the areas of triangles EHK and NBC.

Both approaches can be used in a comparable manner to show that a country may be able to make a net welfare gain by taxing an exported product.

If one accepts the validity of the economic surplus technique, describing the welfare effects of an import tariff therefore amounts to little more than an exercise in geometry. In the previous chapter it was pointed out, in connection with the example illustrated by Fig. 6.1, that an overall comparison of the costs and benefits of a particular government project *or* policy measure could be obtained either by examining the effect on various groups in society or by looking at the aggregate impact upon the value of output available for consumption in the economy. A more intuitively acceptable interpretation of the costs and benefits resulting from the imposition of the import tariff is perhaps provided by the second approach. The effect of the import tariff has been to force down the world market price of a product A (from P_2 to P_1) and to raise the domestic market price (from P_2 to P_3). The country gains an amount P_1P_2FJ because it can now import quantity Q_1 ($= Q_3Q_4$) at price P_1 whereas with free trade it paid the higher price P_2. It loses, however, on account of the fact that it has reduced its quantity of imports beneath the free trade level. It has replaced a quantity Q_2Q_3 by higher cost domestic production and it has reduced consumption by Q_4Q_5. Remembering that the supply curve reflects the increasing marginal cost of domestic production, the area EHK is an estimate of the loss due to producing domestically a quantity of product A which was previously purchased at price P_2 from world markets. If we regard the demand curve as giving an indication of the increasing marginal value to consumers of each unit of product A they give up as they reduce their consumption from Q_5 to Q_4, the triangle NBC measures the loss to consumers of being forced to forego the opportunity of purchasing Q_4Q_5 units of product A at price P_1. So the welfare loss, or *economic cost* of the imposition of the tariff is the sum of the areas EHK (the *production loss*) and NBC (the *consumption loss*).

The general equilibrium treatment of the theory of tariffs allows a clearer illustration of the idea of an *optimum tariff* than is possible in the partial equilibrium case, as well as highlighting the possibility of reciprocal losses due to retaliation. Both of these features are illustrated in Fig. 7.14, which depicts the same food importing country as we encountered in Fig. 7.12. With free trade and world terms of trade OA_1/OM_1, this country maximised welfare by producing *OT* manufactures and *OE* food, and then exchanging *QT* manufactures for *EH* food on world markets. It was assumed in Fig. 7.12 that the quantity of imports or exports by the country did not influence the level of world prices and that it could therefore exchange as much of product M for

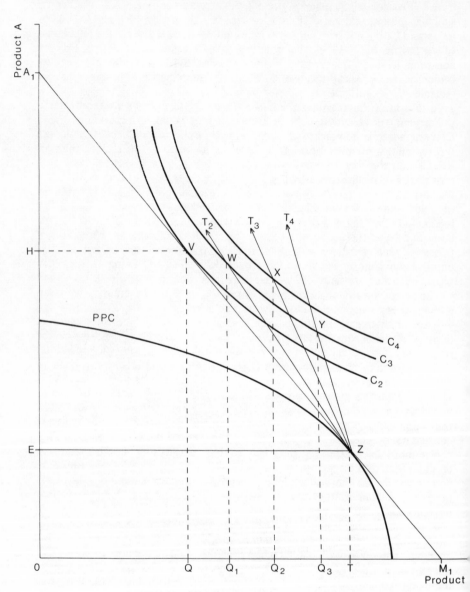

Figure 7.14

product A as it wished at the trading terms indicated by the slope of the line A_1M_1.

Suppose, now, that the quantity of the manufactured product M exported by this country does represent a significant proportion of the total quantity of M traded internationally, and let V be the free trade equilibrium position. (To simplify matters we assume that the price of A on world markets is not influenced by the quantity imported by this country – though it is quite possible to incorporate both monopsony and monopoly power into the kind of example illustrated by Fig. 7.14.) We can now no longer simply draw a straight terms of trade line to indicate the trading opportunities open to the country. A_1M_1 indicates the quantity of A that can be obtained per unit of M exported when exports equal QT units. If more is exported, the price of M in world markets will decline and the quantity of A which can be obtained per unit of M will fall. Correspondingly, if less is exported than the free trade equilibrium quantity of QT, a greater quantity of A per unit of M exported can be obtained. A reduction in the quantity exported of product M to Q_1T units may for example turn the terms of trade in the country's favour to become those represented by the slope of the line T_2. If the country exports Q_1T manufactured products at terms of trade T_2 it is able to attain welfare level C_3 at point W. If a further reduction of exports to Q_2T improves the terms of trade to T_3, the country can attain welfare level C_4 at point X. This, however, is the best it can do by a policy of trade restriction. Although a further reduction in exports to Q_3T still improves the country's terms of trade (to T_4) this allows a welfare level of only C_3 to be reached at point Y.[3]

The danger of attempting to improve welfare by a policy of trade restriction is that other countries may retaliate and introduce their own trade restricting measures. In our example, we can see that if the country imposes its optimum tariff policy and cuts exports to Q_2T, retaliatory measures, which gradually reduce the terms of trade from T_3 back towards A_1M_1, will reduce the country's welfare below C_4 and may reduce it to below the free trade level C_2. It is not difficult to show (see, for example, (18)) that if all countries attempt to improve welfare by restricting trade, they are all likely to end up worse off than with universal free trade – an outcome that was responsible for reciprocal trade restriction being given the name *beggar-my-neighbour policies* (19) during the inter-war depression.

There are nevertheless two ways in which a country might be successful in an attempt to make a welfare gain by altering the terms at which it trades. The first possibility is that the country has such a dominant position in the world market for its imports or exports, compared with the market power possessed by other countries trading in these products, that even including maximum retaliation, it attains a higher welfare level by exploiting its market power than it could achieve if all countries allowed free trade. Few countries do possess this degree of market power but a group of countries having a common interest in the import or export of a product might achieve it if they agree on a combined trade restricting policy. This kind of agreement has appeared attractive to some tropical product exporting countries. The demand for such products is usually relatively price inelastic in consuming countries and production is sometimes concentrated in a small number of countries. Three basic conditions for the operation of a successful *cartel* among exporters of a raw material have been postulated by Jacob Viner (20). They are:

(a) That the cartel should control a large proportion of total supply – two-thirds or more. Otherwise, even if final consumer demand is relatively inelastic, the demand facing the cartel members will be relatively elastic.

(b) The supply from non-participating countries must be relatively inelastic in both the short and long run, or else the advantage to the cartel members of their price raising activity will be eroded as the quantity supplied from non-cartel members increases.

(c) The demand in consuming countries must be relatively inelastic in both the short and long run. The demand for most agricultural raw materials is inelastic in the short run but higher prices may act as an incentive for the development of substitute products in the longer term.[4]

Even if these conditions are met, and a successful cartel is possible in principle, there is still the problem that there will be a great incentive for any one participating country to 'break ranks' and sell more than its allotted quantity of exports at the more favourable terms of trade which have been created by the reduction in exports by the cartel members.

The second way in which a welfare gain might be made by a trade restriction policy is of course if for some reason a country's trading partners do not take up their option to turn the terms of trade back in their own favour. This might apply for example in the case of the tropical product exporting countries mentioned above for the reason that the relevant trade flow is largely from less developed producing countries to high income consuming countries. The exploitation of monopoly power might then be interpreted in consuming countries as a legitimate method of 'encouraging' development aid. This kind of view of the manipulation of primary product export prices is probably becoming more widely accepted and is an important part of what has become known as the *new international economic order*. A report written by a group of experts appointed by the Commonwealth Heads of Government in 1975 contained the statement:

> We accept that the emergence of producer's associations is a reality born out of historical experience. In an unequal world it is understandable that such a development should take place (21).

Apart from agreements among less developed primary product exporting countries the other circumstance where retaliation might not occur is if a country can justify a trade restricting measure as the only way of achieving some general objective of economic policy – an objective which is accepted as a reasonable one by other countries. For this reason, Governments rarely declare that they are about to impose a trade restricting policy 'in order to exploit foreigners' even if this is the real intention; the policy will be applied to 'protect employment', 'to stabilise markets', or whatever.

Although the world prices of many agricultural products are certainly influenced by national government trade policies, it is probably true to say that in most cases any welfare gains via the exercise of international market power have been unintentional. One curious feature of the unintentional exercise of international market power is that retaliation can have the opposite effect upon the terms of trade to that implied by textbook treatments of the theory of tariffs. This has happened when farm income support has been the principal objective of agricultural policy in both food importing and food exporting countries. During the 1960s, for example, the European Economic Community established minimum import prices for most agricultural products which were very high relative to world market prices. The policy reduced the level of EEC agricultural imports beneath the level which would have applied with free trade and this undoubtedly had a depressing effect on world agricultural prices compared with their free trade equilibrium level. The reaction of some food exporting countries, such as the United States, was to increase their subsidies on agricultural exports thus accentuating, rather than reversing, the initial movement in the terms of trade.

The relationship between agricultural policy and farm income support is discussed in the next chapter. It is, however, extremely unlikely that the EEC did make a welfare gain from its trade restricting agricultural policy. The degree of protection was almost certainly well in excess of the optimum level under the theory of tariffs. To benefit from a position of monopsony buying power, a country still has to import a reasonable quantity of the product at its depressed price, and the EEC was itself subsidising exports in the case of some products. There may also have been some retaliation of the more conventional kind. A famous example is the so-called 'chicken war' of 1962–63 when the United States placed controls on imports from the EEC in retaliation against EEC import levies on chicken, and, at a more general level, the EEC's commitment to agricultural protection probably weakened its bargaining position with respect to non-agricultural trade in the GATT (22).

Perhaps the most interesting application of the theory of tariffs to agricultural trade has been made in connection with the post-war argument in the United Kingdom for replacing agricultural imports by domestic supplies 'to aid the balance of payments'. In our simple example of currency exchange (Fig. 7.9) we identified a balance of payments deficit as official borrowing from abroad, or an outflow of official reserves of gold and foreign currency, for the purpose of supporting a currency rate of exchange above its equilibrium level. Such a deficit cannot be sustained indefinitely simply because there are limits to exchange reserves and to the quantity of funds foreign governments and international institutions are prepared to lend. Thus a country must eventually take action to remove a balance of payments deficit, and three broad kinds of policy option are possible. These are:

(a) To allow a currency depreciation.
(b) To apply domestic monetary or fiscal measures designed to reduce the general level of prices in the domestic market relative to prices in other

countries, when these prices are converted at the prevailing rate of exchange.

(c) To introduce measures designed to restrict certain categories of imported products or to increase the quantity of certain categories of exported products.

Economists have traditionally favoured currency devaluation because of the welfare merits of the free trade solution. Whatever method of removing a balance of payments deficit is adopted, a welfare loss relative to the situation where the country was financing part of its imports by overseas borrowing or by the running down of reserves is inevitable. Furthermore, Governments have found that the various methods of restoring international payments equilibrium have differing implications for the pursuit of general economic objectives, such as those applying to employment, income distribution, regional disparities, and economic growth. It is not possible therefore to generalise about the appropriateness of agricultural trade policy measures as a means of removing a balance of payments deficit; this will vary with the circumstances of the country concerned, the origin of the payments deficit, and the kind of agricultural trade policy mechanism employed.[5]

In the United Kingdom, however, the peculiarity of the balance of payments argument for the replacement of imported agricultural produce by domestic supplies has been the way an application of the theory of tariffs has been incorporated into the argument. The assumed ability of the country to turn the terms of trade in its favour has been used to strengthen the case for agricultural import substitution as a means of removing a balance of payments deficit. At the same time the country's balance of payments problem has acted as a smoke screen behind which the argument for a policy of exploiting a position of international market power could hide. It is worth spending a little time examining the evolution of the argument concerning agricultural expansion and the UK balance of payments because it provides an excellent example of the use of economic theory in the public debate which surrounds the formulation of agricultural trade policy.

The debate began in 1950 with an article in the *Economic Journal* by Blagburn (25), who had calculated that it took £123 of the nation's resources to produce £100 of food valued at import prices. In reply, Robinson and Marris (26) argued that, although the value of exports produced by £123 of resources might be as high as £200, 'The extra output must not only be produced, but also sold, and sold almost certainly at worse terms.' They went on to estimate that the elasticity of demand for UK exports would have to be at least 'as high as 2·5' to make a transfer of resources from agriculture to export industries worthwhile.

MacDougall (27) then pointed out that what Robinson and Marris were advocating was an application of the theory of tariffs and that their calculation ignored the dangers of retaliation. Undeterred, Marris (28), in what was an early econometric exercise, attempted to estimate the relationship between the quantity of UK exports and the nation's terms of trade. He satisfied himself that an increase in UK exports would result in a worsening of the terms of trade. Morgan and Paish (29) were not satisfied. They pointed out that since the United Kingdom was a large food importer but exported mainly manufactures, its terms of trade would move with the world terms of trade for agricultural produce. Furthermore, a substantial proportion of UK exports went to primary producing countries whose ability to import manufactures would also vary with world movements in agriculture's terms of trade. Thus an improvement in the world terms of trade for agricultural produce would be associated with a worsening of the United Kingdom's terms of trade but also with an increase in the quantity of UK exports to primary producing countries. Marris did not accept this criticism of his work (30) but he may have been more inclined to do so if he had been able to extend his analysis further into the post-1945 period. During the 1950s and 1960s an increase in the quantity of UK exports was associated with an improvement rather than with a deterioration in the country's terms of trade (31).

In 1958 McCrone entered the arena presenting a formal treatment of the application of the theory of tariffs to agricultural protection (32). He followed this with an observation (33) which although significant in itself was perhaps more important in that it emphasised that the nature of the cause of a balance of payments problem influences whether or not a particular measure represents an appropriate solution. His argument was that the UK balance of payments problem at that time was a shortage of gold and dollar reserves, but that since most imports of temperate agricultural produce came from countries which traded in sterling, reducing these imports would not make a substantial contribution to a build-up of the nation's gold and dollar reserves.

More recently, Ritson (34) has pointed out that the argument that the UK could turn the terms of trade in its favour by a policy of restricting agricultural imports might only be valid in the context of a balance of payments deficit. He demonstrated that, with free exchange rates, a country would not exploit a position of monopoly selling power by the imposition of measures which reduced its quantity of imports. Thus the presence of a balance of payments deficit was critical in the application of the theory of tariffs to agricultural protection, not only because this made retaliation less likely, but also because it was only under conditions of balance of payments deficit that one could assume an inverse relationship between the quantity of exports and the level of domestic agricultural output. The implicit assumption in the Robinson–Marris argument was that, in the absence of agricultural expansion, the country would have no option but to try to increase exports because of the severity of the contemporary balance of payments problem.

By the mid-1960s the ideas originated by theoretical economists concerning the possibility of a country improving its terms of trade by exploiting a position of international market power, plus the dangers of retaliatory trading losses, had permeated sufficiently through the British agricultural establishment for both to receive a mention in the semi-governmental Economic Development Committee for Agriculture's report 'Agriculture's Import Saving Role' (35).

Import saving is not synonymous with the contribution which the increased output may make to the balance of payments. The latter depends not only on the volume of imports replaced, but on any changes in the terms of trade which policy might produce and on the extent to which reduced imports lead ... to a reciprocal fall in British exports compared with the level they might otherwise attain. Generally speaking, the 'terms of trade effect' of agricultural expansion is likely to be favourable, but it may be partly offset or even exceeded by the 'reciprocal effect'.

The Committee did not attempt to include these effects in their calculation. Phillips and Ritson (36), applying their own estimates of the reciprocal trading links between the United Kingdom and temperate agricultural exporting countries, concluded that the net balance of payments contribution of UK agricultural expansion might be only about one-half the NEDC estimate of import saving. 'Reciprocal trading loss' is a broader concept than retaliation, including any reduction in the value of a country's exports which is caused by a reduction in its imports whether or not the export loss is due to the imposition of retaliatory measures by foreign governments.

The successful application by the United Kingdom for membership of the European Community had the effect of bringing to an end (for the time being) applications of the theory of tariffs to UK agricultural trade. This was because of the importance then assumed by administered prices under the Community's Common Agricultural Policy (37). The balance of payments argument lived on, and found a new bedfellow in public debate with a reawakening of interest in UK agricultural self-sufficiency (38).

3.4 Stabilising domestic markets

The case for market stabilising policies is founded upon the view that unstable agricultural product prices lead farmers to take production decisions which are not socially optimum.[6] Two aspects of our discussion in Chapter 2 on producer behaviour under uncertainty are relevant here. First, it was suggested that the risk averse producer might not aim to maximise expected profit. He might instead take production decisions which were intended to provide a level of profit which was less than the maximum when averaged over a number of years, but which would provide less year to year variation in profit. Second, the presence of product price variations, when there is a significant time lag between the decision to supply and produce becoming available for sale, means that production decisions have to be based upon an expected future price. Inasmuch as farmer price expectations turn out to be incorrect, then it is contended that their decisions will lead to departures from the Pareto conditions. Other things being equal, the reduction of product price variations make it that more likely that producer expected prices will approximate to actual market prices.

It should be pointed out, however, that there is much more to the relationship between a price stabilising policy and economic welfare than merely a reduction in producer uncertainty. Perhaps most important is that a movement towards a more stable product market can involve income transfers between different groups within the economy, particularly between producers, consumers, and taxpayers, as well as intercountry transfers. There is also the problem of choosing the appropriate level upon which to stabilise prices, and resources are of course required to administer stabilisation policies. Finally, there is no clear indication that consumers prefer stable prices as such – the difference between the producer and consumer in this respect being that in general there is not a time lag between the decision on the part of a consumer to purchase an item and the actual sale taking place.

These aspects of stabilisation policies have received much less attention than have the potential benefits from reducing producer uncertainty and until such time as they are more fully explored by agricultural economists we must be careful to temper our enthusiasm concerning the merits of stable prices. However, stability *has* been a prominent objective of many agricultural policies, and agricultural trade policy measures are often justified as a means of stabilising domestic markets. The net importing country can dampen product price fluctuations in its domestic market by the imposition of a policy which reduces the quantity of imports below their free trade level when world market prices are relatively low, and which increases the quantity of imports when world market prices are relatively high. Similarly, the country which is a net exporter of a product can stabilise its domestic market by increasing exports when world market prices are relatively low and by reducing exports when world market prices are relatively high.

It is not sensible to review the national measures which influence agricultural trade as if they were stabilisation policies, irrespective of whether or not they happen to be called this by the Government concerned. There are two reasons for this. First, the word 'stability' has come to be used as a euphemism to describe a policy measure which is designed either to support or to restrain agricultural product prices. In periods of rising world prices Governments sometimes introduce policies to 'stabilise' food prices, but the mechanisms used are usually only capable of restricting price rises. More common have been 'price stabilisation policies' which a closer inspection reveals as price support policies. To give just one example, towards the end of the 1960s there began to emerge from the British Ministry of Agriculture the information that it was the intention of the Government to introduce a 'beef stabilisation scheme'. When the scheme itself appeared it turned out to be the imposition of a minimum price for beef imports, which would have the effect of removing the troughs, but not the peaks, from the price fluctuations for beef within the United Kingdom. Thus though it is quite possible to conceive in principle of a 'pure' price stabilisation policy, the great majority of the schemes that have been introduced to stabilise agricultural product prices have attempted to stabilise prices above their longer term equilibrium level. The policy mechanisms which have been used by Governments to stabilise agricultural prices in domestic markets have therefore normally been the same mechanisms as those used to support prices. The next chapter considers these various mechanisms primarily in relation to their price supporting function but also in relation to their ability to stabilise.

The second reason for being sceptical about the claim that certain agricultural trade policy measures are stabilisation schemes is that a national trade policy to stabilise a domestic market is, at the same time, a *destabilising policy* as far as the rest of the world is concerned. The world trading system ensures greater price stability in each domestic market than would be experienced if trade between country markets were prohibited. The reason for this is that unplanned variations in output throughout the world are not perfectly synchronised – good and bad harvests tend to cancel one another out. With free trade, a country which experiences a shortfall of output below the planned level will import more, or export less, than it would if output plans had been fulfilled. As a result, the price rise in the domestic market will be less than if the full extent of the production shortfall had had to be absorbed by domestic consumers. Similarly, in the event of an unusually good harvest, free trade will mean more exported or less imported than in an 'average' year. Inasmuch as comparable unplanned variations in output occur throughout the world, all domestic country markets will be more stable than if domestic markets were isolated from one another.

But for the system to work effectively, it is necessary for each country, not only to accept the benefits of the world market absorbing variations in its own output, but also to be prepared to absorb part of the net variation in world production. Take, for example, a market similar to that depicted by Fig. 7.8 and consider a simple case where output approximates to the planned level in all countries except in country 2, where there is a substantial production shortfall. With free trade this implies a reduction in exports from country 2 and a rise in the world market price of product B. As a result of this rise in price, consumption will be reduced in all other countries (as well as in country 2) and each country will either import a little less or export a little more than they would, had output plans in country 2 been fulfilled. If, however, the Government of any other country reacts to the rise in the world price of product B by the imposition of a policy which prevents any increase in its exports of product B, or any decrease in its imports of product B, the world price will need to rise that much more in order to absorb the impact of the shortfall of production in country 2.

Similarly, in periods of above average world output, world prices will fall less under conditions of free trade than they will if some countries stabilise their domestic markets, preventing any increase in their imports or decrease in their exports.

The European Community's Common Agricultural Policy (see, for example, 40, 41) provides a good, though by no means the only, example of the way a domestic market can be stabilised at the expense of destabilising the world market. For most products the policy aims at a target level of prices within the Community and attempts to regulate agricultural trade so as to ensure that, wherever possible, imports equal the excess of domestic consumption over domestic production at the target level of prices, and exports equal the excess of production over consumption at the target price level, irrespective of whatever the world price happens to be. As mentioned in the previous section, during the 1960s target prices were generally well above world prices and were therefore maintained by levies on imported produce. These levies varied so as to counteract any movement in world prices. During the early 1970s, when some prices on world markets moved above the EEC target level, the system was thrown into reverse and taxes on exports and some subsidies on imports were introduced.

This second aspect of the relationship between the stabilisation of agricultural product prices and national trade policies has led some Governments, albeit reluctantly, to come to the conclusion that the solution to the problem of instability in agricultural markets may lie in the establishment of internationally agreed stabilisation policies – not national policies – and it is on this question that we conclude the present chapter.

4 The international quest for stability

4.1

An international commodity agreement (ICA) may be defined as a scheme, sponsored by some or all of the countries trading in a commodity, which is designed to maintain the price at which the commodity is traded within some specified range. Most internationally traded agricultural products have during the twentieth century been subject to recurrent attempts to establish stabilising trading agreements and there is consequentially a very extensive literature covering the various agreements for individual commodities.[7] Wheat, coffee, and sugar, which are by value three of the most important of all internationally traded goods, have been the agricultural commodities to experience most action. Commodity agreements achieved international respectability after World War II, beginning with the endorsement by the United Nations of the chapter concerning the principles applicable to ICAs in the so-called *Havana Charter*, which had proposed the establishment of an *International Trade Organisation* (*ITO*) 'to promote higher standards of living, full employment and conditions of economic and social progress' (44). The ITO itself never got off the ground, the international organisations concerned with commodity trade eventually to be established being the *General Agreement on Tariffs and Trade* (*GATT*) and the *United Nations Conference on Trade and Development* (*UNCTAD*).

The regulations attached to individual ICAs, as well as the documents describing them, tend to be so complex that it is somewhat surprising to discover that in principle the subject is relatively straightforward. Indeed, two statements summarise most of what there is to be said. First, if an agreement is truly to stabilise prices on an international commodity market, someone somewhere must manage a stock of the commodity so as to even out irregularities in the quantity supplied. Second, nearly every commodity agreement has eventually broken down because it finds itself attempting to stabilise market prices at a level which is either substantially below or substantially above the long run equilibrium level.

Three kinds of international commodity agreement can be distinguished:

(a) Pure stabilisation agreements.
(b) Contractual arrangements.
(c) Export Quotas.

4.2

The distinguishing features of a pure stabilising agreement are: that there must be both a maximum and a minimum price; that the long-term equilibrium price for the market must be within this range and; that the agreement should have the effect of stabilising prices for all countries trading in the product whether or not they participate in the scheme. Figure 7.15 illustrates two possible alternative approaches to a pure stabilising arrangement; the approaches differ on account of the way they treat the stockholding requirement. D_w is the demand curve for the product and S_w the planned supply curve – that is, the

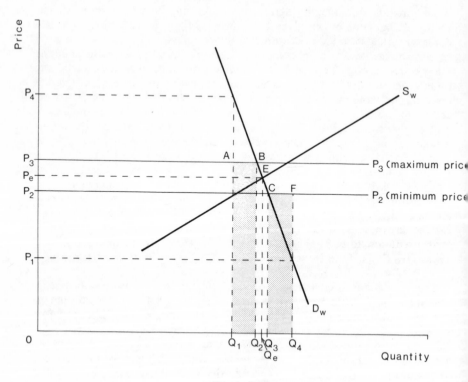

Figure 7.15

quantity that will be supplied to world markets at different prices if production plans are fulfilled. The world equilibrium price is therefore P_e with a quantity of Q_e per time period traded internationally.

Supply is, however, subject to unplanned variations in output, and to simplify matters we will assume that the erratic nature of supply takes the form of a random occurrence of 'good' and 'bad' years. In a good year supply is Q_4, in a bad year it is Q_1, and any year has an equal chance of being good or bad. Figure 7.15 therefore describes the typical primary product market problem of an inelastic demand translating variations in the quantity supplied (between Q_1 and Q_4) into proportionately larger variations in price (between P_1 and P_4).

Consider now the feasibility of an international agreement among countries trading in the product to restrict variations in price to within the range P_2P_3. To achieve this a quantity Q_3Q_4 must be removed from the market in years of good harvest and a quantity Q_1Q_2 must be released from stocks in years of bad harvest. One way of achieving this would be to establish an organisation, the function of which was to purchase the product off the world market once the price fell to P_2 and to sell produce if the world price rose to P_3. The produce stored by such an organisation is known as a *buffer stock* and this is also the name by which the organisation administering the scheme is sometimes known.

As a theoretical solution to market instability the buffer stock appears very neat. In bad years the organisation receives revenue Q_1ABQ_2 and in good years pays out Q_3CFQ_4. As long as the price range within which it must operate is not too narrow, the stock can be self-financing with the excess of the revenue from the sale of the product over expenditure on purchases covering the cost of storage. In spite of its apparent attractions, however, there is in fact no major example of an international buffer stock for an agricultural commodity, though one has operated for tin and the 1972 International Cocoa Agreement included an (initially) unsuccessful buffer stock arrangement.[8]

It would appear that the task of agreeing a set of rules and then providing finance for what must become a semiautonomous body is more than can be expected of Governments. Even if this kind of agreement did prove feasible in political terms, it is arguable that a buffer stock could not last for more than a few years because this kind of agreement is particularly vulnerable to the effects of longer term movements in world prices. A buffer stock can be financed exclusively by either importing or exporting countries. If it is, there will be a strong temptation to take an overoptimistic view (from the standpoint of the countries concerned) of the longer term equilibrium level of prices on the world market. Even if this price is correctly identified, it is likely to change as the balance between world supply and demand for the commodity evolves. The buffer stock authority therefore eventually finds itself with either no money or no stock and as a consequence is unable to prevent the world price of the commodity from moving outside the designated range. Whereas some kinds of commodity agreement can continue being 'half-successful', once a buffer stock ceases activity the scheme is likely to be wound up. To survive, therefore, a buffer stock must aim to stabilise around a trend price, the difficulty of doing so being to identify the trend when the operation of the stock is itself determining the level of international prices for the commodity. One possible way out of this impasse would be to agree to limit the size of the stock to whatever level thought necessary to even out short-term supply fluctuations, and to apply a formula to alter the target price range as the size of the stock approaches either zero or its upper limit.

The alternative to a buffer stock is simply for the countries trading in a commodity to agree not to engage in transactions at prices lying outside the prescribed range. In terms of Fig. 7.15, therefore, in 'good' years production will exceed consumption by Q_3Q_4 and exporting countries must store this excess and/or importing countries must purchase more than they will consume of produce imported at price P_2. In years of shortfall exporting and importing countries must together release a quantity Q_1Q_2 from stocks if the traded price is not to move above P_3. It has been upon this principle that successive *International Wheat Agreements* have been founded, though the individual agreements have approached the matter in slightly differing ways (42, 43).

The obvious weakness of the maximum–minimum price undertaking as a mechanism for stabilising international commodity prices is the lack of any formal agreement on the distribution of the stockholding requirement. The onus tends to fall on exporting countries since stocks have to be accumulated at times of surplus production and it is in the interest of exporters rather than importers to prevent trading prices from falling beneath the minimum level. Importing countries become interested in stocks at times of rising prices since it is then in their interest that there should be plentiful stocks available for release. But this interest tends to evaporate once surplus conditions reappear and the opportunity to build up stocks presents itself.

Although wheat prices remained fairly stable between 1954 and 1971 (below, however, the International Wheat Agreement minimum price from 1966 to 1971) this can be attributed largely to a willingness on the part of Canada and the USA to allow their own stocks to accumulate, to a restriction of their wheat acreages, and to the donation by the USA of large quantities of the commodity as food aid. The declaration by the US Government (48) that it was no longer prepared to carry the full cost of storing grain for the world, plus a period of high agricultural commodity prices in 1972–73, increased the general awareness that a successful international grain stabilising programme must contain an agreement about stockholding as well as an agreement about prices (49).

4.3

Some ICAs take the form of a contract, between one or more exporting countries and one or more importing countries, for the sale of a specified quantity of the commodity at a fixed price. Varying degrees of flexibility concerning price and quantity can be incorporated into the agreement. As long as the exporting country does not contract to sell more than its export surplus in 'bad' years, it can fulfil its contractual requirement without the necessity of holding stocks, selling any excess over its contractual requirement on the free market. Thus the essential point about such contractual arrangements is that, whereas the price is stabilised for the contracting parties, prices are destabilised for countries which continue to trade on the free market. This is because the quantity of produce traded on the free market will be reduced, but this market must continue to absorb the full impact of world fluctuations in production. Clearly, contractual arrangements, *without a stockholding agreement*, cannot stabilise all international trade in the commodity – contracts can work for the countries concerned only because there remains a free market to absorb supply fluctuations.

During the post-1945 period the international sugar trade has been subject to a number of contractual arrangements, such as those between the United Kingdom and a group of Commonwealth countries, between the United States and most non-communist sugar-exporting countries, and between Cuba and Eastern European countries. In all, something like $10\frac{1}{2}$ million tons of sugar has been covered by special arrangements with about 8 million tons traded on the 'free' market. It is therefore this residual market, accounting for only about one-eighth of total world sugar production, which has had to absorb the full shock of variations in world sugar output and demand. A series of *International Sugar Agreements* have attempted to stabilise this market. The agreement of 1968 (43) was a most sophisticated affair with each change of 25 cents, within a price range of 3·25 and 5·25 cents per lb, triggering off some relaxation in the severity of export quotas, the release of stocks, or the extent to which importers were expected to purchase from participating countries. The free market price did remain within the ISA range for about three years, but broke through the 5·25 cents ceiling in December 1971, reached the extraordinary level of 56 cents in November 1974, and had returned to settle around 13 cents by the end of 1975. Contractual arrangements are probably the most resilient of all ICAs in the face of changes in the world balance between supply and demand for the commodity, but many supplying countries did break their contracts and sell sugar on the more lucrative world market during the 1972–74 price boom.

4.4

The most popular form of ICA for agricultural products has been agreements among supplying countries on individual quotas for their exports. These have applied at one time or another to rubber, sugar, coffee, tea, and cocoa. The dividing line between a market stabilising export quota system and an export cartel (which we discussed in section 3.3) is a narrow one. In principle, a quota scheme need not be a cartel. If exporting countries agree on individual quotas which correspond to each country's export surplus in an average year, they accumulate as stocks any excess of their output over their consumption plus export quota, and they release stocks to fulfil their export quotas in years of production shortfall, then what we have is a pure stabilisation agreement. However, export quota commodity schemes have tended to be introduced as much as a defence against declining primary product prices as to stabilise prices.

4.5

We have seen that the major difficulty faced by an international commodity agreement is that of identifying the correct longer term trend of world prices, and that the architects of ICAs often also have difficulty in divorcing the stabilisation function of a particular agreement from their desire to influence the longer term trend of prices. It is not just that a producer- or consumer-dominated agreement may try to stabilise prices against the trend; it is usually only when the trend is moving against it that a country becomes interested in stabilising measures. For most of the post-war period there has been a general belief that the terms of trade for primary commodities were tending to decline, and in this situation predominantly importing countries were generally very content to purchase in an unstable market. A renewed interest in commodity agreements came from importing countries with the sudden rise in commodity prices during 1972. Partly this was merely another instance of the way the word 'stability' is used to mean in reality 'preventing longer term price movements' (see section 3.4); but also it can be regarded as a genuine interest in price stabilising measures against a background in which there were increasing fears in importing countries of commodity shortage and worsening terms of trade. In other words, importing countries prefer stable rising prices to unstable rising prices but they are quite content with unstable, but generally declining prices.

Much of the literature on ICAs has taken it as axiomatic that a longer term relative downward trend in agricultural commodity prices was to be expected. The pressure for stabilising schemes has come mainly from exporting countries and most writers have seen the potential benefits of ICAs as accruing to exporting countries – even if the agreements succeeded only in stabilising rather than supporting prices. The general lack of success of price stabilisation arrangements in the early post-war period led some experts to ask whether the existing agreements were attempting to stabilise the right thing. If the main problem of a successful stabilising agreement was the pressure of changes in the balance of world supply and demand for the commodity, when the agreement had the effect of preventing these supply and demand changes from being translated into world price movements, was it not possible to alleviate the damage of fluctuating prices without stabilising prices as such?

The main casualty of fluctuating primary product prices, it was argued, were the development prospects of low-income primary product exporting countries. Many of these countries were highly dependent on a small number of products for their foreign exchange earnings and variations in exchange earnings meant variations in their capacity to import and thus a damaging 'stop–go' impact upon development planning. What was required therefore was a scheme designed to stabilise the export earnings of these low-income primary product exporting countries and in particular a means of compensating them for the reduction in earnings they experienced in periods of relatively low primary product prices.[9]

In February 1975, some fifteen years after the idea of compensatory finance as an alternative to price stabilisation was first put forward, such a scheme did appear when an agreement was signed between forty-six developing countries in Africa, the Caribbean and the Pacific (the '*ACP States*') and the nine countries of the European Community (54). This agreement, which is called the *Lomé Convention*, and which replaced the *Yaoundé Convention*, a previous agreement between a group of African countries and the six original member states of the EEC, includes a scheme for stabilising the primary product export receipts of the developing countries involved. The agricultural products covered by the stabilisation part of the Lomé Convention (known as STABEX) are groundnuts, cocoa, coffee, cotton, palm products, hides and skins, wood products, bananas, tea, and sisal. (Special arrangements apply for sugar.) The basic principle of the scheme is that the Community transfers funds to individual ACP states in any year if two conditions are met. These conditions are:

(a) That exports of one of the products covered by the scheme have, over the four previous years, constituted at least 7·5 per cent of the country's total export earnings. This is called the *dependency threshold*.

(b) That export earnings have fallen by 7·5 per cent or more beneath a reference amount, this amount being based on the previous four years' export receipts. This is called the *trigger threshold*.

For thirty-four of the least developed, landlocked, or island economies the dependency and trigger thresholds are reduced to 2·5 per cent.

If both conditions do apply, the Community agrees to transfer to the country concerned an amount equal to the difference between actual earnings and the reference amount. For a small number of countries, the economies of which are regarded as particularly weak, the arrangements apply to their exports to all destinations, but in the main the system applies to exports to the EEC only. The relatively more developed ACP countries are expected to transfer back finance to the EEC fund if, because of a price rise, their export earnings exceed the reference amount, but not when an increase in export earnings is attributable to a quantity increase.

In principle, the use of the rolling average approach − that is, the calculation of the reference amount in any given year on the basis of the previous four years' trade − means that the scheme will offset the effects on export earnings of short-term fluctuations in product prices, but will not attempt to combat the effects of longer term price movements. However, because the repayment rules are much weaker than the arrangements for compensation (about half of the countries have no requirement to repay and no country repays when it earns more by increasing the quantity of its exports) there is bound to be a net transfer of funds to the ACP countries, and a limit of 375 million units of account has been placed on this transfer for the first five years of the agreement.

Notes

[1] The term 'international trade' usually refers to the exchange between states of goods and services. The broader term 'international economics' includes the study of all international economic transactions. There are many good textbooks devoted to international economics such as those by Mundell (1), Caves and Jones (2) and, at a more elementary level, Kenen and Lubitz (3). An excellent survey of the contemporary development of trade theory, including a comprehensive list of references, is provided by the contributions of Haberler (4) and Corden (5) to the Princeton International Series.

[2] Strictly, throughout this section, to be consistent we should refer to Oq_p, OP_p, etc., but see Chapter 1, note 3.

[3] In this example, we have further simplified matters by assuming no change in the country's production combination of OE food and OT manufactures.

[4] These conditions will be recognised as similar to the ones we discussed in relation to the exercise of monopoly power by a firm (Chapter 3, section 5.3).

[5] For examples of the kind of calculation which is required, see Phillips and Ritson (23) and Winegarten and Josling (24).

[6] Blandford and Currie (39) provide a careful analysis of the potential welfare gains from a policy which stabilises agricultural producer prices. They include a useful bibliography on the behaviour of firms under uncertainty.

[7] References (42–47) constitute a small selection.

[8] At the time of writing negotiations are taking place under the auspices of UNCTAD to set up a very ambitious buffer stock arrangement covering a number of commodities, but commonly financed.

[9] One of the most concise statements of the compensatory finance argument was Meade's submission to the first UNCTAD (50). Some indication of the extent to which those less-developed countries which are associated with the EEC are dependent upon individual agricultural products for their foreign exchange earnings will be found in Ellis, Marsh and Ritson (51). A study by MacBean (52) has thrown some doubt on the belief that fluctuations in export earnings do seriously damage less-developed economies. For an interesting report on the impact of fluctuating export prices on a high-income country (New Zealand) see Ross (53).

References

(1) Mundell, R. A. *International Economics*. London & New York, Macmillan, 1968.

(2) Caves, R. E. & Jones, R. W. *World Trade and Payments: An Introduction*. Boston, Little, Brown, 1973.

(3) Kenen, P. B. & Lubitz, R. *International Economics*, 3rd edn. New Jersey, Prentice Hall, 1971.

(4) Haberler, G. 'A Survey of International Trade Theory.' Princeton University, 1961.

(5) Corden, W. M. 'Recent Developments in the Theory of International Trade.' Princeton University, 1965.

(6) Heckscher, E. 'The effect of foreign trade on the distribution of income.' *Ekonomisk Tidskrift*, 1919. Vol. XXI (Reprinted in the *Readings in Theory of International Trade* eds. H. S. Ellis & L. A. Metzler). American Economic Association/Allen & Unwin, London, 1950.

(7) Ohlin, B. *Interregional and International Trade.* Harvard University Press, 1933.

(8) Samuelson, P. A. 'International trade and the equalisation of factor prices.' *Economic Journal,* Vol. LVIII, June 1948.

(9) Meade, J. E. *Theory of International Economic Policy.* Vol. II: *Trade and Welfare.* Oxford University Press, 1955.

(10) Kindleberger, C. P. *International Economics,* 3rd edn. Illinois, Irwin, 1963.

(11) Stopler, W. F. & Samuelson, P. A. 'Protection and real wages.' *Review of Economic Studies,* Vol. IX, No. 1, Nov. 1941. (Reprinted in Ellis & Metzler (6).)

(12) Ritson, C. 'Who gets a subsidy.' *New Society,* Vol. 31, No. 642, Jan. 23 1975.

(13) *Self-Sufficiency in Food and Food Commodities. A Provisional Study of the Measurement and Use of the Concept of Self-Sufficiency.* C 75/LIM/1. Rome, 1975, FAO.

(14) *Agricultural Policy in Sweden.* Paris, OECD, 1974.

(15) *Sweden: A Case Study in Agricultural Adjustment.* International Agricultural Adjustment Support Study No. 2, C 73/LIM/2. Rome, FAO, Nov. 1973.

(16) Bickerdike, C. F. 'The theory of incipient taxes.' *Economic Journal,* Vol. XVI, 1906.

(17) Kaldor, N. 'A note on tariffs and the terms of trade.' *Economica* NS, Vol. VII, 1940.

(18) Scitovsky, T. 'A reconsideration of the theory of tariffs.' *Review of Economic Studies,* Vol. IX, 1942 (Reprinted in Ellis & Metzler (6).)

(19) Robinson, J. *Beggar-My-Neighbour Remedies for Unemployment. Essays in the Theory of Employment.,* 2nd edn. Oxford, Blackwell, 1947. (Reprinted in Ellis & Metzler (6).)

(20) Viner, J. *International Economics.* Chicago, Free Press, 1951.

(21) 'Towards a New International Economic Order.' Report by a Commonwealth Experts Group. Commonwealth Secretariat, London, 1975.

(22) Warley, T. K. 'Western trade in agricultural products.' In *'International Economic Relations of the Western World, 1959–71'* (ed. A. Schonfield). Royal Institute of International Affairs/Oxford University Press, 1975.

(23) Phillips, T. & Ritson, C. 'Agricultural expansion and the UK balance of payments.' *National Westminster Bank Quarterly Review,* Feb. 1970.

(24) Winegarten, A. & Josling, T. 'Agriculture and import saving.' *Hill Samuel Occasional Paper,* No. 5, Feb. 1970.

(25) Blagburn, C. H. 'Import – replacement by British agriculture.' *Economic Journal,* Vol. LX, Mar. 1950.

(26) Robinson, E. A. G. & Marris, R. L. 'The use of home resources to save imports.' *Economic Journal,* Vol. LX, Mar. 1950.

(27) MacDougall, G. A. D. 'The use of home resources to save imports: a comment.' *Economic Journal,* Vol. LX, Sept. 1950.

(28) Marris, R. L. 'The purchasing power of British exports.' *Economica* NS, Vol. XXII, No. 85, Feb. 1955.

(29) Morgan, D. J. & Paish, F. W. 'The purchasing power of British exports further considered.' *Economica* NS, Vol. XXII, No. 88, Nov. 1955.

(30) Marris, R. L. 'The purchasing power of British Exports: a rejoinder.' *Economica* NS, Vol. XXIII, No. 89, Feb. 1956.

(31) Ritson, C. 'United Kingdom agricultural support, the balance of payments, and the terms of trade.' Unpublished Thesis. University of Reading, Department of Agricultural Economics and Management, 1968.

(32) McCrone, G. 'The relevance of the theory of tariffs to agricultural protection.' *Journal of Agricultural Economics,* Vol. XIII, No. 1, June 1958.

(33) McCrone, G. *The Economics of Subsidising Agriculture: A Study of British Policy.* London, Allen & Unwin, 1962.

(34) Ritson, C. 'The use of home resources to save imports: a new look.' *Journal of Agricultural Economics*, Vol. XXI, No. 1, Jan. 1970.

(35) Economic Development Committee for Agriculture. 'Agriculture's Import Saving Role.' National Economic Development Office, London, HMSO, 1968.

(36) Phillips, T. & Ritson, C. 'Reciprocity in international trade.' *Journal of Agricultural Economics*, Vol. XX, No. 3, Sept. 1969.

(37) Josling, T. 'The agricultural burden: a reappraisal.' In *The Economics of Europe* (ed. J. Pinder). London, Charles Knight/Federal Trust, 1971.

(38) Ritson, C. 'Should Britain feed itself?' *New Society*, Vol. 34, No. 686. 27 Nov. 1975.

(39) Blandford, D. & Currie, J. M. 'Price uncertainty – the case for Government intervention.' *Journal of Agricultural Economics*, Vol. XXVI, No. 1, Jan. 1975.

(40) 'The Common Agricultural Policy.' Commission of the European Communities, Brussels. (Periodically revised.)

(41) Ritson, C. *The Common Agricultural Policy.* Section III of: *European Economic Community: Economics and Agriculture.* The Open University Press, 1974.

(42) Law, A. D. *International Commodity Agreements.* Lexington, Mass., D. C. Heath, 1975.

(43) Grogan, F. O. (ed.). *International Trade in Temperate Zone Products.* Edinburgh, University of Newcastle upon Tyne Agricultural Adjustment Unit/Oliver & Boyd, 1972.

(44) Tontz, R. L. (ed.). *Foreign Agricultural Trade: Selected Readings.* Part IV: *Trade Stabilisation and Commodity Agreements.* Iowa State University Press, 1966.

(45) Warley, T. K. (ed.). *Agricultural Producers and Their Markets.* Oxford, Blackwell, 1967.

(46) *International Commodity Review and Outlook* (annual); plus series of *Commodity Policy Studies.* Rome, FAO.

(47) *Commodity trade*, Vol. III. UNCTAD, 1965.

(48) Goodman, R. 'The reliability of supply – we all need it.' *Journal of the Farmers Club*, No. 10, Aug./Sept., 1974.

(49) Josling, T. 'Towards an international system of grain reserves.' In *Agriculture and the State: British Policy in a World Context* eds. Davey, Josling & McFarquar. London, Trade Policy Research Centre/Macmillan, 1976.

(50) Meade, J. E. 'International Commodity Agreements.' *Lloyd's Bank Review*, No. 73, July 1964.

(51) Ellis, F., Marsh, J. & Ritson, C. 'Farmers and foreigners: impact of the Common Agricultural Policy on Associates and Associables.' Overseas Development Institute, London, 1973.

(52) MacBean, A. *Export Instability and Economic Development.* Harvard University Press, 1966.

(53) Ross, B. J. 'Fluctuating export prices and economic instability: problems and policies in New Zealand.' *Journal of Agricultural Economics*, Vol. XXVII, No. 1, Jan. 1976.

(54) 'EEC–ACP Convention of Lomé.' *The Courier*, No. 31, Special Issue. Commission of the European Communities, Brussels, Mar. 1975.

CHAPTER 8

Methods of Agricultural Support

1 Introduction

1.1 Policy objectives

In the final chapter of this book we attempt a more systematic approach to the various policy measures which governments use when they intervene in agricultural markets. That is, we now turn to the policy mechanisms themselves, rather than concentrating, as we have done in the previous three chapters, on the underlying economic principles applicable to the analysis and evaluation of agricultural policies. We attempt, first, to categorise policy devices according to the economic variables upon which they operate, and second, to compare the merits of alternative policy mechanisms according to the extent to which they appear capable of fulfilling the objectives which governments set for themselves when they decide to formulate policies towards agriculture.[1]

Governments intervene in agriculture for many reasons, but there is little doubt that it has been the tendency for farm incomes to fail to keep pace with rising incomes elsewhere in the economy that has been largely responsible for the manner in which agricultural policies have developed in most advanced countries since World War II. An OECD report on agricultural policies states that:

> The drive to increase income and improve the standard of living for the agricultural population is so widespread that it must be considered as the predominant aim of agricultural policies (2).

Inasmuch as income support is therefore seen as the prime objective of agricultural policy, then this is the ultimate criterion upon which any policy measure must be judged; and it is by no means certain that all the devices used by governments to raise farm incomes are in fact capable of meeting that objective. For example, as argued later in the chapter, attempts to improve farming profitability may result merely in higher rents for land and higher prices for purchased inputs. Similarly, a policy which attempts to influence agricultural productivity may be confounded by subsequent adverse price movements. Is the policy measure therefore, on its own, or in combination with some other device, capable of raising agricultural incomes?

Second, where it appears that a policy device can be successful in raising agricultural incomes then it might be judged on the basis of the extent to which it is likely to fulfil subsidiary goals of agricultural policy. The stated objectives of agricultural policy in the EEC, the USA and the UK will give some indication of what these subsidiary goals might be.

The common agricultural policy shall have as its objectives:

(a) To increase agricultural productivity by developing technical progress and by ensuring the rational development of agricultural production and the optimum utilisation of the factors of production, particularly labour.
(b) To ensure thereby a fair standard of living for the agricultural population, particularly by the increasing of the individual earnings of persons engaged in agriculture.
(c) To stabilise markets.
(d) To guarantee regular supplies.
(e) To ensure reasonable prices in supplies to consumers.

(Article 39, Treaty of Rome, 1958.)

. . . Stabilising, supporting and protecting farm incomes and prices, . . . assisting in the maintenance of balanced and adequate supplies of agricultural commodities, . . . facilitating the orderly distribution of agricultural commodities.

(Congress declaration, when providing Federal Charter for the Commodity Credit Corporation which operated Agricultural Support Programs in the USA, 1948.)

. . . Promoting and maintaining . . . a stable and efficient agricultural industry capable of producing such part of the nation's food and other agricultural produce as in the national interest it is desirable to produce in the United Kingdom, and of producing it at minimum prices consistently with proper remuneration and living conditions for farmers and workers in agriculture and an adequate return on capital invested in the industry.

(United Kingdom Agricultural Act, 1947.)

Any particular policy device must also of course be seen in the context of the overall objectives of government policy, for example towards employment, efficiency, exchange rates, consumer prices, income distribution, economic growth and relations with foreign countries. Sometimes one or more of these overall objectives of economic policy will be reflected in the stated objectives of government policies towards a particular sector (such as agriculture) but in other cases they will be implicit. The three areas of government interest in the economic affairs of the nation which seem likely to be of most relevance in the case of agricultural policy are the distribution of income, economic efficiency and international relations.

1.2 Income distribution

In view of the fact that a policy of agricultural income support aims to redistribute income in favour of the agricultural population, clearly this will be a relevant area of general government policy; and since the motive for supporting agricultural incomes usually lies in the view that part of the agricultural population is receiving an average level of income which is substantially lower than the national average (rather, that is, than because farmers and farm workers are regarded as, in some sense, more worthy of high incomes) it would seem reasonable to require of a policy directed towards supporting agricultural incomes that it should have the effect within the economy as a whole of transferring income from higher to lower income groups. This means that we must be concerned not only with the aggregate amount transferred from non-agriculture to agriculture, but also with the method by which the transfer is financed and the way the benefits of the support are distributed.

1.3 Economic efficiency

Much of Part II of this book has been concerned with an examination of the meaning and implications of economic efficiency for the assessment of government agricultural policies and projects, and in particular with the extent to which market prices provide a guide to an efficient allocation of the nation's resources. Such great complexities have been raised that it is perhaps necessary for us to remind ourselves that economic efficiency is nevertheless something that cannot be ignored in any comparison of agricultural policy measures. A simple example will serve to demonstrate this. Suppose the British Government decides to support the incomes of farmers in the Scottish Highlands by subsidising the cultivation of bananas. This would probably be 'technically' quite feasible – it has proved so in the equatorial house in Kew Gardens. If a high enough price is guaranteed to producers, banana growing under controlled environment could be profitable in the Scottish Highlands. The suggestion is an absurd one because it would be an extremely inefficient way of pursuing the objective of income support; but without an efficiency criterion there might be no grounds for excluding it.

In this particular case there would be no need to examine the relationship between the price required to make banana-growing in Scotland profitable, and the price at which supplies were available from world markets, in order to ascertain that the proposed measure was inefficient. But it will not always be so self-evident that a policy measure is relatively inefficient so that, in spite of the lack of confidence that will sometimes be attached to them, efficiency criteria are a vital part of the assessment of agricultural policies.

Many of the objectives of government policy which can be regarded as subsidiary to the major objective of agricultural income support are in fact efficiency criteria. These may be divided into static and dynamic aspects. Static efficiency will include the administrative cost of a support system, the extent to which a measure introduces 'stability' as well as 'support' into the market for agricultural products, and the general efficient use of the nation's resources in the sense of the extent to which the conditions required for a Pareto optimum are attained. Dynamic efficiency is concerned with the extent to which a policy measure facilitates or frustrates the longer term adjustment of the agricultural sector.

1.4 International relations

As we shall see, one frequent side effect of a policy to support agricultural incomes is to increase the degree of agricultural self-sufficiency, either replacing imports or adding to exports. The costs associated with foregoing the gains from trade consequent upon the output increasing effects of a policy are covered by our efficiency criteria. There may however be further costs emanating from the international repercussions of the policy in the form of reciprocal trade relationships. We discussed these in the previous chapter in the context of government policies which deliberately sought to make a welfare gain by manipulating the country's terms of trade. However, we suggested that:

> Although world prices of many agricultural products are certainly influenced by national government trade policies, it is probably true to say that in most cases any welfare gains via the exercise of international market power have been unintentional.

But even when a country's agricultural trade is influenced as an accidental byproduct of a policy to support domestic agricultural incomes, there may be reciprocal losses to be taken into account – either because of deliberate trade retaliation, or through more diffuse areas of world economic and political power.

Since the Second World War, international trade in temperate zone products has provided an abundance of evidence of the way in which a policy of protecting domestic agriculture might have adverse repercussions across the entire trade spectrum. In the view of one respected writer, the situation merited the title *World Agriculture in Disarray*:

> Agriculture surely stands out as the most important single case in which the Governments of most industrial countries are willing to permit domestic policy considerations to override so completely their interests in achieving the advantages from increased international specialisation in production. . . .
> In short, a significant fraction of world farm output is being produced in the

wrong place. . . . It is difficult to overestimate the dangers of current trends in agricultural protectionism to the future of trade liberalisation generally (3).

Thus the trade impact of a policy to support agricultural incomes is important for two main reasons – because of the economic costs associated with foregoing the gains from trade, and because of the danger of the application of retaliatory measures by foreign Governments.

2 Cataloguing policy mechanisms[2]

2.1

The existence of such a wide variety of agricultural policy measures means that we must restrict ourselves to highlighting the major characteristics of each device. At the end of the chapter the *deficiency payment* and *variable import levy* methods of supporting agricultural prices are exposed to a more detailed critique.

A first important distinction to be made is between those support measures that attempt to raise agricultural incomes by improving the profitability of farming, and those that do not. Among the latter, there are three main categories:

(a) Government expenditure directed specifically towards rural areas.

This includes a whole array of schemes to improve rural infrastructure, provide social services, subsidise transport facilities, provide water and electricity in isolated areas, and so on. Attractive as these kind of measures undoubtedly are, they may have only a peripheral effect on low incomes as such unless massive expenditure is involved. Where one overall objective of government policy is to maintain the 'vitality' of rural areas, these measures may make a useful additional contribution to the objective of agricultural income support.

(b) Development of farm-based non-farm occupations.

'Part-time farming' occurs to varying degrees in all industrial nations and is particularly prevalent in West Germany. Part-time farming can take many forms, ranging from the 'gentleman hobby-farmer', for whom income from farm sales is incidental, to those small farmers who find it necessary to seek additional employment. It is in the field of tourism that it seems most likely that government assistance and promotion might result in significantly improved incomes for small farmers.[3] One might view the income benefits as a useful bonus while providing tourist facilities, or vice versa, but clearly this kind of solution is a localised one where low income farmers are regionally grouped in attractive areas. There is a second drawback attached to tourism as a method of bringing higher incomes to small farmers. Most benefits (as with many income support measures) may in practice not go to low-income farmers, because they lack the initiative and enterprise required, a point argued succinctly by Wibberly:

If a farmer is having difficulties in managing efficiently an enterprise based on livestock and crops, he will probably have worse management problems if he introduces human beings into the complex. Therefore, one may have to suggest, tentatively and nicely, to some ... farmers, that if they are small because they have had difficulties in getting onto good land and onto big farms, and that their income situation shows that they have been fairly poor managers of resources in the past, it is unlikely that they will get out of that situation by inviting a lot of people onto their places (10).

(c) Direct income supplementation.

It is perhaps somewhat surprising that direct income payments should be such a rare feature of agricultural policy in developed countries in view of the fact that income support is the prime aim of most policies. In principle, direct income supplementation allows both the distribution and the collection of the income transfer to be in accord with the Government's policy towards income redistribution. By supporting agricultural incomes directly it is less likely that the policy will be in conflict with other goals of agricultural policy – in particular the appropriate degree of agricultural self-sufficiency can be determined to a large extent on the basis of 'national interest', rather than as a byproduct of income support. In October 1973, the European Commission put forward proposals (11) for the reform of the Common Agricultural Policy in which direct income support was considered, and rejected, on three grounds – that it would impose substantial administrative problems for member Governments; that it would involve too heavy expenditure from public funds; and that it would hold up structural improvements.

The first of these is difficult to defend as governments frequently do resort to income supplementation schemes when dealing with other aspects of income inequality which are no less substantial and where in some cases the incidence of low incomes may be more difficult to identify. The question of expenditure from public funds is probably a peculiarity of the European Community which has consistently found it politically more difficult to finance a scheme which required Exchequer funds than one which merely involved manipulating consumer prices. On the third point, any scheme which allows a small farmer to enjoy a tolerable existence rather than exposing him fully to market forces will probably impede structural reform, but it is not clear why direct income payments should be more onerous in this respect than support given via the market. Indeed, the contrary may be the case, as the latter method may give rise to false expectations concerning the longer term viability of the farms in question.

It would seem therefore that we must look further for an explanation of the absence of direct income supplementation schemes in the agricultural policies of the developed countries. The answer probably lies in the lack of popularity among the farming community itself for these kind of measures. First, there is the very real possibility that it may be politically more difficult for a Government to apply a direct support scheme, where the full transfer to farming is clearly visible to taxpayers, rather than a method which operates via income from farming. Thus farming pressure groups may regard it as advisable to press for market support, and the Government regard it as expedient to acquiesce.

There is a second argument against direct income supplementation which is worthy of substantial respect – that it may have psychological association with charity. Thus, given the choice of an identical improvement in income either directly, or via farm revenue, most farmers would choose the latter. (If the recipient when receiving the benefit through revenue was unaware that such a choice existed, so much the better.)

If it were possible to give an identical monetary effect by these alternatives, with identical associated market and budgetary consequences, then the choice of the farm revenue option would represent a genuine Pareto-style improvement over direct income supplementation. Unfortunately, the two methods do not have identical budgetary and market implications for a given monetary benefit, and, in particular, it is much more difficult to distribute the benefit of support in accordance with a progressive income distribution via farm profitability. This means, first, that there will be a trade-off between the psychological benefits and other costs. Second, it means that we should be extremely cautious about the supposed lack of popularity (among the recipients) of direct support. In general, for a given level of government expenditure, the better-off larger farmer (who will also tend to be more vocal and better represented on farmer organisations) receives a larger share of the benefit from a scheme that works via farming revenue, than when direct income supplementation is involved.

This last point is so important that it deserves a certain amount of elaboration.

Suppose that, in a particular country, 90 per cent of dairy producers are small peasant farmers owning five dairy cows, and 10 per cent of producers are modern, capital-intensive, large farmers with dairy herds of eighty cows. Assume that the average milk yield per cow is the same for both groups, so that 64 per cent of the milk supply is produced from the large herds and 36 per cent from small herds. If the Government decides to allocate a given amount of finance to dairy producers, then if it is distributed directly and solely to the small producers, they would receive nearly three times as much per producer as they would via a scheme that raised the price of milk. Raising the milk price may, of course, be more compatible with other goals of agricultural policy, but where the objective is raising low incomes in agriculture, it is often difficult to avoid the conclusion that the best idea might not be just to go ahead and raise low incomes.

As already indicated, one advantage of methods of income support which do not attempt to operate via income from farming is that they are less likely to conflict with other policy objectives. It must be emphasised, however, that it will not be possible to escape entirely some impact upon farm production. First, where a scheme described under (a) above improves rural infrastructure and services, one would expect some reduction in the costs of production in that area (e.g. better transport, power and water supplies, etc.). Second, any measure that results in certain individuals continuing to farm, when otherwise they would have discontinued, will have some impact on aggregate farm output. Normally, one would expect this to be a positive impact, but it is possible (where support prevents small farms becoming vacant and being amalgamated into larger holdings) that the impact might be negative – that is, aggregate output would be higher in the absence of the income support.

2.2

Most of the measures adopted by governments with the aim of raising the standard of living of the agricultural population do in fact operate by attempting to increase income from farming. We can broadly classify these measures according to whether they are directed principally towards reducing farm costs, increasing farm revenue, or reducing the size of the agricultural population. In Chapter 2 it was suggested that, strictly defined, the 'cost' of production would comprise the payment for all factors, including those owned by the farm family, but now of course we need to distinguish between costs which are payments for resources owned by the farm family (and which therefore contribute to farm income) and those which are not. When in this chapter we talk about 'reducing farm costs' it is payments for factors of production excluding those owned by the farm family to which we refer. If then we distinguish:

The aggregate cost of agricultural production (C)
The aggregate revenue from agricultural production (R)
The number of individuals earning their living from agricultural production (N)

$R - C$ gives the aggregate income (or net revenue) of the sector (I), and I/N gives average income per head. C is determined by $p \times q$, where p describes the prices farmers pay for their inputs and q the quantity of inputs used.

(More precisely,

$$\left(C = \sum_{i=1}^{n} p_i q_i \right)$$

where p_i and q_i are the price and quantity used of the ith, out of a total of n, inputs.)

R is determined by $P \times Q$, where P describes the prices farmers receive for their produce and Q the quantity of output.

(More precisely,

$$\left(R = \sum_{i=1}^{n} P_i Q_i \right)$$

where P_i and Q_i are the price and quantity produced of the ith, out of a total of n, products.)

In purely formal terms, therefore, it is possible to secure any selected level of income per head by a suitable manipulation of the variables p, q, P, Q, and N. In practice, very severe limitations exist on the extent to which these variables can be adjusted. In particular there are important interdependencies between some of the variables, the most crucial of which are:

The link between p and q in the markets for agricultural inputs
The link between P and Q in the markets for agricultural products
The link between q and Q in agricultural production functions

These various interdependencies mean that it is difficult to categorise agricultural policy devices into watertight compartments, but we shall nevertheless find it convenient to classify the various measures according to whether they are directed primarily towards farm costs (C), farm revenue (R), or the size of the agricultural population (N).

3 Measures which attempt to reduce farm costs

3.1

The main policy mechanism which aims at improving farm incomes by reducing farm costs is the payment of subsidies on inputs. The possibilities for aid in this form are numerous. Subsidies may be given for a specific input, such as fertiliser; refer to a specific activity – such as renovating derelict land or installing irrigation or drainage systems; or more generally, farmers may be provided with access to money capital at preferential rates.

As far as the individual producer is concerned, if the Government pays him a subsidy per unit of an input, this is equivalent to a fall in the price of the input by the amount of the subsidy (as long as the market price of the input remains unchanged). In Chapter 4 (section 2.1) we established that, if all other prices remain constant, a fall in the price of an input would, for the profit maximising firm, result in:

(*a*) An increase in farm profit.
(*b*) An increase in the quantity demanded of the cheaper (in this case, the subsidised) input.
(*c*) An increase in the quantity supplied of the product.
(*d*) Either an increase or a decrease in the quantity demanded of other inputs, depending on whether the tendency for more of all inputs to be used because of the higher level of output outweighs the tendency for the cheaper input to be substituted for all other inputs.

The net effect of an input subsidy upon farm income will thus be very much bound up with the impact of increased supply upon product prices and the changed demand for inputs on factor prices. The problem of aggregate revenue being reduced by the price depressing effect of output increasing policies will be considered in the next section. It is sufficient to note at this stage that an attempt to increase farm income by subsidising input prices may not be successful unless it is combined with a policy towards product prices.

Price changes in input markets, resulting from the application of the subsidy, will depend on:

(a) The extent and nature of competition in input industries. It is possible that the subsidising of a particular input may lead to a substantial increase in the market price of that input if its supply is dominated by a small number of firms.

(b) The extent to which the input is specific to agriculture, and/or the factors of production required for the manufacture of the input are specific to the input industry. We would, for example, expect the supply of fertiliser to be less elastic than the supply of farm machinery. To take an extreme case, there would be little point in attempting to improve average farm incomes by subsidising farm rents. Since the supply of land is more or less fixed, any attempt by farmers in aggregate to use more of the 'cheaper' input, land, would merely result in a rise in rent levels until the effective price paid by producers was high enough to reduce the quantity of land demanded to equal supply – that is rents would rise by the full amount of the subsidy.

For an input subsidy to be successful in raising farm incomes therefore, it may be necessary for there to be an associated policy towards product prices, and subsidies will need to avoid inputs for which the supply is relatively inelastic. Input subsidies may prove attractive if there is a particular farming practice which a Government wishes to encourage – say land reclamation, where there may be longer run social benefits to the community – or the use of a new technique which farmers are being slow (in the view of the Government, they are being unnecessarily cautious) in adopting. Input subsidies also have the advantage that they may provide a convenient way of concentrating income support on a particular group of farmers – say hill farmers. It may be politically more feasible to aid disadvantaged farming groups by subsidising investment on hill or small farms rather than by some other means. Similarly, there are less likely to be adverse effects in factor and product markets when only a small proportion of farmers are affected. Subsidising rents for farms under 20 hectares would in many countries have only a small impact upon rent levels. On the other hand, generalised input subsidies are likely to help most the larger prosperous farmer – the proportion of purchased inputs used tends to increase with farm size.

3.2

In principle, another way in which farm incomes might be raised by a policy directed towards reducing farm costs is if the quantity of purchased inputs used is reduced.

If a profit maximising production plan is in operation, a reduction in the quantity of inputs used will, by definition, reduce aggregate revenue by a greater amount than it will reduce aggregate costs (if prices and the production function remain unchanged), but there are two sets of circumstances in which a reduction in the quantity of inputs might be associated with an increase in net revenue. These are:

(a) By an improvement in agricultural productivity, which reduces the quantity of inputs required for any output level.
(b) Where existing patterns of resource use involve a greater quantity of some inputs than required in the profit maximising solution, and thus profits can be increased by reducing the quantity of inputs used. Such a situation might be thought of as involving an improvement in productivity by better management.

(Restricting the quantity of resources used by agriculture, particularly removing land from production, can improve farm income via the effect on aggregate revenue of the price increase which follows the reduction in output. This however is a form of supply control which is designed to aid incomes by increasing aggregate revenue, rather than reducing aggregate cost, and is discussed in the next section.)

In Chapter 2 (section 4.4) we concluded that, in most cases, a productivity improvement would lead to an increase in the profit maximising level of output for the farm firm if prices remained unchanged. Since a productivity improvement reduces the quantity of inputs required per unit of output, it will not necessarily involve an increase in the demand for inputs, even when output does increase. However, in Chapter 4 (section 4) we noted that much of the productivity improvement that had been experienced in agriculture in the twentieth century had been associated with an increase in the quantity of purchased inputs used in farming. In such circumstances increases in farm income (if any) must have been derived from the sale of more output.

Nevel has estimated (12) that 62–80 per cent of the increase in output per manhour in American agriculture between 1950 and 1966 was attributable to technological change, and 20–38 per cent to increased capital intensity. The latest analysis for the United Kingdom (13) shows that, over fourteen post-1945 years, about 64 per cent of increased output (at constant prices) was attributable to improvements in total factor productivity and 36 per cent to additional inputs used in farming. It would seem therefore that inasmuch as government measures designed to improve agricultural productivity are seen as a means of raising farm incomes, then they should be regarded as measures directed at increasing farm revenue rather than reducing farm costs.

Turning to the second possibility – that farm incomes might be increased by an improvement in management causing a fall in aggregate farm costs – on the face of it there would appear to be every possibility that some producers might be applying inputs beyond the economic optimum. Indeed, it is sometimes suggested in farm management literature that the most profitable farmers may be those who achieve only modest yields, but keep 'a tight rein on costs'.

Although there are undoubtedly some producers who operate profitably in this way, it must be said that the bulk of evidence favours the view that the most profitable farmers are also those who achieve high output levels. For example, data for the southern counties of England (14) shows that the top 25 per cent farms (on the basis of overall profitability) have, in almost every category, higher costs per acre (and much higher output per acre) than the average. Government expenditure on farm advisory and extension work with the aim of helping farms to achieve higher income levels is therefore more likely to involve increased output with little or no change in costs, than reduced costs, with little or no change in output. In short, it would seem that there is little scope to view policies to encourage the more efficient use of resources on farms as a method of improving farm incomes *by reducing costs*. As with technical innovation, such benefits as are likely to accrue to farmers from this kind of policy will depend on the effect of extra output on aggregate farm revenue.

4   Measures which attempt to increase farm revenue

4.1   Two market models

Government policies can aim to raise farm revenue by increasing the prices farmers receive for their produce, by manipulating the quantity of output they produce, or by some combination of the two.

In this section we divide such policies into four groups, namely policies which raise farm output; policies which subsidise farm product prices; policies which exercise control over imported supplies; and policies which exercise control over domestic supplies. We illustrate the impact of the various policy mechanisms considered using the partial equilibrium models of agricultural trade developed in the previous chapter (Figs. 7.5–7.8). There we distinguished between four market situations, depending on whether the country was a potential importer or potential exporter of the product and whether or not the production and consumption of the product within the country was significant relative to the total quantity of the product traded internationally.

Since many price support programmes lead to an increase in domestic supplies, a particular policy measure can transform an importing country into an exporting one – so in this section we use the same diagram to illustrate both the importer and exporter cases. We maintain the distinction between the case where imports or exports by the country are insignificant in world terms (which we referred to as 'country 1') and the case where a change in the quantity of imports or exports by the country does have a significant impact on the world market price (country 2). This distinction can be associated with important differences in the effectiveness of some of the policy devices considered. In Chapter 7 we showed the equilibrium trading position in terms of both the domestic market (the 'a' diagrams) and the world market (the 'b' diagrams). In this chapter we are mainly concerned with the impact of government policies on the domestic market and we do not show the corresponding adjustments in the world market.[4]

4.2 Raising farm output

In Fig. 8.1 the country illustrated does not account for a significant proportion of total world production and consumption of the product, and the amount imported or exported can therefore be regarded as having no perceptible influence upon the world price of the product.

The product is considered at the 'farm gate' stage in the production process, that is, in the condition in which it is normally sold by the farmer, and the demand curve is therefore derived from final consumer demand through the marketing process (See Chapter 3, section 5). The 'world' price (P_w) is the landed price at port of entry and is thus directly competitive with the farm gate price of home supplies. (Where the product is normally traded in a semiprocessed form, e.g. milk products, then the home product would be considered in the equivalent processed state, rather than at the 'farm gate' stage.) We assume, in the first instance, an 'open' economy, that is, the product may be imported and exported free of government regulation.

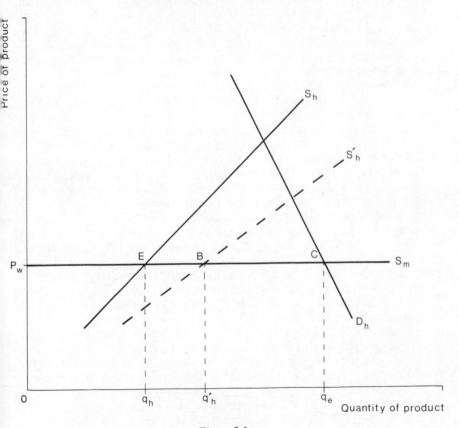

Figure 8.1

With domestic supply curve S_h and demand curve D_h, q_h will be home-produced and q_hq_e imported. OP_wEq_h is the revenue to the farm sector from the sale of this product, and q_hECq_e the amount spent on imports (in terms of domestic currency). The aggregate revenue of domestic producers can be increased by a policy which shifts the supply curve to the right, for example to S'_h where revenue has been increased by $q_hEBq'_h$. As we saw in the previous section, policies directed towards improving agricultural productivity, and policies which give aid in the form of input subsidies, will be likely to lead to just such a shift in the supply curve – producers find it profitable to supply a greater quantity of the product at any given price. In this case, the market price is unchanged, being determined by the price at which supplies are available from world markets and $q_hq'_h$ imports are replaced by home produce.

At first sight, output increasing policies seem a very attractive solution to the problem of low incomes in agriculture, particularly if the supply curve shift is brought about by productivity improvement rather than by a diversion of resources to agriculture from other sectors. Improving productivity is, in any case, usually a goal of general economic policy. If a valuation of the extra output $q_hq'_h$ exceeds a valuation of the extra resources used by agriculture (plus the resources devoted to the research and extension activities promoting the productivity improvement) then the policy might be regarded as nationally worthwhile irrespective of the effect on farm incomes.

However, although this kind of policy may be efficient when judged on the basis of conventional economic criteria, the policy may be extremely inefficient when judged in terms of the primary goal of agricultural policy – raising farm incomes. Public funds are received by research and extension services; benefits to farming are derived from extra output. Such rewards may be slow to be realised. It may require large quantities of public finance to achieve quite modest improvements in average incomes when product prices remain constant but some rises in input prices are experienced. Characteristically, it may be the larger more prosperous farmers who introduce new methods, especially where these favour large-scale production, and for some farmers, whose ability to respond to new techniques is limited, programmes designed to foster better techniques may even make their income problem more acute, if the increase in output by larger farms forces up some farm costs. There may, of course, be exceptions to this generalisation but, by and large, measures to improve agricultural productivity, when seen solely in terms of income support, are less likely to aid the low-income farmer than the equivalent amount of public funds channelled to some more direct form of income support.

Finally, we should note that if a number of countries pursue this kind of policy simultaneously, then although the impact on the world market of each country's action may be imperceptible, this will not be the case when the effect of all the policies is taken together so that the world price will fall as a number of countries increase their output.

The assumption that a country accounts for an insignificant proportion of total world production and consumption of an agricultural product will often be reasonable, but sometimes it will not. For example, for many years the

United Kingdom has been a substantial importer, when viewed in aggregate world terms, of dairy products, mutton, and bacon. (In 1970, the proportion of world imports accounted for by the United Kingdom was 46 per cent for butter, 50 per cent for mutton and lamb, and 87 per cent for bacon.) Australia, New Zealand, Denmark and USA, among others, are significant exporters of a variety of major agricultural products. When one considers a large regional grouping, such as the European Community, which is subject to common agricultural policy measures, the use of a model incorporating a single world price may rarely be appropriate.

In such circumstances our second and somewhat more complicated 'country 2' model is required. This is illustrated by Fig. 8.2 which depicts the same basic market situation as Fig. 7.7a and uses the same notation. P_w is now the equilibrium price on world markets *in the absence of imports or exports from this country*. The aggregate of domestic supply (S_h) and supply of imports (S_m) gives the total supply S_t. The aggregate of domestic demand (D_h) and demand for exports (D_x) gives the total demand from this country's market, D_t. Equilibrium is established with q_e consumed at price P_e. q_h is supplied by domestic producers and q_m ($= q_h q_e$) is imported.[5]

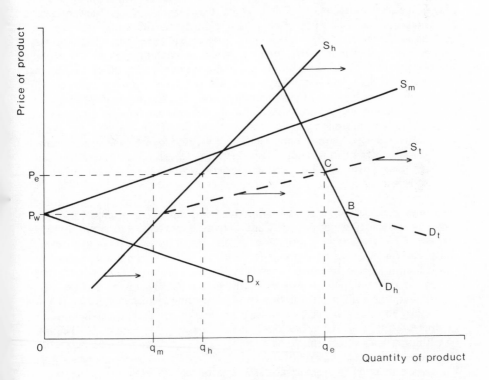

Figure 8.2

If there is now a shift in the domestic supply curve S_h, there will also be a shift in the total supply curve S_t and there will be a fall in the market price of the product, as S_t intersects with a point on the demand curve D_h somewhere between C and B. Imports will be reduced and consumption increased. If the domestic supply curve continues to shift to the right, eventually the country will move into export surplus and the domestic (and world) price will decline as the domestic supply curve intersects the total demand from the country's market, D_t, somewhere below B.

Two factors must therefore be taken into account when considering the income effects of policies designed to raise output for a country which accounts for a non-negligible proportion of world production. First, the increase in aggregate revenue to producers will be diluted because of a decline in product price. Second, the country's agricultural policy becomes a matter of international concern (or at least international interest); the action of one country affects the price received for all world supplies. The extent to which this might imply international displeasure, and perhaps reciprocal trading action, seems to vary as much with the kind of policy device used as with its effect:

(a) Generally speaking, a policy which reduces imports is viewed more favourably by other producing countries than one which increases exports, although the effect they have on the prospects of other exporting countries will be very similar. The point at which a country moves into export surplus may therefore be a more critical one than indicated by the formal model of supply and demand represented by Fig. 8.2.
(b) Policies which involve Exchequer payments to agriculture appear to escape more lightly than measures such as import tariffs or export subsidies which are directed at traded goods.
(c) Measures which aim to improve the productivity of the agricultural sector, though their main income effect operates via raising output rather than reducing costs, are favoured to devices which raise product prices or subsidise inputs.

These considerations indicate that the international repercussions of an agricultural policy which supports productivity improvement are unlikely to be severe. This is especially the case in periods of generally buoyant world markets. For example, an agricultural policy which raises output does not lead to the same chorus of protest from the governments of traditional exporting countries in the mid-1970s as it did in the mid-1960s. This is partly due to the more favourable financial situation facing exporting countries, but also due to an ability to justify an increase in food production when many contemporary commentators take what we termed in Chapter 3 (section 4) the neo-Malthusian view of the future balance between supply and demand on world agricultural product markets. This is, of course, particularly the case when funds are directed to support research into better production methods which might be applicable throughout the world as well as in the domestic economy.

4.3 Producer product subsidies

In the previous section we considered the impact of a policy which promoted an increase in agricultural supply, but left price to be determined by the market. In this and the next section we examine policies which attempt to raise product prices; but just as an important effect of increasing output can be a decline in price, so one consequence of price support may be extra output.

Two alternative methods of subsidising producer prices are to pay farmers a *subsidy per unit of output* or to pay a *deficiency payment*, which makes up the difference between the price received from the market and some specific guaranteed price. Both these methods are illustrated in Fig. 8.3, which uses the same ('country 1') model as Fig. 8.1.

If a subsidy per unit of output, equivalent to $P_w P_g$ ($= BK$), is paid to domestic producers, they can be expected to supply, at any given market price, the quantity they would previously have supplied when the market price was higher by an amount equal to the subsidy. For example, q_g would now be supplied at a market price of P_w rather than P_g. The supply curve, which relates quantity supplied to *market* price, therefore shifts from S_h to S_s.

Alternatively, a price of – say – P_g could be guaranteed and underwritten by a promise to pay a deficiency payment to producers when market prices are lower than the guaranteed price. In this case, the supply curve will be unaffected by the guarantee when market prices exceed the guaranteed price. For all market prices below the guaranteed price, q_g will be supplied so that, in effect, the supply curve becomes the line $q_g BKS_h$.

In our model it is assumed that all producers receive an identical price from the market. In practice, of course, the price received by each individual producer will vary somewhat. The deficiency payment system which operated in the United Kingdom was based on average market prices, rather than the deficiency between each individual producer's price and the guaranteed price. In this way, the incentive for the producer to market the product in the most favourable manner was retained.

Note that the distinction between short- and long-run elasticity of supply (Chapter 2, section 4.5) is particularly important in this kind of policy analysis. In general, it will be the long-run response of supply to a government price support programme which will be the relevant consideration. Also, where a price support programme is simultaneously applied to a number of products, it is necessary to remember that a supply curve normally shows the response of quantity supplied to a change in the product's price, *all other product prices remaining constant.*

Figure 8.3 has been constructed in such a way that, when the supply and demand conditions are as shown, the amount of deficiency payment is the same as the unit subsidy. In both cases, therefore, the quantity of domestic production increases from q_h to q_g and imports are correspondingly reduced. Total revenue to the sector increases from $OP_w Eq_h$ to $OP_g Kq_g$ and a total subsidy payment of $P_w P_g KB$ is transferred from the Exchequer to farmers.

A major contrast between the two methods emerges when we consider what

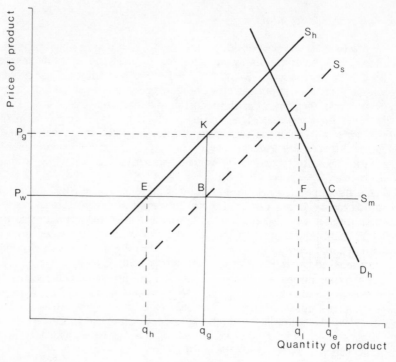

Figure 8.3

happens if the world price fluctuates. With the unit subsidy, producer prices move with the world price, as the subsidy is a fixed amount added to whatever price is received from the market. In the case of the deficiency payment system, the producer continues to receive the guaranteed price unless the world price moves above the level of the guarantee, in which case producers receive the world price, the deficiency payment having been eliminated. The deficiency payment system therefore contains a measure of stability lacking in the unit subsidy system, but, correspondingly, represents a more 'open-ended' commitment in terms of financial support when world prices fall. With either method, there is no reason in principle why the subsidy should not be high enough to take the country into export surplus for the product, although there may be more political resistance to the payment to farmers of subsidies on produce which is not for domestic consumption.

Figure 8.4 illustrates the impact of a deficiency payment system for a country where output of the product accounts for a significant proportion of total world supplies – the 'country 2' model. (In order to avoid cluttering up the diagram, the comparable unit subsidy effect is not shown.) Prior to the application of the guarantee, the intersection of the home demand curve D_h, and the total supply curve, S_t ($= S_h + S_m$), results in a quantity q_e being consumed at P_e price. The application of the guaranteed price P_g leads to a new

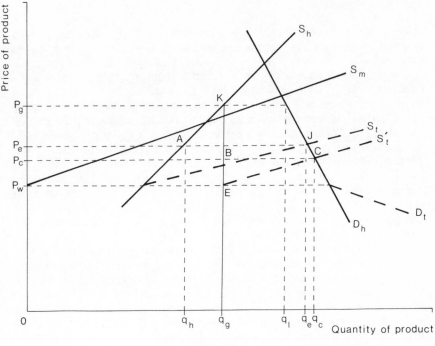

Figure 8.4

domestic supply curve $q_g BKS_h$, shifting total supply to S'_t. Consumption increases to q_c, and the market price falls to P_c. A total subsidy of $P_c P_g KB$ is paid to domestic farmers.

The impact of the application of the deficiency payment differs in this case from the situation where production and consumption of the produce within the country represents an insignificant proportion of world supplies in that:

(a) The price to consumers is reduced, with some resulting increase in consumption.

(b) As the deficiency payment leads to a fall in the market price of the product, the amount of the subsidy is greater.

(c) The country may make a welfare gain, since, by its action, it has reduced the price of a product which it imports and has thereby turned the terms of trade in its favour. (See Chapter 7, section 3.3.) (Figure 7.13 demonstrated how we can compare the various gains and losses to discover whether a net gain accrues. In the case of Fig. 8.4, a net welfare gain is made if the sum of the gain in producer supplies $P_e AKP_g$ and gain in consumer surplus $P_c P_e JC$ exceeds the Exchequer subsidy $P_c P_g KB$.)

(d) The replacement of imports and/or increase in exports brought about by the subsidy may have international repercussions due to the depressing effect of the policy on world prices.

4.4 The control of imports

Prices received by domestic producers can be raised by reducing the quantity of imports. This can be done either by quantitative controls or a tax on imports.

The domestic market price can be raised by applying an *import tariff* (of a fixed amount, or on a percentage basis (known as 'ad valorem')), or by specifying a *minimum import price* and applying a *variable levy*[6] to make up the difference between the minimum import price and whatever price imports are offered at. These mechanisms can be illustrated in Fig. 8.3. The effect of a minimum import price of P_g, or a fixed tariff equal to BK, is identical in terms of increased revenue to producers to the impact of a guaranteed price of P_g or a unit subsidy paid to domestic farmers of BK. In the case of the mechanisms which raise the price of imported supplies, however, the price paid by domestic consumers is increased and consequently there is a reduction in the quantity consumed (to q_1). The Government receives the tax revenue, $BKJF$, rather than paying out the subsidy, $P_w P_g KB$.

The major difference between the variable levy and import tariff mechanisms occurs when there is a movement in world price. Like the deficiency payment system, the variable levy introduces a measure of stability in the domestic market which is lacking with tariffs. In the case of the minimum import price system, the amount of the levy on imported produce varies so as to ensure that, whatever the world market price, imported supplies cannot be sold in the domestic market at less than the minimum import price. (The variable levy system cannot of course prevent the domestic price from rising if the world price rises above the minimum import price.) With import tariffs, the domestic market price moves with the world price, remaining above it by the amount of the tariff.

An alternative to tariffs or levies is quantitative controls on imports. If for example imports were limited to $q_g q_1$ (in Fig. 8.3), the effect on domestic producers would be the same as the minimum import price P_g or the tariff BK. Quotas for amounts aggregating to $q_g q_1$ could take the form of import licences, and if these were distributed by auctioning to the highest bidders, we would expect competition among suppliers to result in total licence revenue of $BKJF$, with suppliers receiving the same price for exports to this country as for sales elsewhere in the world.

Quotas might be distributed in some other way. One common method is for quotas to form part of a trade agreement. The foreign supplier then receives the same price for his produce as do domestic producers, and the country granting the quota aims to receive some reciprocal trading benefit, rather than tax revenue. It might even be possible to come to a 'gentleman's agreement' with traditional suppliers such that they would restrict their exports to this country (or guarantee not to sell produce beneath some minimum price, which, to be effective, would imply the same reduction in supplies). The effect would be to benefit the exporting country to the extent of the higher price at the expense of a (probably relatively small) reduction in its quantity of sales. Consider for example an agreement among exporting countries designed to raise the price to P_g in the domestic market of the country illustrated by Fig. 8.3. Compared with the sale of import licences or the imposition of tariffs or levies, producers in the supplying country rather than the Government of the importing country receive the extra revenue, $BKJF$. On the face of it, one would have thought that this would make the 'gentleman's agreement' method of raising agricultural product prices an unattractive one for the importing country. However, the British Government during the 1960s negotiated a number of such agreements for individual commodities with the UK's main suppliers, limiting the quantity that would be exported and sometimes the price at which it would be sold. One such agreement was the 'Bacon Market Sharing Understanding'. Paul Cheshire quotes the words of the Ministry of Agriculture:

> Under the Understanding the United Kingdom determines annually a total minimum quantity for supplies to the United Kingdom market and a reserve quantity and allocates shares of the total minimum quantity between each of our main overseas suppliers and our own industry. Her Majesty's Government is obliged to use its best endeavours to keep United Kingdom production of bacon at the minimum allocation . . . the other participants . . . accept a similar obligation in respect of their exports to the UK market . . . allocations from the reserve may be made . . . as necessary to satisfy demand while maintaining stable prices at a reasonable level (15).

He then comments:

> These words are almost worthy of the Ministry of Truth. Since the participants accept an obligation to keep supplies to a minimum, the minimum is in fact a maximum.
>
> In plain English this means that the agreement restricts the total amount of bacon coming onto the United Kingdom market in order to keep up the price and stop the Treasury having to fork out too much money to farmers. Instead the money is forked out by bacon buyers via higher prices; higher prices which benefit not only our own farmers but also overseas farmers participating in the restriction of supply. The Understanding does not reveal to whom the price level has to appear 'reasonable' (16).

The system saved the Treasury money because a deficiency payment system was also in operation for pigs. The 'Bacon Understanding' combined import supply control with domestic supply control, which is discussed in the next section. We should also note that, with the United Kingdom accounting for most of the world's imports of bacon, our country 2 model (and not Fig. 8.3) applies in this case and, to be fair to the British Government, there may well have been reciprocal trading benefits resulting from the choice of the 'gentleman's agreement' approach to import quantity control rather than the imposition of tariffs or levies.

Turning now to the second basic model, in Fig. 8.4 we can see that a price level for domestic producers of P_g can be obtained if imports are reduced to $q_g q_1$. This could be achieved by direct quantitative controls, or by taxing imported supplies in such a way as to ensure that, at a domestic market price of P_g, the effective price received by foreign producers was at that level which would induce a supply of $q_g q_1$. (Again, to avoid making Fig. 8.4 too complicated, this particular price raising device is not explicitly shown.)

It is worth noting that the price-raising effect of import controls always operates by reducing the quantity of imported produce, whether the control is on import quantity or price. A tax on imports raises the domestic market price because it results in a reduction in the quantity of imports supplied, not because it raises the market price of the existing quantity of imports. If the supply of imports were perfectly inelastic, then the imposition of a tariff on imports would fail completely to raise the price received by domestic producers. All that would happen would be that part of the price paid for imported produce would be collected by the Government, with quantity and price in the domestic market unchanged.

Finally, we should note something which is perhaps self-evident – that it will not be possible to sustain a market price level by import control on its own if domestic production exceeds domestic consumption. As the European Community has discovered, if the minimum import price is set at a level at which home farmers wish to supply a greater quantity than is accounted for by domestic consumption, a second line of defence is required if the desired price level is to be maintained. For the European Community, this was to remove part of domestic production from the home market, a mechanism of supporting prices which is discussed in the next section.

4.5 The control of agricultural supply

4.5.1
We have now considered measures which attempt to increase farm revenue by raising farm output (section 4.2), by raising producer prices (section 4.3) and by restricting imports (section 4.4).

A fourth method is to restrict domestic supply. When we discussed the feasibility of increasing aggregate revenue by an increase in farm output, it was suggested that the policy might not be very successful if the country was a large enough producer of the product to influence world prices. In this case, part of the benefits to producers from extra output would be offset by the effect of falling prices, but it is most unlikely that this negative effect on revenue would be large enough to offset entirely the positive effect of extra output. However, since in most cases the demand for agricultural products is inelastic, if the domestic market is isolated from world supplies, a given increase in supply will bring forth a more than proportionate fall in price, so that an increase in supply will reduce aggregate revenue. In these circumstances, the possibility emerges that a policy of restricting supply could increase aggregate farm revenue. The circumstances in which the domestic market can be regarded as, to some extent, isolated from world supplies are as follows:

(a) Where the domestically produced product has some marketing advantage over imports. For example, if the cost of transporting the good internationally represents a substantial proportion of final selling price (as it is with liquid milk, which rarely crosses national frontiers) there will be some scope for raising price, within a definitive band, by restricting domestic supply. However, the ability to trade products in a semiprocessed form limits the opportunities for this kind of action. Similarly, the existence of cold-store transport facilities lessens the advantage to the domestic supplier in the case of perishable produce. Another possibility is for a domestic marketing agency to promote the national image of a particular product (e.g. 'English' lamb) but the essential homogeneity of agricultural produce from different world sources means that usually only a slight advantage can be established in this way and a particular foreign country may be the supplier who is able to achieve the premium price. (Danish butter sold in the UK possesses this characteristic, selling at a premium price over other butters.)

(b) Where the subsidising of product prices (as in section 4.3 above) has taken the country into export surplus and the Government regards it as unacceptable to subsidise the price received for produce which is exported. The Government might, for example, fix a *standard quantity* for output upon which it was prepared to pay a deficiency payment. If domestic production then exceeds the standard quantity, the subsidy per unit of output would be reduced to prevent the total Exchequer commitment from exceeding the amount of subsidy required to maintain the guaranteed price for the standard quantity of output. The quantity of output to which the payment of subsidies is limited might in principle be set at any level, but if it is the payment of subsidies to farmers for produce which is not consumed domestically which is the cause of concern, then the appropriate level for the standard quantity will be the amount purchased by domestic consumers at prevailing (i.e. 'world') prices for the product.

The combined deficiency payment/standard quantity policy is illustrated in Fig. 8.5 (which makes the assumptions of our 'country 1' model). The guaranteed price is P_g and the standard quantity q_s, which means that, assuming a constant world price P_w, the Exchequer payment is limited to $P_w P_g BC$. If domestic output increases beyond q_s – to q_t, say – the Exchequer subsidy, upon which a maximum limit has been placed, is distributed over a greater quantity, reducing price per unit of product to P_t (area $P_w P_t EF$ = area $P_w P_g BC$). In these circumstances, a policy of restricting domestic supply would raise the price received by producers, though it could not increase total revenue because exported produce will always add some revenue to the sum guaranteed for the sale of the standard quantity. A policy of restricting supply in excess of self-sufficiency would, however, imply an increase in net revenue, since when aggregate output of the sector is q_t, profit maximisation for the individual producer implies equating marginal cost with P_t whereas the marginal revenue to the sector as a whole is P_w.

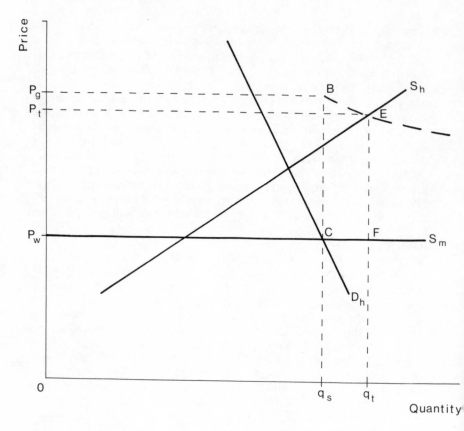

Figure 8.5

(c) The most common background to domestic supply restrictions will be a policy which effectively excludes imports (or at least places a strict quantitative limit on imports). Domestic supply restrictions can then be used to reinforce the price raising effect of import controls. For example, taking the minimum import price of P_g in Fig. 8.3, this can only be sustained by a variable levy as long as domestic supply is less than q_1. If domestic supply exceeds q_1, a policy of restricting any quantity in excess of q_1 from reaching the domestic market can still maintain a domestic price level P_g. If a complete ban on imports is imposed, the domestic market price can be raised above P_g by restricting domestic supplies below q_1.

Domestic supply may be controlled either by restricting the amount which is produced or by ensuring that part of what is produced is not sold on the domestic market. The two most common methods of production control are quota systems and land retirement schemes.

4.5.2 Production quotas

Quotas can take the form of a maximum amount of deliveries by each producer to authorised marketing agencies, with legally enforceable restrictions, or a complete embargo on the product bypassing official marketing channels. Such a scheme will be simpler to operate for a product which requires processing, for example sugar beet, than one for which there are potential farm gate sales, such as eggs and potatoes. In the latter case, or where produce is marketed through various agencies by a large number of producers, and it therefore becomes impossible to operate a quota system by a check on deliveries, it will be necessary to impose restrictions on the area which can be planted to the crop in question (and, in principle, though it rarely applies, to the number of animals in the case of livestock products). It is, however, difficult to check the plantings of every individual farmer. (In the United States, which has the longest experience of this kind of programme, a system of aerial photographs with spot checks was used.) Further, each farmer can step up production by intensifying output per acre.

Two basic disadvantages are attached to any quota scheme. First, they introduce rigidity into the farming sector, preventing expansion by low cost and preserving high-cost producers. Various devices have been suggested to minimise this effect. Quotas can be made saleable, so that the more efficient can buy the right to produce from the less efficient. This creates a capital asset for sitting tenants but involves an additional cost for new entrants or those who wish to expand. It thus represents an impediment to larger farm size as a method of improving the income of some producers, but will aid those small farmers who are granted the quota, whether they realise the benefit by selling the quota or producing the (higher priced) crop. An alternative device would be an annual auction of licences to produce. This permits aggregate production to be controlled, but distribution of production to be flexible. Unfortunately, much of the income benefits of the higher prices would be offset by the need to purchase the quota. Generally speaking, therefore, attempts to improve the productive efficiency of quota systems reduce their efficiency as methods of income support.

A possible compromise between these conflicting goals might be obtained by a two- (or even multi-) tier pricing system. There are numerous conceivable systems of this kind. The basic pattern is that all producers receive a high price for a basic quota and a lower price for any additional output. The high price for the basic quota forms an element of income support for small farmers, whereas the lower price is intended to encourage extra output only when it can be justified in relation to international price levels. An example of this kind of system is illustrated in Fig. 8.6. In the absence of government regulations, q_e is purchased by domestic consumers at the world price P_w, with q_h supplied by domestic producers and $q_h q_e$ imported. A complete ban on imports can raise the price for home farmers only to P_1, but if a quota is placed on domestic production in addition to the elimination of supplies from world markets the price received by domestic producers (and paid by domestic consumers) can be raised above P_1. For example, if a quota of q_h is established, market price rises

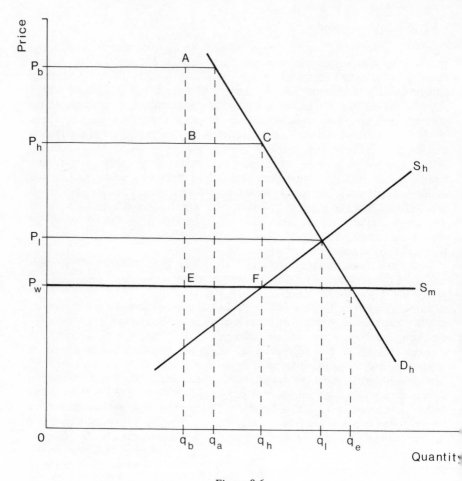

Figure 8.6

to P_h; if the quota is set lower at q_a, the market price is P_b; and so on. However, such a generalised quota system would possess the disadvantages of production rigidities mentioned above.

The two-tier quota system would operate as follows. The Government would require all produce to be sold to a central marketing agency. This agency awards each producer a basic production quota which in total would constitute a supply of – say – q_b units of the product. Producers are informed that they will be paid only the (world) price P_w for any quantity they supply in excess of their basic quota. The total quantity supplied will thus be approximately q_h, with only the larger more efficient farmers finding it profitable to supply more than their basic quota. The marketing agency is able to sell the product for P_h per unit, bringing in a total sales revenue OP_hCq_h. Since it pays farmers only price P_w for the quantity $q_b q_h$, it is able to use the profit it makes on its sales of quantity $q_b q_h$ (*EBCF*) to raise the price paid to farmers for their basic quota to P_b (since $P_h P_b AB = EBCF$).

There are therefore two advantages of the two-tier system over the generalised quota:

(a) A higher price per unit is obtained by small, low-income producers. (It would require a reduction of output to q_a, and thus even higher prices for consumers, if P_b were to be obtained for producers by a generalised quota.)
(b) The marginal output $q_b q_h$ will be supplied by low-cost producers. Although a price of P_h can be achieved by a generalised quota of q_h units, average production costs would almost certainly exceed those that would apply with the two-tier system, simply because of the problem of identifying low cost producers when marginal output is receiving price P_h. (The supply curve indicates that the quantity producers wish to supply at price P_h is about double the quota q_h.)

The other major disadvantage of quota schemes is their administrative cost, which will become greater as both the number of producers involved increases and the scheme attempts to introduce flexibility (if the first disadvantage of penalising the efficient is to be overcome).

The problems associated with quota schemes are well illustrated by the fact that sugar beet is probably the product for which quotas have been most commonly applied. The demand for sugar is generally quite inelastic so that market price is sensitive to the amount supplied. The crop has been particularly subject to modern production techniques, and supply has tended to increase rapidly. As we saw in the previous chapter, international trade in sugar (which mainly takes the form of raw sugar from cane exported by tropical developing countries) is influenced by a variety of international agreements which control the quantities traded. In the main, the crop is grown by a relatively small number of large producers; this reduces administration costs and makes it less likely that a quota system will preserve high cost producers. Finally, the requirement that the crop should be processed in a refining factory means that there are few problems over 'policing' the quantity to which each individual producer is restricted.

4.5.3 Land retirement

Schemes under the general heading of land retirement may aim to divert land out of the production of specific crops or to withdraw land from production of any kind. In either case, all schemes have been voluntary, payments being made to induce farmers to comply. The United States has a long history of paying farmers to withdraw land from production, forming a *soil bank*, and land retirement schemes formed part of both the Vedel report for French Agriculture (1969) (17) and the Mansholt Plan for the EEC (1968) (18). Diverting land from specific crops is only likely to be appropriate if there is scope for replacing imports of alternative products. In the case of generalised land retirement, if the farmer is free to choose which part of his farm he will retire, he is bound to choose the least productive land, and the programme may be relatively ineffective. For this reason, the United States *set aside* programme specified that the land withdrawn must be land normally used for one of the major crops in surplus. In spite of this, when in 1973/74 the United States decided to bring land back into wheat production because of the high price prevailing on world markets, the US Department of Agriculture soon became reconciled to the fact that some land, upon which farmers were being paid not to grow wheat, seemed to have mysteriously disappeared.

A characteristic of paying incentives to farmers to withdraw land from production is that the amount of financial inducement will need to increase in relation to the success of the policy. The policy will be introduced because of low returns per hectare. Quite modest payments might thus induce farmers to withdraw land from production, but as the supply restriction pushes up market prices, so the amount required to induce farmers to continue to withhold land from production increases. For example, a payment of – say – £50 per hectare per annum may initially be sufficient to cause a 10 per cent reduction in the land allocated to a particular crop; but a 10 per cent reduction in supplies coming onto the market may raise prices such that returns per hectare under this crop increase by £50. Other things being equal, one would now expect that a payment of something like £100 per hectare would now be required to sustain the new equilibrium relationship between supply and demand.

One disadvantage of land retirement schemes is that of all agricultural policy mechanisms, the practice of 'paying farmers not to produce' is one which strikes the general public as being particularly absurd. This sentiment was incomparably captured by Joseph Heller in his novel *Catch 22*:

> He was a long-limbed farmer, a God fearing, freedom loving, law abiding rugged individualist who held that federal aid to anyone but farmers was creeping socialism. . . . His speciality was alfalfa, and he made a good thing out of not growing any. The Government paid him well for every bushel of alfalfa he did not grow. The more alfalfa he did not grow, the more money the Government gave him, and he spent every penny he didn't earn on new land to increase the amount of alfalfa he did not produce. . . . He invested in land wisely and soon was not growing more alfalfa than any other man in the country.
>
> He was an outspoken champion of economy in Government, provided it did not interfere with the sacred duty of Government to pay farmers as much as they could get for all the alfalfa they produced that no one else wanted or for not producing any alfalfa at all (19).

4.5.4 The creation of 'surpluses'
An alternative to the control of production is to reduce the proportion of total output which is sold on the domestic market. The Government can pay incentives to divert part of output to use in a non-competing market; government-financed 'intervention agencies' can buy produce off the domestic

market to prevent prices from falling beneath some specified level; or statutory producer organisations can withhold from the market a part of the produce they have purchased from farmers. (The producer organisation must be backed by statute, or there will be no way of ensuring that some farmers do not bypass the official marketing channels, thus benefiting from the action of the organisation in supporting market prices without contributing to the costs of the operation.)

The major problem attached to any policy which attempts to raise farm prices by preventing part of the produce offered for sale by farmers from being sold on the domestic market is simply: What to do with the rest? There are a number of possibilities:

(a) The 'surplus' produce could be destroyed. From an administrative point of view this may well be the most attractive (or least unattractive) alternative. Productive resources are required to administer policies as well as to produce agricultural products. If a choice exists between restricting the amount sold on the domestic market either by restricting the quantity produced by a complex quota scheme, or by destroying any output produced in excess of some specified total quantity, it is not inconceivable that the former might be found more costly. In other words, in a severely constrained 'second best' world, the destruction of food might represent a genuine Pareto-style improvement over the alternatives, and cases where produce has been destroyed (or at least been allowed to destroy itself, when perishable produce is stored) are not entirely absent from agricultural policy in developed countries. But on a permanent basis, the solution is unlikely to prove politically feasible. The destruction of food is too emotive an issue for any government to be likely to choose this method of reducing the quantity of a product sold on the domestic market.

(b) Official 'intervention agencies' can dispose of surplus produce for whatever price it will fetch on the world market, or via specially negotiated trading arrangements with other countries.

This practice may lead to protests from the governments of other exporting countries, who regard their agricultural sectors as being able to produce efficiently for export if the world price were not depressed by 'dumping'. As already mentioned, a policy which subsidises exports seems to arouse a great deal more international displeasure than one which reduces imports. In principle, from the point of view of the impact upon world trade, no particular significance is attached to the point at which a policy of price support changes from causing a net reduction in world import requirements to representing a net addition to world exports.

The practice can also arouse the ire of consumers within the domestic economy, who find themselves paying more than consumers in other countries for the output of their own farmers.

The European Community, which has from time to time purchased large quantities of dairy products, wheat, sugar, beef and wine from its domestic market, has been accused on both counts. In particular, relations between the USA and the Community have been strained over the Community's grain policy, and the sale to Russia in 1973 of 200 000 tons of butter at about 16 per cent of its cost caused something of an uproar among European consumers.

A similar effect to official sales on the world market is to pay private traders export subsidies, and this practice does not seem to attract the same kind of domestic hostility as do cheap official sales. Indeed, the European Commission often gives the impression that the payment of export subsidies under the Common Agricultural Policy is righting some kind of grave injustice which is being perpetrated upon the people of Western Europe when world prices are less than official EEC prices. For example:

> The higher level of official Community prices would make it difficult for Community food exporters to sell their products on world markets. For most products, therefore, export subsidies or restitutions are payable when there is an abundance of home supplies of any commodity. The restitutions bridge the price gap (20).

To describe export subsidies as export subsidies, rather than *restitutions* or *refunds*, is in fact rare within Community circles.

The 'political' advantages of export subsidies as an alternative to official purchases by intervention agencies, may be outweighed by the fact that the practice of paying export subsidies to private traders seems peculiarly prone to fraudulent transactions. For example, in the case of the Common Agricultural Policy,

> There are well-known cases of barges going up and down canals to collect subsidies and which never unload. There are grain-ships navigating between European ports and changing their documents to enable them to qualify for subsidies at each. And there is the notorious case of the 1300 tons of butter sent annually to the 'foreign' territory of the Vatican. If, as is claimed, it was entirely for internal consumption, each inmate of the Curia would be eating 10 lb of butter a day (21).

Thus when the European Commission comes to calculate the quantity of exports upon which subsidies have been paid, and the quantity of exports that have actually taken place, the former may very well exceed the latter.

(c) Produce can be sold in a market which does not compete directly with the original one, and for which there is some scope for replacing imports. A common practice, for example, is to sell a product, which is normally for human consumption, for animal feed. This requires some method of rendering the product unfit for human consumption (sometimes known as 'denaturing') or there is a danger that the product will be purchased at the subsidised feed price and subsequently sold at the higher price in the consumer market. It was for this reason that mounds of purple potatoes could sometimes be found on British farms. The dye was effective in preventing purchases by housewives, but the cows did not seem to mind too much. Similarly, the European Community has subsidised the denaturing of wheat, which is done by the introduction of a dye or fish oil, or just by including as part of a compound feed mixture, and in 1976 it introduced a measure requiring compound feed manufacturers to incorporate skim milk powder in their product. Eggs have been somewhat easier to deal with. The practice of 'breaking', for sale to manufacturers as egg powder, is an irreversible process. Rather like Humpty Dumpty – you can't put them together again.

(d) Surplus produce may be sold cheaply to 'needy' groups within the domestic economy. The European Community has subsidised the sale of cheap butter and beef to pensioners and low-income families. The disadvantages of this solution are twofold. First, the bogus nature of this kind of 'welfare' is manifest, allowing political opponents to argue that if there is a need to aid certain groups then it should not happen as an accidental byproduct of agricultural policy, and that the funds involved in administering the system, together with the subsidy, could be better spent in other sectors of social welfare. Second, the scope for disposing of surplus produce in this way is severely limited because all subsidised sales within the domestic economy will, to some extent, reduce sales in the supported market.

(e) Produce may be donated as food aid to poor countries. It is the United States which has the longest record of food aid as a means of disposing of supplies in order to support domestic price levels. In 1954, the programme was put on a semipermanent basis in the Agricultural Trade Development and Assistance Act, better known as PL 480. More recently the programme has been referred to as *Food for Peace.*[7]

It is possible to distinguish two rather different cases where food aid might be needed. First, there is the case of temporary famine caused by adverse, and localised, climatic conditions. In these circumstances, it will be fortuitous, but none the less welcome, if food surpluses are available as aid at the right time and in the right form. Second, there is the possibility of a widespread tendency for food production to fail to keep pace with population growth in low-income countries. For this contingency, most experts stress the need to give aid directed towards increasing food output in developing countries, and warn of the dangers that intermittent batches of food aid can have in disrupting local marketing systems. One cannot rule out the possibility that there might be a concord of interest between surplus production in developed countries and hunger in the developing world. But the value of food aid will be maximised if it is planned for, donated at the right time, and does not disappear when it is most required simply because world prices happen to be buoyant at the time and little financial cost is involved in disposing of surpluses on world markets.

(f) Finally, surplus produce may be stored in the 'hope' that it may be resold when prices move up again – in other words, storage can be regarded as a national buffer stock. When we discussed buffer stocks in the previous chapter (section 4.2) it was suggested that there was a danger of stocks accumulating, even when the intention was merely to stabilise around a long-term equilibrium price. Clearly, any attempt therefore to support prices over a long period by storing produce removed from the market (i.e. to secure a higher level of revenue when averaged over a number of years) will result in accumulating stocks and a collapse of the policy.

5 Structural policy

5.1

It has increasingly come to be recognised that the problems of agriculture, and in particular the problem of agricultural incomes, cannot be adequately solved so long as the basic structure of the sector remains deficient. (OECD–(22).)

Structural policy aims to increase farm incomes by gradually reducing the number earning their living from farming, so that the aggregate income of the sector is distributed among fewer individuals. Any structural policy must contain two elements: measures directed towards reducing the number of farmers, and measures directed towards increasing farm size.

A programme designed to influence the numbers working in agriculture must operate on either the rate of recruitment, or on the rate of outward migration or retirement. No specifically deterrent action is normally contemplated as far as recruitment is concerned, but the provision of an adequate and broadly based educational system and incentives for firms to invest in agricultural regions gives much wider job opportunities for young people in rural areas. To assist existing farmers and workers to discontinue in agriculture, there can be grants for retraining, payments to compensate for removal costs, or retirement pensions. A satisfactory pattern of outward migration will require action outside the normal span of agricultural policy to ensure that job opportunities, housing and social services match the needs of those who are leaving agriculture.

Hired workers in agriculture tend to be occupationally more mobile than farmers and family workers. Some European countries never had many hired farm workers, but even in the United Kingdom and North America their numbers have been dramatically reduced and many of those remaining are highly skilled and working on modern farms. The number of family workers has also been significantly reduced and, inevitably it is the farmers themselves who are most immobile. Some younger farmers do move to other occupations but generally the fall in the number of farmers occurs through death and retirement. In many countries self-employed people have been to a large extent left outside the general provisions of social security and, in particular, have often not been eligible for old-age pensions. In so far as farmers can usually continue to live on their farms, producing at least a minimum amount of food for their own needs, and often receiving support from their descendants, they have a greater element of security and their need for pensions could be regarded by legislators as less pressing. This has provided the opportunity in some cases for pension schemes to be extended to agriculture in such a way as to encourage the recipients to give up their land. Further, some countries have introduced schemes under which discontinuation payments may be given at any age in order to induce farmers to give up their land at an early stage.

One should not, however, underestimate the problems involved in the use of incentives to increase the rate of migration from the sector. Commenting on these difficulties, Hine states:

> The occupational immobility of the farmers themselves is, in part, attributable to the lack of alternative employment suited to their age, skills and experience and to the natural reluctance of older persons to undergo the considerable upheaval which might accompany a change of livelihood and residence. It is also due to the positive satisfactions derived from farming as a 'way of life' – independent and all-absorbing, if financially unrewarding. In these circumstances, small farmers may continue in farming so long as their incomes remain above the minimum necessary for their survival. This would place a considerable constraint on the structural policies designed to encourage farmers to give up their farms through the use of financial incentives (23).

The land freed by death, retirement and outflow becomes available for transfer to heirs, for sale or for tenancy. Some countries have set up regulations governing the transfer of land to prevent an unwanted concentration in the hands of a few proprietors or to guide the development of farm structures. Measures directed towards reducing the number of farmers will to a certain extent automatically increase farm size, but spontaneous developments on the land market may lead to relatively small enlargements. With a limited number of large holdings available, farmers have to rely on successive expansion from smaller units. The supply of additional land comes mainly from the retirement of elderly farmers and available land may be excessively fragmented and badly sited. The process of expansion is thus complicated and slow.

More specific aids for farm enlargement may therefore be required for a successful policy of structural reform. This involves the identification of farms which are 'potentially viable' and then assisting the acquisition of extra acres and investment in farm buildings and equipment on these farms. The three main types of aid currently used are subsidies to reduce rates of interest on borrowed capital, direct investment grants and guarantee funds to back up bank loans. A selective use of investment aids – giving assistance to farms which have growth prospects and, as important, refusing it to those which do not, can make a significant contribution to structural improvement, but there are difficulties in choosing guidelines for the identification of the farms meriting support. For example, should available land be given in priority to farms which need it to rise above the threshold of viability, or to those already above the threshold, and should the threshold itself represent a size and degree of modernisation which is sufficient to provide some income norm with, or in the absence of, an element of price support?

5.2

Structural policy is designed to assist an economy to adjust to the changing resource conformations which are implied by economic growth. Its attraction as a solution to the problem of low incomes in agriculture is that it alone attempts to deal with the causes, rather than the symptoms, of the problem. The origin of low incomes in agriculture has usually been traced to the failure of the agricultural population to decline with sufficient rapidity in response to the pressures of increased productivity and overall rising living standards (Chapter 3, section 4.2). This problem is 'structural' because of the link between occupational mobility and farm structure. Those countries where farming developed with large numbers of hired workers employed on relatively large holdings have not experienced as severe an income problem as those where the majority of the farm population were employed on small one or two-man peasant holdings. An improvement in agricultural structure is thus part and parcel of the process of reducing the numbers earning their living from farming, so that incomes are raised for those who remain.

A second attraction of structural policy is that it can claim to be self-liquidating rather than self-perpetuating. Of course, inasmuch as the pace of improving productivity in agriculture, and generally rising income levels, continues in the same way as it has in the first thirty or so post-1945 years (and, as mentioned in Chapter 3, there are grounds for believing that the rate of agricultural productivity improvement, and with it the adjustment requirements, may be slowing down), then structural policy will be chasing an advancing structural target. But equally, faced with similar growth conditions, a policy directed towards symptoms will find itself in the deteriorating position either of requiring increasing finance or becoming increasingly unsuccessful.

The main disadvantage of the structural solution is temporal – it leads the agricultural sector towards a solution in five, ten or more years hence, rather than dealing with the political imperative of immediate support of farm incomes. It was for this reason that the famous 1968 Mansholt Plan (18) for EEC agriculture was incomplete.

The Mansholt plan envisaged subsidies for farm improvement, retirement pensions, and so on, partly as compensation for price cuts on surplus commodities. On their own, however, such measures are insufficient to allow price cuts because, inevitably, there will be many farmers who fail to qualify for modernisation expenditure, but yet remain in farming and have to exist on lower prices. Structural policies are therefore usually envisaged in combination with other income support measures, particularly price support.

The precise effect of the general level of agricultural prices on structural change is not clear, but there is little doubt that in the longer run a high level of prices will slow down the outward migration from agriculture. The price level is, of course, only one influence on structural change, and the experience of some countries, which have had high farm prices but also rapid structural development, suggests that rapid growth of non-farm income and employment opportunities can be the overriding factor. However, a high level of price support tends to increase the incentives necessary in discontinuation schemes so that governments are, in effect, bidding against themselves and where there is a budgetary constraint, funds required for deficiency payments, or to finance the disposal of surpluses, reduces the amount available for structural improvements.

In recent years, increasing attention has been given to another, rather different, disadvantage associated with the structural solution to the problem of low incomes in agriculture. This is that the size of the agricultural population and the kind of farming practice which may be regarded as 'ideal', when the terms of reference are narrowly defined in relation to agricultural output and income per head, may be inappropriate if a broader view of social welfare is taken. As the numbers living in rural communities declines, so the cost per head of providing an acceptable level of public facilities in these areas rises and there may be a cost to the nation as a whole emanating from the outward migration of the agricultural population which is not reflected in efficiency when defined in terms of relative profitability between farming and other industries. For example, there may be a minimum expenditure per geographical area required if basic services, such as transport and schools, are to be provided. Once the rural population falls beneath a certain level it is not possible correspondingly to reduce public expenditure on these services. Meanwhile, expenditure may have to increase substantially in some crowded areas where existing services are under pressure. Thus the average cost per head of providing a certain minimum level of public services can increase as the result of migration from agriculture.

The cost of maintaining public services in rural areas is, at least in principle, measurable. Another aspect of rural depopulation is the less tangible costs associated with declining 'vitality' of a region, as the indigenous population ages and traditional rural communities disintegrate. There may also be social costs associated with the other arm of structural policy – the development of a 'modern' farming structure. Bowers (24) has drawn attention to these social costs and assembled a variety of evidence relating to the United Kingdom. These costs, he says, stem not so much from expansion of output, but from the particular form it has taken – the increase in specialisation. Some costs can be expressed as money cost to the community, the most striking of which is the problem of sewage disposal resulting from the breaking of traditional stock/crop rotations, and the rearing of animals and the growing of crops on separate farms. The other major social cost of modern agricultural practice, upon which, as we saw in Chapter 6, it is much more difficult to place a monetary value, is the growing conflict between specialist agriculture and the recreational use of the countryside. Bowers mentions four different aspects of this conflict in the United Kingdom.

First, he says, modern agricultural production damages the landscape. It does this by reducing variety, replacing older buildings, which fit into the English landscape, by obtrusive buildings – silos, grain dryers, etc. Second, it reduces access to the countryside. This is particularly so with intensive arable production, which leads to the ploughing-up and blocking-off of footpaths. Third, intensive agriculture reduces the quantity and variety of wildlife of the countryside. Bowers notes four ways in which this has happened: through the destruction of hedgerows (a 1970 estimate put the loss of hedgerows in Britain at somewhere between 5000 and 10 000 miles per annum), reduction in permanent pasture, extensive drainage works, and the use of pesticides.

Finally, another area where changed agricultural practice has caused damage to amenity is that of archaeological sites. Bowers quotes a number of surveys showing that a substantial proportion of sites scheduled as ancient monuments have in recent years been destroyed or seriously damaged, mainly by ploughing.

Not everyone would agree with this picture of the impact on social welfare of modern farming techniques, and of course it would be incorrect to regard government agricultural policy as solely responsible for the development of new farming practices. But inasmuch as the establishment of a fundamentally modern commercial farming is seen as a solution to the problem of low incomes in agriculture, then it must be recognised that this approach may perhaps conflict with other goals of government policy such as preserving the amenity value of the countryside, maintaining the 'vitality' of rural areas, and minimising the expenditure required to sustain essential public services.

6 Measuring the welfare effects of alternative policy devices: deficiency payments versus import levies – a case study

6.1

In recent years, agricultural economists have increasingly turned towards detailed critical analysis of individual agricultural policy mechanisms as well as making more generalised statements concerning government intervention in agriculture. In this section we return to two of the policy mechanisms discussed, in brief, earlier – the guaranteed price/deficiency payments and minimum import price/variable levy methods of supporting farm product prices – and use them to illustrate the kind of detailed agricultural policy analysis now being attempted by some agricultural economists. These particular policy devices have been chosen because one of the more important consequences of British adoption of the European Community's Common Agricultural Policy (CAP) was the requirement that deficiency payments should be replaced by import levies as the principal mechanism for supporting prices in the United Kingdom. At the same time, continued preference for deficiency payments among British politicians has led to some pressure for their incorporation into the CAP. These events have focused attention in contemporary writings, both in Western Europe and in some temperate exporting countries which have traditionally sold in the UK market, on a comparison of the various effects of the deficiency payment (DP) and variable levy (VL) methods of supporting agricultural product prices.

6.2 Problems with price support

The first thing to note is that, within the broad span of policy devices covered in this chapter, the DP and VL systems are very similar. Both attempt to protect the incomes of agricultural producers by raising product prices. In the case of the United Kingdom the essential similarity of the mechanisms was obscured by the higher levels at which prices were to be supported after the introduction of the levy system, many of the changed circumstances surrounding British adoption of the CAP being wrongly attributed to the imposition of levies rather than the higher support level itself. This chapter has drawn attention on several occasions to some disadvantages of price support as a mechanism for raising agricultural incomes. It would be instructive at this stage to summarise the main points that have been made, and to note that they all apply to either a VL or a DP system, provided both mechanisms are designed to ensure the same level of product prices for producers.

(a) A measure which successfully raises the price received by producers, above the level that would apply in the absence of the policy, distributes the benefit of income support in proportion to the amount produced. If the desire on the part of the Government to support agricultural incomes is taken as being derived from (or at least consistent with) a more general objective of moving towards a greater degree of equality in income distribution, then an essential concomitant of raising the aggregate income of agricultural producers would appear to be a progressive distribution of the aggregate income transferred. The raising of product prices fails to accomplish this as those farmers with highest incomes tend to receive a more than proportionate amount of the support. If prices for farm products are raised to a level which meets the 'socially acceptable' income needs of small farmers, they will, as a byproduct, produce a massive, and arguably socially undesirable, transfer of income to those farmers who are likely to be already relatively wealthy.

(b) Raising product prices stimulates increased supplies. If production in the country accounts for a significant proportion of world supplies, extra output will depress world market prices and this may cause concern among alternative suppliers. The fall in market prices reduces the income benefit when the extent of the support is fixed (e.g. unit subsidy or import tariff), but increases the Exchequer or consumer cost of supporting prices for those mechanisms, such as deficiency payments and variable levies, which attempt to ensure a specific price to producers.

(c) Declining relative agricultural product prices have been the most notable symptom of the pressure experienced by agriculture in the context of rising agricultural productivity and increasing incomes per head. Prices have also acted as a signalling mechanism – to convey the message that the proportion of the population engaged in agricultural production should decline. The effect of the general price level on structural change is far from certain, but it seems likely that the maintenance of a high price level will also make difficult, within a policy of structural reform, the identification of the minimum size required for a 'viable' unit.

(d) High product prices tend to force up farm costs, so that some of the benefit of the support is transferred to input industries. The extent to which this is likely to happen depends on the elasticity of supply of inputs to agriculture, an issue which was discussed in section 3.1 in connection with input subsidies. In particular, we noted that farm rents and land prices are likely to increase. For the owner occupier therefore, part of the benefit of higher prices will be capitalised into land values, but, in the absence of rent control, the tenant farmer will not be so fortunate. High land values make more difficult the process of farm enlargement within a programme of structural reform.

6.3   Comparing the effects of alternative systems of price support

6.3.1
The above arguments apply to any mechanism for supporting agricultural product prices. In order specifically to compare the DP and VL systems, we return to our basic partial equilibrium trade model ('country 1' version) and in Fig. 8.7 reproduce from Fig. 8.3 the market effects of both a guaranteed price, P_g, sustained by a deficiency payment, and a minimum import price, also established at level P_g, sustained by a variable levy. With the aid of this model, we can note the following differences between the impact of a DP or VL system designed to achieve the same level of product prices for producers.

6.3.2   Market effects
The application of a guaranteed or minimum import price at level P_g increases domestic supply by the amount $q_h q_g$. The DP system leaves consumers unaffected but the imposition of the levy, $P_w P_g$, reduces domestic consumption to q_1. Imports are therefore reduced by the additional amount $q_1 q_e$ with the VL system, imports falling by $q_h q_g$ because of the increase in domestic production in both cases. Under the DP system, the Exchequer finances the subsidy $P_w P_g KB$ (area $R + C$), whereas with the VL system it receives the levy revenue $BKJT$ (area V).

6.3.3   Political feasibility
With the DP system the amount of support required to sustain a particular price level is clearly visible in the form of an Exchequer subsidy and will be the subject of public debate. The application of import levies can disguise the extent to which price support is taking place – indeed it is sometimes possible for politicians to give the impression that no element of support is involved when levies are used. For example, the British Minister of Agriculture said in 1970, when explaining the decision of the Government to replace the DP system:

> There is a growing revulsion by the industry at the use of subsidies and as prosperity increases in the nation as a whole, less reason to subsidise

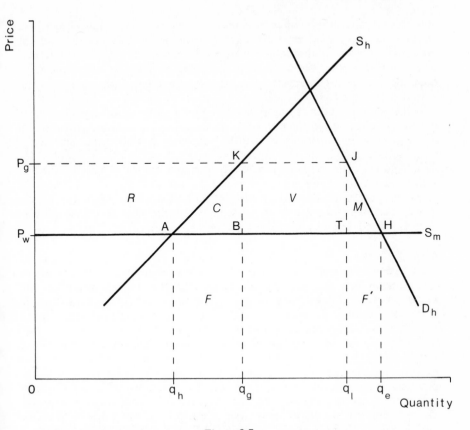

Figure 8.7

everyone's food out of general taxation.... The Conservative Party have always intended to switch from the subsidy system to one in which farmers get their return from the market and the level of prices is controlled by import levies (25).

The Minister was repeating on this occasion a remark that was often heard in connection with British agricultural policy – that deficiency payments were consumer food subsidies. This claim is not easy to substantiate. For market conditions similar to those depicted by Fig. 8.7, deficiency payments do no more than allow consumers to purchase the product at the price at which supplies are available from world markets. However, if one were to argue that, in practical terms, guaranteed producer prices could not be reduced, and that a removal of the subsidy would therefore have had to be accompanied by an equivalent rise in market prices, then the deficiency payment might conceivably be regarded as a subsidy to the consumer. The other circumstance in which deficiency payments might be regarded at least in part as consumer food subsidies, is when the market conditions of our 'country 2' model apply, in which case one would expect the removal of producer subsidies, and the consequent decline in domestic production, to lead to an increase in market prices. For example, if we return to Fig. 8.4, we see that abandoning the domestic producer guaranteed price (P_g) would result in an increase in the market price from P_c to P_e.

It has generally been the case therefore that a Government finds less of an obstacle to giving a specific element of price support to domestic producers by the imposition of import levies than by deficiency payments, because of the semidisguised nature of the former kind of support. This advantage (or disadvantage, depending on which way you look at it) of import levies is somewhat offset by the ability to justify the use of deficiency payments as 'consumer food subsidies'. At times of inflationary pressure, when increases in a published index of retail food prices may assume importance in a political context, the DP system may become the easier to apply.

6.3.4 Stability

Both systems stabilise producer prices as long as prices on world markets remain below the producer guaranteed or minimum import price. The DP system, however, leaves consumer prices free to fluctuate in response to world events. It is open to debate as to which of (i) the increasing Exchequer cost of subsidies, or (ii) the increasing awareness by consumers of the relatively high price they are paying for the product, would put the maintenance of producer prices under the greatest strain in the context of declining world prices. Neither system stabilises in the event of world prices moving above the desired producer support price; both systems then become inoperative and producer and consumer price moves up with the world price. In these circumstances, the Government may decide to apply 'true' consumer food subsidies (of the kind introduced in the United Kingdom in 1974) which allow consumers to purchase both domestically produced and imported produce at less than the price implied by free market conditions.

Note that it is international trade which leads to a distinction between *producer* and *consumer* food subsidies. If our 'country 1' model applies, then a subsidy paid to producers will not lead to any fall in consumer prices, and, correspondingly, a subsidy injected at the retail level will not lead to any rise in producer prices. If our 'country 2' model applies, a subsidy paid to producers (which leads to an increase in quantity supplied) will result in some fall in consumer prices. Correspondingly, a consumer subsidy, which leads to an increase in quantity demanded, will mean some rise in producer prices. If the domestic market is isolated from the world market the distinction between consumer and producer subsidies disappears. The payment of a subsidy on a product, at whatever stage in the marketing process, will lead to a rise in producer prices and a fall in consumer prices, the distribution of the benefit depending upon the price elasticity of farm supplies and the price elasticity of consumer demand. Also, unless the supply of 'marketing services' is perfectly elastic (see Chapter 3, section 5), some of the benefits of the subsidy would also, in this case, accrue to the processing and distributive sector.

One possible difference in the stabilising potential of the two systems occurs if the country is approximately self-sufficient in the product at the support price. If the world price moves above this level, then prices to both domestic consumers and producers can be prevented from rising with the world price by prohibiting exports. A slight extension of the VL system can achieve this – reversing the system and applying negative import levies (export taxes). This action has in fact been taken by the European Community, and with the EEC more or less self-sufficient in many food products, spokesmen for the Community are able, with some justification, to claim that the CAP stabilises rather than merely supports agricultural product prices. For example:

> If high world prices have relieved the financial pressures they have also shown up how the Common Agricultural Policy can and has acted to stabilise prices in an upward as well as a downward direction. It is no longer tenable to say that the CAP pays only lip service to the interest of consumers. About a year ago, world cereal prices started rising above Community levels. Export levies were immediately applied with the effect that the consumer not the producer enjoyed the benefit. It may be noted in passing that the deficiency payments system of support is not capable of producing the same effect, as the Community has experienced for instance in the field of vegetable oils and fats. The Community system works remarkably well standing on its head, as it has done for most of this year for both cereals and sugar. It may be calculated that during the cereal year 1973/74, the UK consumer benefited to the extent of £135 million between August last year and June this year as a result of Community wheat prices being lower than the world market level (27).

However, as argued in the previous chapter (section 3.4), this method of stabilising internal markets destabilises the world market.

6.3.5 Income distribution

As already noted, the distribution of the benefit of both systems will be similarly regressive and will probably increase the inequality of income distribution within the farming sector. However, the systems differ in the way they raise the revenue to be transferred to agriculture. In the case of the DP system the cost of the support (area $R + C$ in Fig. 8.7) is part of Government expenditure, whereas, with import levies, consumers pay the higher price P_g, with the Government collecting the levy revenue V. A system which increases consumer food prices is likely to involve a regressive redistribution of income because of the well-known tendency, discussed in Chapter 1, for the proportion of income spent on food products to decline as income rises.

Estimating the distributional impact of financing the transfer to agriculture out of central government expenditure is more problematical. Some taxes (such as income tax) are progressive, others (such as many purchase taxes) are regressive. On balance, a tax system may be more or less neutral (28) with the implication that the burden of supporting agricultural prices is distributed approximately in proportion to incomes throughout the economy. Further, there may be effective constraints on the level of overall government spending so that subsidies to agriculture may mean, not a small increase in income tax, but less spent on some other aspect of government policy. Conceivably, such a reduction in government expenditure elsewhere in the economy might represent more of a burden to lower income groups than the alternative of high food prices (and of course the VL system raises revenue for the Government which might mean more expenditure on, for example, social services).[8]

6.3.6 International effects

The deficiency payments policy is commonly regarded as consistent with a liberal trading policy whereas the support of prices by the imposition of import levies is regarded as protectionist. If we return to Fig. 8.7 we can see that the only difference in the trading impact of the two policies is that imports are reduced by the extra amount q_1q_e with levies, both systems replacing q_hq_g imports by home production. Since we may expect demand to be generally inelastic, the quantity q_1q_e is likely to be a relatively small addition to the reduction in imports which results from the increase in domestic supply. In practice therefore, there is probably little difference between the impact that the two systems have on world trade (though deficiency payments do seem to create a somewhat better impression). If import saving is an objective of government policy, then it can be noted that with the VL system there is the additional foreign exchange gain (area F').

6.3.7 Efficiency

In Fig. 8.7 the imposition of a variable levy on imports, which raises the market price from P_w to P_g, has the effect of reducing consumer surplus by P_wP_gJH. Extra resources, valued at $F + C$, are attracted into production of the product, and producers benefit by the amount R. Tax revenue is increased by V, so that the amount of consumer loss, $R + C + V + M$ exceeds the sum of the benefit to producers and the Exchequer ($R + V$) by an amount $C + M$. Areas C and M can be interpreted as the economic costs derived from a government policy which prevents the economy from attaining its free competition Pareto-style conformation of resources and production – a movement away from the 'welfare frontier'. The supply curve between A and K gives us the marginal cost of producing each extra unit of output between q_h and q_g, whereas imported produce is available at price P_w. Similarly, area M is a cost associated with consumers adjusting their expenditure patterns in the face of a price rise when produce could be available at price P_w.

Now, turning to the DF system, the sum P_wP_gKB (area $R + C$) is a subsidy by the Exchequer, but of this, R represents a benefit to producers, and C the loss associated with the extra resource cost of supplying quantity q_hq_g domestically, compared with the import cost P_w. Thus it can be argued that the DP system is more efficient than the VL system, because the imposition of levies results in an extra economic cost by distorting consumer expenditure patterns, as well as production patterns, away from the perfect competition Pareto-style optimum.

6.4 On choosing an optimum policy

6.4.1

This comparison of the deficiency payment and import levy systems does not therefore lead to any firm conclusions as to which policy is superior. Given a primary objective of accomplishing a specified level of agricultural price support, whether it is appropriate to use a DP or VL system will depend on to which subsidiary objective agricultural policy is related. Where there is no obviously decisive ranking of objectives, no rational choice between the mechanisms can be made. In his much quoted article 'A Formal Approach to Agricultural Policy' (29) Josling drew attention to this problem and, mentioning that 'recent work in the theory of economic policy has indicated that a necessary (though not sufficient) condition for the reaching of a number of quantitative objectives is that one employs a similar number of policy instruments', proceeded to show how a solution might be found in a combination of the deficiency payment and variable levy mechanisms.

Josling's article was concerned with the relative efficiencies of alternative methods of price support and used a numerical example based on the UK wheat market. During the mid-1960s import saving was a major objective of UK agricultural policy and so various policy devices were considered in relation to both import saving and income support. The DP system was demonstrated, for the reason explained above, to be more efficient than the VL system for effecting a given income transfer to the farming sector, but the VL system was shown to be the more efficient method of saving imports. This can be seen quite easily if we return to Fig. 8.7. Consider the VL policy which saves imports, valued at $F + F'$, at an economic cost $C + M$. A DP system, guaranteeing an equivalent price to domestic producers, saves imports of value F. If a DP system is to increase import saving by an extra amount equal to F', then it can only do this by a further increase in domestic production (and not a reduction in domestic consumption). The resource cost of increasing domestic output by a quantity equal to q_1q_e (represented by an extension of area C between the supply curve and world price) must necessarily exceed area M.

Now suppose that specific objectives are established for income transfer to agriculture and saving of foreign exchange. These can be measured in Fig. 8.7 by increase in producer surplus, R, and value of imports replaced, F (or in the case of the VL system, $F + F'$). Economic cost is measured as C, or for the VL system, $C + M$. In Fig. 8.8, in the right-hand quadrant, the levels of foreign exchange saved are plotted against economic cost as the level of the deficiency payment or levy rises. The VL curve is above the DP curve, reflecting the greater efficiency of levies for import saving.

Similarly, in the left-hand quadrant of Fig. 8.8, the relationship between gain in producer surplus and exchange saving is shown for the two policies.

Assume that there is some target transfer, R^*, corresponding to a level A deficiency payment or level B levy. The associated exchange saving (E and E') is shown on the vertical axis and the same level of DP and VL (A' and B' in the right-hand quadrant) gives the economic cost of achieving R^* by either DP

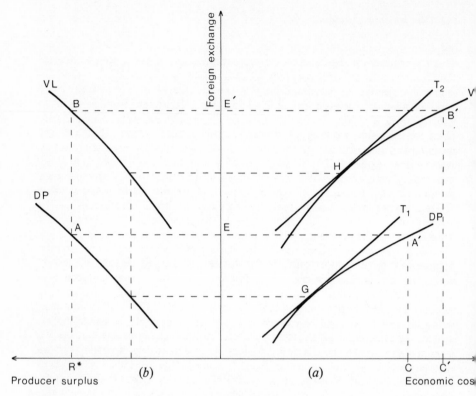

Figure 8.8

or VL systems (*C* and *C'* respectively). The import saving objective can be expressed in terms of marginal gain in foreign exchange to either the imposition of levies or payment of subsidies (i.e. as long as one extra unit of economic cost is associated with a gain in foreign exchange which exceeds some specified amount, the policy is regarded as worthwhile).

In Fig. 8.8a this critical marginal relationship between economic cost and import saving is shown by the slope of the lines T_1 and T_2 drawn tangent to the *DP* and *VL* curves, and the points *G* and *H* thus show the optimum application of subsidy or levy in order to meet the import saving objective. (The fact that import saving exists as an objective implies that there is a tendency for a trade deficit to develop at prevailing exchange rates. Thus domestic market prices 'incorrectly' reflect prices on world markets and the relationship between economic cost and foreign exchange saving indicated by the slope of lines T_1 and T_2 in Fig. 8.8a is one way of representing the relevant *shadow exchange rate* – see Chapter 6 (section 3.4.3).)

Now, it would be only the merest chance if this optimum level of VL or DP were the same as that which accomplishes the transfer *R**. In this particular example, however, there is a simple solution. Since the desired level of income transfer is associated with a higher levy or subsidy than that required for the optimum amount of import saving, a deficiency payment policy at the level which produced the required income transfer, combined with an import levy scheme set at the (lower) level required for optimum import saving will mean that both objectives are fulfilled.

6.4.2

The 'conventional wisdom' concerning the economic cost of agricultural policies of income support, then, is that import restriction is inefficient relative to the same degree of support given by deficiency payments (and, one might add, that deficiency payments are in turn thought to be less efficient than direct payments not related to the amount produced). Josling has recently returned to this question (1) and, in taking the link between agricultural policy analysis and formal welfare economics further than hitherto, has succeeded in turning the result on its head to come up with the conclusion that the VL mechanism may in fact be the more efficient method of income support. The crucial new element that he introduces is to recognise that farmers, as well as consumers, pay taxes. This means that a specific transfer to agricultural producers can be achieved by a lower levy than deficiency payment, because the latter involves a net loss and the former a net gain to the Exchequer.

We again use the basic model illustrated by Fig. 8.7. The various transfers which result from the application of a particular level of subsidy or levy can be reproduced as in Fig. 8.9. This measures consumer surplus (CS) along the horizontal axis and producer surplus (PS) on the vertical axis, so that any point in the diagram represents a particular combination of CS and PS (which will vary inversely as the price level alters). If there were a combined mass of CS and PS, which could be transferred at no cost by a price change, then this inverse relationship would be represented by a single straight line, such as W, drawn at an angle of 45 degrees to the axes. However, as we have seen, any attempt by the Government to depart from the distribution between consumers and producers which emerges with free competition involves an 'economic cost', so that, in terms of Fig. 8.7, the application of a levy attempting to redistribute $P_w P_g JH$ consumer surplus to producers and the Exchequer involves the loss $C + M$. In Fig. 8.9 this means moving to a position somewhere inside the boundary of W.

For example, suppose that point A represents the distribution under free trade. If a price P_g is guaranteed to producers, then producer surplus increases (in Fig. 8.7) by R, and this can be represented in Fig. 8.9 by the distance AC. The Exchequer pays a subsidy $P_w P_g KB$ (Fig. 8.7) and if we assume that only consumers pay taxes, then this can be represented by a movement from C to D in Fig. 8.9, point D lying inside the W boundary (on W') by virtue of the 'production loss' (area C in Fig. 8.7, distance DJ in Fig. 8.9). Similarly, consider the variable levy maintaining the minimum import price P_g. This increases producer surplus by the same amount as the deficiency payment, but in this case consumer surplus is reduced by the amount $P_w P_g JH$ (Fig. 8.7),

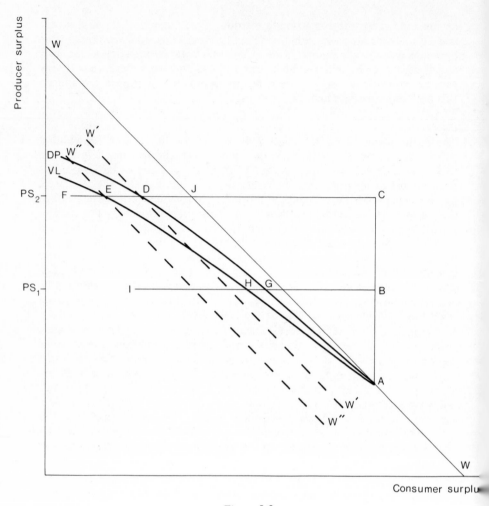

Figure 8.9

which is equal to distance *CF* in Fig. 8.9. Consumers, however, receive the benefit of the levy revenue, which takes their position back to point *E*, which lies on a lower *W* line (*W″*) than with the deficiency payment because of the extra 'consumption loss' (area *M* in Fig. 8.7 – distance *ED* in Fig. 8.9).

By taking a number of different levy and subsidy levels (such as that represented by the increase in producer surplus *AB* in Fig. 8.9) we can construct two lines, *A-VL* and *A-DP*, which show both the distribution and efficiency effects of alternative levy or subsidy policies. The greater efficiency of the deficiency payment system is shown by the fact that the *A-DP* line lies above the *A-VL* line, so that to attain a specified increase in producer surplus, say to attain level PS_2, consumers are better off (by an amount ED) if the DP rather than the VL system is used.

However, so much is only reworking the conclusion already reached – that the DF system is more efficient than the VL system because of the consumption loss occurring when market prices are increased with levies. Figure 8.10 shows what happens to the welfare/distribution possibility curves (A-VL and A-DP) when we recognise the fact that agricultural producers, as well as consumers, pay taxes. In Fig. 8.10a deficiency payments raise producer surplus from A to C, but the cost of the subsidy is redistributed back along the line CK which indicates the ratio of the marginal propensity to pay taxes out of real income for the two groups. Point K must lie on the same W line as point D, since we assume that the amount of economic loss is not altered by a change in the assumption of the burden of taxation. Thus, the A-DP line is pulled downward (A-DP to A-DP').

Similarly, in Fig. 8.10b the levy revenue is distributed in the same ratio as that indicated by the slope of CK in Fig. 8.10a, taking us to position M, rather than E, but still on the same welfare line (W''). The new welfare/distribution line for the variable levy (A-VL') will be above the previous one and have a pronounced curve, since the levy revenue declines at higher tariff levels. *Thus the A-VL line may move above the A-DP line, the extent of the movement depending on the incidence of taxation between producers and consumers.* According to Josling, 'If producers bear any significant portion of their own subsidy costs through taxation and receive a part of the distributed tariff revenue in the form of extra consumption of public goods, then the subsidy locus [i.e. A-DP'] lies inside the tariff locus [A-VL']' (1).

Figure 8.11 shows four possible alternative objectives towards distribution:

(a) A minimum level of producer surplus, PS_1.
(b) A minimum level of consumer surplus, CS_1.
(c) A target distribution ratio, R.
(d) A general social welfare function, represented by the set of welfare contours W_1, W_2, etc.

These objectives will be recognised as similar to some of those suggested in Chapter 5 in connection with our simple two-person economy, and the A-VL and A-DP lines are based on the same ideas concerning what we called 'the conflict between distribution and efficiency' as our 'feasible redistribution line' in Fig. 5.5.

In each case the levy proves superior to the deficiency payment. In case (a) a higher level of surplus for consumers is accomplished with the levy assuming a target producer surplus, PS_1. The levy is thus a Pareto improvement over the subsidy in the sense that a switch from subsidies to levies makes consumers better off without producers being made worse off. Similarly, in case (b) the levy is also a Pareto improvement over the subsidy. In case (c), under the objective of a target distribution ratio between producers and consumers, both groups can be made better off with the levy rather than the subsidy, and in the case of the social welfare function (case (d)), the levy allows the economy to attain a higher welfare contour.

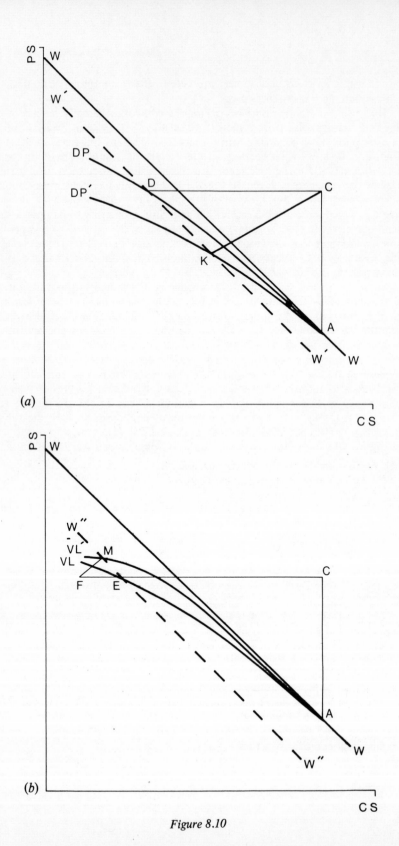

Figure 8.10

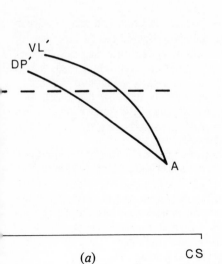

(a)

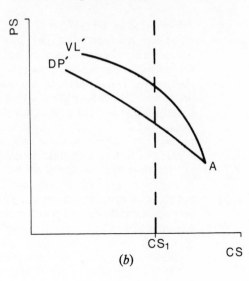

(b)

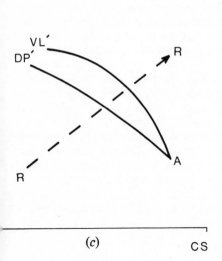

(c)

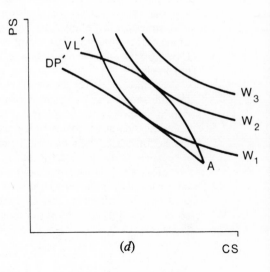

(d)

Figure 8.11

7 Conclusion

It would, perhaps, be sensible to end on a note of caution.

The process of agricultural production affects the welfare of a country's population in a number of ways – by providing income from employment, supplying food for consumption, and regulating the landscape – as well as having implications for aspects of general economic activity and international relations. Since World War II, in most developed countries, and increasingly in some less-developed countries, the dominant force behind the development of agricultural policy has been the desire to support agricultural incomes. During this period Governments have taken the view that agricultural markets, left to themselves, would result in an unacceptably low level of income for many producers. For this reason, a chapter that attempts to show how economic principles can be used to compare the relative merits of different policy devices would find it difficult to proceed in any way other than by viewing agricultural policies, first and foremost, as methods of income support.

But it would be a mistake to assume automatically that the preoccupations of the past will continue to be those of the future. For example, one development that might radically alter the prevailing priority of agricultural policy objectives would be the kind of longer term rise in terms of trade between agricultural and other goods on world markets discussed in Chapter 3 (section 4.3). Such an event might lead to greater priority being given to objectives such as increasing agricultural self-sufficiency and protecting consumers from some of the effects of rising food prices.

Many of the policy devices, and techniques for evaluating them, discussed in this chapter can be adapted to meet objectives other than income support. To give just one example, the methodology discussed in section 6.4.2 could easily accommodate a policy designed to increase consumer surplus (a movement down rather than up from point A in Fig. 8.9) by the imposition of negative levies (export taxes) and thus a reduction in producer surplus below free market level.

Agricultural policy however is unlikely in the foreseeable future to lose income support as at least one of its major objectives. For the small farmer, a rise in the prices of agricultural products on world markets has as little impact upon his income as does a policy of price support. Meanwhile, a buoyant world market increases the incentive for governments to stimulate the development of modern agricultural enterprises to replace traditional farming patterns. Thus the pressure on Governments to operate programmes of structural reform, combined with measures to protect the incomes of small farmers, is likely to continue to influence the character of agricultural policies in developed countries and may become of increasing significance in the developing parts of the world.

Notes

[1] This approach to the analysis of agricultural policies corresponds to what Josling calls in his review of agricultural policies (1), 'A rather stylised conception of policy analysis involving (a) the definition of objectives, (b) the choice of policy instruments, and (c) the monitoring of the performance of the policy'.

[2] It is not the intention of this chapter to describe the particular bundle of agricultural policy devices adopted in individual countries. The agricultural policies of OECD member states are periodically described in OECD agricultural policy reports (1, 4, 5). The policies of all developed and some less-developed countries are

summarised in three publications of the Foreign Agricultural Economics Service of the US Department of Agriculture (6, 7, 8). For a shorter summary see Chapter 4 of Fernon (9).

[3] Mountain farms in Alpine regions have long been regarded as a tourist attraction worthy of support, but this is a rather different case, with support channelled through agricultural production for two compatible goals – income support and maintaining a prosperous farming system in tourist areas.

[4] The student might find it a useful exercise to consider for himself what would be the impact on the 'b' diagrams of the various policy devices discussed.

[5] If you do not understand this, return to Chapter 7 and read section 2.2 again.

[6] It is conventional to use the term *tariff* to refer to a tax on imported produce which is either a fixed sum or a percentage of its supply price, and the word *levy* to refer to a tax on imported produce which varies according to some formula.

[7] For a discussion of this topic see Chapter 8 ('Food Surpluses of Industrial Countries and Food Needs of Developing Regions') of Johnson (3).

[8] Some of these issues are discussed in a study (28) which attempts to estimate the change in income distribution that would have occurred in the United Kingdom in 1969 following an instantaneous switch from the DP to the VL support system, and which employs the Gini coefficient method of measuring income distribution described in Chapter 1 (section 6).

References

(1) Josling, T. E. 'Agricultural policies in developed countries: a review.' *Journal of Agricultural Economics*, Vol. XXV, No. 3, Sept. 1974.

(2) *Trends in Agricultural Policies Since 1955*. Paris, OECD, 1961.

(3) Johnson, D. G. *World Agriculture in Disarray*. London, Fontana/Collins in association with the Trade Policy Research Centre, 1973.

(4) *Agricultural Policies in 1966*. Paris, OECD, 1967.

(5) *Agricultural Policy in – – – – – [country volumes]*. Paris, OECD, 1973–75.

(6) 'Agricultural Policies in the Western Hemisphere.' Foreign Agricultural Economic Report No. 36. Washington, US Department of Agriculture, 1967.

(7) 'Agricultural Policies in the Far East and Oceania.' Foreign Agricultural Economic Report No. 37. Washington, US Department of Agriculture, 1967.

(8) 'Agricultural Policies in Europe and the Soviet Union.' Foreign Agricultural Economic Report No. 46. Washington, US Department of Agriculture, 1968.

(9) Fernon, B. 'Issues in World Farm Trade: Chaos or Co-operation?' Trade Policy Research Centre, London, 1970.

(10) Wibberley, G. P. Opening discussion on paper by M. Dower: 'Recreation, tourism and the farmer.' *Journal of Agricultural Economics*, Vol. XXIV, No. 3, Sept., 1973.

(11) Commission of the European Communities. 'Improvement of the Common Agricultural Policy.' Memorandum Agriculture 1973–78. European Commission – Directorate General for Press and Information, Nov. 1973.

(12) Nevel, R. O. 'Technological change in agriculture.' *Agricultural Economics Research*, Vol. 21, No. 1, Jan. 1969.

(13) Beynon, R. V. H. & Houston, A. M. 'Productivity, The Concept, Its Measurement and a Literature Review.' Annex to the report 'Farm Productivity.' National Economic Development Office, London, Nov. 1973.

(14) *Farm Business Data* (annual). Department of Agricultural Economics and Management, University of Reading.

(15) House of Commons. *Select Committee on Agriculture (Evidence)*. London, HMSO, 1969.

(16) Cheshire, P. 'Management of the Market: the economic arm of agricultural policy.' In *Decision-making in Britain: Agriculture*, Block III, Parts 1–6. The Open University Press, Milton Keynes, 1972.

(17) 'Perspectives à long terme de l'agriculture françoaise, Paris Ministère de l'Agriculture 1969.' Summary of Chapter 1 – analysis; and part of chapter 3 – policy proposals, given in 'Current Agricultural Proposals for Europe,' Federal Trust for Education and Research, London, 1970.

(18) European Commission. Memorandum on the Reform of Agriculture in the EEC (The Mansholt Plan) Brussels. Commission of the European Communities, 1968.

(19) Heller, J. *Catch 22*. London, Cape, 1962.

(20) European Commission. 'The Common Agricultural Policy.' Directorate General for Press and Information, Brussels, 1973.

(21) Beloff, N. *The Observer*, 15 July 1973.

(22) *Structural Reform Measures in Agriculture*. Paris, OECD, 1972.

(23) Hine, R. C. 'Structural policies and British agriculture.' *Journal of Agricultural Economics*, Vol. XXIV, No. 2, May 1973.

(24) Bowers, J. 'Economic efficiency in agriculture.' In *Decision-making in Britain: Agriculture*, Block III, Parts 1–6. The Open University Press, Milton Keynes, 1972.

(25) Prior, J. MP. Addressing the Country Landowner's Association. Reported in *The Guardian*, 22 Oct. 1970.

(26) Ritson, C. 'Who gets a subsidy.' *New Society*, Vol. 31, No. 642, Jan. 1975.

(27) Franklin, M. D. M. 'The Common Agricultural Policy, 1974.' *Journal of Agricultural Economics*, Vol. XXVI, No. 1, Jan. 1975.

(28) Josling, T. E. & Hamway, D. 'Distribution of costs and benefits of farm support policy.' In *Burdens and Benefits of Farm Support Policies*. Trade Policy Research Centre, London, 1972.

(29) Josling, T. E. 'A formal approach to agricultural policy.' *Journal of Agricultural Economics*, Vol. XX, No. 2, May 1969.

Index